THE PRICE OF LIBERTY

THE PRICE OF LIBERTY

AFRICAN AMERICANS AND THE
MAKING OF LIBERIA

CLAUDE A. CLEGG III

The University of North Carolina Press | Chapel Hill and London

© 2004 The University of North Carolina Press

Designed by April Leidig-Higgins
Set in Minion by Copperline Book Services, Inc.
Manufactured in the United States of America

**Publication of this work was aided by a generous grant from the
Z. Smith Reynolds Foundation.**

The paper in this book meets the guidelines for permanence and
durability of the Committee on Production Guidelines for Book
Longevity of the Council on Library Resources.

Library of Congress Cataloging-in-Publication Data
Clegg, Claude Andrew.
The price of liberty: African Americans and the making of Liberia
/ Claude A. Clegg III.
p. cm. Includes bibliographical references and index.
ISBN 0-8078-2845-9 (cloth: alk. paper)
ISBN 0-8078-5516-2 (pbk.: alk. paper)
1. African Americans—Colonization—Liberia. 2. African
Americans—North Carolina—History—19th century.
3. Liberia—History—To 1847. 4. Liberia—History—
1847–1944. I. Title.
DT633.C58 2004 966.62'01—dc22 2003019659

cloth 08 07 06 05 04 5 4 3 2 1
paper 08 07 06 05 04 5 4 3 2 1

TO THE ENDING OF
MAN'S INHUMANITY TO MAN

CONTENTS

A section of illustrations follows page 112.

MAPS, FIGURES, AND TABLES

MAPS

FIGURES

TABLES

ACKNOWLEDGMENTS

SPACE WILL NOT ALLOW for an exhaustive listing of individuals who facilitated the completion of this project, but several warrant specific mention. I
am grateful for the assistance of a number of colleagues in the history department of Indiana University, who shared their insights on various matters
and supported this work in a number of ways. These individuals include John
Bodnar, George Brooks, Ann Carmichael, Larry Friedman, and Steve Stowe.
Graciously, Dave Cecelski and Amos Sawyer offered helpful suggestions for
improving the first draft of this study. Special thanks to anthropologist and
Africanist Svend Holsoe, who allowed me access to his voluminous collection
on Liberia and provided useful comments on the manuscript. Marie Tyler-
McGraw, Tom Parramore, and several others encouraged this project in various ways. I am most indebted to my wife, Alfreda, without whose patience
and support this book would not have been possible. Finally, my mother and
father have been lifelong inspirations to me, and their ongoing interest in my
work and well-being are appreciated beyond words.

In addition to these individuals, this book project benefited from funding
from several institutions, including the Munson Institute of Mystic Seaport,
the North Caroliniana Society, the Arts & Humanities Institute of Indiana
University, and the Office of International Programs, also at Indiana. Additionally, a number of libraries, archives, and other institutions were instrumental to the research and writing of this study. These include the Archives
of Traditional Music and various libraries of Indiana University, the Southern Historical Collection and North Carolina Collection of the University of
North Carolina at Chapel Hill, the Special Collections Library of Duke University, the Hege Library at Guilford College, the North Carolina Department of Archives and History, the National Archives II, the University of Virginia Library, the Tennessee State Archives, the Chicago Historical Society,
the Pasquotank-Camden Library (in Elizabeth City, N.C.), the Lawrence

Memorial Public Library (in Windsor, N.C.), and the Bertie County Court-house. Many thanks to editor Sian Hunter and the staff of the University of North Carolina Press for their good work on this project. Of course, whatever mistakes this book may contain are my sole responsibility.

Bloomington, Indiana
November 2003

THE PRICE OF LIBERTY

INTRODUCTION

WHEN CHARITY HUNTER and her three children ventured from North Carolina to Norfolk, Virginia, during the winter of 1825, the port was a colonial-era town on the brink of dramatic changes. Well situated with deep harbors and natural shelter from Atlantic winds, Norfolk offered sites and experiences that would have fascinated the young mother and her small family. Though her place of origin in North Carolina is unknown, Charity likely would have marveled at the sheer size of Norfolk, which was more than twice as populous as the largest town of her home state. Over the next decade, the port would become even more distinctive in character with the opening of the United States naval dry dock at Gosport and the concomitant expansion of both residential and commercial sectors. Hotels, churches, taverns, banks, steam mills, and tanyards would line its paved streets, and timber and naval stores from North Carolina would supply its burgeoning shipbuilding industry. Characteristic of its modernizing tendencies, a railway would eventually connect Norfolk to Wilmington and Raleigh in the south, and regular steamboat circuits increasingly integrated the port into the commercial worlds of Baltimore, New York, and Boston to the north. In many ways, Norfolk in the 1820s was more progressive and urban than anything that Charity would have been used to, assuming she had lived her twenty-two years solely in North Carolina. Her young children—ages six, four, and two—would have been even more intrigued by the bustling port and the restless waters flowing through its veins.[1]

For all its structural maturation and maritime energies, the Norfolk that the Hunters encountered in 1825 was still very much a southern town, configured with institutions, demographics, and mores typical of other urban areas of the region. The family of four had recently been freed from bondage by a Mr. Hunter of North Carolina, and thus Charity was almost certainly cognizant of how the worlds of slavery and freedom intersected and diverged in the ebb and flow of life in Norfolk. As passengers bound for the young colony of Liberia in West Africa, aboard a brig ironically named the *Hunter*, she and her children unavoidably caught a glimpse of how white mastery interfaced with black servitude in the port town. In a population of approximately nine thousand, whites accounted for half of the town's residents, with slaves comprising fully a third of the inhabitants. Free African Americans, most of whom lived their lives within the narrow interstices between bondage and liberty, made up less than 10 percent of the total.

During their brief stay in Norfolk, Charity and her small companions, along with the other sixty-four emigrants of the *Hunter*, were treated generously by the free black community of Norfolk, which was becoming accustomed to witnessing Africa-bound ships, chartered by the American Colonization Society, leaving Chesapeake waters. By way of the *Hunter*, local African Americans donated "sundry small presents" to the Liberian colony, including seventy yards of cloth for the "Sunday African School" there. In years to come, prospective immigrants to Liberia would continue to rely upon the good will of black Norfolk for everything from lodging and subsistence to companionship and moral support. Although the Hunters were the first black North Carolinians to emigrate, they would merely be the first of a stream of over two thousand African Americans from the state, who would over the course of the nineteenth century seek refuge in Liberia. Norfolk, because of its navigability and geographical superiority to North Carolina ports, would be their primary port of embarkation, thus allowing for a continuous cross-fertilization of African American cultures and interests between Virginia and its southern neighbor.[2]

If the hospitality of free blacks was refreshing, Charity likely found the banality of Norfolk slavery and slave trafficking extremely repulsive. By the 1820s, the town was an exporting emporium for the domestic slave trade. As cotton monoculture spread westward and the frontier demand for slaves increased, Upper South states with an abundance of bondpeople, such as Virginia, North Carolina, and Tennessee, sold slaves by the shiploads and coffles to the insatiable markets of the Lower South. Perhaps as many as eight hundred thousand slaves were part of these interregional migrations between 1820 and 1860. Although it is unknown what features of this system were witnessed by the Hunters, they scarcely could have avoided seeing some aspect of this trade in people.

As it turned out, the young family was in Norfolk during the slave-exporting season, when planters in the New Orleans market and elsewhere had enhanced purchasing power due to the sale of the previous year's crop. Given this unfortunate coincidence in timing, the Hunters could have easily passed within earshot of a slave depot, where hapless captives wailed for mercy from a plenitude of tortures. Similarly, they could have observed whole families manacled and marched through the streets of Norfolk, with a small cavalry of drivers inflicting a coarse discipline with each serpentine lash of the bull-whip. It is even probable that the last memory the Hunters had of America was the riveting stench of slave ships anchored alongside their own transport in Norfolk harbor. Whatever the case, the modernizing impulses of the port town were intertwined with routinized spectacles of brutality and inhuman-ity, which were moored in the culture—were, indeed, the raison d'être—of Norfolk. It was perhaps not so much that Charity and her children were ex-posed to man's capacity for cruelty and unbounded avarice; they had surely been privy to this in North Carolina, where many of the slaves in Norfolk's market originated. What was different was the scale and ordinariness of the dehumanization, as well as the occasion. These were the closing images, the last feelings, that they would take away from the land of their birth.[3]

As the *Hunter* sailed through Hampton Roads on February 2, Charity Hunter and her North Carolinian shipmates had, in the mere act of embarking for Liberia, decisively injected themselves into an intensifying and critically im-portant debate over the future of southern slavery, African Americans, and national unity. Although their eyes were now turned eastward toward the pos-sibilities of Africa, their migration facilitated a shift in many North Carolini-ans' perceptions of who they were and what they were destined to become. Conventional paradigms of race, freedom, slavery, citizenship, and progress were losing their constancy under the weight of a complexity of forces, rang-ing from demographic trends and the maturation of capitalism to political expediency and evolving moral sensibilities. Charity Hunter and her emi-grating cohort were squarely at the center of these transformations.

PERHAPS UNBEKNOWNST TO Charity Hunter and many of her fellow so-journers, the idea of black Americans emigrating from the United States, vol-untarily or otherwise, as a solution to racial conflict was as old as the repub-lic itself. As early as the Revolutionary period, Thomas Jefferson proposed relocating African Americans beyond the boundaries of the new nation. Similarly, as late as the Civil War, Abraham Lincoln still envisioned a great black exodus that would purge the country of African Americans once and for all. Colonization, as this idea became known, rested upon the contention that blacks and whites—due to innate racial differences, polarized societal statuses, and pervasive racism—could not live together in social harmony and political equality within the same country. To many of its advocates, col-onization was an ideological middle ground between the immediate, nation-wide abolition of slavery, which seemed an ever remote possibility, and per-petual black bondage, a proposition that even some southern slaveholders found discomforting. During the nineteenth century, the colonization movement was largely spearheaded by the American Colonization Society (ACS). A self-styled philanthropic enterprise, this organization labored to relocate African Americans to the West African colony of Liberia, which the U.S. government had helped establish in 1822 as a settlement for Africans "recaptured" from transatlantic slave ships. The ACS and its colonizing mission were part of the outburst of social reformism that characterized the Era of Good Feelings and the Second Great Awakening. Most pertinently, it was a product of the failure of abolitionism—even of the most gradual sort—in the South following the American Revolution.

In spreading their message, colonizationists appealed to a range of groups with often contradictory interests. For example, they packaged their program as a temperate form of abolitionism to attract antislavery activists, or to at least deflect their criticism. Some ACS spokespersons argued that removing free (and freed) blacks from the United States would make slavery more secure, since many whites believed that free African Americans instigated slave unrest. In appealing to free blacks themselves, colonizationists portrayed immigration to Liberia as an opportunity to experience unbounded liberty in a country of their own. Despite such enticements, African American spokespersons, including Richard Allen, Frederick Douglass, and Martin R. Delany, typically rebuffed ACS gestures. Many free blacks were quick to point out the number of slaveholders among the founders of the group, as well as the patronizing, even racist bent of its publications and pronouncements. Before audiences of white northerners and southerners, the colonizationists often passionately asserted that black removal was the only way to resolve growing sectional tensions over slavery. Significantly, they held that the government was obligated to have a hand in sending blacks to Africa for both their own good and the well-being of the country. In line with this rationale, colonization advocates counseled private citizens that it was their patriotic, humanitarian duty to support the relocation of this despised, degraded people to the land of their ancestors.

With their large African American populations and deepening commitment to slavery, southern states were the primary sources of Liberia-bound emigrants during the antebellum period and beyond. Of all the states involved in this black exodus, North Carolina best exemplified the diversity of opinions, motives, activities, and expectations within the colonization movement. Interestingly, the colonization enterprise in the Tar Heel State gained its first adherents among an insular religious sect, the Society of Friends, which hoped to send nominally free blacks in their custody abroad where they could supposedly enjoy a fuller measure of freedom. Eventually, individuals ranging from desperate governors to even more desperate slaves would find black immigration to Liberia an attractive, if fantastical, strategy for ad-

dressing the ongoing crisis of race and slavery in the state. By the eve of the
Civil War, the ACS's vision would inspire some of the state's wealthiest slaveholders to send hundreds of liberated bondpeople to Liberia, thus spawning
a historical drama upon African shores that reverberates to this day. Notably,
no state more consistently supplied the colonization movement with emigrants, funding, and ideological support throughout the nineteenth century
than North Carolina. Yet, as it turned out, the Tar Heel State was perhaps
most representative of how slavery and abolitionist impulses tore the social
fabric of the South in ways that colonization ultimately could not mend.

The North Carolina colonization movement, as elsewhere, was tied to economic conditions, tending to peter out during hard times due to declining
donations. It was also attuned to the tenor of race relations, surging during
periods of notable slave resistance and white repression. The movement affected almost every part of the state in some fashion but found its most fertile ground in the eastern agricultural counties with their high concentrations of blacks, both enslaved and free, and proximity to the Atlantic. Although
the Civil War precipitated a temporary decline in Liberian emigration, the
failure of Reconstruction to substantially reconfigure power relations between African Americans and whites revived the appeal of the ACS. By the
1870s, Liberia had to compete with increasingly popular midwestern states as
destinations of disaffected black North Carolinians. Nonetheless, hundreds
of black Tar Heels continued to cross the ocean in search of freedom in Africa
until the turn of the century. Ultimately 2,030 blacks left the state between
1825 and 1893 to take up residence in Liberia.

For almost a century, Liberian emigration connected black North Carolinians and others to the broader cultures, commerce, communication networks,
epidemiological patterns, and historical evolution of the Atlantic world. Their
relocation to Liberia challenged conventional notions of race, citizenship,
nationality, gender, and, above all, the very meaning of freedom. Additionally, this migration revealed the protean nature of the emigrants' identities
and self-consciousness as they sought to invent and reinvent communities
on two very different continents. The ways in which they reimagined themselves as Liberians, as free people, and as settlers once they left the United
States remained informed by their black American past. Along with Virginians, Marylanders, Georgians, and others, black North Carolinians created
culturally rich, hybrid communities in Liberia, consisting of an often politically unstable mix of American newcomers, indigenous people, and Africans
"recaptured" from westward-bound slave ships. In the process of forging the
world's second black-ruled republic, they also constructed a settler society
marred by many of the same exclusionary, oppressive characteristics common to modern colonial regimes.

The very idea of immigrating to Africa encouraged a diasporic consciousness among black North Carolinians, embroidered with romantic imaginings of a pristine ancestral homeland and a global, transcendent black kinship between people of African descent everywhere. For many, dreams of a Pan-African utopia in Liberia were instantly shattered when they arrived in the country only to be confounded by their utter unfamiliarity with Africa and Africans. Their evolving political and material interests as Christian, "civilized" settlers complicated their troubled relationship with the Africans whom they dispossessed of vast territories. Likewise, widespread penury, disease, and death made their adjustment to their new environment all the more difficult. Colonization saved over two thousand black North Carolinians— along with fourteen thousand other African Americans—from U.S. slavery and racial oppression over the course of the nineteenth century. Still, it doomed many to lives of misery along an unforgiving tropical frontier, lives too often shortened by a virulent, endemic strain of malaria. Prepared or not, this was the price that thousands paid in their quest for liberty in Liberia.

This book is the first to probe deeply into both the American background and postmigration experiences of a significant number of Liberian emigrants. Of several themes germane to this study, identity construction (and malleability) is among the most central. This book posits that African American immigration to Liberia—and the fluid, ever-changing identities of the emigrants themselves—must be understood as being enmeshed in the constantly evolving meanings of slavery, freedom, colonialism, race, citizenship, and migratory patterns that characterized the development of nineteenth-century Atlantic cultures. The manners in which black North Carolinians experienced bondage and liberty in particular are focal points, along with the historical conditions and variables that made immigration to Liberia a feasible option for over two thousand of them. Conceptually, this study is located at an intersection of United States and West African history. While it focuses on the experiences of black North Carolinians as a representative case study, this work is also concerned with the broader, national debate over colonization, slavery, and abolition, and the voice and place of African Americans in that discourse. Just as important, this study illuminates the dynamics of community-building in Liberia, which even today—in its architecture, educational institutions, and political ethos—bears the unmistakable imprint of a black American past. Thus, based upon extensive archival research, government documents, emigrant rolls, ethnographic sources, genealogical records, period newspapers, and many other materials, *The Price of Liberty* aims to advance the current state of knowledge regarding black life and culture in the Atlantic world.

ONE. ORIGINS

LIKE MUCH OF THE North Carolina Piedmont, Guilford County was a rolling, picturesque plateau during the eighteenth century, adorned with deciduous forests and a matrix of winding streams and natural clearings. The soils were rich enough for a variety of purposes, and indigenous peoples, namely the Saura and the Keyauwee, found it possible to subsist without substantially altering the ecology. European settlers who entered the area by midcentury found the pastoral ambiance of the area alluring, as well as the possibility of hewing a life from this terrain. Gradually, the region, having been designated a county and named after Lord Francis North, the first Earl of Guilford, was adapted to the new rhythms of white immigrant cultures. By the 1770s, a frontier studded with oak cabins, water-powered gristmills, cultivated fields, and a courthouse was etched into the land, and yeoman communities emerged among the toiling newcomers.[1]

Of the German Lutherans, Scotch-Irish Presbyterians, and other groups who settled in what became Guilford County, the Society of Friends (or "Quakers") would eventually become the most influential. These largely English immigrants came in steady waves between 1750 and 1775, hailing from several places, including Virginia, Maryland, Pennsylvania, and Nantucket Island. Accompanied by trains of cattle, sheep, and hogs, they brought farm implements and housewares in their canvas-covered wagons, cultural mark-

Above: New Garden, Guilford County, N.C. (Photograph by author) ers of an agrarian past. Significantly, they also carried ideas about family, worship, education, and civic life, which would inform their efforts to create a viable community in the Piedmont. Similar to other European immigrants, they named their settlements after existing places, thus inventing a sort of imagined familiarity that perhaps added meaning to their migration. The New Garden settlement, established in 1750 and named after Quaker enclaves in Pennsylvania and Ireland, was the first and principal town, hosting the Friends' monthly meetings as early as 1754. As the Quaker presence in Guilford County grew, their Piedmont villages displaced the older communities of Friends in the eastern counties of Pasquotank and Perquimans as the primary centers of the faith. By 1790, New Garden regularly sponsored the North Carolina Yearly Meeting of the Quakers, setting the tone for the continuing evolution of the group's views and practices.[2]

Immigration and natural growth necessitated the founding of other settlements in Guilford County, which had assumed a distinctively Quaker character by the Revolutionary period. The Jamestown community on Deep River emerged as one of the more substantial villages by the 1790s, taking full advantage of its proximity to water to power sawmills, gristmills, and other enterprises. Much labor was, of course, expended on the necessary daily regimens of clearing land, planting crops, building houses, and spinning cloth. Nonetheless, Jamestown did develop a small retail and service sector, which produced guns, hats, and other goods. Additionally, a social life unfolded outside of the meetinghouse, which led to the establishment of fraternal orders, a temperance society, and a literary club. By the turn of the century, Jamestown boasted a number of brick structures, and a federal road coursed through the settlement. Only the county seat of Greensborough (later Greensboro), created in 1809, seemed to eclipse the Quaker village in civic importance, the former becoming a self-governing town in 1824.[3]

On the surface, there appears to have been a methodical simplicity to Quaker life in Guilford County. From the founding of small farming villages in New Garden and Jamestown to their ascetic social life, Friends embraced an ethos that stressed restraint and reflection in public and private matters. This observation is especially pertinent regarding the group's mode of worship. The architecture of their meetinghouses lacked the ornate pretensions of other Protestant sects. There was no stained glass or church bell, benches were without backs, and musical instruments had no place in services. Worship itself was wholly meditative, with no pastor leading prayer or choir offering song. It was not unusual for a meeting to commence and adjourn with not a word spoken by anyone. Even in their most sacrosanct of collective rituals, each worshiper remained an individual capable of experiencing a transcendent connection with God that required no audible expression. Those moved to speak were always free to, though economy of language and forbearance were highly regarded. Typically, silence prevailed during most Quaker services, compromised only by the irrepressible sounds of nature that occasionally echoed through their sylvan sanctuaries.[4]

If the Friends' manner of worship appeared sedate, even uninspired, to observers, the issues addressed in their business meetings certainly revealed a rigorous engagement with communal concerns that could sometimes be contentious. Generally held on Saturdays, these sessions were occasionally segregated by sex, with men and women deliberating on matters that were supposedly best resolved along gender lines. Important issues that affected numerous persons or required an evocation of communal values and authority were often open to discussion by both sexes. Consistent with their moderate, deliberative approach to most matters, the Friends countenanced a range of questions and concerns in their business meetings. Illustratively, marriage proposals were routinely scrutinized to discern the "clearness" of prospective spouses as a precaution against bigamy. Moreover, itinerant Quakers were frequently required to submit to investigations to determine whether they were reputable enough to represent the group in other communities. Potentially scandalous reports of bastardy probably always gained some attention, though no New Garden man was censured for siring a "base-born child" until 1805. Although other, more serious topics certainly preoccupied Guilford County Quakers during the late eighteenth century, no issue more consistently embroiled North Carolina Friends during this period than slavery. In a singular way, African American bondage challenged the essence of what the Quakers believed about themselves and the structured, insular worlds that they had struggled to erect in New Garden and elsewhere. Unlike the marriage or bastardy cases they handled, often with some difficulty, man's ownership of man was a problem, a grating dilemma, that rented the fabric of Quaker life and faith for not only years, but generations.[5]

By the late eighteenth century, when slavery became a common topic of discussion in Quaker meetings, the institution was over a century old in North Carolina. Geography and natural resources substantially determined both the nature and diffusion of slavery across the state. The lack of readily accessible seaports resulted in African slaves entering the area largely through Norfolk and Charleston. Attitudes toward slavery, ranging from advocacy and indifference to abhorrence of the institution, were also imported from adjacent states by white immigrants who introduced the first slaves to North Carolina in the seventeenth century. Notably, the state often patterned its laws regulating black bondage after the statutes of Virginia, South Carolina, and other states. While eastern agricultural counties, such as Bertie, Northampton, Halifax, New Hanover, and Warren, became heavily dependent upon slave labor for producing tobacco, rice, naval stores, and later cotton, North Carolina never developed a plantation economy comparable to its neighbors' in size and overall importance to the state's economy. In 1790, only 25 percent of the state's population was composed of African American slaves, compared to 43 percent in South Carolina, 39 percent in Virginia, and 32 percent in Maryland.[6]

As in other colonies, African bondage in North Carolina was socially articulated and legally codified over time, affected by variables such as geography, economic conditions, migratory patterns, slave resistance, and evolving cultural concepts of racial difference. In 1669, the Fundamental Constitutions of the Carolinas recognized the right of a master to exercise "absolute power and authority over his negro slaves, of what opinion or religion soever." Statutes passed by the colonial government in 1715 and 1741 further elaborated on the shape and texture of chattel slavery in North Carolina by prohibiting unauthorized commercial exchanges between enslaved and free people, establishing "slave courts" to punish a variety of offenses, and mandating that manumissions be approved by county officials. The constitutional guarantee of masters' "absolute power and authority" over their bond servants in practice allowed slaveholders much latitude over their property. Prior to 1774, even the willful killing of a slave by his or her master was legally permissible. Furthermore, individuals who murdered the slaves of others could only be sued for damages based on the bondperson's market value as determined by the courts. As the number of black slaves in North Carolina increased from approximately 800 in 1712 to 100,783 in 1790, notions of race and the realities of African American bondage were becoming reified in the developing character of the state's culture and politics, as well as its long-term economic trajectory. Shaped by a myriad of forces that resulted in a highly uneven distribution of bondpeople throughout the state, slavery, and its profits and perils, fostered an array of correspondingly uneven interests and ideals that both strengthened and contested the institution's growing presence.[7]

During the eighteenth century, the Quakers of North Carolina and the larger Atlantic world came to envision slavery as an aberrant relationship between human beings, void of socially redeeming value. Although they would eventually become known as the Christian group most inalterably opposed to black bondage in the United States, their early experiences with slavery betrayed little that was suggestive of any natural antipathy toward the institution. For instance, in seventeenth-century Barbados, where Quaker influence blossomed amidst thriving sugar plantations, slaveholding Friends offered few moral critiques of their investment in African thralldom. Similarly, Pennsylvania, a Quaker stronghold, passed numerous acts regarding bonded and free blacks, such as a 1725–26 law that rivaled the draconian slave codes

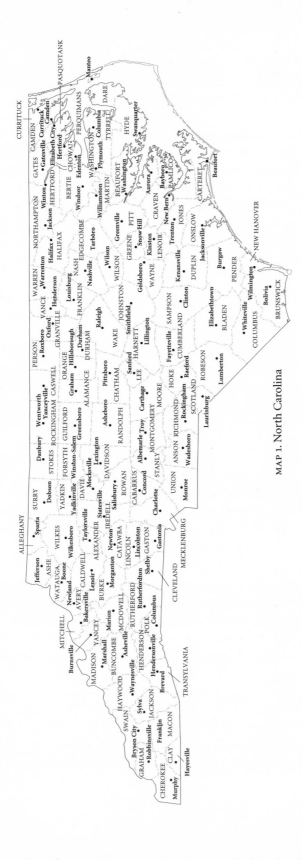

MAP 1. North Carolina

of southern colonies. Friends were deeply involved in the slave trade out of Philadelphia and Providence as late as the 1760s, and slaveholding among members of the North Carolina group lasted well into the nineteenth century. Prior to the 1750s, most Quakers accepted or at least tolerated the existence of slavery, even when they were not directly complicit in its perpetuation. There were, of course, Friends, like William Edmundson, who were appalled by the treatment of slaves by Quakers in Barbados and elsewhere. These radical humanists forthrightly proclaimed the ways in which African bondage contradicted core values of the Society, such as pacifism, the brotherhood of man, and the primacy of the salvational Inner Light. Nonetheless, few were listening to the likes of Edmundson in the seventeenth century, and such compunctions about slavery guided the activities and lifestyles of few Friends of that period.[8]

Much of the Quakers' accumulating discomfort with slavery during the eighteenth century was a matter of degree and was not distinguished by any sudden turn toward abolitionism. It was an evolutionary phenomenon and by necessity had to be, given the slow, consensus-building style of decision-making that characterized the group's contemplation of any major change of policy. Since the most important reforms required the sanction of the Yearly Meetings, issues facing the group sometimes went unresolved, or even candidly discussed, for long periods of time. This inertia had the effect of diminishing, at least symbolically, the urgency of the matter at hand and precluding a rash, hastily derived conclusion. Still, a decisive tilt occurred in Quaker views of slavery, which allowed for the advancement of a new logic that recast the institution in a way that made it less morally digestible.

From firsthand experience and observation, Friends—master and non-slaveholder alike—had witnessed the ways in which African bondage had corrupted their faith. Slavery violated the precepts of marriage, denying legally recognized marital unions between slaves and the legitimacy of their offspring. It allowed, indeed, encouraged violence borne of fear, retribution, and sadistic whims since every slave code included provisions for the corporal punishment of slaves and offered owners power over life and death. In most colonies, the slave was refused access to intellectual improvement through literacy. Further, Christian instruction, where such religious teachings were allowed, was emphatically uncoupled from the notion that the slave, as a Christian, might be entitled to the legal status of person. As a people who had experienced religious persecution and who self-consciously attempted to level social distinctions among themselves, the ill fit of slavery with the Christian ethics of brotherhood, equality before God, and the possibility of redemption from sin was glaringly apparent to many Quakers by the 1750s. If black slaves were ignorant, savage, degraded, and immoral as many observers believed them to be, slavery had allowed, even forced them to be so. If the bondman was mired in sin because slavery, through law, custom, or practice, reduced him to such, then slavery, some began to reason, must be a sin in itself. This moral equation, not wholly an invention of eighteenth-century Quakers, informed the gradual shift of the Society away from slave trafficking and slaveholding. A century in the making, this formula for stigmatizing slavery itself—and not just the refusal of certain masters to become kinder managers of their property—became the framework for the most potent philosophical attacks on the institution during the next one hundred years.[9]

While the Friends' moral bearings regarding slavery were in adjustment, the materialist, secular context of these changes both spurred and made possible this reimagining and assertion of Quaker religious convictions. It was perhaps easier to think about the feasibility of disassociating oneself from owning and trading Africans once the economics of continuing slave importation made less fiscal sense. Pennsylvania, the North Carolina Piedmont, and other Quaker bastions had limited uses for slave labor by the 1750s, for no pervasive plantation cultures existed in these areas that required huge concentrations of bonded agricultural labor. Nonslaveholding Friends who found themselves competing with the slaves of their neighbors in farming endeavors and trades had fewer qualms about entertaining opposition to slavery. However, their objections to the institution were as reflective of economic self-interest as they were of humanitarian concern. Further, given that the cost of servile insurrection, such as those that tore through New York City in 1712 and Stono, South Carolina, in 1739, could be appallingly steep, the need to limit the importation of Africans into their communities was a rational decision for a people whose pacifist doctrines disavowed the kind of armed vigilance and systematic terror that controlling unfree laborers required. Thus, it should not be surprising that the Friends chose to assail the buying and selling of slaves, which enhanced the numbers of Africans in their possession, before seriously considering the emancipation of those whom they already held in bondage. These were two separate issues for the Quakers, the dichotomy relating directly to their financial dependence on slaveholding and their countervailing desire for physical and psychological security against a profitable trade that might have demographic and social consequences that could lead to their utter undoing.[10]

Under the collective, conflicted pressures of their Christian ideals, economic interests, psychic needs, and corporate identity, the Quakers began to incrementally repudiate slave trafficking and holding over the course of the eighteenth century. To be sure, there had been early criticism of slavery by dissenters such as William Edmundson during the previous century. Quakers in Germantown, Pennsylvania, stated unequivocally in 1688 "that we shall doe to all men like as we will be done ourselves; making no difference of what generation, descent or colour they are." However, the most significant official changes came in the 1750s when the Yearly Meetings in Philadelphia and London issued strong denunciations of slave trading. By the 1770s, when many Quakers found it morally imperative, and economically feasible, to distance themselves from complicity in the enslavement of Africans, the policy of the Friends had become overtly emancipationist, certainly in no small way influenced by the liberative rhetoric of the American Revolution. Now, slaveholding was a disownable offense, warranting the excommunication of recalcitrant masters from the Quaker fold. Unlike the Methodists and the Baptists, the new sensibilities of the Friends were not fleeting and subject to sectional compromises. The group had officially turned its back on slavery, deeming it an insufferable sin that its members should no longer inflict upon others.[11]

In addition to their tendencies toward internal conformity and deliberated joint action, the Society's communication networks and commercial connections throughout the Atlantic world facilitated both its collective shift away from slave trading and slavery and the creation of an international antislavery ideology. Thus, just as Philadelphia, London, and Nova Scotia Friends were arriving at their conclusions about the inconsistency of African bondage with their beliefs and interests, Quakers in North Carolina were involved in the same dialogue and moving toward similar positions. In 1768, Piedmont Quakers resolved to avoid trading in slaves "in any case that can be reasonably avoided." After the 1772 Yearly Meeting, only endogenous trafficking in bondpeople was allowed, guaranteeing that the number of enslaved Africans among North Carolina Quakers would not increase artificially, at least not due to foreign importation. Three years later, Friends were required to obtain the consent of their local monthly meeting before purchasing or selling slaves, and in the following year members were encouraged to manumit their remaining bonded Africans. Given the synchronism of Quaker ideological transitions and policy changes regarding slavery, it is probably not coincidental that North Carolina Friends made slaveholding a disownable transgression in 1780, the same year that Pennsylvania passed "An Act for the Gradual Abolition of Slavery."[12]

Despite their own harmonized actions, Quakers of the Tar Heel State undoubtedly understood that North Carolina was not Pennsylvania, especially regarding the issue of slavery. Too many had invested too much in the institution for too long for it to be so emphatically, if gradually, legislated away. Absent laws that positively provided for a sweeping emancipation of enslaved African Americans, Quakers were left with moral suasion as their primary weapon against ongoing bondage in Revolutionary North Carolina.

Accordingly, in 1787, the year that the Northwest Ordinance prohibited slavery in territories beyond the Ohio River, the Quakers appointed committees to "labor with such Friends as remain in the practice of holding their fellow men in a state of slavery." Over the next several decades, this nudging approach would become their preferred method for convincing coreligionists to relinquish their ownership of slaves.

In an effort to add momentum to the emancipation process, members of the Society petitioned the newly formed North Carolina legislature for approval to manumit their remaining bondpeople "under certain rules and restrictions." After being read in the House of Commons, however, the petition was summarily rejected. Starting with this plea, every subsequent Quaker entreaty for the liberalization of emancipation laws was ignored, and an acrimonious atmosphere pervaded the relationship between the Friends and the government in Raleigh. Although perhaps partially due to Quaker insularity and their refusal to take up arms during the struggle against England, this hostility was most closely linked to both slaveholding interests in the state government and legally questionable manumissions that Friends had recently performed. Additionally, news of the massive, protracted slave rebellion that began convulsing the French colony of St. Domingue in 1791 did nothing to make state officials more receptive of Quaker petitions. In fact, though North Carolina temporarily banned the importation of slaves "by land or water" in 1794 as a security precaution, the Friends and other advocates of black liberty would have few allies in the capital at the turn of the century.[13]

In addition to the philosophical strife between Friends and the state legislature, the Society's antislavery activism aroused the ire and suspicion of local governmental bodies. In 1776, Quakers in the northeastern counties of Pasquotank and Perquimans freed forty slaves, apparently without following the established legal procedure requiring that manumitters prove before county courts that "meritorious service" had been performed by the bondpeople in question. To the horror of the Friends, the freed blacks were later apprehended by authorities and resold under a statute passed the following year. The Quakers sued for relief, but the capture and sale of the emancipated slaves were upheld by the legislature in 1779. After these events, conflict between local officials and the Quakers became notably more commonplace and acerbic. In 1795, a Pasquotank County grand jury lambasted the Society for publicly discussing the subject of emancipation. Not only were enslaved African Americans "greatly corrupted and allienated from the Service of Their Master" by Quaker agitation, Friends also allegedly encouraged and even sheltered fugitive bondmen. Raising the specter of a slave revolution on North Carolina soil, the jurors pointed out that unsolved arsons had become a problem and that the Friends' actions had placed the state in "great peril." Moreover, they charged the Quakers with a recklessness oblivious to the "miserable havock and massacres which have taken place in the West Indies, in consequence of emancipation."[14]

In a 1796 effort to stir the conscience of the legislature with yet another petition, Quakers excoriated state officials for allowing freed blacks to be sold back into bondage. "For a legislative body of men professing christianity, to be so partial, as thus to refuse any particular people the enjoyment of their liberty," the petitioners asserted, is "incompatible with the nature of a free republican government, and repugnant to the spirit of the christian religion." The Friends' appeal went on to call for an act that would allow "conscientiously scrupulous" masters to free their slaves, who would in turn be protected from seizure. A similar petition submitted the following year was more measured in tone and seemed designed to mollify whatever apprehension legislators harbored regarding the motives and objectives of the Society. "It is not to enjoin a general emancipation, or to compel any to liberate their slaves, that we have solicited you," the petitioners argued, "but only that liberty of conscience in . . . respect [to private manumission of slaves] may be tolerated." In signaling both its disregard for Quaker-style humanitarianism and new fears occasioned by insurrection scares in northeastern counties and Virginia in 1800, state officials refused to dignify the solicitations of the Friends with even token measures. Instead, the legislature tightened manumission laws in 1801, requiring prospective emancipators to post a bond of one hundred pounds for each slave freed.[15]

In the face of a defiantly proslavery state government and a generally indifferent or even hostile populace, the North Carolina Quakers confronted a dilemma that would thwart many of their emancipation efforts until the Civil War. Having moved doctrinally and in practice toward a complete renunciation of slavery, the Friends were stuck with scores of black slaves whom they neither wanted as bonded labor nor could legally emancipate, at least not en masse in an expeditious manner. To free them outside of the law meant exposing them to the likelihood of being arrested and auctioned back into slavery. To maintain them in a state of bondage was morally abominable, not to mention fraught with risks, such as the possibility of insurrection. Their civil status as slaves as well as Quaker exclusivism and racial prejudices made assimilating them to any meaningful degree undesirable, even if conceivable. Provisions for black auxiliary meetings, supervised by white Friends, had been considered as early as 1758, but not much seems to have become of this proposal. While one person—"a mixed coloured man" named Isaac Linagar —was admitted to the Deep River monthly meeting in June 1801 after three years of delays, the racial integration of white and black friends' religious and social lives was an option hardly considered by North Carolina Quakers. Racial segregation was simply not viewed as the sin that slavery had become, and neither was the self-righteous paternalism that lingered in Friends' perceptions of blacks long after the chains of slavery had fallen away.[16]

Given both the difficult realities and the Quaker penchant toward studied moderation, it was, almost inevitably, a middle course that prevailed. Instead of outright liberty or perpetual bondage, the Friends settled on bestowing a kind of quasi-freedom upon blacks in their custody. In 1808, the North Carolina Yearly Meeting assigned a committee to supervise African Americans whose masters had transferred them to the protection of the Society. Although the nominally liberated blacks would enjoy some control over their social and personal lives, appointed agents would have the authority to hire them out, garner their wages, and dispose of their earnings in ways that ideally improved their condition. This arrangement often included religious instruction, a rudimentary education, and more secure familial ties, all designed to inculcate in quasi-freedpeople the Quaker moral code and work ethic. Ultimately, the general goal was to prepare the blacks in Friends' care for full liberty whenever legal restrictions on manumission were relaxed, or whenever other places of residence outside of North Carolina became viable options acceptable to their African American dependents. Until then, the legal status of the partially emancipated blacks was in limbo, as was their future. For the Quakers, a half-century of antislavery activity still had not entirely extricated them from an institution they had come to despise.[17]

WHEN THE NINETEENTH CENTURY dawned in North Carolina, both change and continuity characterized its evolution. As in North Carolina's sister states, agriculture continued to be central to its economic and cultural development, but in highly differentiated ways. In the counties along the Virginia border, tobacco commanded much of the arable land. Eastern counties, such as Bertie, Edgecombe, Martin and Pitt, and southwestern counties, such as Mecklenburg, Iredell, and Union, would devote an ever-expanding acreage to cotton production, but the state did not nearly approach a monocultural dependence on the crop as did those further south. The Lower Cape Fear region, which was geographically and climatically similar to lowcountry South Carolina, proved to be wet and fertile enough for rice growing. Further inland, the sandhills were the center of turpentine production. Additionally, a host of other commodities, including lumber, naval stores, corn, peas, beans, and pork, were produced in several areas of the state. Generally, early nineteenth-century agriculture in North Carolina was quite similar to the farming production and techniques of previous decades. Compared to its southern counterparts, the state remained unremarkable in this regard, largely due to its scarcity of navigable waterways and seaports and its subsequent dependence upon Norfolk and Charleston for access to external markets.[18]

Unlike agrarian pursuits, manufacturing enterprises in North Carolina were in their nascency during the early national period. As of 1815, only one cotton mill and three paper mills were in operation throughout the whole state. Several iron works, turpentine distilleries, corn mills, and other establishments existed, which produced items such as hats, gunpowder, and textiles; however, little distinguished the state as a center of industry and economic progressivism. As in the case of agriculture, the development of a formidable manufacturing tradition in North Carolina was greatly hampered by a long, jagged coastline, accented with shoals, reefs, and winding inlets, which also stunted the growth of a vibrant maritime trade and populous port towns. North Carolina merchants often found it easier to trade their wares through Virginia and South Carolina, which typically resulted in higher freight costs and smaller profits. Marginal roads and infrequent infrastructural improvements compounded the backwardness in manufacturing and depressed property values, wages, and the overall standard of living of the state's population. Urban development in North Carolina, tied to access to trade and transportation networks, lagged behind other states. Unsurprisingly, the biggest towns were in the eastern counties, with their larger concentrations of waterways, slaves, and wealth. Still, even the three largest urban areas—New Bern, Fayetteville, and Raleigh—contained an aggregate population of less than ten thousand in 1820, a sharp contrast to Baltimore (62,738), Richmond (12,067), Norfolk (8,478), and Charleston (24,780). While geographical peculiarities constricted agricultural and manufacturing pursuits, the resultant feeble rate of urbanization helped ensure a depressing cultural poverty, marked by a dearth of schools, libraries, theaters, and major newspapers.[19]

If North Carolina entered the nineteenth century in eighteenth-century garb, its demographic appearance underwent stunning changes during this period. The overall population of the state increased 62 percent between 1790 and 1820, from 395,005 to 638,829 people. During this same period, the white population rose from 289,181 to 428,948, a 48 percent increase. Very significantly, the enslaved population, numbering 100,783 in 1790, grew to 204,917, jumping 104 percent. Similarly, free African Americans, always insignificant in number, reached 14,701 in 1820, up 192 percent from 1790. Both free and enslaved blacks were largely concentrated in eastern agricultural counties, such as Bertie, Craven, Halifax, Hertford, Northampton, and Wake, unlike the white population, which was more evenly distributed throughout the state. While North Carolina was greatly surpassed by Lower South states in the growth of its slave population, it ranked third in the number of bondpeople in 1820, topped only by Virginia and South Carolina. It was also third among southern states in the number of free African Americans, behind Maryland and Virginia. Overall, the black population represented 34 percent of the state's inhabitants by 1820, up from 27 percent in 1790, with several counties having black majorities.[20]

In many quarters of the white community, the accelerating growth of the black population, both free and enslaved, was cause for concern, even alarm. Between 1790 and 1820, the national slave population had grown by 120 percent, from 694,207 to 1,529,012. Although the white population had increased 152 percent to 7,929,957, this growth rate was dwarfed by the 288 percent rise in the free African American population, from 59,196 to 229,620 people. The increase in the slave population was solely due to the expansion of bondage in the South. Emancipation laws passed in northern states after the American Revolution primarily accounted for the substantial augmentation of the free black population, though there was significant enlargement of this group in the Upper South states of Virginia, Maryland, and Delaware. Much of the anxiety over the growing black population was sectional, as slavery and the African American presence became even more distinctive features of southern culture, politics, and economic life. Also, an ever-deepening fear of slave revolts haunted many southern slaveholders, particularly since mounting evidence revealed that servile conspiracies were becoming more elaborate and better organized by the nineteenth century. Surpluses of bondpeople in Upper South states, coupled with the spread of cotton's supremacy westward, resulted in an interstate slave trade that perhaps abated some white fears of insurrections in exporting states, such as North Carolina and Virginia. However, these states remained heavily populated with slaves, despite the thousands they sold south and westward. Additionally, both of these states had relatively substantial free black populations, which, for many slave masters, were a source of irritation, since the presence of African Americans enjoying liberty, however circumscribed, might encourage black bondpeople to more actively pursue their own freedom.[21]

By the Revolutionary era and certainly by the nineteenth century, wholesale liberation of slaves, or even gradual emancipation measures similar to those passed by northern states, was never seriously considered anywhere south of Pennsylvania. The demand for slaves on plantations being carved from the frontiers of Georgia, Alabama, Mississippi, and Louisiana made such propositions economically seditious in the deep South. Likewise, Upper South states had invested too much of their wealth and historical development in African American bondage to jettison a system that so profoundly undergirded their culture. Nonetheless, if emancipation, in any guise, was an extreme proposal to the majority of those southerners whose opinions were most readily translated into laws and customs, the idea of perpetual black slavery could also be disconcerting.

To many who reflected on slavery's expanding presence in the country, the ideological incongruity between black bondage and the democratic and egalitarian ethos of the republic and its literature, including the Declaration of Independence, was glaringly obvious. Legalized chattel bondage did extreme violence to the American ideals of personal freedom and civic equality. Furthermore, it posed a discomforting dilemma for many of those who had so loudly and eloquently denounced British tyranny and hailed the French Revolution, but who had been more reticent about the daily despotism practiced on their own slave-worked plantations. In addition to the omnipresent fear of a coming reckoning when white mastery would be obliterated by black vengeance, the new vitality that cotton production had injected into slavery meant a sharpening of the contradiction between the professed meaning of American republicanism and the stark realities of American bondage. This complicating development portended that any feasible resolution, any middle ground, was steadily being expropriated by slavery's westward march.

The same economic forces, mentalities, and historical patterns that made both immediate abolition and eternal bondage unacceptable conceptions of America's future stimulated, in some quarters, alternative ways of thinking about race and slavery in the United States. The idea of African Americans migrating from the country, voluntarily or otherwise, as a solution to the dilemma of black bondage in the midst of white freedom trickled into the national discourse as early as the colonial period. The proposition that blacks could be removed and colonized elsewhere was imagined by some as not only an avenue for addressing the moral and economic conundrum that slavery presented to the emerging republic; colonization, unlike outright abolition, evoked the possibility of closure of the tragic, exploitative encounter between the European and the African in North America. Moreover, black removal seemed to offer the opportunity to eradicate from the country's maturing economy, incipient republican institutions, and developing social structure the unsettling inconsistencies and dangers that a tortured history of race relations and chattel slavery had produced. To many advocates of colonization, the logic was irresistible, and the problem of African thralldom in America was clearly reversible. History could, indeed, be undone, and the future cleansed for white posterity.

In line with this reasoning, many colonizationists held that abolition alone was not enough, for it left too many troubling uncertainties, even creating new dilemmas. Slavery, while a central concern, was not the core of the problem. Instead, the primary issue was the whole conspicuous presence of an alien black people in America, toiling to expand the empire of King Cotton, swelling the lower classes of proliferating cities, meandering along the edges of the white body politic. Even among those colonizationists who could imagine a completely free and multiracial United States, white racism seemed too widespread and incorrigible to accommodate such a vision. Thus, for all intents and purposes, any durable remedy had to remove the physical presence of black people, enslaved and free, and thus exorcise the ontological meaning, indeed, the complication of blackness as a troubling counternarrative. It would have to guarantee that the republic could clear its conscience of slavery and bathe itself in ideological fictions that conceived and celebrated the nation as a neo-European preserve.

Predictably, Virginia, the prototypal state that had set the tone and pace of colonial settlement, American republicanism, and plantation slavery, was the crucible from which the colonization idea first emerged. By the early nineteenth century, the state had more slaves than could profitably be employed, and its free black population by 1810 was second only to that of Maryland. More ominously for slaveholders, servile resistance was becoming bolder and better planned, as illustrated by the 1800 conspiracy organized by a Virginia slave named Gabriel. Of the thirteen colonies, the ideals of the American Revolution found their most articulate spokesmen in Virginia, though these principles were flagrantly flouted there as well. Among those torn by the antipodal relationship between their democratic ideals and their tyrannical dominion over slaves, and thus attracted to the concept of black removal, was Thomas Jefferson, author of the Declaration of Independence, third president of the United States, and Virginia planter.

As early as 1776, Jefferson, as a member of the Virginia legislature, had come to the conclusion that the migration of blacks beyond American borders might resolve his own moral dilemma as a revolutionary slaveholder and free the country from this unflattering quandary as well. Between 1801 and 1804, a lively correspondence between then President Jefferson, Virginia governor James Monroe, and others regarding the procurement of "lands beyond the limits of the U.S. to form a receptacle" for blacks disclosed a keen interest in colonization among both state and national leaders. Largely due to Jefferson's encouragement and influence, the Virginia legislature resolved in January 1805 to instruct the state's senators in the U.S. Congress "to exert their best efforts" to acquire a portion of the Louisiana territory for black colonization. The proposed settlement would ideally serve as "the residence of such people of colour as have been or shall be emancipated in Virginia, or may hereafter become dangerous to the public safety." Nothing came of this proposal, but six years later, Jefferson held that "*nothing is more to be wished than that the United States would themselves undertake to make such an establishment* [of African Americans] *on the coast of Africa.*" Pertinently, this statement anticipated the future of the colonization movement, but would not be acted upon for several more years.[22]

Notwithstanding the assorted motives behind white interest in colonization, African Americans were among the first to propose relocating to Africa. Often employing the lofty language of liberty and equality that was in such abundance during the Revolutionary period, slaves petitioned whomever would listen to their pleas for relief. In April 1773, four bondmen beseeched the Massachusetts colonial assembly for emancipation so that they and their compatriots could "from our joynt labours procure money to transport ourselves to some part of the Coast of *Africa*, where we propose a settlement." Twenty years later, blacks in Providence, Rhode Island, seriously entertained migrating to the newly established British colony of Sierra Leone, West Africa, but were frustrated by the machinations of a local white clergyman. During the early nineteenth century, there was much fascination among some African Americans regarding the prospect of immigrating to Haiti. The island republic, forged from a successful slave revolution that concluded in 1803, offered liberty and nationality, and its first ruler, Jean-Jacques Dessalines, actively encouraged black American immigration to the new nation. However, advocates of a black exodus from the United States most frequently and consistently assumed that Africa, the ancestral homeland, was the optimal destination, though Haiti, Canada, and a few other places would sporadically attract new attention during the nineteenth century. Among black proponents of migration to Africa, no single individual energized the colonization movement more than Paul Cuffe, a New England sea captain and Quaker.[23]

Born free in Massachusetts in 1759, Cuffe embarked upon a seafaring life in New England as early as age sixteen. He and his brother, David, purchased a small ship during the American Revolution and engaged in commerce along the coast of New England. Although David shortly returned to a life of farming on the family's lands, Paul reinvested his earnings in ever larger ships. By 1795, he was setting sail in the *Ranger*, a sixty-nine-ton schooner. Eleven years later, he owned and commanded a 268-ton sloop called *Alpha*, though his favorite vessel was his brig *Traveller*. Cuffe's enterprising spirit and wanderlust served him well financially and took him to the outer edges of the Atlantic world. He whaled, hauled lumber, and transported foodstuffs and other commodities throughout New England, routinely stopping at New Bedford, Martha's Vineyard, and Nantucket. Journeys to Philadelphia, Baltimore, and Wilmington, Delaware, placed Cuffe in the thick of interstate coastal trade networks. Importantly, several voyages as far south as the West Indies and as far east as the Baltic Sea offered him a view of the world that few African Americans had access to.[24]

Partially because of his maritime peregrinations, Cuffe was very sensitive to the rank oppression that pervaded so much of the eighteenth-century world. Maturing during an age of revolution, he became actively involved in efforts to attain suffrage and educational opportunities for Massachusetts blacks. His sensitivity to the human condition probably led him to become a member of the Society of Friends in 1808, though his parents had been previously affiliated with the group. Undoubtedly, the ripening abolitionism of the Quakers, along with their pacifism and far-flung business connections, also figured into Cuffe's application for membership. Regardless of the specific motivation, affiliation with Quakers helped Cuffe, and Cuffe, in turn, helped the Quakers. For instance, when the captain planned a voyage to Africa in June 1810, the Friends of Westport, Massachusetts, authorized the trip and gave him a letter of recommendation, a necessary item for an African American when sailing through slave trading areas. At around the same time, Massachusetts Quakers benefited materially from their association with Cuffe, who donated six hundred dollars in money and goods to finance a new meetinghouse in Westport. These observations are, of course, not meant to suggest that the relationship between Paul Cuffe and his white coreligionists was wholly, or even principally, predicated upon a mundane *quid quo pro*. Nonetheless, both parties were fully aware of the rarity of black people within the Society of Friends and, thus, were almost certainly cognizant that other factors, outside of spiritual affinities, influenced Cuffe's application and admission into the Society.[25]

The humanitarian bent and civic activism of Cuffe were most evident in his opposition to slavery and the slave trade. Fortunate enough to have never been in bondage himself, he was still deeply sympathetic to enslaved African Americans. As a veteran sailor, he was aware of the ongoing illicit importation of African slaves at various eastern ports and the growing shipments of cotton that entered northern harbors, thanks to the entrenchment of Lower South slavery. Moreover, he had personally been a frequent victim of racial discrimination in an oceanic commercial culture more used to black men as property and cargo rather than as ship's captains. For these reasons and others, Cuffe was not at all sure that slavery was terminally ill in the United States, even though his native state had abolished it and the transatlantic slave trade was legally closed in 1808. By the time he spoke at the Newport Yearly Meeting in 1810—perhaps becoming the first black man to speak at any such Quaker gathering—he had arrived at the opinion that slave trafficking might best be combated at its source, Africa, thus inhibiting the growth of the institution in the United States. Also, in the absence of any meaningful governmental intervention, he felt that private efforts might have an impact on both the continuing slave trade and the degradation of bonded African labor across the expanses of the Atlantic.[26]

With the official endorsement of Westport Friends, Cuffe traveled to Sierra Leone in 1811–12. During a three-month visit, he established the Friendly Society, an organization patterned after the Society of Friends with the objective of strengthening "legitimate" trade between England, Sierra Leone, and the United States. Additionally, the group was intended to facilitate the demise of the slave trade by transplanting industry, civilization, and Christianity to Africa. Like many of his American contemporaries, Cuffe's cultural framework and understanding of civilization was thoroughly Western in orientation. He believed that blacks like himself, tutored in the English language, Christian theology, and Euro-American notions of social etiquette, economic organization, and political thought, had much to offer Africa and Africans, whose development had supposedly been stymied by heathenism, illiteracy, and the depredations of the slave trade. Actually, this trip was more than a sightseeing venture with missionary undertones. Cuffe wanted to discern whether the British colony, which had been established in 1787 as a settlement for black "loyalist" refugees of the American Revolution and London's "Black Poor," was viable enough "to encourage some sober families of black people in America to settle among the Africans." These emigrants would ideally instruct Africans in the art of civilization and the glory of the Gospels, thus leading them away from the alleged savagery and spiritual darkness that had made the slave trade and a host of other evils possible. Importantly, migration to Sierra Leone or elsewhere in Africa would also provide an outlet for African Americans fleeing U.S. slavery and racial oppression.[27]

Sailing from Westport in December 1815 with the blessings of local Friends, Cuffe journeyed once more to Sierra Leone in the *Traveller*. While this was a commercial voyage involving a cargo of tobacco, flour, and naval stores, the nine families aboard—eighteen adults and twenty children—being transported for settlement in the British colony represented a turning point in the evolution of an active, American-based African colonization movement. For the first time, the ubiquitous rhetoric advocating black removal and settlement outside of the United States fused with the will and means to begin this work. Not only was this relocation of African American families to Sierra Leone significant for launching a larger program of colonization; it was conceived, financed, and realized almost solely by the efforts of a single black individual, Paul Cuffe. This was no minor achievement. Given that free African Americans in particular would eventually become the most vociferous opponents of colonization schemes directed by whites, Cuffe's initial efforts were met with approbation in many quarters of the black community, largely because of his racial background and the fact that his motives were uncomplicated by reliance upon antiblack, slaveholding interests. The captain may have only slightly exaggerated when he informed white colonizationist Samuel J. Mills that in 1816 "I have had so many applications for taking more [African Americans to Africa] that I believe I could have had the greater part out of Boston." Conscious that his efforts had attracted a wide audience, Cuffe also transported to Sierra Leone a Senegalese man named Anthony Survance, who had been a bondman in St. Domingue before relocating to Philadelphia during the slave insurrection against the French. Thus, his epic 1815–16 voyage to Sierra Leone was truly Pan-African in scope and appealed to a protonationalism developing among blacks, which would be further elaborated during the 1850s. Notably, the trip, at least in regard to Survance, included passengers who were literally going "back to Africa," the symbolism of which was not lost on those who believed that continent should be the natural focus of colonizationist energies in the United States.[28]

It is impossible to predict where the African colonization movement would have gone if Cuffe himself had not died on September 7, 1817. Yet, it is clear that his efforts did inspire others who were contemplating the feasibility of African colonization. Quakers, many of whom by now had become preoccupied with the plight of African Americans, determined to build upon the foundation that Friend Cuffe had laid. Actually, the idea of removing blacks beyond the country's boundaries had been percolating for some time in various Quaker communities. For instance, as early as 1773, Anthony Benezet had suggested removing blacks to lands between the Alleghany Mountains and the Mississippi River. Interestingly, he was against colonizing African Americans in Africa since that "would be to expose them, in a strange land, to greater difficulties than many of them labor under at present." Similarly, at the turn of the century, Maryland Quaker John Parrish posited sending free blacks to "unoccupied" western lands where their progress would encourage a wave of manumissions, thus hastening an end to American bondage. Colonization as a palliative for the open wound of slavery that still troubled the republic was an almost natural fit for the Society of Friends. It appealed to both their inclinations toward moderation and the racially exclusive tendencies of the group, which had resulted in Paul Cuffe, even in death, being interred in a secluded corner of a Quaker cemetery, away from the graves of white Friends. For the Society's members in North Carolina, black colonization was the virtually inevitable answer to their manumission dilemma. Restrictive state laws left them with little choice but to conflate emancipation with removal, or risk seeing the quasi-free blacks currently in their custody apprehended by local authorities and sold to owners who had fewer scruples regarding slavery.[29]

Only two months after Paul Cuffe returned from Sierra Leone, North Carolina Quakers decided to act more decisively on their emancipationist impulses. On July 19, 1816, thirty-one Friends met at Center Meeting House, Guilford County, to craft the state's first antislavery organization. Representing the four Quaker churches at Center, Caraway, Deep River, and New Garden, the assembly inaugurated the General Association of the Manumission Society of North Carolina and elected Moses Swain, a local Friend, president. On the following day, the constitution of the organization was drafted and presented, officially proclaiming the aims of the group. The moralistic language of the document was deeply inspired by the republican philosophy of the American Revolution, as well as by Christian ethics and abolitionist sentiments. In candid terms, the constitution took the country to task for allowing slavery to exist "where the principles of freedom are so highly professed." It quoted the "golden rule" and the Declaration of Independence, but its most eloquent and pertinent lines evoked a universalist vision of human equality and liberty. "The human race however varied in color are Justly entitled to Freedom," the authors asserted, adding that "it is the duty of Nations as well as Individuals, enjoying the blessings of freedom to remove this dishonor of the Christian character from among them." Undoubtedly with an eye to their past difficulties with authorities regarding their antislavery activities, the founders decided to temper their abolitionism, at least on the surface, by changing the name of the organization to the Manumission & Colonization Society of North Carolina (MCS). This alteration acknowledged the state's hostility toward emancipation without removal and similar apprehensions among some of the Friends themselves. Additionally, the limiting of membership to "free white [Quaker] males" likely quieted concerns that the new organization might be viewed by outsiders as advocating social equality as well as abolition.[30]

The MCS apparently did not meet again until year's end. When the members finally did get together on December 20, their conference at Deep River was unremarkable except that it revealed how pragmatic the Quakers were willing to be in attracting allies to their cause. Illustratively, the conferees resolved that the organization should be interdenominational and that "the Baptist, Methodist, Presbyterian, and Moravian Societies" should be invited to join. Also, the gathered members again implicitly recognized that rapprochement with the Raleigh government might be necessary in order to advance their agenda. Private efforts alone could not liberate and transport the nearly two hundred thousand bondpeople in North Carolina, not to mention the dozens of quasi-free blacks in Quaker custody, without the acquiescence, indeed, active support of the state government. Thus, the organization found it feasible to package its program in ways that would be palatable to the legislature, which it would eventually have to approach for aid. To this end, the conferees expunged an article from their constitution allowing for the impeachment of members running for legislative office "who [were] not in favor of the emancipation of Slaves."

As evidenced by these gestures, the MCS leadership had few illusions about the magnitude of the task before them. Along with strategizing to stir up local and government support for manumission and relocation, the Piedmont Friends also found it expedient to look elsewhere for assistance. At their April 28 meeting, MCS officials reported that contact had been established with a kindred organization in Tennessee. Most significantly, however, a proposal "recommending the opening [of] a communication with the American Society at Washington City for Colonizing the free people of color" was presented and approved. Although it was probably not apparent to anyone at the time, the passage of this proposal was the single most consequential action that North Carolina Quakers had yet taken to free themselves from their manumission woes.[31]

TWO. BETWEEN SLAVERY AND FREEDOM

ON DECEMBER 21, 1816, a group of white men met in the hall of the U.S. House of Representatives to discuss the future of African Americans. It was a distinguished crowd by any standard, including some of the highest-ranking officials in the federal government. The meeting was the culmination of colonizationist sentiments that had been efflorescing in some quarters of the country since the American Revolution. It was a private coming together of powerful men to candidly discuss the meaning and texture of American freedom, property rights, and sectionalism, and the personal interests that each of the attendees had bound up in these topics. But the great question of the day, which had only been temporarily and partially overshadowed by the War of 1812, was overbearingly present, if delicate and controversial, and informed most of the meeting's agenda. It was a question that the framers of the U.S. Constitution had found too unpleasant to meaningfully address and that even when whispered, echoed in discordant tones through the august seat of American democracy. It was, simply stated, *whither slavery?*

Above: U.S. Capitol, Washington, D.C. (© PictureNet/CORBIS)

The discussion that ensued about colonization was lively and telling. Henry Clay, a congressman from Kentucky and Speaker of the House of Representatives, was called upon to chair the meeting and did not mince words regarding his purpose for attending. Colonization, he asserted, held out the promise of ridding "our country of a useless and pernicious, if not a dangerous portion of its population": free blacks. Furthermore, once jettisoned to Africa, this same group could be instrumental in spreading "the arts of civilized life, and the possible redemption from ignorance and barbarism of a benighted portion of the globe." Clay failed to clarify how African Americans who were "useless and pernicious" in the United States could become vectors of civilization and progress in Africa by merely crossing the Atlantic Ocean. He was perhaps proceeding from the premise that Africa was so low on the scale of human achievement and cultural development that even the "dangerous portion" of America's population would have something to offer the continent, given U.S. blacks' exposure to Western culture and Christianity. Whatever the case, the paradoxical language of Clay and other colonizationists regarding free African Americans would, for decades to come, incorporate a tortured logic geared more toward effecting their ends than to proving the intellectual cogency of their position. In revealing his personal investment in the idea of free-black removal, Clay, one of several slaveholders present, informed his audience that he had only agreed to attend the meeting on the condition that any discussion of the abolition of slavery be off-limits.[1]

The next speaker, Elias B. Caldwell, the secretary of the U.S. Supreme Court, insisted that racial prejudice and concerns for "the Safety of the State" would forever preclude free African Americans from enjoying the rights and immunities enumerated in the Constitution. While "there ought to be a national atonement for the wrongs and injuries which Africa has suffered," he was convinced that enfranchisement and racial equality were not possible remedies. Instead, Caldwell suggested that sending free blacks to Africa would be appropriate, if incomplete, recompense. He personally felt comfortable enough with this notion to assure his listeners that, once informed of the plan, prospective emigrants would not object to removal.[2]

Following Caldwell's remarks, John Randolph offered comments that would resonate for years following the meeting. A U.S. representative and Virginia planter, Randolph believed that the establishment of a colony for free blacks in Africa would encourage masters to liberate their slaves, thus relieving "themselves from the cares attendant upon their possession." Conversely, however, such a safety valve for drawing free African Americans out of the country would also "materially tend to secure the property of every master in the United States over his slaves." In Randolph's estimation, colonization could be both abolitionist, albeit gradual and voluntary, and proslavery. It could be a compromise solution to the American race problem, since the idea of removal sat squarely in the middle of the debate over emancipation and bondage. Its respect for property rights and individual discretion made colonization protean enough to become whatever individuals desired it to be. Thus, it could not be wholly and accurately characterized in any singular way and subsequently might transcend growing sectional differences over the issue of slavery. To the chagrin of many future colonizationists, it was not Randolph's sop to abolitionists that would be memorable to critics of removal. Instead, it was the proposition that transporting free blacks from America would rivet the chains of slavery tighter. To many free African Americans and others, this idea was the selfish, operative motive behind this slaveholder-supported plan, and it was this motive which would inevitably provoke their loudest and most unrelenting scorn.[3]

The December 21 meeting turned out to be merely a high-profile hashing out of ideas regarding the efficacy of colonization. A week passed before the opinions expressed by Clay, Randolph, and others took on a life of their own. On December 28, another group of white patricians gathered at the House of Representatives to hear a report proposing the establishment of a new organization. The committee charged with presenting a draft constitution was composed of an array of notables, including U.S. Supreme Court Justice Bushrod Washington and local lawyer and national anthem composer Francis Scott Key. In unembellished prose, the document called for the creation of "the American Society for Colonizing the Free People of Color in the United States." In cooperation with individual states and the federal government, the Society's primary purpose was "to promote and execute a plan, for colonizing (with their consent) the free people of color residing in our country, in Africa, or such other places as Congress shall deem most expedient." The report and constitution were unanimously adopted by the gathering. During a subsequent meeting on January 1, 1817, Bushrod Washington was elected president, and Elias Caldwell became the secretary of the Society. Additionally, thirteen vice presidents were also elected, representing nine states and the District of Columbia. Ever conscious of the need to appeal to a broad spectrum of individuals and interests, the Society's founders tried to balance vice presidencies between different sections of the country, choosing five from four northern states (Massachusetts, New York, New Jersey, and Pennsylvania) and seven from five southern states (Maryland, Virginia, Tennessee, Kentucky, and Georgia). Finally, to ensure access to reputable and influential circles, the members elected well-known individuals to serve as vice presidents, including Henry Clay, General Andrew Jackson of Tennessee, and political theorist John Taylor of Virginia.[4]

The purposeful balancing of sectional representation within the organization, which became known as simply the American Colonization Society (ACS), was indicative of the national appeal that the group's ideals initially enjoyed. When Clay, Caldwell, and others gathered in Washington in late 1816, their sense of timing could hardly have been better regarding the creation of an organizational structure for the various colonizationist ideas that had been floating around since the 1770s. Not only were a number of the principal men of the country ready to lend their weight to the concept of free-black removal, but several state governments eagerly anticipated the advent of such a group as the ACS. Illustratively, only days before the December 21 meeting, the Virginia legislature requested that the governor contact President James Monroe about "obtaining a territory on the coast of Africa," the North Pacific, or elsewhere outside of the United States for colonizing free blacks and those later emancipated. In 1818, the legislature of Maryland unanimously resolved to request that the governor there express to the state's congressional delegation "the expediency, on the part of our National Government, of procuring, by negotiation, by cession, or purchase, a tract of country on the Western Coast of Africa, for the colonization of the free people of colour of the United States." New Jersey's legislature passed a resolution suggesting that foreign colonization would allow for a complete, though gradual, demise of slavery. Connecticut lawmakers concurred with New Jersey's stance, as did the Ohio legislature in 1824.

Interestingly, no state south of Tennessee, which adopted a position similar to Maryland's, issued resolutions in favor of colonization. This conspicuous silence was an early indication that the Lower South states, still hungry for imported slave labor and with a collective free black population of less than fourteen thousand in 1820, would have little interest in anything that savored of abolition, even if organized by slaveholders. North Carolina, which was unrepresented among the group that founded the ACS, also refrained from offering legislative approval of the aims of the colonizationists. Nonetheless, a robust auxiliary of the Society appeared in Raleigh by the summer of 1819, with John Branch, the state's governor, as president.[5]

Notwithstanding its uneven appeal, the ACS emerged within the context of a burgeoning nationwide reformism that sought to impose order on segments and practices of society that seemed at variance with the vision of a progressive, industrializing Christian democracy. Infused with missionary impulses occasioned by the Second Great Awakening, a number of movements and institutions arose during this "Era of Good Feeling," including temperance, antiprostitution activism, penitentiary systems, insane asylums, almshouses, and antislavery. Colonization, though a complex and conflicted phenomenon, came out of this burst of experimental philanthropy and activism, which sought to remedy social ills that electoral politics, the free market, and eighteenth-century notions of benevolence failed to resolve, or even address.[6]

Central to the idea of colonization was the concept of irremediable difference, indeed dysfunction. This idea, advanced by Jefferson and others, characterized the races as absolutely distinct and dissimilar in nature, interests, and aspirations, and consequently unsuited to coexist as equals. Thus, not a problem amenable to conventional reformism, many proponents of black removal viewed antagonistic race relations as redressable only through the asylum version of correction—that is, the separation of the (black) deviant from the (white) mainstream. The problem, according to these colonizationists, was larger than slavery, and thus abolition was not considered the primary solution. It alone would not suffice since blackness itself, burdened with all of the degrading, brutalized, guilt-ridden meanings that bondage and history had encumbered it with, was the problem. Even among those colonizationists who were not wholly convinced of the innate inferiority of blacks or the impossibility of an interracial republic free of slavery, removal seemed to provide the most direct route to black liberty and citizenship, which were putatively unattainable within the United States.

Associated either directly or implicitly with this notion of irreconcilable racial difference, other ideas, motives, and agendas shaped the colonization movement, giving it both a multifaceted ideological foundation and a diverse network of adherents. Religious antislavery types, such as the Quakers, were drawn to the ACS due to their moral aversion to slavery and their limited ability to legally free their bondpeople. Some evangelical Christians of Methodist and Baptist persuasions also found slaveholding spiritually problematic by the nineteenth century, and thus viewed the possibility of ending the institution through colonization worth exploring. Parallel to these religiously inspired rationales for black migration to Africa, a missionary strand of thought was evident in many of the pronouncements of colonizationists. Some individuals believed that sending Christian African American immigrants to Africa was the best way to spread the Gospel and civilization across a supposedly savage continent while at the same time imparting to the settlers freedom in the land of their ancestors. Several advocates of colonization even ventured that such an enlightened immigrant outpost on the west coast of Africa might serve as a commercial conduit for facilitating trade between Africans and the United States.

While the colonization movement did appeal to those concerned about the morality of slavery, it also attracted individuals who were more preoccupied with the long-term political, economic, and social implications of African American bondage—and the black presence in general—in the

United States. Federalists and Whigs, such as Upper South congressmen Henry Clay and Charles Fenton Mercer, favored colonization as a balm for a country increasingly separated into free and slave states. Clay, in particular, viewed slavery as an awkward, premodern mode of production that would have to be gradually abolished through colonization if the South was ever to escape its economic backwardness and dependence upon the industrial North. By midcentury, Free Soilers and Republicans, including Abraham Lincoln, supported colonization for similar reasons, as well as their opposition to the western expansion of slavery. Proslavery individuals, whether Democratic politicians or southern slaveholders, sometimes supported removing free(d) blacks to Africa as a means of protecting racial slavery from its starkest contradiction —the unregulated growth of a vital free black community. Even among ordinary whites of no particular political bent, colonization had an allure, if only for its promise that deported free(d) blacks would not be able to compete with them for jobs, housing, status, or social space.

Complicating the array of motives behind the colonization movement, many of the perspectives outlined here were often alloyed with others, and thus an individual might be attracted to the cause for a variety of intertwined reasons, not all complementary. For example, those who spouted religious rhetoric about the possibility of christianizing Africa with black American settlers could also oppose increasing the U.S. free black population, despite its increasingly Christian character. Moreover, those who disapproved of slavery on philosophical or moral grounds were not necessarily at odds with those who despised blacks as a race or used the banner of Free Soil to prohibit African Americans, free or enslaved, from migrating to the Midwest. For many, colonization was not to be wholly equated with either abolitionism or the perpetuation of slavery, though it could sometimes seem conducive of both ends. In the view of many of its proponents, colonization was inherently respectful of property rights, mindful of sectional strife, and above all, moderate. Consequently, emerging from this mosaic of ideologies, motives, and interests, the ACS seemed a kind of national therapy, versatile enough to soothe dilemmas ranging from slavery and white anxieties over free blacks to sectional differences and African barbarism. Starting in 1817, this was the nostrum that the organization was selling across state lines and sectional divides, and for one long historical moment, much of the nation was listening.[7]

But, of course, not everyone was buying. From the outset, the ACS's demonization of free blacks as a tactic for winning white support disaffected African Americans, especially in northern states. Hardly were they attracted to an organization founded by slaveholders that so frequently characterized them as "wretched," "predatory," "contaminated," "vicious," and "evil." Predictably, following its creation, many free blacks became inalterably opposed to the

ACS and its program. The first of their many organized protests against the Society took place in Philadelphia during January 1817, the same month the ACS was officially established. Attended by three thousand people, including Rev. Richard Allen and businessman James Forten, the group resolved that "any measure, having the tendency to banish us from her [America's] bosom, would not only be cruel, but in direct violation of those principles, which have been the boast of this republic." In a direct reference to Henry Clay's recent calumny, they repudiated the characterization of free blacks as "dangerous and useless." They further resolved not to "separate ourselves voluntarily from the slave population of this country" since "they are our brethren by the ties of consanguinity, of suffering, and of wrong." Emphatically, they distanced themselves from the notion of migrating "into the savage wilds of Africa." To the contrary, "we . . . feel ourselves entitled to participate in the blessings of her [America's] luxuriant soil," they asserted, "which [our ancestors'] blood and sweat manured." Until the American Civil War, the 1817 resolutions of Philadelphia blacks typified the most common objections that African Americans would have to colonization.[8]

It had not always been the case that blacks were overwhelmingly averse to relocation outside of the United States. As described earlier, there was some sympathy for the idea during the colonial period. Actually, "back-to-Africa" sentiments likely existed among every group of first-generation Africans shipped across the Atlantic for a life in American slavery. By the nineteenth century, however, opposition to migration had reified among free blacks in particular. Probably a substantial majority of this population, many of whom had always believed colonization to be a specious solution to racial discrimination and slavery, saw removal as a disingenuous scheme of proslavery interests. Although the attitudes of slaves or even illiterate and impoverished free blacks regarding colonization were much less clear, African American spokespersons and writers, almost without exception, shunned the objectives of the ACS and similar organizations. Consequently, despite efforts by the Society to portray itself as the fulfillment of Paul Cuffe's dream, most African Americans seemed to want no part of the new movement.

Apparently, for a significant number of free African Americans to even consider leaving the United States, emigration would have to be both voluntary and coordinated by blacks, à la Cuffe's model. It could not be white-controlled removal and certainly not deportation directed by the slaveholders and southern politicians who led the ACS. For some, colonization might be appealing for the same missionary ethos and capitalist opportunism that motivated some white advocates. Above all, any acceptable plan for removal would have to promise what slavery and racial oppression in the United States could not: respect for the integrity and unity of black families, legally recognized and protected personhood, and access to the basic freedoms and opportunities routinely denied to African Americans on racial grounds. Colonization could only be meaningful to a substantial number of African Americans if it addressed these issues forthrightly, a requirement that many believed the ACS wholly incapable of satisfying.

According to several free African American spokespersons, white colonizationists were seeking to deny them full citizenship in the land of their birth by maintaining that they had no proper place in the United States. Even more insidiously, they were attempting to insulate slavery by hauling away its most glaring and enduring contradiction: the existence of a free African American community that explicitly demonstrated that blackness and liberty were not mutually exclusive. On a number of occasions, ACS officials, such as John Randolph, admitted that their brand of colonization might have this effect. In an unabashed effort to straddle sectional fences, the 1819 annual report of the organization acknowledged its "irresistible appeal . . . to all the powerful sentiments of the heart—the most sordid and degrading, as well as the most benevolent and exalted." Of course, these confessions did nothing to quiet the rising indignation that free blacks felt toward colonization. If anything, these statements confirmed their worst fears regarding ACS motives.[9]

If the Society did not enjoy widespread support among African Americans, it did have enough friends and momentum to begin actively pursuing its plans. In addition to black cooperation, two assets essential to the success of its program—financial backing and territory—were among the most pressing needs following the founding of the organization. However, timely legislation passed by Congress in March 1819 seemed to at least partially address both of these issues. An outgrowth of the same slavery-tempered abolitionism that would lead to the Missouri Compromise the following year, this act authorized President Monroe to remove "beyond the limits of the United States . . . all such negroes, mulattoes, or persons of colour" taken from slave ships intercepted by naval patrols. The "recaptives," as such people would later be known, were then to be delivered to an agency to be established "upon the coast of Africa" for their settlement. Financed with an initial appropriation of one hundred thousand dollars, this act provided for the creation of an American-sponsored colony in Africa. Although primarily designed to curtail the illicit and ongoing importation of African slaves into the United States, the measure was interpreted by ACS leaders as a clear sign of federal interest in at least the basic premise of their plan. Without hesitation, the Society—assisted by supporters in Congress—quietly began merging its efforts with the new agency to be created in Africa.[10]

Prior to this congressional act, the ACS had already actively explored the

BETWEEN SLAVERY AND FREEDOM

possibility of acquiring territory in Africa for an immigrant settlement. After consulting Paul Cuffe in December 1816, Samuel Mills and Ebenezer Burgess made an exploratory trip to West Africa on behalf of the Society. Much of their time was spent in Sierra Leone and Sherbro Island to the immediate south, meeting with various African potentates to gauge their willingness to cede land for an American settlement. Writing from the British colony in May 1818, Mills informed the managers of the ACS that "I am every day more convinced of the practicability and expediency of establishing American colonies on this coast." However, as an ill omen of things to come, the agent died of fever on June 16, necessitating that Burgess finish their report alone. Despite this setback, ACS officials wanted to show supporters and detractors tangible results of their program and decided to move forward with their vision. In late January 1820, the *Elizabeth*, carrying eighty-eight free blacks from mainly New York and Philadelphia, set sail for Sierra Leone. Officially, the passengers—none of whom were recaptives—were under the authority of the federal government and were to help organize the recaptive agency once land was purchased in West Africa. As it turned out, the government and the ACS, having shared both agents and information, commenced to establish a colony with the dual purpose of receiving recaptured Africans and settling black emigrants from the United States.[11]

From the time of their arrival along the West African coast on March 9, nearly everything that could have gone wrong for the immigrants did. Although the ACS, which held its third annual meeting only days before the departure of the *Elizabeth*, assured members that Africans were "impatient to receive" American immigrants, such was not the case. Difficult negotiations with indigenous leaders at Sherbro Island and elsewhere revealed that African rulers had little interest in colonization. In fact, immigrants, even black ones, would be distinctly unwelcome as permanent neighbors. As the newcomers shuffled between Sierra Leone and Sherbro Island in a desperate search for agreeable terms of settlement, the rainy season found them inadequately sheltered, and malaria ravaged their ranks grievously. By late November, at least twenty of the original immigrants had died, in addition to Samuel Crozer, the ACS agent, and two U.S. government officials. A year after their departure from New York, there was still no established colony for immigrants, not to mention recaptives.[12]

Caught off guard by "these abundant causes of sorrow," ACS leaders in America put the fate of their plans in the hands of a rash navy lieutenant named Robert Stockton. Accompanied by Dr. Eli Ayres, the Society's new agent in Africa, the lieutenant was able to get Dei monarch, King Peter, to cede Cape Mesurado to the ACS, but only after leveling a gun to his head and threatening to pull the trigger. This pistol diplomacy netted the Society malar-

ial land south of Sierra Leone worth "one million of dollars," in Ayres's estimate, at a contracted expense of about three hundred dollars in tobacco, beads,
knives, pots, and other items. In the near future, there would be much steeper
costs attendant to this kind of violent expropriation of lands, sealed by "fee
simple" treaties that meant little to Africans whose notions of land tenure
precluded the permanent cession of territory to foreign interlopers. For now,
however, the band of surviving immigrants, supplemented by the emigration
of thirty-three free blacks from Virginia and Maryland in March 1821, took
formal possession of the cape on April 28, 1822. Facing yet another insalubrious rainy season and surrounded by African polities offended by the aggres-
sive methods of ACS operatives, the colony, anemic and hemorrhaging, teetered
precariously on its perch overlooking the Atlantic. Its future was as much intertwined with events transpiring thousands of miles away as it was bound
up in the unpleasant circumstances that presently portended its demise.[13]

Fortunately for the ACS, this calamitous episode in Africa did not occur
before the organization aroused sufficient interest and garnered enough political support and financial resources to weather such a crisis. Shortly following the founding of the Society, enthusiasm for colonization crested
throughout the country. In North Carolina, the Quaker-dominated MCS wrote
a laudatory letter to the ACS in May 1817, seeking further information about
its goals. Curiously, nearly a year passed before Elias Caldwell, the secretary
of the Washington-based group, sent a reply. He seems to have assumed that
the ACS's preoccupation with removing free blacks to Africa, along with its
association with slaveholders, might be offensive to the MCS. In politely ex-
plaining the sectional balancing act that the ACS was undertaking, Caldwell
stressed that the goal of his organization "requires great Delicacy and Cau-
tion" in regard to the South. Alluding to the group's reliance upon proslavery
interests, he asserted that "persons of opposite oppinions on certain subjects
are to be conciliated, and unless we can move with the assent of the Slave
Holders nothing of Importance can be done by this Society."

Responding on behalf of the MCS, Richard Mendenhall, a prosperous Jamestown Quaker, wrote in July 1819, "our intention and object is in the most gentle and pacifick manner gradually to promote the abolition of Slavery . . .
under a hope that Some way will open for the relief and Instruction of these
unhappy beings." Referring to past Quaker conflict with the state of North
Carolina over emancipation, he assured ACS officials that "we are well aware
of the Importance as well as the Delicacy of the Subject and that it must work
of Time is the only thing expected or Desired." Reflective of the ideological
affinity between the MCS and some members of the ACS as well as the debilitating impact of the former's manumission crisis, Guilford County Friends
meeting at New Garden in November decided to make a one-thousand-

dollar donation to Caldwell's group. Six months later, as the emigrants of the *Elizabeth* were being consumed by the "African fever," the Quakers deposited eight hundred more dollars in the State Bank of Fayetteville for use by the ACS. Over the next decade, North Carolina Friends would become more invested, financially and philosophically, in the aims and outcome of the African colonization movement than any other group in the state.[14]

Aside from the practical purpose of circumventing restrictive manumission laws, one of the principal reasons that North Carolina Quakers and others were attracted to the ACS had to do with the nature of nineteenth-century benevolence. During this period, religious organizations became the mediums through which humanitarian activities were often organized. As church-based groups were spearheading the temperance, educational, and missionary movements of the day to check any perceived erosion of public morality —a role government had largely declined to assume—they were also concerned with race relations and slavery, making African Americans the subjects of their philanthropy. Consequently, the merging of Quaker antislavery with the quixotic reformism of the ACS, especially given their somewhat complementary goals, was not only imaginable, it was hardly avoidable.

White colonizationists, whether claiming that their work would redeem the republic from the stain of slavery or impart Christianity to "benighted" Africans, often coated their rhetoric of black deportation with religious undertones, which appealed to the era's spirit of reform. Quite significantly, many of the early spokesmen and agents of the ACS, including Samuel Bacon, Robert Finley, Ralph R. Gurley, William McLain, and Lott Carey, were clergymen, whose colonizationist sentiments were a mix of their theological, political, and personal interests, as well as their racial views. Along with the Society of Friends, other Christian denominations found the near-fantastical program of the colonizationists, with its allusions to the biblical themes of exodus, redemption, and the millennium, alluring. For instance, the Presbyteries of Fayetteville and Orange County both sent enthusiastic messages to the ACS soon after its founding, the latter church expressing "sincere and peculiar satisfaction" with the group's goal of removing free blacks. They hoped that the colonization enterprise would eventually fulfill an "anxious wish to the hearts of the humane, and the charity of the Christian." Similarly, in 1825, the Methodist Conference of North Carolina and Virginia passed a resolution stating that they "highly approve the object of the American Colonization Society, and recommend it to their congregations." As auxiliary branches of the movement sprouted around North Carolina, it was clear that religious leaders and institutions were to be intimately involved in the work of black removal.[15]

Local chapters of the ACS appeared initially in the central Piedmont region of the state. The first auxiliary society was started in Raleigh in June 1819.

Reverend William Meade, an itinerant agent of the parent organization, was instrumental in forming this group, assisted by local leaders who convinced prominent residents to join the movement. As mentioned earlier, Governor John Branch became the president of the Raleigh group, and Joseph Gales, editor of the *Raleigh Register*, assumed the role of secretary. Shortly after its advent, the auxiliary society busied itself with soliciting donations—raising $1,277.50 in just a few months—and petitioning the legislature for government support of the ACS. In addition to the Raleigh organization, sister auxiliaries emerged in Chapel Hill and Fayetteville by 1820 and in Greensboro by 1821, though the latter chapter was a Quaker-led derivative of the MCS.[16]

In the eastern counties, a number of ACS branches blossomed by 1825. In April of that year, an organization was formed in Edenton, with Josiah Collins as president. Collins's election was suggestive of the influence of slaveholders in the ACS, given that Collins's seigniorial plantation on the banks of Lake Phelps would be home to over three hundred bondpeople by 1860. Other auxiliaries in the east included one in Hertford County, which met in Murfreesboro, and another Quaker-inspired branch in Pasquotank County, led by Isaac Overman. In general, the auxiliary societies were patterned after the parent body, with a president, a number of vice presidents, a secretary, and a treasurer. In the case of the Pasquotank and Greensboro chapters, there were also managers, reminiscent of the evolving bureaucracy of the national ACS. The branches were funded by subscriptions from supporters and other donations, and were, of course, beholden to the constitution and policies of the parent organization. All officers were male, presumably white, and often members of the professional community. Unsurprisingly, clergymen were well represented among the leadership of auxiliaries, and at least one of these societies, the Chapel Hill group, was led by a minister, the Rev. Joseph Caldwell.[17]

While the infrastructure of the colonization movement was being constructed in North Carolina, the situation among the quasi-free blacks in Quaker custody continued to develop in unpredictable ways. Although their voices are largely silent in historical documents, some of the experiences of African Americans among the Friends can be gleaned from extant sources. Based on Quaker reports, their supervision of the nominally liberated blacks tended to be paternalistic and doctrinaire. Great concern was expressed during Yearly Meetings regarding the need to encourage each quasi-free African American to live "a virtuous life." Also, educating the African Americans in their care was a core component of the Friends' plan for intellectually uplifting them. In 1818, Quakers in the eastern counties reported that their efforts had led to "some advancement" in the spread of literacy among blacks in their custody. Concurrently, Piedmont Friends agreed to take steps "to extend the Education of the males so far as to Read, Write, and Cypher as far as the Rule of

Three, and those of the Females to read & write." Besides efforts to instruct African Americans, Quakers were preoccupied with eliminating any residue of slavery and slave trading among themselves. Tales of Friends holding, selling, and hiring bondpeople were discussed at annual gatherings, and egregious cases of "ill usage," perhaps reported by blacks themselves, were taken "under care."[18]

Despite their exertions to improve the lives of the quasi-free, the Quakers still had not resolved their basic dilemma: their inability to legally emancipate the African Americans in their charge. To complicate their predicament, the number of blacks under their protection continued to grow. In addition to natural increase, a number of slaveholders transferred controlling interest in their bondpeople to the Society of Friends during this period. In 1816, Thomas Wright, recently deceased, willed his slaves to the New Garden monthly meeting, along with his personal property, which was to be sold and the proceeds distributed among them. In 1822, the Yearly Meeting reported that John Kennedy had assigned thirty-six people of color to the Society, Joseph Borden had given eighteen, and the heirs of Thomas Outland transferred fifty-nine more. By this time, over four hundred quasi-free blacks were under the "care and direction" of the Friends, and there was little cause to believe that the number would not soon increase.[19]

Pleading once again for official relief, the MCS sent petitions to the state legislature, one in particular arguing that manumission laws were denying citizens "liberty of conscience" and depriving bondpeople of legitimate marriages and legal protection for "the chastity of female Slaves." Another petition requested that "Virtuous citizens . . . be enabled to Liberate such persons of colour as may be considered Suitable to be colonized." To the dismay of the Friends, Raleigh lawmakers still had little interest in making emancipation easier and consequently did nothing to placate the MCS. Frustrated at nearly every turn, the Quakers still continued to act as if a remedy for their situation was forthcoming. The quasi-free blacks were still given work assignments and their earnings held in trust, some of which were used for their upkeep and to pay taxes. As evidence of both their desperation and how domineering Quaker paternalism could be, the 1819 Yearly Meeting decided to give up "to a course of Law" any African American who refused to fully abide by the Society's custodial arrangements. That is, "after necessary care has been taken," recalcitrant individuals would be delivered to local authorities who would almost certainly reduce them to outright slavery. While there is no evidence that this rather extreme measure was ever resorted to by the Quakers, it was definitely a stark reminder to their black wards that they were not wholly free.[20]

By the early 1820s, the situation among Guilford Friends in particular seemed to be steadily deteriorating. To their moral discomfort, slavery was still part of the fabric of the local culture. Although only one in ten of the county's 14,500 residents was in bondage, ghastly images of the institution's inhumanity were easy to come by, including lethal floggings of enslaved men, the separation of enslaved mothers from their infants, and coffles of bond-people being herded to market for sale. Probably few Quakers harbored illusions of decisively ending the institution through the polite, deportationist abolitionism that they had unsuccessfully proposed to the state government. Moreover, news of the unfolding tragedy afflicting the emigrants of the *Elizabeth* did not inspire confidence in the ACS's initial search for a colony in West Africa. To steel their resolve in the face of these unpleasant realities, Friends would occasionally take on a cause célèbre, such as the case of Penny, "a mulattoe girl . . . supposed to be freeborn," who was being threatened with enslavement. Eastern Quakers, including Exum Newby of the Pasquotank auxiliary society, were assigned to provide for her defense, which promised to be financially costly. Aside from such largely symbolic public battles against bondage, many Friends undoubtedly experienced a gnawing helplessness regarding their failure to dissociate themselves completely from the sin of slavery. The language of their petitions and meeting minutes reveal as much. However, there were others who were becoming more militant in their anti-slavery activities, largely as a result of the manumission impasse that had embroiled the Society since the 1770s.[21]

Actually, the actions of slaves themselves were instrumental to the radicalization of a number of Friends during the 1820s. According to Levi Coffin, a Guilford Quaker, fugitive bondmen "used frequently to conceal themselves in the woods and thickets in the vicinity of New Garden, waiting opportunities to make their escape to the North." Sympathetic to their efforts, Coffin, along with others, became deeply involved in what would become the Underground Railroad, secretly assisting runaways in their attempts to escape bondage. In 1819, John Dimrey became the first African American in Guilford County to elude enslavement in this fashion. Dimrey had recently been liberated by his owner in another region of North Carolina before deciding to settle in New Garden. After his former master passed away, his heirs appeared in Guilford County and apprehended the freedman. With the help of the Coffin family, however, Dimrey escaped to Richmond, Indiana. Following this incident, the Underground Railroad was active in Guilford County until the 1850s, and Levi Coffin became especially well known in abolitionist circles as a central figure in its operation. Not to be completely outdone, county commissioners established a slave patrol in 1830, which had the authority to mete out up to fifteen lashes to any bondman who failed to "give a satisfactory account of himself" when caught out after dark. Although the

Underground Railroad continued to run through the Piedmont region, regardless of this crackdown on slave mobility, not all Friends were receptive of fugitives. In the perhaps not-too-uncommon case of Elmina Foster, a Quaker who grew up in Guilford County during the 1830s, there was nothing she feared more than "mad dogs, snakes and run-a-way niggers."[22]

The bold and illegal participation of a number of Quakers in Underground Railroad activities revealed ideological cleavages that were emerging among the Friends and within the MCS specifically. The failure to persuade the state legislature to allow voluntary manumissions and the slow, uncertain headway that the ACS was making in Africa inflamed abolitionist sentiment among some Guilford Friends. This divergence in the views and tactics of the MCS membership was most apparent at a meeting at Deep River in July 1824. After ruefully observing that "the present situation of our Society . . . [is] not the most agreeable," Aaron Coffin, a relative of Levi Coffin, drew an unfavorable comparison between the MCS and the more active Tennessee Manumission Society. "I also think," he added, "the title ought to be in the future, the Manumission Society of North Carolina." Anticipating rigorous objections to the dropping of the word *colonization* from the group's title, Coffin suggested that the alteration was a minor one, since "our primary object as a Society, is the relief of oppressed humanity." At a meeting in October, the name of the organization was officially changed to the "Manumission Society of North Carolina, for promoting the Gradual Emancipation of Slavery, and for Meliorating the condition of the African race among us."[23]

The issue did not rest, though. At a subsequent meeting held in neighboring Randolph County, the idea of predicating manumission upon colonization was the subject of near-hostile debate. According to Levi Coffin, slaveholders who were present favored the linking of the two acts, while others were against requiring the removal of liberated slaves. After much discussion over whether free blacks should be compelled to migrate to Africa, a slender majority of those in attendance voted in favor of changing the group's name back to the "Manumission and Colonization Society." According to Coffin, the passage of this motion convinced him and other less proremoval abolitionists "that the slave power had got the ascendancy in our society, and that we could no longer work in it." Following the meeting, which ended "in confusion," the New Garden faction of the MCS seceded from the parent body to pursue its own antislavery agenda.[24]

Coffin's recollection of these events perhaps overstated the level of opposition to colonization that existed among New Garden Quakers during the mid-1820s. Undoubtedly, there were those who, like him, were "conscientiously opposed and against" the coupling of emancipation with removal. If given the opportunity, the Piedmont Friends would have likely liberated most, if not all, of the African Americans in their custody, with no stipulation that they migrate elsewhere. However, considering that state law made most manumissions prohibitively expensive, time consuming, and uncertain, the Quakers as a group remained pragmatic and did not generally repudiate colonization as a condition of emancipation. In fact, the Society of Friends in New Garden and elsewhere would continue to make large contributions to the ACS, even though none of the quasi-free blacks in their care would migrate to Africa prior to 1826.

During this period, all options were left open in regard to possible destinations for liberated African Americans. In November 1823, the Yearly Meeting appointed agents to take blacks to Ohio, Indiana, and Illinois "as fast as they are willing to go," after finding no discriminatory laws that prohibited them from entering these states. Nine people in Friends' custody had already migrated to Indiana, and more were to follow. Yet despite the growing interest in the Ohio River Valley and Africa, North Carolina Quakers were not primarily looking west or east for prospective places for blacks to relocate to. In 1824–25, they were instead looking south, toward the tropics, where a black revolution had utterly annihilated a slave regime a generation earlier.[25]

AS PREVIOUSLY MENTIONED, the government of Haiti had expressed interest in African American immigration to that country since its independence in 1804. It was hoped that such an influx of people would bring needed skills and talents to bolster industry and agriculture, as well as provide potential recruits for the military. Furthermore, by cultivating a relationship with the United States, leaders of the island nation believed that a strategic alliance between the two countries might discourage France from attempting to recapture its erstwhile colony. Against this background, the subject of black American immigration to Haiti took on a new urgency during the 1820s. At the beginning of the decade, English abolitionist Thomas Clarkson broached the idea to Haitian monarch Henri Christophe as part of a geopolitical strategy designed to forestall a possible French invasion. Clarkson suggested that the United States might be persuaded to purchase Santo Domingo, the Spanish colony that shared the island of Hispaniola with Haiti, and cede it to the Haitians if Christophe were to agree to receive African American immigrants. While some evidence exists that indicates that the Spanish were amenable to such a sale and that France was still a potential threat to Haitian independence, nothing of note became of Clarkson's proposal. Besieged by political enemies at home, Christophe himself committed suicide in 1820 before any further plan could be elaborated.[26]

Jean Pierre Boyer, who came to power in the wake of Christophe's death, proved to be an active supporter of African American immigration. As with previous governments, a preoccupation with French intentions was central to Boyer's foreign policy. Anxious to avoid being isolated during a Franco-Haitian conflict, he pushed for American formal recognition of his West Indian republic. Failing in these efforts, he implored the United States to remain neutral in the event of hostilities with France. By the mid-1820s, Boyer's anxieties about war were so acute that he found it expedient to play to American racial biases in order to gain consideration. In particularly obsequious gestures, he offered to prohibit Haitians from visiting states below the Potomac River and stated his willingness to send diplomats "such in color as not to offend the prejudices of the country." In 1825, French recognition of Haiti calmed many of Boyer's fears, though the price—an extorted indemnity of 150 million francs for property lost by French slaveholders during the revolution—was obscene and hardly affordable to the impoverished Caribbean nation. Nonetheless, during this time, one of the major initiatives of the Haitian government involved forging closer ties with the United States through the encouragement of African American immigration.[27]

The emigration agents that Boyer sent to the United States found that blacks in northeastern cities exhibited the most avid interest in Haiti. Promised land, high wages, and free passage, thirty Philadelphia families immigrated in August 1824 alone. Of southern states, North Carolina seems to have had numerous African Americans who were willing to immigrate to Haiti. According to Prince Saunders, a Haitian who helped organize prospective emigrants, correspondence he received "from an association of black people" in the state asserted that fourteen thousand free African Americans "were desirous of going to Hayti with all possible dispatch." Saunders believed that once a period of political stability settled over the Caribbean nation, a huge number of American blacks would migrate there. Considering the demographic evidence, it is very likely that the Haitian agent was misinformed about the prevalence of emigrationist sentiments. In 1820, only 14,701 free blacks lived in North Carolina, and most were probably not interested in immigrating to Haiti. Despite this embellishment, Saunders's information was not wholly in error. A number of North Carolinians were, in fact, paying close attention to the Haitian government's offer of free transportation and land.[28]

In September 1824, the MCS met to seriously discuss Haiti as a destination for the quasi-free blacks in their custody. Aaron Coffin, who had two months earlier proposed striking the word *colonization* from the group's title, made a fervent plea for Haitian emigration. In his estimate, the Haitian government was being quite generous in its offer to "take any number" of African Americans as immigrants, especially since it was prepared to defray much of the cost of transportation, exempt newcomers from taxation for a year, and provide them sustenance until they became self-sufficient. "What more can be asked?" he queried rhetorically. Coffin further claimed that southern states would not agree to abolish slavery without deporting "a considerable number" of blacks. "And as the distance is so much less to Hayti than Africa, & more likely to be adopted," he argued, "I think we ought to stand forth as advocates for the plan of removing them where we are most likely to succeed." Coffin's remarks did not fall on deaf ears. During the Yearly Meeting in November, the Quakers decided to contact Haitian emigration organizers to ascertain how best to proceed toward the goal of sending to the Caribbean nation as many of the seven hundred African Americans now in their care "as are willing to go." Two hundred dollars was appropriate for the initial implementation of this plan, and a motion was passed to start raising funds for the project.[29]

The idea of relocating the quasi-free blacks to Haiti, and thus resolving their manumission troubles, energized North Carolina Friends. Prior to 1824, the MCS had been in a malaise, unable to accomplish anything of significance regarding slavery. The restrictive emancipation laws of the state were largely to blame for this organizational inertia, but the Quakers' slow, deliberative style of decision-making was also responsible for their stagnant activism. Many issues that the group discussed in meetings were put off until later meetings or dropped altogether. Nearly everything that the organization expressed an interest in accomplishing, no matter how minor, was first assigned to appointed committees, which inhibited expeditious action. Even in regard to issues like slavery that aroused their moral indignation, a certain stilted formality pervaded many MCS proceedings. The voices and interests of those most affected by their decisions, in this case African Americans, were usually not recorded in the meeting minutes, suggesting that decision-making processes were typically exclusionary and shaped by the agendas of those allowed to participate. Additionally, with the exception of the radicalized Friends who assisted the Underground Railroad, Quaker antislavery activism was characteristically observant of state laws and was thus largely confined to symbolic flourishes, such as memorials and an occasional lawsuit.[30]

With the advent of the Haitian emigration movement of the 1820s, a certain urgency seemed to grip the MCS. The incessant meetings that tended to resolve little gave way to a new dynamism that was undoubtedly generated by both years of pent-up frustrations and the discovery of a willing and able partner in Boyer's government. To be sure, the gradualism in Quaker antislavery, a pragmatic necessity in North Carolina, still was quite evident in the mid-1820s. The MCS still believed in the prudence of coupling emancipation with colonization. Yet during this period, even their gradualism seemed accelerated, as witnessed in their pronouncements requesting that the state prohibit further slave importation, provide for the education of bondpeople, and eventually pass a statute mandating that "after a certain time, all persons shall be born free." Aaron Coffin's optimistic advocacy of African American relocation to Haiti perhaps best reflected the programmatic and psychological revitalization of the MCS, which had roughly 1,150 members by September 1825. "From the situation of things among us," he declared, "I think it is time to be up and a doing."[31]

Notwithstanding the growing appeal of Haiti to MCS members, the hundreds of quasi-free blacks among the Quakers were not of one mind regarding immigration to the Caribbean nation or anywhere else. According to an opinion poll conducted by the Friends in 1826, only 110 of the 729 African Americans in their care in five eastern counties were interested in migration to Haiti. Interestingly, 270 of those polled were willing to go to the ACS colony in West Africa, 101 were amenable to migrating westward to Ohio or Indiana, 14 wished to go to Philadelphia, and 99 wanted to stay in North Carolina. Complicating matters for a number of the blacks, many individuals among them were intermarried with slaves owned by people other than Friends. Moreover, scores of children belonged to these "mixed" families, which made issues of status and rights even more complex. It appears that perhaps a majority of these non-Quaker slaveholders were unwilling to liberate bondpeople for the purpose of migrating. Predictably, a number of African Americans refused to leave the state without family members, choosing instead to stay near enslaved spouses and children.[32]

Certainly coming as no surprise to the Quakers by this time, at least a few blacks were "not disposed to be under the care of Friends" at all, perhaps having had enough of white paternalism, even of a relatively benign sort. One man, upon hearing rumors of his imminent removal to Haiti, allegedly assailed his Quaker master, forcing the latter to agree not to ship him off to the West Indies. Given the magnitude of changes and adaptations that migration to Haiti and other places would have required of African Americans, it was probably not uncommon for them to have reservations about, or even to resist, suggestions by the MCS and the Friends in general to permanently leave the country. While the extent of black efforts to control their destiny among the North Carolina Quakers cannot be fully ascertained from surviving records, the Yearly Meeting of November 1825 did make reference to "people of colour under friends' care [who] will not be persuaded by the advice and council of friends." The Quaker response to this situation underscored their communal tendency toward conformity, as well as a lingering inclination to control the bodies and choices of black people. In dealing with quasi-free African Americans who refused their guidance, the meeting resolved "that they may be subjected by the most moderate means that will effectually reduce the object to industry for the benifit of him or herself." The exact meaning of "moderate means" was left undefined in the meeting's minutes, imply-ing that individual Quakers had some discretion in this matter.[33]

Although the idea of sending African Americans to Haiti had circulated among MCS members since 1824, it was not until 1826 that their deliberations became action. The Meeting for Sufferings, a Friends' charity group, dispatched Phineas Nixon and John Fellows to recruit emigrants in counties with high concentrations of quasi-free blacks. Concurrently, Benjamin Lundy, the Quaker editor of the *Genius of Universal Emancipation*, journeyed to Haiti to negotiate terms of settlement with Boyer's government. Lundy had recently traveled through North Carolina and had met a man who offered to free his slaves on the condition that Lundy relocate them somewhere "they could enjoy their rights." Other masters who were privy to the Friends' Haitian em-igration project also offered their slaves to the MCS, including John Stafford, who transferred an enslaved woman named Barbary and her seven-year-old daughter, Lilly, to the Guilford Quakers. Even among Friends themselves, sim-ilar transactions were taking place. George C. Mendenhall sold a family of eight slaves to his son Richard for the token price of eighty shillings for the purpose of sending them to Haiti or another place "where Slavery is not toler-ated." The arrangement was almost certainly designed to circumvent state man-umission laws, though the senior Mendenhall was one of Guilford County's largest slaveholders and would continue to own bondpeople into the 1850s. While the work of recruiting emigrants had hindered the MCS from sending blacks to Haiti earlier, raising funds for transporting them also slowed things down. Adding to these difficulties, the Haitian government, after having been defrauded by unscrupulous agents, rescinded its offer to pay for emigrant pas-sage in April 1825. Consequently, the Quakers had to raise the money among themselves and their supporters in order to finance African American immi-gration to Haiti.[34]

After assembling 119 emigrants and enough money to pay for their jour-ney, Nixon and Fellows made arrangements to disembark from the port of Beaufort during the spring of 1826. The emigrants were largely from eastern counties, with fifty-four sent by the North Carolina Yearly Meeting and fifty-five sent by individual Friends who had liberated them for the purpose of emigration. Of the remaining ten, eight were free blacks who had married bondpeople, and two were slaves who had been liberated and conveyed to the Quakers by nonmembers. On May 31, George Swain, a Greensboro Friend and president of that city's auxiliary of the ACS, arrived in Beaufort to super-vise the voyage preparations. A 105-ton schooner called *Sally Ann*, owned by Captains Samuel Douglass and Henry Cooke, was chartered for the passage to Haiti, but conflict over accommodations nearly derailed the arrangement. Upon touring the ship, Swain had noticed that the *Sally Ann* was crammed with commercial cargo to be sold in the West Indies. These goods included one thousand planks, one thousand pounds of leaf tobacco, ninety-eight barrels of tar, and seventy-five thousand shingles. This cargo was in addition to several barrels of flour, bread, pork, beef, rice, and other foodstuffs that were to be rationed to the emigrants during the trip. Finding the cramped passenger accommodations unsatisfactory, Swain complained to Captain Thomson, the man assigned by the owners to pilot the ship during the voyage.[35]

The Greensboro Quaker learned quickly that the *Sally Ann*'s captain was both temperamental and contemptuous of the Society of Friends and its abolitionism. In response to Swain's comments about space, Thomson retorted that he was aware of "how negroes ought to be used," since his father had owned eighty of them. Furthermore, he denounced Quakers who "loved negroes better than white people." At this point, the language of the seaman became violently disrespectful, and his disdain for both the Friends and African Americans was flagrantly displayed. As a small crowd gathered to witness the quarrel, Thomson roared that he would take pleasure in seeing forty of the emigrants "tied round [Swain's] neck and all throwed into the gulph stream together." Cooke, a co-owner of the vessel, had overheard some of the combative words of his employee and tried to smooth things over by making light of Thomson's tirade. Swain, thoroughly disgusted by the captain's antiblack and anti-Quaker attitude, insisted that Thomson had to be replaced as commander and passenger arrangements liberalized before he would proceed with chartering the *Sally Ann*. Unable to shake the Quaker's resolve with a threat of a lawsuit, Cooke's co-owner, Captain Douglass, agreed to take over the helm, and a modest amount of space, still insufficient in Swain's view, was created for the passengers. On June 11, the *Sally Ann* and its 121 passengers, including Nixon and Fellows, set sail for the Republic of Haiti under light westerly winds.[36]

The voyage was unfortunately eventful. Rain drenched the ship for the first week of its journey, and head winds lengthened its time at sea. An outbreak of measles afflicted twenty-five of the emigrants, but claimed no lives. According to Nixon, the water on board was "extremely bad, both as to taste and smell." Altogether, the *Sally Ann* was at sea for twenty-five days before landing at Aux Cayes on July 6. Haitian officials at the scenic port cordially welcomed the newcomers, notifying them that "comfortable homes" would be prepared for them in the countryside where they were expected to take up farming. Also, four months of rations were to be given to them at the government's expense to facilitate their acclimation. Finished with their work, Nixon and Fellows returned to North Carolina, satisfied that the immigrants would be well provided for in their new homeland.[37]

Unbeknownst to them at the time, the *Sally Ann* expedition was the first

and last Haiti-bound migration that North Carolina Quakers would sponsor. A number of factors would make the island nation less attractive to both
the Friends and the quasi-free blacks. First, the relocation of just 119 immigrants to Aux Cayes proved to be quite expensive. The Quakers alone were
responsible for a bill of over fifteen hundred dollars. Second, there had not
been much initial interest among black North Carolinians regarding relocation to Haiti. Liberia and the free American states seemed to be more popular destinations, according to polls taken by the Friends. Finally, those who
had emigrated aboard the *Sally Ann* did not fare well in their new land, and
news of their discontent reached North Carolina soon after their arrival.[38]

In 1826, the British consul general in Haiti encountered sixty of the North
Carolina immigrants working the farm lands of the commandant of Aux
Cayes. Although they said kind things about their employer, they had grievances regarding the purloining of their property by Haitians, as well as the
cultural intolerance they had experienced. Similarly, Thomas Kennedy, a
Wayne County Friend, made an investigative visit to Haiti in 1829 and found
that the black North Carolinians there were "unpleasantly situated, and very
much disappointed." Having been grossly cheated out of wages by landowners, they told Kennedy that they preferred North Carolina slavery to their
treatment in Haiti. In common with some of the estimated thirteen thousand other African Americans who arrived in Haiti during the 1820s, the
Sally Ann immigrants found adapting to the Caribbean country most difficult. Cultural barriers, especially regarding language, religion, and social values, hampered assimilation. Moreover, the political chaos and widespread
poverty certainly made citizenship in the black republic less dignifying than
many had perhaps imagined. Ironically, as racism and slavery had created a
migration to Haiti, discrimination and deprivation there provoked a reverse
migration back to the United States. As early as 1825, two hundred African
American immigrants had already returned to their land of origin with
enough unpleasant tales to make others think twice about leaving. In that
same year, the governor of North Carolina, ever watchful of the activities of
blacks and Quakers, suggested to the legislature that it pass a law forbidding
immigrants to re-enter the state from Haiti. Only one generation removed
from the great slave insurrection against the French, he was convinced that
"our own safety and tranquility seems to require this prohibitory measure."[39]

While they had been galvanized by the thought of sending African Americans in their custody to Haiti, the North Carolina Friends had remained
open to other avenues through which they could terminate their direct association with slavery. In September 1825, though they focused on Boyer's republic, the Quakers resolved to continue encouraging African colonization,
if only "to give the Emigrants a choice in countries." Three months later, they

reiterated their support for the ACS, authorizing Richard Mendenhall and two other Friends to correspond with the Washington-based organization. By this time, the group's colony seemed to be evolving into a viable fixture on the West African littoral. Emigrant ships were regularly depositing colonists into the settlement, who had thus far proved able to fend off the irredentism of their African neighbors. In North Carolina, the colonization movement had become respectable and, according to a Virginia agent of the ACS, "has many warm-hearted and influential friends" there. Indeed, the group had several auxiliary societies in the state, supported by some of the bluest blood in the South.[40]

Motivated primarily by self-interest, the ACS had been critical of African American immigration to Haiti as early as 1820. During their third annual meeting, the white colonizationists denounced the religion, language, and "military despotism" of the Caribbean nation in favor of the promise of Africa, where colonists could "impart their own [American] manners, religion, laws, and language." Having less to do with the ACS or what Africa might promise and more to do with what Haiti could not deliver, the Haitian emigration movement turned out to be a learning experience for the African colonization movement. For the Quakers, their short-lived Caribbean project provided valuable experience in raising funds, recruiting emigrants, and chartering and outfitting ships. It moved them away from long-winded deliberations in their meetinghouses and into a hands-on mode of resolving their manumission problems through migration. For African Americans, the lessons of Haiti were much less inspiring. The emigration movement had raised unreasonable expectations regarding the possibilities of a fuller freedom, a black nationality born of revolution, and economic opportunities. More than anything else, it demonstrated just how despised they were in their native land and how their Americanness did not necessarily serve them well abroad. Thus, for the Quakers, Africa was an answer to a morally exhausting riddle. For the quasi-free blacks, it was an open question, just as their lives and status in North Carolina had been.[41]

IN EARLY 1825, over a year before the *Sally Ann* carried its 119 sojourners to Haiti, the brig *Hunter* approached the coast of West Africa with the first of thousands of black North Carolinians who would migrate to the ACS's colony there during the nineteenth century. In addition to the aforementioned Charity Hunter and her three children, who had seen so much in Norfolk prior to embarkation, the ship carried John Williams and his family of ten from Pasquotank County. Like Charity, John, a forty-year-old father and husband, was looking to build a new life for himself and his family on the other side of the Atlantic. Unlike the Hunters, however, the Williams clan had never been in bondage and were thus not migrating to escape North Carolina slavery but instead the low quality of black freedom in the state. The thirty-nine-day voyage to Africa gave all aboard plenty of time to ponder their past experiences and the new identities available in their tropical destination. Every morning as they looked anxiously eastward for land, North Carolina realities were steadily eclipsed by imaginings of Africa and a host of new uncertainties.[42]

On March 13, Cape Mesurado, covered with misty forest, rose in lush majesty before the approaching *Hunter*. The colony that the ACS had planted here was officially given the name Liberia a year earlier, meaning "a settlement of persons *made free*." In tribute to President Monroe, who had allowed white colonizationists to interject their agenda into the recaptive agency authorized by Congress in 1819, the first immigrant town was dubbed Monrovia and established atop the promontory of Mesurado. Like North Carolina, this part of Africa had some of the most beautiful shoreline on the planet, but was void of natural harbors that would allow ships to easily dock close to the settlement. As a response to this geography, a maritime industry of ship-to-shore transportation evolved along the coast, dominated by the Kru, an African ethnic group with communities based several miles to the southeast. It is impossible to know what John Williams thought as the African landscape filled his eyes, or as the sounds of a continent full of life and lore reverberated in his ears. What is certain was that his future lay on shore, and whatever had happened in North Carolina to drive him to this place now existed only in the realm of memories. For John and the others, Liberia was both an ending and a beginning.[43]

THREE. THE FIRST WAVE

MUCH OF THE EARLY STORY of African American immigration to Liberia is embedded in the history of Pasquotank County from whence the Williamses hailed. Bound by Chowan County on the east and Perquimans County to the west, Pasquotank is one of North Carolina's oldest counties, having been established as a precinct in 1670 and named after local Native Americans. Its topology is perhaps its most striking feature. The Albemarle Sound forms its southern boundary, providing access, though not unobstructed, to the ocean. The northernmost portion of the county descends into the Great Dismal Swamp, which straddles the border between northeastern North Carolina and Virginia. Forests of oak, pine, maple, and cypress overshadow much of its terrain, and streams and rivers further accent its watery character. Rich soils, naturally irrigated and favored by temperate weather, suited the county for an array of agricultural pursuits, and the abundance of woodlands made it a valuable source of lumber for various markets.[1]

By 1800, the principal town of Pasquotank was Elizabeth City, which also became the county seat in that year. Established on the banks of the Pasquotank River, it had access to several tidewater counties bordering the Albemarle Sound, as well as Norfolk, by way of the Dismal Swamp Canal. A steamboat circuit connected the town to New Bern by 1817, and stagecoaches regularly passed through it en route to Norfolk and Edenton by the follow-

Above: Ruins of slave quarters, eastern North Carolina (Photograph by author)

ing year. The communal and cultural life of Elizabeth City centered around the courthouse, a multi-purpose institution that hosted recreational events, religious gatherings, political affairs, and the business of the town commissioners. In addition to these functions, quarterly court sessions were held here, guaranteeing a lively traffic in its halls during judicial proceedings. When President Monroe visited the town in 1819, it boasted a City Hotel, where he stayed, and a maturing system of riverine travel and trade. Over the next decade, Elizabeth City became even more commercial with the founding of general stores, a tobacco factory, and a tannery. Importantly, the expansion of the Dismal Canal in 1828 further opened its navigable arteries to a brisk circulation of people, goods, and information to and from Norfolk and other eastern cities.[2]

Predictably, Pasquotank County's connections to the Chesapeake, its fertile lands, and its patterns of commercial development made it, along with its sister counties along the Albemarle Sound, an early site for experimentation with slave labor. Although not nearly as dependent upon black servitude as some of its neighbors, such as Bertie, Halifax, and Northampton Counties, slaves comprised 33 percent of Pasquotank's population of 8,008 in 1820, roughly the same as the state's percentage for that year. Legal and customary measures for controlling enslaved as well as free African Americans, who numbered 532 in 1820, accompanied the growth of these populations, and officials in Elizabeth City were especially vigilant in regard to demarcating the limits of black life in the town. In 1813, county authorities forbade blacks from selling "spirits, cakes, or any other articles" on the premises of the courthouse during sessions. In 1830, the state legislature banned slaves from establishing households in the town that were not situated on property owned by their masters. Bondpeople accused of serious offenses were subjected to a range of punishments, some of the most barbarous penalties dating back to the colonial period. Whippings, torture, and imprisonment were among the most common punitive acts imposed upon slaves, but ear croppings and castrations were still inflicted throughout the late eighteenth century. At all times, insurrection, planned or realized, was a capital crime and was routinely punished as such.[3]

In large part due to such repressive mechanisms designed to ensure their subjugation, bondpeople resisted their masters with all available means. A favorite method was to take advantage of the geography to escape enslavement altogether. Absconding by way of the Albemarle Sound was certainly attempted on numerous occasions, but fleeing to the murky recesses of the Great Dismal Swamp became a preferred form of resistance by slaves of Pasquotank and adjacent counties. Throughout the settlement of the region, hundreds of fugitives took refuge in the marshes during any given decade, some residing there as long-term runaways, or maroons, who established communal bases and preyed upon local plantations. By the nineteenth century, the swamp was a central motif of the lore of black resistance in the state, taking on greater cultural meaning with each failure of patrollers to quickly capture fugitives. Consequently, the Great Dismal allowed Pasquotank slaves to breach the confines of their thralldom in ways not available to most North Carolina bondpeople.[4]

Somewhat complementary of this legacy of black rebelliousness in Pasquotank was a tradition of white antislavery, though it developed in a slower, more halting fashion. Quaker communities along the Albemarle Sound had existed since the late seventeenth century, with perhaps the oldest in Perquimans and Northampton Counties. Similar to the Friends of New Garden and elsewhere, abolitionist sentiment among Pasquotank Quakers emerged from generations of slaveholding and a gradual reckoning with the iniquities of the practice. By the Revolutionary period, Friends in the Albemarle region were freeing their slaves with a frequency that aroused a counterresponse from local and state officials, who were becoming increasingly indignant about the group's emancipationist philosophy. In close collaboration with Piedmont Friends, Quakers in the eastern counties settled on colonization as a compromise solution for ridding themselves of quasi-free blacks who could not be fully and safely manumitted without provoking retaliatory state action. Even more than their Piedmont counterparts, Friends in the eastern agricultural counties witnessed the brutality of slavery and the difficulties of manumission in stark ways, since African American bondage was concentrated in their area of the state. Thus, it is perhaps not surprising that they, at least as much as their Guilford brethren, saw a divine influence in their colonization work within counties with a third, or more, of their populations in bondage. "Verily I believe this to be his cause," rhapsodized Caleb White, a member of the Pasquotank auxiliary society, in 1827. "He led the children of Israel out of Egypt, & in a way similar I believe he will lead the poor sable Africans from amongst us & may the colonizing plan be compared to Moses."[5]

In November 1825, North Carolina Quakers gathered at New Garden for their Yearly Meeting. While Haitian emigration was still a fresh topic of discussion, African colonization, as well as black removal to "free governments" (nonslave states) within the United States, drew the most attention. Several hundred quasi-free African Americans were still in the custody of the Friends, many of whom preferred migrating to Liberia as opposed to Haiti. In light of this, the conferees unanimously agreed to raise one thousand dollars to fund future migrations, which would be largely spent on emigrant expeditions to Liberia. Considering the dearth of surviving MCS, ACS, and Quaker records detailing the preparations that were made, it seems that the first Friends-sponsored migration of North Carolina blacks to Africa the following year was hastily arranged. The group's increasing zeal for colonization and willingness to experiment with a number of options superseded, at least momentarily, their penchant for deliberative gradualism and delay. As a result, very little can be known about the people whom they so eagerly desired to send to Liberia or the manner in which they, in conjunction with the ACS, orchestrated this seminal expedition.[6]

Despite this shortage of documentation, information contained in the emigrant roll and other extant sources do allow for a cursory look at the African Americans who migrated to Liberia on the ship *Indian Chief* on February 15, 1826. In regard to their origin, all of the 121 North Carolina emigrants, with 6 possible exceptions, were from the northeastern counties. Sixty were from Pasquotank alone, and most of the others were from Bertie (17), Camden (16), and Perquimans (15). A slight majority (66) of the emigrants were female, and a few of the families, such as the Morrises of Pasquotank and the Sandlings of Bertie, were headed by women. There was a wide age-range among the emigrants, the youngest being infants less than 1 year of age and the oldest in their 60s. The average age of the group was 20.7 years, and the modal ages were 3 and 25, with 8 persons of each age. All but one emigrant, Sampson Taylor, a 60-year-old shoemaker from Camden County, were listed as free born, though this was certainly not the case, despite the fact that fifty emigrants sent by the Friends had lived nominally as free people.

In reference to occupations, thirty of the emigrants, including fifteen farmers, are listed as having trades or skills. Of the remaining number, there were four weavers and two spinsters, all of whom were women; three shoemakers, two carpenters, a sawyer, a wheelwright, and a fifty-year-old midwife, Milly Taylor of Camden County. While most of the emigrants are listed with no particular skill or vocation, it can be assumed that adults and older children were previously engaged in agricultural and domestic labor, considering their counties of origin. Finally, the rudiments of literacy were apparent among a minority of the emigrants, at least partially reflective of Quaker efforts to instruct the blacks in their custody. Seventeen individuals are listed as being capable of spelling, eleven could read, and two were noted as being able to write; one of the latter could cipher as well.[7]

Behind this interesting though sketchy statistical profile of the *Indian Chief* emigrants are lives and experiences that were largely unchronicled and thus lost to history. Most of these people, originating from predominantly rural and illiterate communities, were not retrievable historical personalities until their names and other information were entered on the rolls of ACS-chartered ships. They are, therefore, only knowable because they chose to immigrate to Liberia. Even with this information, the vast majority of the emigrants on the *Indian Chief*, and subsequent Africa-bound ships, must remain primarily in the shadows of history, though basic descriptors—names, ages, occupations, and so forth—give them a vaguely discernible historical presence. Notwithstanding the unfortunate limitations of source materials, occasionally a fuller picture of particular emigrants can be rendered from existing sources. For the emigrants of the *Indian Chief*, one such life, that of Priscilla White, can be characterized in some detail.

Apparently born in slavery in 1766, Priscilla had lived her early life in Perquimans County during a most tumultuous time. She was only ten when her master, Caleb White, a Quaker, resolved to free her, along with "Luke, Zilpha, and Nancy." She perhaps had some sense of the evolving sensibilities of the Friends regarding slavery, as well as the dissonance between the ideals of the coming revolution and the ongoing servitude of African Americans throughout the Albemarle Sound. Whatever the case, her life was certainly complicated by a 1777 law that was construed by local officials as reversing her manumission by White. In what must have been a horrific experience for an eleven-year-old girl, the county court ordered that she and the other emancipated slaves be "exposed to sale to the highest bidder, for ready money, at the courthouse door" in July. In response to an appeal that was probably initiated by White or other Quakers, a superior court in Edenton overturned the order in May 1778. This favorable ruling held that Priscilla and the other liberated slaves "were sold and enslaved by order of the said court, in express violation of the constitution of this State, and contrary to natural justice, and that there are manifest errors and irregularities in said proceedings." What transpired in her life between this verdict and her departure in the *Indian Chief* is undocumented. Nonetheless, Priscilla appears to have been the sixty-year-old matriarch of a clan of Whites who emigrated from Perquimans and Pasquotank in 1826, which also included a Caleb White, almost certainly named after Priscilla's benefactor. Her time in Liberia is similarly obscure, though her last days were spent in the Caldwell settlement on the St. Paul's River. In 1828, she died in the colony of what was officially listed as "decline."[8]

Like Charity Hunter and her children a year before, Priscilla White and the other North Carolinians left America by way of Norfolk. They had arrived in the city in the late fall of 1825 and were housed there until the *Indian Chief* arrived. Thus, it seems likely that they, too, may have experienced Norfolk and its urban, maritime, slave-trading culture in ways similar to the passengers of the *Hunter*. In addition to carrying 121 North Carolinians, the ship also transported two dozen emigrants from Virginia and Maryland, states that had been sending blacks to Africa since the voyage of the *Elizabeth* in 1820. Also aboard was Dr. John W. Peaco, an employee of the U.S. government who was to serve as the resettlement agent for recaptured Africans, assistant to the ACS representative in Liberia, and colonial physician. As part of its cargo, the *Indian Chief* carried the frames of five buildings that were to be the foundations of recaptive housing in Liberia, along with the frames for two schooners meant for use in the West African coastal trade. Ostensibly, there was little that was unusual about the voyage of the *Indian Chief*. The ship arrived off Cape Mesurado on March 22, though most of its passengers were taken to the new agricultural settlement of Caldwell, a few miles east of Monrovia. As would be proven time and again, there was certainly nothing atypical about the strain of malaria that frightfully afflicted the North Carolinians, "without a single exception," upon arrival in Liberia. Most of the twelve lives immediately claimed by the scourge were those of female children under the age of eight from Perquimans and Camden Counties. As discussed at length in Chapter 7, there were many ways to die in Liberia, but the *Anopheles* mosquito was, by far, the principal destroyer of those seeking liberty in the African tropics.[9]

Just as dreams of a Caribbean homeland for their black wards had galvanized Quakers earlier, the qualified success of the *Indian Chief* reignited their interest in African colonization. In some ways, it was logical that the Friends would focus their attention on Liberia by 1826. According to their poll of over seven hundred African Americans in their custody during that year, a plurality preferred the African colony over other destinations. Furthermore, without the financial assistance of Boyer's government, immigration to Haiti proved costly, and following the voyage of the *Sally Ann*, it became unpopular among prospective emigrants as well. Migration to midwestern states appealed to a small portion of the quasi-free blacks and others. However, this region, and Indiana in particular, was becoming a less welcoming destination for black North Carolinians.[10]

In 1826, New Garden Friends received reports that racism was as prevalent in Indiana as it was in the Tar Heel State. Moreover, the Quakers themselves were not immune to antiblack prejudices. Although they claimed to be against slavery, Indiana Friends did not want African Americans to migrate among them. These attitudes could hardly have caught the New Garden group completely off guard, given that even among them, racial segregation and paternalist control were routinely imposed upon blacks in their custody. Nonetheless, if these sentiments alone were not enough to dampen enthusiasm for black migration to the Midwest, laws passed by a number of these states did have this effect. Ohio adopted measures in 1804 and 1807 to discourage black immigration, as did Illinois with its "Black Law" of 1819. Twelve years later, Indiana, which experienced a 300 percent increase in its African American population between 1820 and 1830, required blacks migrating to the state to post a five-hundred-dollar surety against indigence and bad behavior. Those convicted of either a crime or misdemeanor forfeited the money.

As antiblack biases fanned across the lands north of the Ohio River, similar feelings seethed in northeastern cities as well. Even in the Quaker capital of Philadelphia, African Americans were personae non gratae in many quarters. Evidently, many Friends and others outside of the South viewed slavery and race as peculiarly southern problems. From a distance, they could indulge their benevolent proclivities and passionately advocate abolition, civil rights, and Inner Lights. Yet their own liberalism and tolerance were sorely tested when it was they who were confronted with the prospect of having to interact personally and daily with black people, who did not easily fit into their phenotypical, cultural, and socioeconomic frames of reference or their leveling, conformist vision of the ideal society. On this score, it becomes comprehensible that Philadelphia Quakers would be among the biggest financial contributors to the colonization cause by the late 1820s. Likewise, these observations illuminate at least some of the reasons Pennsylvania would send more blacks to Liberia than any other state north of Maryland and the Ohio River.[11]

If it was becoming clear to black North Carolinians that interstate migration and an exodus to Haiti were in many respects uninviting alternatives to staying put, their feelings about relocating to Liberia were certainly not uniform. During their 1826 survey of several hundred African Americans regarding their destination preferences, MCS members and other Quakers gained a good sense of just how diverse and complicated black views of Liberia were, as well as knowledge of present circumstances among blacks in eastern North Carolina. For example, a number of African Americans could not conceive of migrating anywhere without being accompanied by family members. Rhoda Jordan, a quasi-free mother of four, refused to leave the state without her husband, who was a bondman of a non-Quaker, for fear of rupturing her "snug little family." An elderly woman, owned by Quaker Catherine White, was in a similar situation, but intimated that she and her enslaved husband desired that their six children migrate to Liberia without them. Sarah Davis, thirty-four, was reluctant to relocate to Africa with her husband and nine children, but asserted that she would rather migrate than "fall in slavery." Perhaps predictably, active resistance to the prospect of migrating to Liberia was not difficult for the Quakers to find in the several eastern counties that they canvassed. In one instance, Fanny Taylor assented to being colonized in Africa, "but Ran away and Decived Friends." One man belonging to Catharine White followed his enslaved wife to Alabama, where she had apparently been sold. In a terse statement of his fate, the MCS noted that having acted "against the council of his Friends, he is said to be kill[d]."

Some of the blacks interviewed by Quakers simply desired more information about Liberia before deciding whether to quit the state. Many had determined not to make any decision before hearing "good news" from the people who had left on the *Indian Chief*. Although the scarcity of reliable information about Liberia discouraged emigration, it did not prevent African Americans from conjecturing about Africa and the life they were likely to find there. Some of their comments may have seemed of questionable accuracy, even fanciful, to their interviewers, but they are, nonetheless, valuable evidence of the meaning of the continent and its peoples to nineteenth-century black southerners. In the case of Ferebee, twenty-five, and Nanny, twenty-three, both women were disinclined to leave primarily because their husbands were still in bondage. Notwithstanding this consideration, apprehensions regarding the sanitation of African water gave them further reason to pause, as did rumors "that the Guinea folks are Troublesome." An elderly man, in contemplation of embarking for Liberia, informed Quakers that he "understands there are elephants in Africa that can catch Rats and that no body can stop them when they start their course." A darker and more realistic concern was expressed by one group of blacks who mentioned hearing of "a Dreadful Flie that comes about in Liberia once in 7 years." In a not-so-veiled allusion to the vectors of malaria endemic to the colony, these individuals believed that if the insect "bit one child all the family would die." In most cases, it is impossible to know how often such beliefs prevented people from leaving for Liberia, since Quaker chroniclers did not typically list the full names of those interviewed or their subsequent actions.[12]

By late 1826, the Friends had heard enough from black North Carolinians to conclude that another expedition could be arranged. The national office of the ACS in Washington, inundated with inquiries from all over the country, was of this opinion as well. In September, John Ehringhaus of the Pasquotank auxiliary society informed ACS secretary Ralph R. Gurley that the North Carolina Quakers hoped to send as many as one hundred of the blacks in their custody to Liberia during the fall, assuming that the parent organization could secure a ship. Concurrently, the Friends endeavored to raise the necessary funds to assist in outfitting a second expedition. In November, the Meeting for Sufferings proposed raising two thousand dollars to meet the cost of black migration, and within two months, eight hundred dollars had been turned over to the ACS for this purpose. The rapidity of the Quakers' actions here, unfettered by the hesitancy of the past, was suggestive of the urgency that they now associated with their colonization work.[13]

Although there were other instances such as this when large sums of money were all at once donated to defray the cost of Liberian migration, this was not the most common method of fund-raising. Much of the money raised by Guilford, Pasquotank, and other communities of Friends was in the form of small contributions, which accrued into formidable sums over time. Donations such as the two dollars that the Pasquotank auxiliary society sent to the ACS in September 1826 or the ten dollars that the Greensboro organization forwarded the following month were the typical sums received by the ACS and its branches. Also, subscriptions to the ACS's new organ, the *African Repository*, generated modest, though steady, revenue. Many of the smaller donations were sent with letters of support for the cause and regrets that more could not be collected. Some remittances were accompanied by passionate gushes of antislavery and colonizationist sentiments that were, of course, characteristic of North Carolina Quakers by this time. Illustratively, in sending Gurley two dollars in March 1827, Mary Mendenhall of Guilford waxed, "may your Society grow stronger and stronger and your colony may flourish as the cedars of lebanon so that consciencious men may not die hampered with thier Slaves." Aside from the usual incremental pattern of fund-raising, North Carolina Friends did raise significant sums of money quickly during the late 1820s. Still, the Pennsylvania philanthropist and Philadelphia Friends who donated $2,914.19 and $3,000, respectively, for the removal of North Carolina blacks in 1826–27 had no counterparts in the Tar Heel State during this period.[14]

In November 1826, the Yearly Meeting charged Caleb White with recruiting emigrants for an expedition that fall. Little, however, was accomplished before January, when several Pasquotank blacks indicated a willingness to embark for Liberia. To be sure, the delay in sending an expedition was not due to a lack of interest in colonization among North Carolinians. The ACS had previously received numerous inquiries from people all over the state desirous of information about their African colony. In September, Joseph Gales of the Raleigh auxiliary had reported that several African American men in that area appeared amenable to migrating. Similarly, a Hillsborough slaveholder was described in a letter to Gurley as "extremely anxious" to send her young bondman to Liberia, the latter allegedly interested in going. Yet the ACS privileged the Quaker settlements of the Albemarle Sound, with their high concentrations of quasi-free blacks, as primary sources of emigrants for their chartered ships. The Friends, experienced fund-raisers and philosophically committed to colonization, provided the momentum and financial backing behind the movement in North Carolina, and the ACS dutifully deferred to their timetables for sending emigrants during this period. Accordingly, in early January 1827, thirty-seven African Americans from Northampton County, formerly under Friends' care, loaded their belongings on three wagons and began the northeastward journey to Norfolk. They were joined by four or five blacks from neighboring Hertford County who had also lived among Quakers. The Pasquotank emigrants, thirty-eight in number, departed for the Virginia port shortly afterwards. Traveling by boat, they braved

the frigid waters and billowing fog of the Dismal Swamp Canal, the most direct water route to Norfolk.[15]

Despite the fact that background information on particular individuals is
scarce, the emigrant roll for this group discloses a number of salient and sub-
tle features regarding this migration. As with the North Carolinians who departed on the *Indian Chief*, this expedition was mostly composed of family
groups, the largest clan being the twenty Peeles of Northampton County. Of
the Pasquotank blacks, there were the seven members of the Brozier family,
twelve Tisdales, and nine Whites. Most of the younger children in the party
were listed as free born, and only the Wheeler family of five from Northampton County appears to have been liberated for the expressed purpose of colonization in Liberia. Insofar as ACS officials apparently encouraged the migration of nuclear families in the hope of fostering a balanced sex ratio in the
colony, the Pasquotank and Northampton groups were almost evenly divided by gender, with an aggregate of thirty-eight males and thirty-five females. Colonizationists hoped that this pattern of emigration would promote natural population growth and social stability in Liberia as well as shield
them from accusations that their operation, like slavery, divided black families. Further indicative of the desire to establish a self-reproducing colonial
populace, the emigrants were a relatively youthful group, with an average age
of 17.6 years and modal ages of 1 and 4, of which there were 7 of each. Thirty-
nine of the emigrants were eighteen years of age or younger, and only six
were over forty. Primus Peele of Northampton was the sole sexagenarian.[16]

Occupationally, this group was, at least on the surface, much less diverse in
talents than the *Indian Chief* emigrants. While it can again be assumed, considering their origins, that most of the adults and older children had experience in agricultural or domestic work, only twenty-two of the emigrants are
listed with vocations. Of this number, twenty-one were farmers, two of whom
—Jacob and James Pritchard of Pasquotank—were also sawyers. Of the
seventy-five emigrants who would eventually embark at Norfolk, only one,
Peter Johnston, a forty-year-old Pasquotank farmer, was listed in the emigrant roll as literate in any manner. Considering that a majority of these African Americans had at one time been in Quaker custody, which often included
at least basic instruction in reading or writing, the rate of literacy among this
group was likely underreported. Possible reasons for this oversight include a
reluctance on the part of blacks to implicate Friends or incriminate themselves by acknowledging their level of education in a cultural atmosphere
that was generally hostile to African American literacy. Additionally, the un-
derreporting could also have been due to the failure of ACS officials in North
Carolina and Norfolk to routinely inquire about the prevalence of literacy
among emigrants, especially among black children. This possible lack of in-

terest in such information-gathering may also explain the dearth of vocations and skills recorded in emigrant rolls.[17]

The Northampton and Hertford emigrants arrived in Norfolk on January 16. Although preparing for its annual surge in slave trading, the city was in a recuperative mode, having only recently been released from a yellow fever epidemic, which crested during the previous September with fifty-seven deaths. Currently, ice was crystallizing in the port's waterways, significantly blocking maritime traffic. John McPhail, the ACS agent in Norfolk, was responsible for housing the party, a charge made all the more imperative by the inclement wintry weather. He and Virginia agent John Kennedy unsuccessfully tried to rent a house in the city and eventually ended up allowing the emigrants to stay in a residence owned by McPhail, which was "undergoing some repair." While they were able to protect the group from exposure, the colonization agents were less effective in screening other influences. To Kennedy's dismay, a number of local African Americans and whites attempted to discourage the party from departing for Liberia. In his correspondence with Secretary Gurley, he offered no specifics about these entreaties but was satisfied that none of the migrating North Carolinians "will now fly the course." Of more pressing concern, the party from Pasquotank County, which was traveling via the Dismal Swamp Canal, was delayed by frozen waters that were clogging the southern end of the passage. On January 20, Kennedy sent two covered wagons to retrieve the stranded emigrants, hoping to have them in Norfolk that afternoon.[18]

By early February, the *Doris*, the English-built brig that had been chartered to make the voyage to Liberia, had yet to arrive from Baltimore. Several of the emigrants occupied their time by working low-paying jobs, perhaps saving some of their earning for life in Africa. Kennedy reported that the newcomers "still hold on in good Spirits," but later lamented that pleurisy and colds afflicted the group by the third week of February. When the *Doris* finally arrived to collect a contingent of ninety-four passengers, including twelve emigrants from Maryland and seven Virginians, the Murfreesboro people of Hertford County were forced to remain behind in Norfolk due to a lack of space aboard ship. Departing on February 24, the expedition barely missed seeing Norfolk razed by fire on March 9, which consumed seventy thousand dollars in property, including sixty homes, an Episcopal church, and a Lancasterian school. Although avoiding this calamity, on April 11 the emigrants landed in Monrovia on the eve of "the rains," the most unhealthiest of the region's two season.[19]

The colonial agent in Liberia, Jehudi Ashmun, wrote euphemistically about the malarial plague that ambushed the *Doris* emigrants within days of disembarkation at Monrovia. "In regard to the natives of North Carolina," he informed the ACS board of managers, "all the change they have undergone seems to be less of a *disease, than a salutary effort of nature* to accommodate the physical system of its subjects, by a safe and gentle process of attenuation, to the new influences of a tropical climate." Colonization officials were quick to reprint Ashmun's disingenuous letters in the *African Repository* and to incorporate them into the report that was issued following their 1828 annual meeting. In the latter document, the organization's leaders even commended themselves on having established a colony in an "admirably selected" location. Predictably, they were less forthcoming about the atrocious mortality that decimated the company of the *Doris*.

Of the seventeen victims of malaria, all were North Carolinians, who suffered a 23 percent death rate from the disease. All of the deaths occurred among those who were sent from Monrovia to Caldwell on the St. Paul's River, and every family suffered at least one loss, the Peeles witnessing six of their number waste away in feverish exhaustion. The liberated Wheeler family, which stayed in Monrovia probably to facilitate Samuel Wheeler's search for employment as a carpenter, was miraculously spared tragedy, considering that the capital tended to be slightly more malarial than upriver settlements. Similarly, none of the Virginians and Marylanders perished from malaria, despite also having remained in Monrovia. In due time, news of this epidemiological catastrophe would reach North Carolina and have a withering impact on the willingness of African Americans to migrate to Liberia. Meantime, however, the ACS pushed for more expeditions and more colonists, ravenously annexing additional tracts of malarial lands to accommodate its African vision.[20]

The fate of the *Doris* emigrants, and dozens of others who had been sent to Africa since 1820, raised troubling questions for the Quakers and others who had supported the ACS for largely humanitarian reasons. Leading colonizationists who refused to camouflage their proslavery motives for championing the organization tarnished whatever emancipationist veneer that the ACS had achieved since its founding. Whether it was the ranting of Henry Clay, who slandered free blacks as "contaminated," "vicious," and "evil" at the annual meeting in January 1827, or colonial agents who dismissed malarial mortality as an acceptable cost of colonization, skepticism of the motivations and operation of the ACS accumulated rapidly in many quarters. At a meeting of the MCS in September, ideological fissures in the organization were laid bare during a contentious debate over the integrity and morality of the Washington-based organization. Some were of the opinion that Liberian colonization was worthy of support and that the ACS was "congenial" enough to warrant a merger. Others argued that the ACS was animated by principles inconsistent with the mission of the MCS and, thus, undeserving of its further consideration. The meeting ended with a resolution praising "the existance of the *American Colonization Society*," suggesting that colonizationists still held sway in the organization. It was even agreed that the token sum of twenty dollars be donated to the ACS. Notwithstanding these gestures, the Quakers were not immune to dissension regarding colonization, and in this instance the divisions never softened.[21]

Regardless of the qualms individual Quakers and others were having about the ACS, canvassing for a new company of emigrants commenced shortly after the departure of the *Doris*. Nathan Mendenhall and Phineas Albertson, both Guilford Quakers, were appointed by the "Committee for the Removal of the People of Color under Friends' Care" to recruit emigrants for the next North Carolina expedition. Beginning in August, they traveled a few hundred miles across the eastern counties, eventually enrolling between sixty and seventy blacks who had expressed an interest in migrating. Concurrently, James Nourse, the ACS agent for North Carolina, also toured the state in the hope of arousing colonization sentiment among whites. Nourse's journey included stops in the Albemarle towns of Elizabeth City, Edenton, and Plymouth, as well as in areas farther south and inland, such as Raleigh, New Bern, and Fayetteville. By early 1828, the itinerant agent had found that North Carolinians had widely divergent views of the ACS and its goals. His task was easiest in the northeastern counties, where colonization had its most attentive audience. In the Pamlico Sound city of New Bern, Nourse encountered clergymen who were amenable to black removal but found "many others" who were opposed to it, thus precluding the founding of a local auxiliary society. The agent received a more hospitable reception in Fayetteville, Chapel Hill, and Rowan County, where ACS branches were reestablished after years of stagnation. In Hillsborough, people were "friendly" to the cause, according to Nourse, "yet decidedly averse to the *open discussion* of the subject in any way."[22]

In Raleigh, Nourse's mission generally met with disappointment. Initially, it seemed that the city, centrally located and politically valuable to the ACS cause, would provide the necessary conditions for the growth of a unified statewide movement based in the capital itself. On December 28, 1827, the Raleigh auxiliary society, during a poorly attended meeting, voted to create the "North Carolina Society for Colonizing the Free People of Colour of the United States." Governor James Iredell was elected president of the group, and Reverend Dr. Joseph Caldwell and a Dr. Beckwith were made vice presidents. The new state society resolved that the national organization "is worthy of the patronage and assistance of the citizens of North Carolina," and in January commissioned Nourse to serve as its agent, in addition to his ACS duties.

Despite these optimistic signs, the much-sought-after state support that the colonizationists hoped for continued to elude them. In 1826, the legislature had again displayed its distaste for emancipation and colonization by refusing to act on yet another Quaker memorial. Instead, the state Senate chose to contemplate a bill that would have outlawed manumission societies in North Carolina altogether, an explicit challenge to the Friends. While this proposal was never passed, a law was enacted that banned free blacks from entering the state, setting a penalty of five hundred dollars and up to ten years of enslavement. The following year, the state Supreme Court ruled, in *Trustees of the Quaker Society of Contentnea v. Dickerson*, that the Friends could not hold slaves in a state of quasi-freedom with the intention of manumitting them at first opportunity. The justices held that only "meritorious services" could warrant emancipation and that "the idea that a collection of [slaves] will perform such services . . . is quite chimerical." When James Nourse reached Raleigh in the early winter of 1827, the cumulative weight of these governmental measures had created a political climate that was thoroughly hostile to African Americans, Quakers, emancipation, and colonization. Whatever popularity the ACS had previously enjoyed in the capital had by then largely dissipated.[23]

Upon arriving in Raleigh, Nourse found it difficult to locate a single legislator friendly enough to his cause to present an ACS memorial to the General Assembly. After calling on members of the Raleigh auxiliary society for assistance, the agent was able to persuade the speakers of the Senate and House of Commons to bring the petition before their respective bodies. In a letter to Gurley, Nourse stated that although "many friends" of colonization lived in North Carolina, "I have found violent opposers to the operation of the Soc^y in every form." Not only did the organization not have an influential advocate in the legislature, but, according Nourse, "the Quakers & every thing connected with emancipation & colonization is unpopular in the state." The memorial, while receiving an "attentive hearing," was assigned to a joint select committee, where it was tabled. Particularly galling to the agent, "proposed friends" of the ACS voted against the petition, leading him to conclude that "nothing will be done." In acknowledging just how widespread disdain for the ACS was, Nourse reported to Gurley, "You cannot imagine the jealousy which emits in many counties of this state against our cause." To his surprise, he learned that even Governor Iredell, recently elected leader of the new state colonization society, desired no open affiliation with the movement. "I am willing to pay my subscription," he informed Nourse, "but as I know the [colonization society] to be unpopular with most in the Legislature . . . I do not wish to do anything which may displease my constituents." Having accomplished nothing of consequence in the capital, the agent journeyed to other parts of the state, conscious of the fact that the ACS had lost a major battle in its propaganda war to win government support.[24]

As Nourse's mission was foundering in Raleigh, the Quakers moved ahead with preparations for a new emigrant expedition to Liberia. In November 1827, John McPhail, the agent at Norfolk, notified Gurley that fifty-seven emigrants had arrived from Northampton County. Assisted by Nathan Mendenhall, the party was, according to McPhail, "better provided for than any that came from Carolina before." By early December, 164 emigrants, including 144 North Carolinians and 20 Virginians, had gathered at the port to await embarkation on the *Nautilus*, a double-decked brig of 200-ton burden commanded by McPhail's brother-in-law. The ship made four attempts to break through Hampton Roads, the port's main passageway to the ocean, before severe weather and northeasterly winds drove it back into the harbor. It was not until December 20 that the *Nautilus*, propelled by "a fine breeze," sailed past the cape into the Atlantic. Well supplied with pork, beef, Indian meal, tea, and other items, the emigrants were at sea for two months, during which time three children died, including a four-year-old boy who was eviscerated by dysentery. Reaching Monrovia on February 19, most of the North Carolinians stayed only briefly in the capital before eighty were relocated to the new settlement of Millsburg on the St. Paul's River. Of the remaining emigrants, thirty-eight were settled at Caldwell.[25]

A statistical portrait of the *Nautilus* expedition reveals much about the North Carolina emigrants and their migratory experience. Fifty-nine of them were from the northeastern border county of Northampton, which had a 55 percent slave majority in 1820, with only 725 of its 13,242 inhabitants consisting of free blacks. The forty-five members of the Peele family, newly liberated and related to the Peeles of the *Doris* expedition, comprised most of the emigrants from this county. A company of forty-seven people had come from Wayne County, the Outland clan of twenty-seven making up most of their number, along with ten Davises and eight members of the Kennedy family. Of the remaining emigrants, twenty-one originated in Perquimans County, including twelve Fletchers who were freed by the will of William Fletcher after his schooner, *Perquimans*, disappeared at sea. As had been the case with the *Hunter*, *Indian Chief*, and *Doris* parties, Pasquotank blacks were represented in this expedition as well, including eight members of the White family and six Jordans. In regard to their prior condition, only the liberated statuses of the Fletchers and Peeles were listed in emigrant rolls, although other families had probably known bondage or ambiguous statuses at some point, particularly those from Quaker communities in Pasquotank, Perquimans, and Northampton Counties. Additionally, the gender composition and age spread of the expedition favored females and young adults. The sex ratio was

1:1.15 (77 females and 67 males), and the average emigrant age was 17.4 years. Ninety-six of the 144 North Carolinians were age 18 or younger, and only 16 were 40 or older. Modal ages were one and twelve, with eleven instances of each.[26]

Similar to the *Doris* company, the North Carolinians migrating in the *Nautilus* were not an educationally or occupationally distinguished group, according to the ship's emigrant roll. Given that the entire party, like previous expeditions, had been gathered from eastern agricultural counties, it was very likely that most of the adults and teenage children had experience in cultivating tobacco, corn, cotton, or other crops, in addition to ancillary skills. Whatever the case, only sixteen people were listed with occupations, perhaps an undercount reflective of the low value ACS officials placed on recording detailed information about the background of emigrants. Of this group, fourteen were recorded as farmers, along with Wiley Reynolds, a twenty-four-year-old clergyman from Murfreesboro, and Dempsey Fletcher, a fifty-one-year-old blacksmith who had been freed by the will of the aforementioned Perquimans slaveholder. Rather remarkably, not a single emigrant of this party is listed as literate in any fashion. While it is entirely possible that this could have been the case, it is probable that a few of these people were at least functionally literate, though they could have intentionally avoided disclosing their proficiency to ACS officials due to the suspicion that black literacy aroused in the slaveholding South.[27]

Finally, the *Nautilus* emigrants proved no more immune to malaria than the previous expeditions. Actually, this company suffered the highest mortality rate of any North Carolinians who migrated to Liberia, losing a full quarter (36) of their number to the disease within a year. Factoring in their numerical preponderance, female emigrants perished in a slightly higher percentage than males, the latter accounting for only fourteen of the deaths. Yet it was not sex, but age, which was the most important determinant of one's susceptibility to a fatal bout of malaria. Generally, the young and elderly were killed by the disease, a pattern indicative of their respectively immature and deteriorating immune systems. Illustratively, only one person between the ages of nineteen and forty-one died from the sting of the *Anopheles* mosquito. Three of the four infants under one year of age perished, and the oldest emigrant, seventy-seven-year-old Cambridge Toms of Perquimans, was terminally afflicted by malaria as well. This age-related pattern of death was common among all black Americans who were colonized in Liberia. In this particular instance, immigrants who moved to the riverside settlements of Millsburg and Caldwell or stayed in Monrovia died in comparable percentages. This finding suggests that most people were either fatally exposed to malaria dur-

THE FIRST WAVE

ing the initial stop in Monrovia, or they settled in areas of the three towns with similar disease environments.

For North Carolinians, the *Nautilus* was their death ship. Again, no other emigrant party from the state endured a higher incidence of terminal malaria. The 25 percent mortality rate suffered by this company was above the 20 percent of all American immigrants who died of malaria between 1820 and 1843, the only years for which reliable records are available. Most shocking, the malarial mortality rate of North Carolinians traveling on the *Nautilus* even exceeded the percentage of disease deaths noted for the emigrants of the *Elizabeth*, whose ill-fated pioneering expedition of 1820 sustained only a 19 percent rate of death. While ACS publications predictably made no references to the African deathtrap these North Carolinians had been caught in, some Quakers, during the outfitting of the *Nautilus*, had expressed concern as to whether emigrant parties were being sent to Liberia "too rapid[ly] for the Colony to support." Once information about the *Nautilus* company and the perils of colonial life in general, began trickling into North Carolina, the tide turned decisively against the colonization movement in the state. For over a generation, black interest in an African homeland ebbed.[28]

EVEN BEFORE PRINTED CRITICISM of the ACS and its African experiment was circulated widely during the early 1830s, communication networks linking black North Carolinians throughout the state with the outside world had been carrying news of Liberia for years. Early on, colonizationists had recognized the importance of tapping into African American information structures to publicize their program and, on a number of occasions, had suggested to national officials that a Liberian immigrant from the state be allowed to return for recruitment purposes. However, by the time this proposal was seriously considered by the ACS leadership, black North Carolinians and many others in the state had soured on colonization.

In November 1828, Nathan Mendenhall informed Secretary Gurley that "few people of color will migrate from under our care the present year." Not only had Quaker finances thinned during the recession of the late 1820s, but African Americans in Fayetteville, Guilford County, and elsewhere refused to countenance removal. Even in Pasquotank County, the state's premier source of emigrants, a colonization agent was compelled to report in early 1830 that "I . . . find the cause quite neglected by the people in general, & no coloured people inclined to go." Those blacks who were disposed to going to Liberia at this time often stipulated conditions for their departure. For example, an agent recruiting for the *Nautilus* expedition noted that African Americans in eastern counties were unwilling to make a decision about leaving until they received news about the fortunes of the *Doris* expedition. In one curious instance, Gurley received a letter from the southcentral county of Robeson alerting him to the existence of a group of "free mulattoes" whose "pride seems to revolt at the idea of being colonized & equalized with the Blacks." Alternatively, they were willing to consider migrating "*provided* they could have a colony to *themselves*." To be sure, there was still scattered interest in colonization following the departure of the *Nautilus*, but not nearly enough to warrant another expedition for the next two years.[29]

In addition to oral dissemination of colonization news, print media was instrumental in stirring up anti-ACS sentiments in North Carolina. The *Raleigh Register*, the state's leading newspaper, had been an early advocate of the Liberian colony with its editor, Joseph Gales, even serving as treasurer of the ACS during the 1830s. Other periodicals, such as Benjamin Lundy's *Genius of Universal Emancipation*, had been laudatory of various migration schemes, and most notably the black-owned *Freedom's Journal* abruptly embraced the African colonization movement in February 1829 after months of abrasive criticism. Despite these early endorsements of the ACS cause, most newspapers directed toward African American audiences were staunchly anticolonization by the 1830s, which probably accurately reflected the feelings of most free blacks on the subject. The *Rights of All*, published by Samuel Cornish, an erstwhile editor of *Freedom's Journal*, led the charge against the ACS. Writing in September 1829, he asserted that "we view the efforts of the colonization society . . . as unwished for on our part, uncalled for by circumstances, as injurious to our interests, and as unrighteous and meddlesome on the part of the society." Almost without exception, the budding abolitionist press that Cornish represented was inalterably opposed to removing from the United States free blacks whom the press believed had every right to remain in the land of their birth. Second only to slavery, the ACS, its motives, and objectives were more frequently and roundly denounced in the black press than any other institution or program.[30]

Notwithstanding the efforts of Cornish and others, one of the writers most responsible for gutting whatever credibility the ACS enjoyed among blacks and many antislavery proponents was David Walker. Born free in Wilmington, North Carolina, Walker had lived in Charleston during the time of Denmark Vesey's failed slave conspiracy of 1822 before moving to Boston roughly two years later. There, he found work as a clothing retailer and became increasingly active in the political and organizational life of the city's black community. In 1827, he assisted in the founding of *Freedom's Journal*, the first African American newspaper, which helped him to hone his own skills as a polemicist. In late 1829, Walker published his *Appeal to the Colored Citizens of*

THE FIRST WAVE

the World, a lengthy pamphlet that employed biblical imagery, ancient history, and pointed language to denounce American slavery.

In addition to characterizing whites as "unjust, jealous, unmerciful, avaricious and blood-thirsty," the *Appeal* predicted and encouraged an apocalyptic slave uprising that would engulf many of those who held African Americans in bondage. Notably, Walker's vision was not only rooted in the "eye for an eye" retributive justice of the Old Testament, it also evoked a pan-Africanist vision of black liberation. "I advanced it therefore to you," he proclaimed in the righteous anger that coursed through his diatribe, "that your full glory and happiness, as well as all other coloured people under Heaven, shall never be fully consummated, but with the entire emancipation of your coloured brethren all over the world." Unlike the gradual emancipationists of his day, Walker assumed that slavery would not fade away over time, but instead, would have to be violently extirpated by those most aversely affected by it, the slaves themselves.[31]

Although the *Appeal* is primarily the work of an immediatist abolitionist preoccupied with excoriating black bondage, it also contained one of the more devastating assaults on the colonization movement to date. Proceeding from the familiar argument of free blacks that America "is as much ours as it is the whites," Walker lambasted the ACS as seeking to perpetuate slavery. The organization was putatively directed by "a gang of slave-holders" who hoped that by removing free African Americans to Liberia, bondpeople "may be the better secured in ignorance and wretchedness, to work their [masters'] farms and dig their mines, and thus go on enriching the Christians with their blood and groans." Walker seemed to be at a loss in trying to understand why blacks would voluntarily migrate to Liberia. He sympathized with those who might leave for British dominions, where slave emancipation was currently being considered, or Haiti, where the people "are bound to protect and comfort us." However, the assertion that a black exodus to Africa was a rational response to racial oppression in the United States was a non sequitur to him. "What our brethren could have been thinking about, who have left their native land and home and gone to Africa, I am unable to say," Walker confessed. Like so many other free blacks by this time, he took umbrage at the notion that slaveholders, while often damning the very existence of African Americans who were not the property of others, should be so bold as to call for their removal under the guise of philanthropic benevolence.[32]

Walker's *Appeal* reached North Carolina by the summer of 1830, apparently having first slipped in through Wilmington and then passing through hands farther inland. In August, the magistrate of the city alerted Governor Owen that the discovered pamphlet described the experience of southern slaves "in most inflammatory terms." The official also alleged that a recent investigation had discerned among local free blacks and bondpeople the existence of a conspiracy to liberate slaves in Wilmington. Owen took the magistrate's report seriously and dispatched letters to law enforcement officials around the state, as well as to state senators from thirty-two eastern counties, informing them of Walker's writing and the rumored conspiracy. He encouraged them to implement "the most vigilant execution of your police laws" and requested that they inform him, "with as little delay as possible," of any agents suspected of distributing the pamphlet. In a message before the legislature in November, Owen described Walker as having distorted biblical teachings in order to instigate slave resistance. He also disclosed that free blacks had been implicated in the dissemination of the literature.[33]

Owen's efforts to suppress the *Appeal* and other abolitionist literature came at a time when reactionary proslavery interests were launching their most massive offensive of the period against free blacks. Walker's exhortation to rebellion arguably triggered the avalanche of legislation that sought to smother African American liberty in the state, but other factors, such as rumors of uprisings in eastern counties and a free black population that had grown by a quarter since 1820, contributed to the repression. As cash-crop production proliferated in the state's agricultural east, the entrenchment of slavery, always accompanied by fears of rebellion, almost naturally made free African Americans problematic to whites with an interest in controlling black labor. In this light, it should not be surprising that Pasquotank and Craven Counties, with the second and third largest communities of free African Americans respectively, were believed by whites to be focal points of conspiracies. In the latter county, Miles White, a Quaker colonization agent, reported in September that free blacks had been "ill treated & their privileges abridged" due to hysteria over the Walker pamphlet. Thus, not singly but taken together, these evolving political, demographic, and economic circumstances aroused vigorous and sometimes violent opposition to free African Americans and the alleged threat that their presence posed. Consequently, the General Assembly, both responding to and generating this anti-free-black persecution, devoted a substantial portion of its 1830–31 session to greatly reducing the civil liberties and mobility of this group.[34]

Among several acts passed to better control both free and enslaved African Americans, one statute the General Assembly passed made illegal the teaching of slaves to read and write, with the exception of numeration. Policymakers believed that such instruction "has a tendency to excite dissatisfaction in their minds and to produce insurrection and rebellion to the manifest injury of the citizens of this state." Furthermore, to supplement the 1826 law prohibiting free blacks from entering the state, a measure was enacted that banned free African Americans from disembarking from ships that were docked in

North Carolina ports. Free blacks of the state were forbidden interaction with those aboard quarantined ships, and imprisonment was stipulated for those visiting blacks who violated the law by coming ashore. Perhaps most significantly, the General Assembly once again narrowed the passageway between slavery and freedom by making manumission more cumbersome to slaveholders. To initiate the emancipation process, the 1830 law mandated that masters submit a petition to a superior court which included the slave's name, age, and gender. If the court upheld the petition, the master was then required to post notice of his intention at the county courthouse and in the *State Gazette* at least six weeks before any scheduled hearing. If no one came forward with a claim against the value of the bondman, the slaveholder at that point had to post a one-thousand-dollar bond for the slave, which was subject to forfeiture if the bonded person did not "honestly and correctly demean him[self]" while still in the state. The liberated individual then had to leave North Carolina within ninety days of being freed, "never afterwards [to] come within the same."

The only exception to these otherwise onerous manumission rules applied to masters who desired to emancipate slaves over age fifty. In these instances, the slaveholder had to give a full exposition of the reasons why the person merited liberty and swear under oath that he had not been motivated by a bribe from the person to be manumitted. These freedpersons of advanced age were the only ones allowed to remain in the state after their emancipation. Of course, the effect of the law on most masters and would-be liberated slaves was obvious and intentional. Only the wealthiest and most persevering slaveholders would be able to manumit bondpeople, and almost never in groups. Moreover, only the oldest slaves would likely be granted their freedom, which many would not be able to fully enjoy, since it would be most difficult for them to provide for themselves in their waning years.[35]

If Walker's abolitionist pyrotechnics inflamed white hostility toward free blacks in North Carolina, his damning critique of the ACS virtually extinguished the already faint pulse of colonizationist sentiment among African Americans in the state. Ironically, however, the legislative and extralegal repression that followed the appearance of the pamphlet created conditions that produced dozens of refugees who were willing to employ colonization as a means of fleeing the state. Writing from Raleigh in October 1830, Josiah Polk informed Secretary Gurley that the *Appeal* "has been doing the cause much harm in this state as well as other parts." Yet he recognized an opportunity during this period of increased racial tension and advised Gurley to send an agent to various places "whilst the free negroes are suffering under those suspicions & the whites in dread." In Pasquotank County, where a number of indignities had been recently visited upon free blacks, forty people expressed a willingness to migrate to Liberia by October, whereas agents could not find a single prospective emigrant there only months earlier. In addition to this group, several others intended to emigrate from the county after selling their lands, corn crops, and other properties but did not dispose of these possessions in time to depart with the party of the *Valador* in January 1831. In the case of free blacks, their sudden interest in colonization directly correlated to their threshold of pain and ability to withstand abuse at the hands of agitated whites. When Miles White reported to Gurley in November 1830 that as many as one hundred blacks in the vicinity of Elizabeth City could be ready to migrate by January 1, this estimate, representing a tenth of the county's free black population, definitely suggested that many had been abruptly motivated to leave by gross violations of their most basic rights.[36]

In Northampton County, a different dynamic was at work, which apparently squelched all interest, even of the refugee sort, in colonization. Sandy Peele, a twenty-five-year-old farmer who had immigrated to Liberia on the *Doris*, had returned to the state around 1830. In October of that year, he was apprehended and incarcerated in the Northampton County jail just before returning to Africa. He appealed for assistance to a local white man, John Wheeler, who in turn notified John McPhail, the ACS agent in Norfolk. Wheeler did not believe that Peele, who had at one time been in quasi-free limbo among Quakers, was claimable as the property of anyone and thus requested that the Washington-based organization send an agent to secure his release. Although it is not known whether the ACS actively intervened, Peele was freed shortly afterward.

Instead of immediately departing for Liberia, Peele remained in Northampton County. According to one colonization agent, he had "a very unhappy influence" on blacks under Friends' care in the area, warning them against migrating to Liberia. Among other things, he told them that letters from the colony that described life there in favorable terms were manufactured by whites. Predictably, the ACS official labeled him as "evil minded" and a "very worthless fellow" for speaking ill of the African settlement, but Peele actually had much to complain about. Having lived in the colony for only three years, he had already lost fourteen of his family members to malaria, over a fifth of the sixty-four Peeles who migrated in 1827 and 1828. Beyond the grief that the clan suffered, frontier life in Liberia was extremely difficult, especially for the vast majority of immigrants who took few if any resources to Africa. Local indigenous people had not been very welcoming of permanent colonists, and many items readily available in America were prohibitively expensive in Liberia. The account of the African colony that Peele offered to the people of his former home county must have been a poignant one, with layers of tragedies, uncertainties, and longings. In any event, his reappearance in Northampton had a lasting impact on blacks there. According to ACS records, no other person from the county migrated to Liberia during the rest of the nineteenth century.[37]

During the lull in the North Carolina colonization movement between 1828 and 1831, one noteworthy development did take place in the state legislature in addition to the slew of antiblack statutes that emanated from its chambers. Against the backdrop of several unsuccessful efforts by the ACS to convince the federal government to extend financial aid and U.S. sovereignty to its colonization program, the North Carolina General Assembly finally took up the issue of sending free blacks to Liberia. In December 1830, a joint select committee presented a bill that called for an additional eight-cent tax on all blacks subject to taxation in the state. The new levy was to last ten years, during which time a fund would be created for "the removal of free persons of color from the State to Liberia." The money was not to be used to transport individuals over the age of forty unless the person in question was departing with children under that age. The bill did not mention whether deportation would be voluntary or otherwise and did not raise the constitutional and logistical questions that were involved in such a massive, unprecedented governmental undertaking. The proposal passed the state Senate but went no further. With public support for colonization shaky at best, the legislature proved unwilling to go into uncharted waters in pursuit of a solution that had no antecedents and would prove to be costly in a variety of ways. For once and for all, hopes for a state-sponsored colonization movement died on the floor of the General Assembly, pummeled to death by slavery and abolitionism, and by their increasingly irreconcilable defenders.[38]

IF ANY GROUP CLEARLY BENEFITED from the first phase of colonization activity that swept North Carolina during the late 1820s, it was the Society of Friends. The Quakers had wagered much on the ACS and its Liberian program, hoping to reap both earthly security and spiritual renewal through the resolution of their manumission deadlock. As of 1830, the church had spent $12,769.51 on sending 652 African Americans to free governments, a majority of whom ended up in Liberia or Haiti. For all intents and purposes, the Friends *were* the colonization movement in North Carolina during this time, with their headquarters in Guilford and Pasquotank Counties. Between 1825 and 1830, no other state sent more people to Africa than North Carolina, and no other group more consistently devoted resources of various sorts to recruiting, safeguarding, and transporting emigrants than the Quakers. In December 1830, 402 blacks were still in the custody of the Friends, and according to one estimate, they could have received two thousand more from various sources if transportation to Liberia could have been secured.[39]

It is unclear what happened to all of the quasi-free African Americans who remained in Quaker care after 1830. Several more were sent to Africa, some undoubtedly found niches in the Midwest, and others ended up in northern cities, such as Philadelphia. Certainly, a significant number of them, perhaps a majority, remained in North Carolina, living and dying between slavery and freedom. What is apparent is that the Friends had largely excused themselves from the colonization business by the early 1830s. In March 1830, the once robust MCS had sank into a "lethargic spirit" and could hardly attract a quorum to its meetings. Four years later, it disbanded for lack of members and finances. Similarly, the Quaker-dominated Pasquotank auxiliary of the ACS was virtually defunct by the time white repression in the wake of Walker's *Appeal* spurred a refugee stream from the county in late 1830. Many of its members had either died or migrated to the Midwest, away from the problems of slavery and race that continued to ensnare southern life and development. Except for a brief surge in refugee migration during 1831–32, black North Carolinians would not depart for Liberia again in significant numbers until the 1850s. In the meantime, people from the state who had emigrated during the colonization heyday of the 1820s recreated and invented communities from what they brought from America and found in Africa.[40]

FOUR. INVENTING LIBERIA

FROM THE VANTAGE POINT of an arriving ship, Cape Mesurado eases over the horizon like a great forested mound, eventually towering nearly three hundred feet above the ocean. For black emigrants from America, this was the first image of Africa: breathtaking expanses of profuse greenery bounded by white beaches awash in glistening foam. The second image that greeted the newcomers was onrushing Kru men. With a spirited athleticism, these African mariners lunged across the surf in their dugout canoes, their well-toned musculature bathed in a lustrous sheen of perspiration and brine. To them, emigrants were both interlopers and employment. West Africa's dearth of natural harbors allowed the Kru to monopolize the essential business of transporting people and goods from ships to shore. Navigating their light wooden boats alongside the much larger transoceanic vessels, they boarded without hesitation or difficulty, assured of both their skills and the demand for their services. It was these first encounters, which were routine and work-related for the Kru, that initiated the acculturation of African American emigrants to life in Liberia.

These first interactions were a curious meeting of cultures. The Kru, clad in muslin loincloths, were actually cultural middlemen as well as boatmen and stevedores. Their work interfaced with the polyglot economies of the Atlantic, and so did their identities. Some learned English and other European languages to facilitate social intercourse, even answering to nicknames such

Above: Cape Mesurado, Liberia (From Maugham, *Republic of Liberia*)

as "John T. Chew Tobacco" and "Sam Coffee" to ingratiate themselves to potential employers who refused to learn the pronunciation of their real names. In addition to their maritime talents, the Kru distinguished themselves in appearance for both aesthetic and practical purposes. From their hairlines to their noses, they were marked with a dark blue tattoo one-half inch in width, which made them ethnically recognizable to others. This conspicuous scarification helped tighten Kru control over the transport industry and also provided protection against enslavement, since most foreign vessels, even slavers, valued their services and therefore could not afford alienating them. By the first decades of the nineteenth century, these cultural and economic transactions had reached a level of sophistication that necessitated that the Kru carry "books," or small leather pouches in which they stored recommendations from past clients. Ultimately, the consummate skills of these seafaring laborers, along with the navigational limitations of deep-hulled Western watercraft, guaranteed the Kru steady employment throughout the period.[1]

Although the Kru were based in tidewater communities spread along the Grain Coast (much of which was later annexed by Liberia), they were more or less at home anywhere in western Africa, from Monrovia to Angola. Some Kru males were at sea for years, working at various points along the coast for whomever would pay them for their labor. In working for foreigners, they rarely allowed the particularist politics or moral sensibilities of one employer to limit their ability to work for others. For instance, a Kru team might work for a Spanish or French slaver on one occasion and seek employment with a British cruiser attempting to suppress slave trafficking as the opportunity arose. Beyond this kind of work, much of the riverine trade in West Africa was conceded to these African mariners, since large sailing vessels dared not venture into the region's shallow, narrow waterways. Indicative of the universal acknowledgment of their usefulness, passing ships sometimes allowed Kru to ride free of charge between their residences and various European establishments along the coast. Like their European counterparts, finding a niche in the commercial networks of the continent and the oceanic economy was critical to Kru longevity in the coastal marketplace. Opportunity and opportunism were key components of their strategy in this ever-changing maritime world where one's misfortune could easily be another's gain. Illustratively, when European ships wrecked along the coast or were vulnerable in other ways, it was understood that they were fair game for those seeking plunder. The Kru certainly appropriated their share of such booty, having greater access to such sites than most others.[2]

When not plying the African littoral, the Kru spent their days in villages, such as Settra Kru, southeast of Monrovia. Political authority among them tended to be decentralized and scattered throughout clusters of related patrilineal communities, which accommodated the high mobility of male seafarers. Women among the Kru were relatively sedentary, and it was they who were responsible for much of the child-rearing, gardening, and household chores. Despite copious verdure, their settlements were well ordered and produced many of the foodstuffs and other items that were needed for subsistence. Generally, villages were small, with few having more than a hundred people. However, like most other African communities that would eventually fall under the authority of the Liberian colony, the Kru were a branch of a larger language group, namely Kwa-speakers, which began migrating into the area from the east around the sixteenth century. Little is known about early Kru settlements along the Grain Coast or the reasons for their migration. One can only speculate that the group may have been fleeing despotic rule, economic turmoil, or demographic pressures. Whatever the case, the Kru had become immersed in the waterborne world of the Atlantic by the nineteenth century, thoroughly attuned to its fisheries, trade networks, and rhythms. Very significantly, these were the people who imparted the first meaning of Africa to American emigrants upon their arrival and who vividly demonstrated the cultural fluidity of coastal peoples.[3]

Regardless of the month in which emigrants landed in Liberia, they found a landscape rich with evergreen growth. Mangrove swamps twisted and tangled along the ocean and rivers, alive with fertility and the whine of the *Anopheles* mosquito. Dense rain forest covered rolling hills that rose to significant heights further inland, and alluring flora delicately harmonized even the most chaotic undergrowth. The soils that produced this botanical collage were of varying texture and quality. Primarily sand blanketed the shoreline and kept the Atlantic at bay, but this terrain gradually turned into a ruddy clay further north and eastward. River banks were often carpeted by a dark mold with a formidable fecundity, and other, drier areas were covered with a more lightly colored clay, which spawned a range of vegetation. Additionally, the fauna of Mesurado and its environs consisted of a wide spectrum of animals, such as elephants, leopards, hippopotamuses, snakes, crocodiles, and apes. Smaller creatures inhabiting the region included sloths, chameleons, and numerous kinds of lizards and ants. Indigenous people, and later colonists, kept a variety of domesticated animals, such as sheep, goats, swine, and chickens. However, cows, oxen, and horses were rarely seen among the colonial population, largely due to tsetse flies that caused an often fatal sleeping sickness in such livestock. Thick with vibrant life and natural beauty, Liberia, a quintessential tropical locale, knew no dead season and offered no respite from its endless cycle of growth compounded by growth.[4]

Unlike the mostly temperate United States, Liberia required immigrants to acclimate to a land with fairly constant annual temperatures. They mainly had to adjust to rainy and dry seasons, as opposed to the annual cycles of cool and warm climate that characterized North America. At approximately six degrees north latitude, Monrovia was squarely in the Torrid Zone, with no equivalent of the defoliating autumns or frosty winters that seasonally settled over states such as North Carolina. Beginning in May, drenching downpours of rain incessantly watered the Liberian landscape, with occasional clear days and a period known as the "middle dries" during the latter part of July. The dry season commenced in November and lasted through April, its most eventful feature being the "Harmattan Wind," which blew Saharan dust across coastal areas from December through February. Of the two seasons, the dry period was the hottest, with temperatures routinely in the mid-nineties in February and March. During the wet season, temperatures averaged between seventy and eighty degrees, being somewhat cooler at night.

For immigrants, the rainy season was the most insalubrious, insofar as it was most conducive to the spread of malaria. Moreover, overflowing rivers and inundated roads made both travel and work more difficult and dangerous, forcing many to be less productive than at other times. To be sure, the dry season had its share of inconveniences, even perils. The hazy dust clouds of the Harmattan sometimes lethally affected humans, animals, and vegetation, and the interminable heat of the season's middle months must have come as an unpleasant surprise to many emigrants who had left America in the midst of winter. Also, rain and malaria were not wholly confined to the months of May through November. Still, aside from these observations, the wet season meant moisture, whether in the form of flood waters, stagnant pools, or vaporous mist, and thus heralded the cyclical ascendance of the anopheline pestilence. For immigrants who survived their first year in Liberia, adapting to this new climatic pattern was probably among the more discomforting adjustments that life in Africa required. Colonists from the American South, who comprised the vast majority of all immigrants, were at least somewhat accustomed to the heat and humidity that Liberia perennially offered. Yet they, too, would have been unprepared for other meteorological peculiarities of the region. For example, even the new celestial and geographic perspective could be disorienting. Liberia's proximity to the equator alone meant the motion of the tides, the nature of seasons, and the length of the workday were all unfamiliar to transplanted North Carolinians.[5]

It was in this cultural and natural environment that African American immigrants, directed by their ACS sponsors, attempted to plant a colony in tropical Liberia. For the purpose it was meant to serve, the territory turned out to be a poor choice for a settlement. Congested stretches of intractable forest covered most of the hilly peninsula, and rocky terrain made any substantial agricultural activity impossible. Even the most fertile lands of the cape were

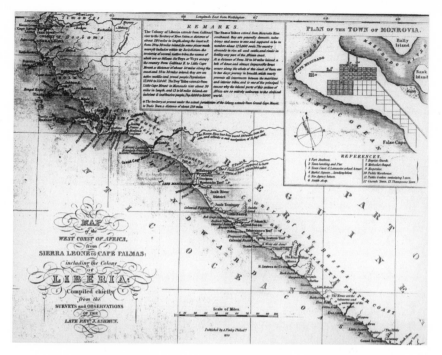

MAP 2. Liberia, ca. 1828 (From *African Repository*, March 1830)

subject to flooding, which often resulted in pools of standing water, ideal breeding grounds for mosquitoes. In 1826, the colonial agent Jehudi Ashmun estimated that only 550 acres of the 24 square miles of land that had been reserved for municipal development on the cape was arable. Consequently, this scarcity of cultivable land encouraged the ACS to seek other, more productive territories to erect settlements on, along with more emigrants to populate these acquisitions.[6]

Early colonists, faced with the daunting tasks of constructing homes, fashioning communities, and staying alive, scratched out a settlement upon stony, tree-shrouded Cape Mesurado, creating Monrovia and demarcating the first Liberian frontier. Located three-fourths of a mile from the cape's summit and eighty feet above sea level, the site was partially shielded from the ocean breeze by the incline of the promontory. By the time shiploads of North Carolinians began arriving in the late 1820s, the immigrant village boasted a number of structures and institutions, which actually made it not so different from some rural towns of the American South. The settlement itself had been cleared of a square mile of undergrowth, and by 1830 ninety residences and stores were situated along its wide, grassy streets. Two churches had been established by this time, in addition to a market house and an agency building, where the chief colonial official resided. A receptacle or communal house for newly arrived immigrants, which could accommodate 150 people, had also been constructed. Rudimentary educational facilities were available as early as 1826, and within a decade six day schools for children were in operation throughout the colony, along with an evening school for adults. A female school in Monrovia was instructing seventy pupils by this time, and older students were receiving training in grammar and geography. The Ladies Liberia School Association, based in Philadelphia, confidently reported in 1835 that a majority of the latter group "read, spell, and write very well." To further assure his superiors in Washington that culture indeed did exist in Liberia, Ashmun cheerfully informed them of the new Colonial Library that had been established a few miles away on the St. Paul's River. Housed in an older agency building, the repository was said to hold over fifteen hundred volumes.[7]

To protect the colonial population and trading ships doing business with the settlement, several measures were taken to enhance the defensive capacity of the colony, which had been sorely tried on a number of occasions. Fort Stockton, named after the impetuous naval lieutenant who had coerced the Dei into ceding Mesurado to the ACS, was the oldest outpost, overlooking Monrovia from the edge of the cape. Fifteen carriage guns and three pivot guns were in the colony's arsenal, and a double battery, located at the extremity of the cape, was under construction in 1827 to protect vessels in Mesurado Roads. The small colonial militia, composed of fifty artillerymen and forty infantry, was meant to fortify the settlement against attack but would have been hard to muster at any given time due to high mortality, communication and transportation difficulties, and a typically strapped colonial treasury. During a time when neighboring African polities were still testing the mettle of the settlers, the ability to amass men and materiel rapidly was both a necessity and a challenge for the struggling colony.[8]

What passed as the military establishment of the colony was much less striking than the settlement's prospects as a trading outpost. The ACS leadership envisioned the colony as being actively involved in coastal trade, and from the beginning colonists were engaged in Atlantic commerce. Several colonial trading ships hauled goods along the coast, and many colonists dropped their hoes and hammers in order to barter with neighboring Africans and passing ships. While some immigrants defined freedom as the opportunity to own land, a sizable number of people who had come to Liberia conceived of freedom as liberty *from* the often demeaning field labor that they had known so well in America. When given the opportunity to earn money or acquire goods more quickly and with less physical exertion, there were those who found the appeal of trading irresistible and who devoted much more time to these transactions than to agriculture. Colonization officials often la-

INVENTING LIBERIA

mented that immigrants were neglecting the soil and purchasing food and other items that they could produce themselves. Despite these concerns, many colonists were simply not bound by the ACS's vision of a colonial yeomanry centered around farms and cash crops.

Actually, the Liberian colony was founded at a propitious time when legitimate trade was gaining ground in West Africa, gradually challenging the dominance of slave trafficking. Ambitious immigrants found it possible to insert themselves as middlemen between Africans and foreign traders, some achieving substantial wealth in the coasting trade in camwood (valued for its red dye derivative), coffee, palm oil, and other products. In 1830–31, the colony exported $88,911.25 in goods and was visited by forty-six ships, twenty-one of which were American in origin. Over time, success in commerce became easily convertible into political influence and social standing. This is not to say that agriculture did not pay. Indeed, under the right economic, climatic, and geographic circumstances, those who tilled the soil, or hired others to do so for them, could garner huge rewards, although the most successful farmers generally brought resources and skills from America. Nonetheless, trade was the fastest way to earn a profit in a land covered in rain forest, rocky soils, and malaria, often requiring little in the way of skills, resources, or prior experience to realize results.[9]

Notwithstanding its Western dressing, Monrovia was not a quaint little southern town that had been transplanted into the shrubby crest of Cape Mesurado. It was much too tropical, too organically African—from its ecology to the Kru men who serviced its incoming ships—and too frequently visited by death to have much of an American character about it. Notable differences certainly existed between the colonists and their African neighbors, but not to the point that the colony developed in isolation. There was a constant dialectical struggle between attempts by the immigrants to adapt the African environment to their needs and the necessity that they adjust to material and cultural realities of a land that they could not truly master. By 1830, evidence of their triumphs was discernible, most significantly the town they had raised on Mesurado and the commercial and maritime networks that infused it with life. Their problems, too, were equally conspicuous: the colony, poor and dependent, was still being bled by malaria, which had yet to be addressed in any systematic, preventive fashion.

While sustained largely by continuous immigration, Monrovia was growing slowly, and natural growth was still a future possibility. In some respects, the town was acquiring a rather cosmopolitan feel, insomuch as it was a crossroads for immigrants from various American states, Africans of different ethnic backgrounds, and European missionaries, traders, and sailors. Colonists from North Carolina made up only about 8 percent of its estimated population of seven hundred in 1830, though the state was second only to Virginia in total number of people sent to the colony. Migrating in large numbers by the late 1820s, North Carolinians were not primarily settled in the capital, but instead in its sister towns of Caldwell and Millsburg. Established some miles up the St. Paul's River, these agricultural villages would be indelibly imprinted with the culture and experiences of African Americans from the Tar Heel State. The stewards of the ACS, disappointed with the progress of colonization on the cape, hoped that the North Carolinians and other colonists on the St. Paul's would be able to avoid some of the trials and difficulties associated with Monrovia's development. They gambled that these riverine experiments would both realize their vision of a colony of prosperous freeholders and be easier to wean from dependency on the organization's coffers.[10]

Flowing perpendicular to the shoreline, the St. Paul's River winds in a southwestward direction across the breadth of modern Liberia. As it moves toward the ocean, its banks rise to heights of ten to twenty feet, uneven in many places and shifting in texture between a rich loam, bulbous clay, and sheets of sand. Rapids and falls accelerate its movement at several junctures, and an occasional island parts the waters into parallel streams. Thick vegetation, including palm and plantain trees, line the river's edges, sometimes giving way to clearings, where the thatched roofs of African villages become visible. About three miles from its mouth, the waterway splits, with the primary vein continuing toward the Atlantic and the other merging with the Mesurado River, just before it pours into Stockton Creek, behind the cape. The forking waters of the St. Paul's River bound Bushrod Island, roughly eight miles in length and two in width. Ranging from one-quarter to three-fourths of a mile across with an average depth of twenty feet, the river was a major corridor for both people and goods prior to colonization and would later connect several American settlements with both Monrovia and the larger world.[11]

The founding of the Caldwell settlement on the southern bank of the St. Paul's River was an acknowledgment by the ACS leadership that the environment of Mesurado was both too infertile and malarial to support the kind of self-sustaining, agrarian settlement they hoped to forge in Africa. Seven miles from Monrovia, this tract of land, like the capital, was ceded to the colony by top Dei officials for a cash payment in May 1825. According to Ashmun, in the days following the sale "a slight ferment" stirred among some Dei leaders, who had apparently not been consulted before their lands were sold to the ACS. Nothing, however, materialized from their "violent remonstrances," at least for the time being. At the close of the rainy season in November, Ashmun assigned residential and farm lots to a group of colonists and dubbed the site St. Paul's. Africans in the area receptive of the newcomers rented two houses to them until the construction of their own homes was completed. Shortly after its establishment, the town was given the surname of Elias Caldwell, the corresponding secretary of the ACS who had recently died. At the founding meeting of the organization in 1816, Caldwell had suggested that colonization in Africa would serve as substantial recompense for the wrongs suffered by black Americans at the hands of white men. From the perspective of these pioneering immigrants, his idea of reparations must have seemed dubious as they stood on the banks of the St. Paul's River. Not only were they faced with the grueling task of hewing farms from overgrown mangrove, but they also inherited with these lots the palpable hostility of the Dei and an unwanted complement of *Anopheles* mosquitoes.[12]

In historically reconstructing community life among North Carolina immigrants in Caldwell, it is useful to refer to emigrant rolls and the colonial census in order to delineate the general demographic character of the population that settled there. In 1830, North Carolinians comprised approximately 40 percent of the town's residents, with the balance made up of Virginians, Marylanders, and Georgians. By the end of the following year, 281 people from the Tar Heel State had been relocated to Caldwell. Not surprisingly, all of these immigrants, with the possible exception of seven whose counties of origin were not recorded, hailed from the northeastern region of the state. The vast majority were from the Quaker-populated counties of Pasquotank (167), Northampton (46), and Perquimans (31), while the rest had come from the neighboring counties of Camden (16), Bertie (9), and Chowan (5). Their origins in the agricultural lands around the Albemarle Sound certainly helped condition the group for a river-centered, agrarian lifestyle on the St. Paul's banks, but did not necessarily prepare them for the realization that many American crops, such as corn, did not grow well in tropical environments. In regard to prior status, only twelve immigrants, including the Fletcher family from Perquimans, were known to have been slaves previous to their migration to Liberia. Two hundred and three others are listed in emigrant rolls as free born, but given that most of them arrived from Pasquotank County, a significant portion of this group had almost certainly known only quasi-freedom among Quakers. While most people settled in Caldwell in family groups, the gender ratio of the North Carolinians slightly favored females, with 148 settling there, as opposed to 130 males. (The gender of three infants was not recorded.) Additionally, the age makeup of this population was skewed toward youth, with 158 individuals migrating at age 19 or younger and only 26 over the age of 40. The average age of the group was 18.6 years, and the modal ages were 4 and 22, with 13 instances of each.[13]

Predictably, the primary talents and skills North Carolinians brought to Caldwell were concentrated in the realm of agricultural production. Of the sixty-five people listed with one or more vocations, forty-nine were farmers, and all but one—twenty-two-year-old Betsey Spellman of Pasquotank County—were male. Undoubtedly, this figure underrepresented the number of people, including women, who had some experience in crop cultivation and perhaps only reflects the proportion of individuals who previously owned their own land or solely provided for their own subsistence through farming. Individuals engaged in other occupations included four weavers, three spinsters, a midwife, and a domestic, all of whom were female; and three sawyers, three shoemakers, two carpenters, a blacksmith, a wheelwright, and a sailmaker, all male. Relative to their proportions, emigrants from no particular county dominated the trades.

In reference to literacy, only thirty-four North Carolinians were listed as lettered before disembarking at Caldwell, with nineteen recorded as capable of spelling, twelve as knowing how to read, and two as trained in writing. All but two of the forty-nine farmers were ostensibly illiterate, and about half of the other skilled individuals were unlettered. Only one of these individuals is not listed as free born, and the gender percentage was almost even, with sixteen females listed as reading or spelling but none as capable of writing. Overall, the literacy rate of this group, broadly defined, was 12 percent, which was probably not unusual compared to others of similar circumstances and backgrounds in their home counties or other Liberian settlements. Furthermore, literacy seems to have been predicated upon age and accessible mostly to adults. The average age of those listed as lettered in some fashion was twenty-four, and only three individuals under age twelve were recorded as literate, all being free-born spellers.[14]

Carved from mangrove swamps and dense woodlands, life in Caldwell was overwhelmingly rural, arduous, and monotonous. Upon arrival in Liberia, immigrants were housed in the receptacle at Monrovia, or some other facility, until lands were allotted to them. The ACS offered each adult coming into the colony a "building lot" and five acres of farm land. A nuclear family was additionally entitled to two more acres for the wife and one for each child, not to exceed a total allotment of ten acres per family. Up to six months' supply of rations was provided to the newcomers in the hope that they would become self-supporting in the interim. Once relocated to their designated settlement site, the immigrants preoccupied themselves with the essential tasks of clearing land, sowing fields, and constructing suitable shelter. More often than not, they toiled without the assistance of draft animals and found that many tasks had to be completed without the appropriate tools. To acquire a fee-simple deed to the land, one had to erect a house within two years and bring at least two acres under cultivation, which were no small accomplishments. In falling short of these expectations, one's claim to the property could terminate in forfeiture, with the land reverting back to the ACS.

Under these conditions, seventy-seven plantations had been established in Caldwell by June 1826, and the North Carolina immigrants displayed "good proof," according to Ashmun, of their ability to create a viable settlement. By the following year, forty families had fulfilled the prerequisites for receiving titles to their lands, though a number of others risked forfeiture due to their more limited success. Lott Carey, an African American immigrant from Virginia and vice-agent of the colony, was less laudatory in his appraisal of the settlement's progress. While he informed the ACS managers that Caldwell was "rapidly advancing in farming, building, and I hope, industry," he noted that the colonists found it easier to set up farms than to build homes. "Some of them are very slow," he lamented in a June 1828 letter, despite the fact that they had received his personal assistance.[15]

Such were the rustic dimensions of early frontier life in Caldwell. The ruralism of the settlement, evinced in the wide distances between residences and the absence of a central commercial district, made it hard for the casual observer to distinguish it as a town. Yet for the North Carolina people, this was not a wholly unfamiliar spatial or communal style of living, given that they had come from one of the least urban of American states. There were, of course, events and developments that broke the desolation and dullness of settler life. Notably, Caldwell farmers, both cognizant of the need to share agricultural information and desirous of fellowship with others, established an Agricultural Society in 1826, which met weekly to discuss practical farming techniques and the general progress of the settlement. Educational facilities were opened in the town by the 1830s, including a female school. According to one report, the growth of the latter institution quickly outpaced its funding, and the fifty-eight students in attendance had made the sole teacher "anxious to have an assistant." Other happenings, such as weddings, the birth of children, and the arrival of new immigrants, occasionally mitigated the numbing routine and boredom of country life. Unfortunately, though, the monotony was not always interrupted by pleasant distractions.

Caldwell, according to one Virginia immigrant, was mired in poverty. Little currency was in circulation, and the prices of imported foodstuffs could be outrageously high. Around 1830, pork sold for eighteen dollars a barrel and flour for ten to twelve dollars, but "Tobacco can't be had for neither Love nor money." To be sure, a barter economy existed among colonists and local Africans, the latter offering camwood and ivory in exchange for beads and what little tobacco there was in circulation. Also, a variety of indigenous produce was available, including cassava, plantains, yams, pineapples, and palm oil, as well as the staples of rice and fish. Still, some merchants were gouging customers for 200 percent profits, and little could be had without paying dearly for it. Perhaps echoing the sentiments of other immigrants, Malinda Rex, a former slave who emigrated from Raleigh in 1839, despaired of the poverty of Caldwell and informed acquaintances in North Carolina of her disappointment. "I have not found notthing as they said and never will," she complained in a letter to the executor of her former master's estate. "If I had of known myself [about the poverty] I would not of been so willing to come."

Between the incessant clearing, weeding, sowing, and harvesting of land and construction of buildings, the shadow of death hung low over Caldwell. Under a sun that typically burned four degrees hotter than in Monrovia, town residents were continuously planning or hearing about funerals. Degenerative, respiratory, and gynecological ailments annually claimed many lives, and a few unusual deaths certainly attracted much attention. The smothering of one-year-old Scipio Peele in 1827 probably scandalized that clan from Northampton County, and the murder of Wilson Taylor of Camden by a Spanish slave trader three years later definitely sparked outrage. Yet, the malarial pestilence prostrated Caldwell more consistently than anything else. It was responsible for 30 percent of the deaths that occurred among North Carolina immigrants between 1825 and 1831 and affected nearly every family that came to the place. Perhaps fortuitously, the predatory vectors largely carried off the youngest and oldest members of the community, disproportionately sparing adults in their prime laboring and reproductive years. Nonetheless, one can only imagine that this observation was of little comfort to the Tisdale family from Camden County, who watched three of their children die in 1827, or the Peeles who agonized over six diseased corpses that same year.[16]

Collectively, the penury, isolation, hardship, and death that stymied its early development bestowed upon Caldwell one defining characteristic: vulnerability. The town's residents and ACS officials in Monrovia and Washington realized this early on, as did the Dei and other Africans who watched as their former lands were scoured of trees to accommodate the farms of foreigners. In recognition of this weakness, Lott Carey, the colony's de facto head after a terminally ill Ashmun departed in early 1828, embarked upon a program to fortify the town with the construction of a "Gun House" and other defensive assets. In a June letter, he told ACS managers that gun carriages had been completed for the mounting of cannon, which had been indispensable to the preservation and expansion of the colony. Undoubtedly, North Carolinians were active participants in these preparations, for two, Bennett Demery, a thirty-eight-year-old sailmaker and carpenter from Chowan County, and Matthias Bowe, a farmer from Pasquotank, served as

Directors of Public Labor. Stationed at the front line of defense was Lieutenant Jonathan James, a literate wheelwright from Bertie County. He was entrusted with the command of the loftily titled Caldwell Infantry Corps, which was more of a militia than a standing force. At bottom, this militarization of the settlement was nothing more than desperate overcompensation for the economic stagnation and malarial devastation that symbolized Caldwell's unenviable predicament. Strategic placement of guns and symbolic military pomp may have impressed upon neighboring African polities the martial power of the town. However, the anxieties behind this preoccupation with defense disclosed the fragility of the Caldwell community and the hollowness of the treaties that had supposedly given it the right to exist.[17]

Perhaps of some consolation to those in Caldwell preparing for an African siege, another immigrant settlement was founded on the St. Paul's River in 1828. Named after Samuel Mills and Ebenezer Burgess, the ACS's first colonial agents, the settlement of Millsburg was established some fifteen miles upriver from Caldwell on the northern bank. Dei leaders had ceded this sparsely populated real estate for the rather small cost of one hundred bars, or approximately twenty-five dollars, and on February 12, immigrants arrived to claim lots. Similar to Caldwell, the town was to be primarily a settlement of farming families but at the same time was to serve as a commercial outpost, mediating and prospering from trade between the coast and African communities further inland. A public factory was to be established to warehouse goods, and a lumber business was created to take advantage of the abundance of woodlands. Upon visiting Millsburg in June, Carey described the site in glowing terms, commenting that the colonists, "with two or three exceptions," had built homes strong enough to withstand the rainy season and had even established farms. Although optimistic about the progress of the town, he recommended to his superiors in Washington that immigrants be allowed to continue receiving rations beyond the standard six-month period, since cassava and other produce were in "great scarcity." In 1830, the settlement had 200 inhabitants, less than half of the 560 individuals believed to reside in Caldwell at that time. By the end of the following year, eighty North Carolinians had arrived in the town, which they shared with blacks from Georgia and Maryland.[18]

While there were, of course, similarities, the North Carolinians who settled in Millsburg were a different lot compared to those who ended up in Caldwell. Emigrant rolls and census data render a portrait of a group much less diverse and fortunate in a number of ways. In relation to origins, forty-seven of these eighty individuals were from Northampton County, with the remaining thirty-three hailing from the southeastern county of Wayne, where 34 percent of the population in 1830 was enslaved. Males comprised a slight majority (41) of the immigrants, and the prior status of most was not recorded, aside from the thirty-three liberated members of the Peele family who migrated from Northampton. Regarding age statistics, the North Carolinians of Millsburg were proportionately more youthful than their Caldwell counterparts, with fifty-eight being younger than twenty years of age and only five listed as over forty. The average age for the group was 15.5 years, and the modal age was one, of which there were seven such instances. More intriguing than these figures, only five persons were recorded as having occupations. All were farmers, four of whom were of the Peele clan. Rather amazingly, not a single individual was noted as literate in any manner, which did not bode well for a settlement that was intended to be a hub for interregional commerce. It is entirely possible that the whole group was accurately listed as unlettered, though their rate of literacy would have been well below that of black North Carolinians in general and residents of both Monrovia and Caldwell. Given the agrarian nature of both Northampton and Wayne Counties, it is very unlikely that the listed farmers were the only individuals with experience in agricultural work.

Among North Carolinians migrating to Liberia, the *Anopheles* mosquito visited an unprecedented mortality upon those who settled in Millsburg. Twenty-four percent of these immigrants were fatally afflicted with malaria, compared to 16 percent residing in Caldwell and 22 percent of those living in Monrovia. Eleven of the 19 victims were female, and the average age of the deceased was 9.5 years. All but two deaths occurred among people eighteen or younger, indicating that maturer immune systems stood the best chance of surviving a bout of the disease. In all three settlements, the age—and secondarily gender—of North Carolina immigrants was the most decisive factor in determining susceptibility to malaria. Not surprisingly, Caldwell, which had the lowest proportion (56 percent) of North Carolina immigrants younger than twenty, had the lowest malarial mortality. Monrovia had both the second highest mortality and the second highest proportion (61 percent) of immigrants younger than twenty. Finally, Millsburg had the highest percentage of colonists from North Carolina under twenty (72 percent) and suffered a commensurately higher death rate due to malaria.[19]

These observations are suggestive of a few things. First, since all of the immigrants from North Carolina initially landed in Monrovia, many could have first contracted malaria there, before moving to sites on the St. Paul's River. This would help explain the uniformity of the disease's impact on various migrating parties, adjusted for both age and gender variables. Second, it appears that Caldwell and Millsburg were as malarial as Monrovia, which also would explain the relatively uniform incidence of the illness. Given that one could easily contract the disease in any damp, unelevated area of the region, residents of riverine settlements were quite vulnerable to exposure. If ships transporting North Carolinians to Liberia had bypassed all three settlements and proceeded directly to elevated sites away from waterways, rates of malarial deaths would have been lower altogether. Especially since all of the people emigrating from the state between 1825 and 1831—with the exception of the nineteen who left in the *Criterion* in July of the latter year—arrived in Liberia during the dry season, survival rates would have almost certainly been much higher if disembarkation sites had been more judiciously chosen. Interestingly, the ACS board of managers had reached many of these conclusions within the first decade of colonization, based on a study of malarial mortality in the three towns. By 1832, they recognized the impact of season of arrival, site elevation, and proximity to wetlands on malarial infection and death rates. Nevertheless, well into the second half of the century, they continued to send African Americans to the colony during the unhealthiest months, and emigrant ships regularly touched at Monrovia, at least partially for commercial reasons, before delivering passengers to other settlements.

Among North Carolinian immigrants, county of origin had no significant impact on malarial mortality. Their home state lacked a sizable environment where the disease could flourish and offered very few opportunities for prospective emigrants to acquire a tolerance of West African versions of malaria prior to departing. To be sure, *vivax* malaria, a rarely fatal strain of the disease, was endemic to low-lying coastal areas, marshy environments such as the Great Dismal Swamp, and other locales with sufficient warmth, stagnant water, and *Anopheles* mosquitoes. Moreover, epidemic outbreaks of *falciparum* malaria, the deadliest variety of the disease, occasionally occurred in wet, humid parts of the state. However, the malarial vectors seasonally present in parts of North Carolina by the nineteenth century carried little, if any, of the specific strain of parasitic *Plasmodium falciparum* that was hyperendemic to Liberia and so lethal to newly arrived African American immigrants. Thus, while Millsburg immigrants from Northampton County endured a slightly lower malarial mortality (21 percent) than those from Wayne County (25 percent), the age spread of immigrants determined their susceptibility to Liberian *falciparum* malaria more than their county of origin. The proportion of people younger than twenty among the Northampton group (67 percent) correlates directly with its lower death rate, and the portion in that age range among the Wayne group (77 percent) correlates with its higher mortality.

Despite these state-specific observations, from a national perspective region of origin did matter. The twenty-seven Georgians who settled in Millsburg in 1828 suffered only a 15 percent rate of fatal malaria, which was lower than the North Carolinians, even after adjusting for the fact that only 55 percent of this party was younger than twenty. This suggests that immigrants from more humid, Lower South states enjoyed better resistance to Liberian malaria than those from more northern areas, perhaps due to previous exposure in coastal and riverine areas and a stronger presence of *falciparum* malaria, which thrived best in hotter climates. This point regarding origins is further supported by the horrific experience of the Claget family, who migrated to Millsburg from Maryland in 1830. All four of their children—ages twelve, nine, six, and two—were killed by malaria, representing a 100 percent mortality for Maryland immigrants under twenty. Although this instance is too small a sampling to conclude anything definitive about Millsburg, Maryland, or the relationship between state of origin and susceptibility to Liberian malaria, North Carolinians in Millsburg suffered only a 29 percent mortality for immigrants in the age range of the Claget children.[20]

Along with the three settlements of African Americans at Monrovia, Caldwell, and Millsburg, a fourth town was established in the colony, but under different circumstances. In July 1827, approximately 143 people landed at Monrovia, having sailed from the United States in the government-sponsored ship, *Norfolk*. The party was wholly composed of Africans who had been intercepted by a naval patrol a decade earlier as they were being shipped into bondage by the Spanish slaver *General Ramirez*. Originally landed and detained in Georgia, a number of these people had been sold into bondage in accordance with state law. To preclude further sales and to promote its colonization program, the ACS took an early and active interest in the case, hoping to send the Africans to Africa before Spanish claimants had a chance to transport them to Cuba or elsewhere. After years of legal and political maneuvering, the U.S. Supreme Court ruled, based on the 1819 law calling for a recaptive agency in West Africa, that the Africans should be turned over to the custody of the president for repatriation. Despite this putative victory, the subsequent embarkation of scores of these people at Savannah was bittersweet.

Although able to avoid a lifetime of slavery in the Americas, a number of the Africans were permanently severing ties with relatives and friends who had been sold into bondage during their protracted ordeal in Georgia. The families of at least three men were forced to depart without them, the men having been turned over to Spanish litigants. Given that most of the *Norfolk* emigrants were female, it is likely that more adult males, who would have commanded the highest purchase prices, were sold away during their detention in Georgia than females or children, though no data exists to substantiate this contention. In announcing the return of the 143 Africans to their native continent, the *African Repository* optimistically predicted that with "prompt exertions" by concerned observers, the families would be reunited and spared "so distressing a calamity." Unfortunately, it is unknown whether they ever were.[21]

Shortly after their arrival in Monrovia, the Africans were relocated to a site on Bushrod Island that became known as New Georgia, named after the state of their erstwhile captivity. Eventually, other recaptives joined them, including 150 Africans who had been liberated by black American colonists from Spanish slave factories along the Liberian coast. Extant records reveal very little about the demography of this group. In addition to being composed of about 78 females, the initial 143 recaptives who founded New Georgia were listed as primarily illiterate, at least in English, with only two capable of reading. Interestingly, by the time they reached Liberia, they had all either adopted or been given Western names, such as Boston Waldsburg, Margarett Bartlett, and Susan Young, suggesting both a degree of acculturation while in America and pressure to assimilate in Liberia.

Occupationally, a number of the males were farmers, along with several listed as sawyers. Since no ages were recorded for any of the emigrants, determining the nature of their experience with malaria is difficult. Of the passengers of the *Norfolk* and the ninety recaptives landed in March 1830 by the *Heroine,* only five are recorded as having died of fever. It is possible, even probable, that a number of the Africans had lived in malarial environments previously, whether in Africa, Georgia, or elsewhere, and thus had acquired a degree of resistance to the disease. Also, there may have been few children among the emigrants who would have been particularly susceptible. In the case of the Richardson family who emigrated from Pasquotank County to New Georgia via Monrovia in 1832, only one person, three-year-old Lydia, died of fever, though five of the nine family members were younger than thirteen. Undoubtedly, the arrival of the Richardsons and the recaptives during the healthiest months of the year encouraged their longevity.[22]

Located between colonial Monrovia and African-ruled territories, the recaptives were geographically, culturally, and symbolically a people between two worlds. Some of them had readily adopted elements of Western cultures, such as names, languages, dress, and other trappings, or had simply acquiesced to the perceived cultural exigencies of their new lives as Liberians. However, these recently sculpted identities were merely, and sometimes temporarily, in the foreground of a vaster African experience that served as a frame of reference for at least those who had been taken from the continent as adults. Even the people who had spent a decade in Georgia were not American in the ways of those who had generations of ancestry in the United States. Culturally disoriented and geographically dislocated by the slave trade and resettlement in Liberia, this mix of people was forced to create new identities, new families, and different cultural tools, based both on what they brought to New Georgia and on what they found there. As subsequent waves of recaptive emigrants shored up this population, the resultant cultural fragmentation, adaptation, and reformulation produced new values, relationships, and aspirations. Consequently, New Georgia and its people came to exist on a middle ground between the culture and authority of the ACS and its colonists and an African environment that they were neither wholly familiar with nor alien to.

The cultural paternalism and political pragmatism of the colonial administration of Liberia, which typically managed the U.S. receptive agency there, expressed itself most vividly in regard to New Georgia immigrants. As in other settlements, American-style educational institutions were established in the town, which had schools for adults and children by 1835. But entirely unique to receptive settlements, the offspring of these relocated Africans were parceled out to colonists, among whom they were to be assimilated. As early as 1826, forty receptive children under age fourteen lived in the homes of American immigrants, and over subsequent decades this number would dramatically increase. The purpose of this practice was less to enfranchise the receptives as Liberians, enjoying the rights and privileges of citizenship, than to create a cultural and communal buffer zone between the American colonists and the much more numerous indigenous Africans, such as the Dei, who surrounded them. Thus, while these liberated people were generally not invited to participate in the political, religious, and commercial structures of power in the colony, they were in much demand as cheap labor and as an auxiliary military force for guarding immigrant settlements against African encroachment. Lacking other viable economic opportunities, many of these people serviced the colony in this fashion, which, of course, did not endear them to groups indigenous to Liberia. In fact, their intermediary role increased their dependence on Monrovia, which may have been the outcome intended by the colonists and the ACS. Whatever the case, this alliance encouraged a certain political and cultural distance between receptives and neighboring African communities and was readily activated at times when the colonists were most in need of assistance.[23]

Beyond employing and deploying receptive men and incorporating their children into their households, African American colonists also created similar networks of dependence with indigenous people. One visitor to Cape Mesurado in 1827 observed that numerous Africans were employed by colonists to "act as servants and perform all the drudgery." In addition, he noted that most immigrant families kept indigenous children who had been sent to Monrovia by their parents to "learn the fashion of white man." Around this time, at least sixty African children had been "adopted" by the colony. Due to a scarcity of firsthand accounts, one can only speculate about the experiences of these children. Yet the motivations of both the colonists and their parents can be more easily discerned. Some immigrants, along with ACS officials, believed that imparting a Western-style education to African youth was a benevolent act that would improve the quality of life of these young people. Others may have viewed these children as possible replacements for their own who had been so tragically ravaged by malaria. The presence of these youths in Monrovia and elsewhere certainly opened lines of communication between immigrants and Africans which undoubtedly facilitated trade, diplomacy, and other interactions. These linkages spread both colonial culture among indigenous people and African cultures among immigrants and provided a bit of security for the latter. It was undoubtedly reassuring to colonists that local communities, even when aggrieved, would probably think twice before beginning hostilities with people who had custody of some of their children.

For parents who allowed their offspring to live among immigrant families, several considerations likely shaped their decisions. To many, learning "the fashion of white man" meant helping their children acquire enough of an understanding of colonial culture, especially its social organization and the English language, to prosper in an environment increasingly influenced by coastal events and foreign powers. Also, by extending their kinship networks, they broadened their influence and access to power and resources. In at least some instances, the whole practice of attaching indigenous children to immigrant families resembled the local tradition of pawning. This custom allowed people to satisfy debts or legal judgments against them by conveying children or wives to another party as servants. Typically, these family members were redeemed, or freed, once the two parties agreed that the issue that had resulted in their servitude had been redressed. African parents probably sometimes understood the relationship between their children and their immigrant hosts within this context, even if the colonists did not recognize or acknowledge the similarities between the practices. From this perspective, the educational instruction of these children would have been purchased by the services they performed as pawns of immigrant families. Additionally, there were instances in which African parents pawned their children to colonists as sureties for monetary loans.

Perhaps from the beginning and certainly over time, colonists adopted children who were consanguineously related to them. As early as 1832, one colonial official reported that a number of immigrant traders had "formed connections with the native women," which often resulted in them having to make payments to male kinsmen or face imprisonment. Traditionally, African leaders along the coast had allowed valued visitors, such as traders, to marry indigenous women in order to incorporate these men into certain families and communal networks. As part of a reciprocal relationship between coastal landlords and foreign visitors, these marriages guaranteed hospitality and protection for the stranger. In exchange, African village heads and others gained gifts, political alliances, middleman privileges, and other benefits. The offspring of both reciprocal arrangements and illicit unions between immigrant men and African women bound colonists and indigenous people together in intimate ways. Although the extent of these relationships is largely undocumented, their social, cultural, and economic implications both promoted and complicated the interaction between the two communities.[24]

In all of these cases, the presence of African children and adult laborers in colonial settlements allowed for substantial contact between immigrants and indigenous people. The preponderance of Africans in the environs of the colony and the necessity of adjusting to both its cultural and natural context meant that the newcomers, albeit often reluctantly, absorbed at least a few local ideas, values, and customs while disseminating their own. For example, immigrant children learned African languages, which smoothed social intercourse between settlers and native speakers. In late 1831, the managers of the ACS passed a resolution calling for the employment of "a native African Teacher to instruct a class of young men in the colony in the Arabic and other languages of the interior." Obviously, the organization was principally concerned about ways to enhance diplomatic and commercial relations with inland communities. Still, the notion that indigenous people should be approached on at least some of their own terms revealed an appreciation for the dominance of African cultures in Liberia and their utility as mediums of expression.

In addition to learning their languages, colonists had many other contacts with local people, which were negotiated on the cultural terrain of the latter. Palavers, or conferences, between immigrants and Africans almost always followed African protocol, and colonial housing, diets, and kinship networks were sometimes modeled after indigenous traditions. While the frequency and overall significance of such cultural and interpersonal interactions are hard to quantify, it is unlikely, as one North Carolina immigrant maintained in the late 1830s, that for every African converted to Christianity "five Americans have pulled off their clothes and gone naked." What is known is that cultural production and transference were a two-way process in Liberia due to convenience and necessity. Even if the ACS chose to stress in its annual meetings how much "heathen children" had benefited from educational instruction and "Christian example," its colony was a crucible of dynamic cultures, which were continually being smelted and recast.[25]

Related to this porous cultural environment, individual and group identities were also subject to transmutations in Liberia. The act of migration itself, along with the evolving political geography of the colony, had given new meanings to the way immigrants thought about themselves and their new land. By no means were the constructions of identities uniform or stable; they were subject to the influence of a number of factors, including prior experience in America, past status, the experience of emigrating, and place of settlement. Beyond being known as colonists and immigrants, these people were also engaged in figuring out to what degree they were still North Carolinians, Virginians, and Georgians. Towns such as Monrovia and Caldwell derived their populations from several states, which perhaps created a more integrated social vision that was more cosmopolitan and less culturally erected around a state-centered past. In contrast, settlements later founded by state colonization societies, such as the Maryland colony at Cape Palmas, were probably more self-consciously provincial in the way their inhabitants understood their origins. Decades of migration of people from a single state to a single town in Liberia likely renewed and strengthened a settlement's ties to a particular region of the United States and created a collective memory that fostered a communal consciousness based on shared origins. To many observers, these distinctions were not self-evident and were less meaningful than the more generally American origins of the immigrants. For instance, many Africans simply thought of the colonists, culturally, as white men who just happened to have dark skin. Nevertheless, these markers of origin and political identity were important to immigrants on a number of levels, whether as signifiers of one's previous status as a free person or as indicators of one's likelihood of dying from malaria.

The Americanness of the colonists filtered into Liberia in different ways. In some instances, the architecture, diets, clothing, language, political ethos, and spiritual values of immigrants, as well as their efforts to preserve these pillars of culture, revealed that their attachment to the land of their birth was quite substantial. Some became more consciously and chauvinistically American, at least in their self-conceptions, as they interacted with Africans, recaptives, and other non-Western people. Moreover, a nomenclature of nationality eventually developed over the course of the nineteenth century which disclosed the conflicted nature of identity development among immigrants. For example, the term *Liberians* was initially used to describe those who had emigrated from America. However, by the late 1800s, this identifying label had been modified to *Americo-Liberians* for the purpose of culturally and politically differentiating the ruling minority from the vast African majority that lived within the boundaries of the incipient nation-state. Sometimes, immigrants and their descendants were simply referred to as *Americans* or as residents of the American colony of Liberia. At no time did they commonly label themselves as Africans or any hyphenated derivatives of that term.

Despite the general tendency to emphasize their American roots, not all immigrants were quick to entirely repudiate ties with Africans. During the national period, Liberian presidents, such as Daniel B. Warner (1864–67), began calling for the political and social integration of all the country's peoples. Likewise, Edward Blyden and Alexander Crummell, leading members of the Liberian intelligentsia, often rhapsodized about the "indissoluble bonds" that tied all blacks together as a single branch of the human family. Blyden, in particular, believed that "there can never be any proper or healthful development of national life . . . without the aborigines." Writing to an ACS official in 1871, he held that immigrants would undoubtedly bring their American cultural mores to Liberia, but would find that they would have to be "Africanized" in order to maintain communal "vitality and growth." Aside from Blyden and other high-profile flirtations with a more inclusive vision of Liberian citizenship, immigrant culture continued to generally define Africans as outsiders. By the end of the century, indigenous people would be subjected to a colonialism that unfortunately resembled the means being employed by European imperialists to partition Africa among themselves.[26]

In addition to the developing self-image of the American colonists, the identities of recaptives landed in Liberia certainly underwent some significant alterations. Illustratively, within the span of a month, one could be a Temne, Akan, or Congolese farmer one week, an anonymous bondman on a Spanish slaver bound for the Americas the next week, a "Recaptured African" on a U.S. naval cruiser the following week, and finally a New Georgian with an English name by month's end. To confuse matters even further, soon after these transplanted people started arriving in Liberia during the 1820s, they became known among American immigrants as "Congoes," a term which indicated the origin of only some recaptives. The psychological implications of this harrowing odyssey of capture, recapture, and colonization were, of course, different for each person who endured it. However, the process of unscrambling and reinventing one's notion of self would eventually be experienced by thousands of recaptives landed upon the shores of Liberia.

As mentioned earlier, this dislocated population tended to gravitate toward the world of the American colonists. Undoubtedly, recaptives were motivated by a certain opportunism, perhaps believing that an alliance with the ruling class might ameliorate their shattered, disheveled lives. To some extent, their near ensnarement in American slavery gave them a degree of common ground with immigrants from the United States, though apparently not enough to make them initially palatable as first-class colonists. While serving, even imitating, Liberia's immigrant population, recaptives did forge relationships with neighboring African communities. According to one colonial official, intermarriage between male recaptives of Ibo and Pessay backgrounds and women from inland areas was common by the 1830s, with the latter adopting many of the cultural habits of their husbands. Besides lingering ethnic ties, little bound recaptives together as a group other than their shared ordeal in the holds of slave ships and their subsequent communal life in Liberia, which was constructed around their unique narrative as a people saved from bondage. These distinctive experiences influenced many of the ways in which recaptives interacted with American colonists and Africans until substantial intermarriage, cultural exchanges, and the passage of time gradually merged their identities with those of American immigrants and indigenous peoples.

Along with recaptives, there were a few cases in which immigrants from America were either literally returning to Africa or were at least no more than two generations removed from the continent. Sixty-six-year-old Sally Ogon Hollister of New Bern, North Carolina, was more than likely one of these returnees. Although listed in the emigrant roll as free born, her middle name suggests that she, or an immediate ancestor, had Yoruba origins, having probably lived in what is now southwestern Nigeria before being shipped into American slavery. In February 1833, Sally settled in Monrovia as the matriarch of a family of seven and was evidently still alive a decade later. Emigrant data shows that she and most of her family acquired literacy in English while resident in the United States but enjoyed very little resistance to malaria, given that two of them died upon arrival in Liberia. Sally's views of Africa and Africans are unknown, as are the opinions of most immigrants. Still, assuming that she was genealogically closer to the continent than the typical colonist, her perspective may not have been very different from those of the recaptives who left Georgia in 1827 aboard the *Norfolk*.[27]

In spite of the intertwining of experiences, customs, and histories in Liberia, the ACS, along with many immigrants, hoped to politically and culturally transform the colony and its environs into an American preserve less conspicuously African. One way in which this was attempted was through giving Western names to the land's geographical features and creating political units and boundaries tailored to the patterns of colonial expansion. Three of the major rivers of what became Liberia—the St. Paul's, St. John's, and Cavalla—had been previously named by the Portuguese centuries earlier, and these designations, and some others, were retained, though Anglicized. Yet colonization inaugurated a sustained effort by the ACS to leave its imprint on the political geography of the area. Most of the towns and much of the natural terrain became an eponymous roll call of ACS officials and white benefactors, starting with the naming of Monrovia and followed by Caldwell, Millsburg, Buchanan, Clay-Ashland, Edina, Marshall, Harper, Arthington, Brewerville, and several other invented places. Bushrod Island, behind the cape, was named after the first president of the ACS, and Stockton Creek honored the rash naval lieutenant who had initially coerced the Dei into opening their lands to colonization. Additionally, several states involved in colonizing African Americans assigned their names to later settlements, including Maryland, Virginia, Kentucky, and Louisiana. Very few of these places, besides Careysburg and Robertsport, were named after black colonists, which suggests that the right to name may have been one of the prices that immigrants were forced to pay for continued white financial support of the colony.

Africans, of course, knew all these places by their traditional names, regardless of what ACS cartographers were manufacturing. Nonetheless, they, too, were affected by the cultural imperialism of renaming, from Kru workers who answered to aliases such as "Pot of Beer" and "Drawbucket" to Dei kings who signed their marks on treaties beside monikers such as Peter, George, and Jimmy. Seemingly fitting, the naming of the colony's first site, Cape Mesurado, has been a source of contention among scholars, just as the territory itself was a cause of conflict between the early colonists and the Dei. All have assumed that the name *Mesurado* is Iberian in origin, but several have offered definitions ranging from "moderate, diminished, quiet" to "measured" and "miserable." The correct interpretation is probably *monte cerrado*, meaning a dense or jagged hill. Perhaps not wholly apocryphal, one tale attributes the naming of the cape to the comeuppance suffered by Spanish slave traffickers who landed there during the early transatlantic trade. After an unsuccessful battle with their intended victims, the hapless Spaniards allegedly cried, "Misericordia! Misericordia!" before being set upon by vengeful Dei. Thus, in this version of the naming, Mesurado represented an African victory against foreign aggression, though later it would become known as the place where American colonization first gained a foothold.[28]

Besides employing naming as a cultural tool for westernizing the African terrain of Liberia, ACS officials also tried to institute policies that would help create their version of an ideal colonial society. As reform-minded men, issues of morality and social progress, variously conceived, preoccupied their thinking about immigrant society and informed many of the measures that they put in place to shape life in the colony. Subsequently, much of their vision was incorporated into the colonial constitution and the digest of laws implemented in 1824, which offers insight into how these men thought about the operation and objectives of colonization. With few democratic pretensions, these documents placed policy-making powers securely in the hands of the Washington-based managers and their agent in Monrovia. Judicial proceedings were patterned after Anglo-American models, and U.S. common law was resorted to in situations where the constitution was silent. Furthermore, colonial statutes required that "every able bodied male" contribute labor to public works, though slavery was explicitly banned. While notably failing to enfranchise the colonists, the constitution did assert that they were "entitled to all such rights and privileges as are enjoyed by the citizens of the United States." The document even went so far as to forecast a time when the immigrants would be allowed self-government but in the meanwhile condemned as "high misdemeanors" political activities that smacked of sedition or insubordination.

Along with installing political and legal institutions in the colony, the ACS attempted to legislate morality by criminalizing a number of behaviors and activities that it deemed degenerate. "Sabbath breaking," profanity, and lewdness were characterized as offenses against public order, as were disturbing the peace and rioting. All felonies, including grand larceny, were punishable by whipping, incarceration, or hard labor. In an age when temperance was an increasingly popular reformist cause, the ACS tried to limit the consumption of alcohol in the colony. The digest of laws prohibited drunkenness on pain of fines, imprisonment, and flogging, and the board of managers encouraged colonists to minimize "the use and the sale of ardent spirits" among themselves and Africans. Despite these gestures, alcoholic beverages continued to flow in and out of the colony. ACS efforts to enforce regulations were often lukewarm, allowing private firms to market liquor with little interference. Moreover, in the face of criticism, some officials argued that alcohol served medicinal purposes in the colony and could not be entirely banned. Beyond this usage, intoxicating drink, especially rum, had proven essential to negotiations with Africans, lubricating everything from nonaggression pacts to land sales.[29]

Aside from the very limited success of their temperance policy, ACS officials had even less luck in halting the slave trade, the greatest moral evil that existed in the area of the colony. Considering that reducing this traffic was the primary official purpose of the colony and the recaptive agency, the failure of the colonial administration and immigrants to significantly abate the trade was both embarrassing and damaging to the colonization movement. As late as 1823, an estimated two thousand slaves were taken from the lands between Monrovia and Grand Cape Mount every year. At their annual meeting in January 1831, ACS managers noted the "undiminished atrocity and activity" of slaving establishments along the West African coast, positing that nine hundred slaves had been exported from the territory bordering Sierra Leone during the previous summer alone. British patrols had provided some relief, occasionally capturing Spanish "Guinea Men" and other slave ships before they could depart with their cargo. Yet, notwithstanding these interdictions, slavers came and went along the Liberian littoral just as emigrant ships did. To the particular chagrin of the ACS, not only was its colonial schooner too small and ill-equipped to deter slave traders, but rumors of colonists participating in the trade began to circulate with increasing frequency. This news was greeted with "grief and astonishment" by the organization's leaders, who decided to react strongly to preserve whatever credibility they retained regarding suppressing the trade. In November 1830, the board of managers resolved to sentence any immigrant convicted of slave trafficking to a year in prison, in addition to a fine of "not less than one thousand dollars." Individuals convicted of a second offense were to "suffer death," making slave trading a capital crime in Liberia.[30]

Regardless of the "too little, too late" nature of some of their policies, ACS officials still hoped to create a colonial regime and culture that produced law-abiding, self-supporting farmers and craftsmen, whose economic success would entice other African Americans to emigrate. Autocratic, paternalistic, and conservative, they sincerely believed that their dominion over the colony, with the cooperation of those they ruled, was essential to bringing this vision to fruition. More than any other person, Jehudi Ashmun, the colonial agent from 1822 to 1828, had proven to be indispensable to the implementation of their plans and had greatly influenced the manner in which his superiors responded to events in the colony, including the slave trade. He was central to determining the trajectory of colonial development during the tumultuous early years and was largely responsible for the image of Liberia that reached America. His letters, reports, and decrees, many of which were reprinted in the *African Repository*, render a view of colonization predicated on the assumption that immigrants could recreate an American community in the tropics. Like many self-styled philanthropists of the period, he and other white colonizationists believed that they were bestowing upon colonists, and by extension Africans, cultural mores and social structures that would raise them above the rather low level of civilization and refinement that they had allegedly become accustomed to. He believed that this feat was possible despite his generally low opinion of colonists, whom he felt lacked "established moral habits," and the corrupting influences of neighboring Africans, who were supposedly unfamiliar with notions of integrity, moderation, and "the simple idea of *moral justice*."

From his perspective, a proliferation of settlements, populous and thriving, along the St. Paul's River was easily conceivable. Although he despaired of the inability and unwillingness of the colonists to instantly transform the colony into grand plantation estates, he believed that their slowly expanding towns would inevitably control the riverine trade. In regard to relations with local peoples, he argued that it was possible for the colony to exist and grow without dispossessing Africans of "*their chosen settlements and villages*." Indigenous people did, in his view, occasionally warrant chastising for "insolent" behavior, but could, unlike American Indians, survive "the march of civilization" that he was leading through annexed territories. Ashmun's reassuring missives to ACS officials were definitely intended to assuage any compunctions they might have had regarding the colony's rapid expropriation of surrounding lands. However, the glaring incompatibility of colonial expansion with indigenous sovereignty was not lost on American critics of colonization. Nor were Africans oblivious to the practical implications of Ashmun's dubious claims.[31]

PETER BRUMLEY DIED a bitter man in 1832. As a Dei king, he had seen much transpire over the last decade of his life and, even on his deathbed, had not wholly formulated a way to respond to several crises that lay before him. One conclusion that he had arrived at was that the central problem of his people was the American colony at the cape, which had begun to creep eastward up the St. Paul's River. In his view, few benefits had come from the establishment of foreign settlements on Dei lands. Actually, Dei territory was smaller and more landlocked now than it had been in generations. Early on, Brumley had been one of several Dei leaders who understood the political and economic ramifications of the advent of an alien maritime power on the Grain Coast. Shortly after the first immigrants set foot in what became Monrovia, he, in alliance with other kings, attempted to violently repudiate the cession of Mesurado which King Peter had acquiesced to while under duress. Their offensive against the colony in November 1822 inflicted, in Ashmun's words, "considerable injury," but it ultimately failed to dislodge their American foes. Following this defeat, Brumley witnessed further annexation of his people's lands and was actually present when King Peter and others signed away the territory between Stockton Creek and Caldwell in 1825. Such dispossessing treaties were often the result of pressures exerted on indigenous authorities by colonial officials but were occasionally products of the shortsighted politics and avarice of individual monarchs who, without consulting others, ceded huge tracts of land in exchange for tobacco, rum, and other perishable items.[32]

While Ashmun and other agents delighted in informing ACS managers of the "profound tranquillity" that supposedly characterized the colony's relationship with neighboring African polities, Brumley's bitterness regarding the creation of Liberia ran deeper than they could have imagined. Too often had the colonists and their administrators added insult to injury, followed by more humiliation. Increasingly, Monrovia seemed to deal with indigenous people with the arrogance of a conqueror. For example, when Dei monarch Long Peter, an erstwhile ally of Brumley's, appealed to the colony for protection in the wake of political conflict that followed the death of King Peter in 1829, he was asked to relinquish his sovereignty. Colonial agent Joseph Mechlin stipulated that the ruler not only had to renounce his title before his request could be granted, he also had to accept a subordinate appointment as "head-man" and tell his people to henceforth "consider themselves Americans." Just as this fellow potentate agreed to what amounted to protectorate status, some of Brumley's peers saw their influence erode in other ways.

King Allen, who had participated in the Dei war against the colonists in 1822, was ruinously affected by the colony's occasional efforts to suppress slave trafficking in its vicinity. According to Mechlin, his domain on the Mesurado River had become "wretchedly poor . . . in consequence of the breaking up of the slave trade." It perhaps seemed hypocritical to Brumley, or at least ill timed, that the same white men, whose rapacious appetite for slaves had fueled the trade a generation earlier, were now trying to end a business that Africans had become so dependent upon as suppliers. To him, it must have seemed a tortured logic. Nevertheless, for Brumley, the most unsettling truth was that Dei power and authority were on the decline, steadily being overwhelmed by force of arms, concessionary treaties, and the enticing wares of interlopers. From his deathbed, the monarch was witnessing, to his consternation, the collapse of a world that had been centuries in the making.[33]

Similar to the Kru, the Dei were part of the Kwa-speaking communities that migrated from the east around the sixteenth century. They eventually settled along a fifty-mile-long strip of territory between the Mesurado River and Little Cape Mount (northwest of the mouth of the St. Paul's River), which extending almost twenty miles inland. Along with other peoples of the area, the Dei came under the authority of the Mandingo-led Kondo confederation, with its capital at the inland town of Bopolu. Known as skillful traders and couriers of Islam, the Mandingo tied the region together commercially, which assisted the integration of markets for textiles, ivory, firearms, and slaves. It is possible that the Dei did not become an agricultural people until they settled in coastal lands where rice could be cultivated for both internal consumption and export. Moreover, the group did not create a strong centralized state or a significant urban culture subsequent to their relocation. Instead, the Dei founded a number of villages with from a few dozen to several hundred inhabitants, each governed by a paramount leader and several vassals. Although each of the rulers had absolute power over his subjects, they occasionally consulted one another, especially during crises, and routinely selected a chief spokesman from among their ranks. Around 1819, King Peter was chosen to lead the Dei, who numbered as many as eight thousand by this time. Accordingly, his town of Gawulun, on what would become known as Bushrod Island, served as the group's capital.[34]

Dei society was stratified and organized around systems of service and obligation. Within households, polygamy was often practiced, and women, who perhaps made up 60 percent of the population, were responsible for many of the domestic chores, child rearing, and agricultural work. On any given day, a woman might make soap or cooking oil, haul wood, create pottery or baskets, wash clothes, or tend a garden, as well as supervise children. Men typically made cloth, wove rattan baskets, and prepared rice and cassava fields during the late dry season, but much of the household and farming work was left to women. In addition to gender-based labor arrangements, other customary means of securing service from others included pawning and slavery. The former usually involved the transfer of women or children to satisfy debts or legal obligations. In some communities, maternal uncles could pawn nieces and nephews. Generally, this condition was a temporary one for those pawned, ending whenever both contracting parties were in agreement that outstanding debts or other obligations had been settled. Pawns could not redeem themselves from servitude, but unlike slaves, they could not be sold unless guilty of serious crimes.[35]

The kind of slavery that existed among groups such as the Dei was complex and varied. Prisoners of war were most commonly used as bondmen. However, free people could also be reduced to slavery for criminal acts, though this was apparently infrequent. As property, slaves could be disposed of as their owners saw fit, and thus could be given as tribute, sold to traders, or killed with impunity. Adapted to the needs and values of each village, slavery was a malleable institution among the Dei and neighboring peoples, sometimes resembling pawning and occasionally reminiscent of serfdom. The institution usually incorporated practices and expectations integral to both free and bonded labor systems and was predictably not immune to contradictions. Slavery, like migrations and trade networks, occasionally softened real and imagined differences between various groups and challenged whatever notions of ethnicity that existed among coastal peoples. For example, Gola or Kpelle women purchased as slaves by Dei men might bear children for their masters, who would be socialized in the culture of their fathers and become identified as Dei. Similarly, a Vai bondman in the possession of a Mandingo trader might become proficient in Arabic, leading to conversion to Islam and the adoption of Muslim dress and other cultural trappings. In these ways, and many others, slavery and slave trading accelerated ethnic and cultural intermingling among the Dei and others, though bondage itself could range from beneficent forms of service to brutish subjugation. As it turned out, it was this integrative, exploitative institution that caused incessant friction between the Dei and newly arrived American colonists, sparking new hostilities by the end of 1831.[36]

In relation to this conflict, the triggering event was the escape of several of King Brumley's slaves to a recaptive settlement in the colony prior to their sale to Spaniards in the Gallinas, bordering Sierra Leone. Desirous of reclaiming the runaways, the monarch sent his son and heir apparent, Kai Pa, to negotiate the return of the slaves. Unexpectedly, colonial agent Mechlin refused to discuss terms with the prince and informed him that only an appearance by the king himself would incline him to "make such arrangements as would be mutually satisfactory." Brumley, terminally ill and likely incensed by the agent's demand that he travel to the cape over such a matter, died before issuing a response. Upon his father's death, Kai Pa assumed command of his kingdom, inheriting both his name and his problems. The new ruler was fully aware that his legitimacy as Brumley's successor, and the authority of nearly every other Dei leader, was substantially tied to the nature of his relationship with the colonists and his ability to be firm when aggrieved by them. In this instance, not only had he been aggrieved and rebuked by Mechlin, but so had his recently deceased father, whose loss of property to the colony was interpreted as a matter of honor which necessitated action.[37]

Although in earnest, Kai Pa Brumley followed local protocol in organizing an offensive against the colony. In early 1832, he consulted first with other Dei kings and found that several would back his war effort. A number of Gola leaders, who had just watched Monrovia absorb some neighboring lands, agreed to allow their subjects to fight with the Dei but declined to openly ally themselves with Kai Pa, hedging themselves against the possible consequences of defeat. Probably assuming that his own capital would eventually be attacked by vengeful colonial forces, Kai Pa designated the village of King Willey, a Dei ally, as a redoubt, fortifying it with a barricade to forestall an invasion. Once this avenue of escape was secured, his military operations started, initially as harassment. His soldiers captured and mistreated a number of colonists and recaptives as immediate retribution for Mechlin's unwillingness to release the absconded slaves of the late King Brumley. News of this provocation arrived first in Caldwell, relayed by one of the detained recaptives who had, despite spear and knife cuts, managed to escape from his Dei captors. In response to this report, the colony sent a message to King Willey's town calling for the release of prisoners being held there. Reminiscent of Mechlin's refusal to treat with Kai Pa earlier, the latter's representatives dismissed this demand and told the messenger to notify the colonial agent that the Dei intended to capture and imprison every colonist they could.[38]

The following day a detachment of Dei soldiers arrived at the banks of the St. Paul's River, opposite Caldwell, and challenged the colonists to meet them on the battlefield. Mechlin, after hearing that the force had blown war horns and discharged muskets in its efforts to provoke a confrontation, immediately solicited the advice of a number of colonists whom he believed were knowledgeable about Dei culture and politics. All agreed that Kai Pa and his army were deadly serious about marching on the colony. However, Mechlin underestimated both the strength of Dei and Gola forces and the tactical skills of Kai Pa. On March 17, the colonial agent organized a unit of one hundred recaptive soldiers and sent them across the river to King Willey's town. He had received intelligence that Dei officials were meeting to discuss battle strategy and hoped to capture the principal leaders who were heading the offensive against the colony. The plan was both daring and doomed. The recaptive contingent happened upon a larger force of Dei soldiers during their approach to the town. A skirmish ensued, and the African army repelled the would-be invaders with such violence that they were forced into "a precipitate retreat," suffering the loss of one of their number. Pleased with the results of this initial battle, Dei leaders informed the colony that if its forces did not "speedily meet them in the field," assaults on both Caldwell and Millsburg would follow.[39]

Mechlin had for some time suspected that military conflict might break out between the Dei and the colony. In December, he had asked ACS secretary Gurley to send a substantial amount of war materiel to Liberia, including two six-pound cannon, three hundred muskets, and several barrels of gunpowder "such as is used in the army or navy." Despite his plea, it was not until their April 9 meeting that the board of managers resolved to send weaponry to Mechlin and then only half of what he had requested. Of course, this was too late to bolster the colony's war effort against Kai Pa and his allies. Mechlin, fearing a generalized conflict involving "the whole of the Dey and [Gola] countries," quickly organized a volunteer force of eighty men in Monrovia and proceeded to Caldwell on March 20. Reaching the riverside settlement that afternoon, the unit was joined by volunteers under the command of Captain Jerry Nixon and members of the local militia led by Lieutenant James Thompson. This latter group of 70 men and a recaptive company of 120 soldiers—almost certainly drawn largely from the force that had been recently humbled at King Willey's town—joined the assembled units. With a total troop strength of 270, the army encamped at Caldwell that evening before crossing the St. Paul's en route to the territory of Kai Pa.[40]

Given that roughly 40 percent of Caldwell's residents were from North Carolina, a substantial number of the men who gathered to fight the Dei and Gola likely originated from that state, many having come from Pasquotank County. Captain Nixon, a thirty-two-year-old carpenter, had emigrated from that area in 1826 aboard the *Indian Chief.* While his trade and ability to read served him well in a nascent agricultural colony desperately in need of such talents, he probably had little choice regarding whether to participate in the Caldwell militia. All past conflicts with Africans were recent memories for colonists, and the St. Paul's settlements were, indeed, now threatened by forces that could devastate their populations and property. Whether Nixon had any sympathy for Dei grievances over loss of lands is unknown. However, he almost certainly opposed the practice of slavery among indigenous people, having been born free, or quasi-free, among Friends and having witnessed or experienced bondage firsthand. If he had ever been partial to Quaker pacifism, it was apparently a fleeting affinity. Frontier life in Africa had proven hard, sickly, and dangerous, and colonial expansion was necessarily an exercise in force, both threatened and exerted.

Although he was a member, even a protector, of a society that was dispossessing others of vast territories, it would be simplistic and perhaps even inaccurate to assume that this reality was Nixon's primary frame of reference for understanding his life and role in Liberia's unfolding history. He had immigrated to the colony with three females who were probably relatives. Arriving at ages twelve, sixteen, and twenty-six, they had all survived Caldwell's 16 percent malarial death rate, which was quite a feat for females entering the colony at such young ages. Six years older and acclimated, Caldwell had become their home and future; there was no returning to Pasquotank, at least not as free blacks. While his lands, livelihood, and sense of civic duty certainly were factors, Nixon probably took up arms with Judy, Rachel, and Lydia foremost in his mind. Imagining them as captives of the Dei or as refugees in Monrovia was probably more than enough to motivate him to serve. Similarly, many of the other North Carolinians who crossed the river with him to stand against Kai Pa almost certainly believed themselves to be making sacrifices for reasons just as dear.[41]

When the force arrived at King Brumley's town, it found that the village had been conceded to them, for no garrison had been stationed there to defend it. The colonial army decided to stay the night there to prepare for the siege on King Willey's town but found that spies were watching them under cover of darkness, undoubtedly to ascertain their number and the nature of their arms. The next morning the colonists slowly journeyed to the Dei stronghold, their progress greatly impeded by trees that had fallen, or been placed, along the path connecting the two towns. The recaptives, who were used as frontline shock troops, were the first to engage Dei and Gola forces in volleys of gunfire during the early afternoon. Unable to advance on the Africans' position behind an elaborate barricade of heavy logs that guarded the entrance to the town, colonial soldiers pushed a light cannon within thirty yards of the fortification and opened fire. After a number of blasts, the Dei and Gola defenders retreated from their position, allowing the besieging army to enter the town after hacking through the breached barricade.

Waiting for the invaders behind a second barricade of logs and dense foliage was a much larger force which hoped to ambush the immigrant army as it took possession of the village. The Africans, however, failed to benefit from the element of surprise, being immediately discovered and fired upon by the recaptive unit. In the fighting that followed, fifteen African soldiers were killed and several others wounded. The casualties of the colonial army were much lighter, with only Lieutenant James Thompson of Caldwell losing his life as he tried to charge the Dei and Gola position. While the invading troops won a rather lopsided victory, the battle could have easily turned out quite differently. To dramatically assert both his royal power and to avenge both family and country, King Kai Pa Brumley had personally planned to fire a three-pound cannon at enemy soldiers as they advanced on the second barricade. To his dismay, before he could ignite the powder, he was shot in the shoulder and could not complete the cannonade. The colonists realized the extent of their good fortune only after examining the weapon later. According to Mechlin, it had been "loaded nearly to the muzzel with bits of iron bolts, pot metal," and other items and positioned in such a fashion as to maximize carnage. Failing to repulse the intruders with either musket or cannon, the African army was routed, and King Willey's town taken.

The recaptive soldiers, who had apparently endured the brunt of the African defensive attack, exacted a fiery vengeance against the Dei. Before the colonial army could encamp at King Willey's town for the night, this unit razed the village, necessitating that the entire force retire to Kai Pa's deserted capital. But as they proceeded to establish quarters there, the recaptives again applied the torch to Dei dwellings. The resultant conflagration spread rapidly, and the army was obliged to flee the town "precipitately," finally ending up in Caldwell where they stayed until the following day. Whether the recaptives acted out of the passions of the moment or hoped such excesses would please their American superiors, their actions, which Mechlin "found impossible to restrain," revealed a brewing antagonism between the Dei and the segment of the colonial population closest to them culturally. This mutual hostility, no doubt, served the purposes of Monrovia, which had so readily deployed the recaptives first during every battle. It facilitated the colonial administration's efforts to control both populations and discouraged alliances between the two.

With his town in ashes and his authority in question, King Willey, along with a military ally, King Brister, sued for an unconditional peace on March 26. Exercising the prerogatives of victors, Mechlin demanded that all the defeated Dei leaders appear before him in Monrovia to learn his decision regarding the terms of their surrender. Four days later, several high officials arrived at the cape to meet with the colonial agent, including Kings Brister, Sitma, and Ba Bey (Long Peter), along with Willey's envoy, Baugh, and Kai Pa's representative, Kai. Although the war had been brief and more costly in treasure than blood for the colonists, the peace promised to be a vindictive one in which the Dei would again be forced to cede sovereignty. In addition

to officially ending the military conflict, the treaty forbade the Dei from acting as middlemen between inland African communities and the colony. Previously, the group had required traders in territories east of Monrovia to conduct their business with coastal clients through Dei brokers. Now, the latter
were barred from acting in this capacity. With the signing of this accord, the
implications of the whole affair were clear. Not only had the colonists illustrated their ability to invade and take a fortified town, but they had also
opened an artery of trade that could only damage the economic well-being
of their most persistent nemesis, the Dei. The war and the peace had demonstrated the determination of immigrant communities to exist, as well as their
power to regulate and control the affairs of their African neighbors. As Mechlin observed after issuing his terms to the vanquished kings, "The consequences of this war will prove highly advantageous to the colony."[42]

As for Kai Pa Brumley, who had been conspicuously absent from the pro-
cession of monarchs and dignitaries that Mechlin had summoned to Monrovia, his authority and rule, though undoubtedly shaken by the humiliation
of defeat and personal injury, survived this war with the colony. He would go
on to become the paramount king, or spokesman, for the Dei and would
continue to have brushes with colonial authority over the next several years.
Ironically, Kai Pa's reign ended in 1847, the same year that the colony declared
its independence. With faltering credibility and mounting enemies, he survived an attempted poisoning in February of that year, before succumbing to
a second effort in August. If his conflict with the colonists revealed the increasing vulnerability of his people to foreign encroachment, it disclosed even
more about the evolving character of colonial rule and immigrant society.[43]

Battles against Africans nurtured a siege mentality among colonists, which
had been a part of their identity since initial conflict erupted with the Dei in
1822. This laager mind-set encouraged them to invent communal, and later
national, notions of belonging and citizenship based upon their increasingly
romanticized role as pioneering insiders of a noble but difficult colonial experiment. Differences between colonists and indigenous people in language,
religion, dress, and social organization became rationalizations for a cultural
arrogance toward all things African and convinced many immigrants of both
their superiority and the alleged providential nature of their migration to
Africa. Over time, a colonial lexicon and ideology of domination would become pivotal to the way successive Liberian administrations and many immigrants understood and interacted with Africans. Unfortunately, these self-
serving views would be employed to validate some particularly unsavory
attitudes and practices.

Rooted in existing Western ideas about civilization and race, this termi-
nology and mind-set separated colonists and indigenous people into com-

peting categories, justifying the former's presence and the latter's subjugation and, relatedly, declaring the one's supremacy and the other's lesser humanity. Thus, this immigrant-centered language of conquest conjured up *Liberians*, who were forging a nation of republican freeholders, and *natives*, who were shorn of an identity, save that of the static, corporatist tribe. Furthermore, it allowed that only colonists could mobilize infantry, soldiers, and troops; the African, regardless of skill and rank among his own people, could aspire to be little more than a warrior or a "head-man" in the pages of colonial reports about hostilities. The immigrant brought civilization, the gospel, and light; the Dei, Gola, Kru, and others waited for salvation in a deep darkness of witchcraft, superstition, and heathenism. In essence, the colonist thrived on high culture and reasoning; the African, impulsive and carnal, was satisfied with his ignorance and curious about nothing.

In support of colonial expansion, even the continent itself, for all its natural beauty, was readily employed to draw sharper lines of distinction between the immigrants and indigenous populations. Like its people, Africa was depicted as wild and unbridled, as evidenced by its thatch villages, its deadly fevers, and its dearth of plantation agribusiness and incipient industrialization. Ultimately, the alleged backwardness, the depravity, was cyclical, allowing neither the continent nor its people an argument against colonial intervention. The land, with its heat and humidity, its rains, its tropical flora and fauna, was savage, and the attempts by Africans to rationally alter and accommodate the harshness of the environment were savage as well, necessitating the injection of outside civilizing influences. This mythological construction of a culturally denuded Africa was central to the ideological imperatives of colonization. This view sought to legitimize the psychic needs of many black Americans to control their own lives (and those of others), to make the foreign familiar through the practice of renaming, and to justify their presence in territories acquired through military conquest and dubious treaties. This mentality, of course, poisoned much of the future dialogue between immigrants and Africans and alienated the latter from recaptives who had been so flagrantly manipulated as both a buffer people and as a cudgel for suppressing indigenous opposition. Consequently, as early as the 1830s, these belligerent relationships threatened to stigmatize Liberia with all the negative connotations that the term *settler colony* would eventually evoke by the twentieth century.

THE WORLDS OF Captain Jerry Nixon and King Kai Pa Brumley intersected at angles that could not have been charted a generation earlier. By the time their armies tried to exterminate each other at the barricades of King Willey's town, the political and cultural terrain of what was becoming Liberia had changed dramatically over just a decade's time. The colonial towns of Monrovia, Caldwell, Millsburg, and New Georgia had sprouted along its mangrove-bound waterways, and two thousand immigrants had become major players in the politics and economies of centuries-old kingdoms. Although established with grueling labor on unforgiving malarial lands, Liberia was primarily an idea, a fantasy, of men who lived thousands of miles away and who were seeking to remake their own world before it slipped into the abyss of social upheaval. Planted first at Cape Mesurado and spreading outward from there, the colony was undoubtedly African in its geographic and climatic texture, its long histories of internal migrations and settlement, and its mixture of peoples, values, and practices. Yet, it was also something more.

By the second decade of its existence, the colony was a meeting ground of cultures, blended, distilled, and transformed daily by innumerable contacts, collaborations, and conflicts. To the Kru, Liberia meant a burgeoning stevedore and transport business, but for the Dei, territorial diminution and fractured sovereignty. American immigrants might come there for freedom, farms, and personhood only to suffer a premature death by the sting of the *Anopheles* mosquito, but indigenous youths might adopt "the fashion of white man" while serving in Monrovian households. Kings and colonial agents vied to define the political ethos and boundaries of the colony as well as to control its trade networks and relations with both inland Africa and the Atlantic community. Despite the denials of ACS officials, Liberia meant both slavery and abolition, pawning and free labor, and a range of practices in between. In perpetual tension, the colony was a patchwork of all these things, exhibiting stark contradictions and timeless continuities. But for the generation of Jerry Nixon and Kai Pa Brumley, Liberia mostly meant mutual suspicion and endless conflict along an ever-shifting, ever-bleeding frontier.

Historical marker for New Garden, Guilford County, N.C. (Photograph by author)

Historical marker for Quaker community, Perquimans County, N.C. (Photograph by author)

Historical marker for
Moses A. Hopkins, U.S.
minister to Liberia,
1885–86, Franklinton,
N.C. (Photograph by
author)

Slave house, Pasquotank County, N.C. (Photograph by author)

African American housing in North Carolina, late nineteenth century
(North Carolina Collection, University of North Carolina Library at Chapel Hill)

African American images on North Carolina currency, 1859
(Special Collections Library, Duke University, Durham, N.C.)

FREEDMEN'S GREAT
Mass Convention

The "North Carolina Freedmen's Emigration Aid Society" will assemble at the CITY HALL, in Raleigh, N. C.,

ON THE 18th & 19th OF OCTOBER, 1877,

In the interests of said Society. Let every County in the State be represented. Some of our number expect soon to embark for Liberia.

ROBERT ORR,
Pres't N. C. F. E. A. S.

SHERWOOD CAPPS,
Secretary.

Meeting announcement, 1877 (Reel 116B, RACS)

A New Bern woman, 1884 (William G. Reed Collection, Special Collections Library, Duke University, Durham, N.C.)

A Mandingo woman, ca. 1900 (From Johnston, *Liberia*, vol. 1)

"Vai Town" near Monrovia, Liberia (From Johnston, *Liberia*, vol. 1)

Vai princess and prince (Library of Congress)

Kru mariners off the Liberian coast (From Johnston, *Liberia*, vol. 1)

Joseph J. Roberts, first
president of Liberia
(Library of Congress)

Bushrod Washington, first president of the American Colonization Society (From Richardson, *Liberia's Past and Present*)

Presidential mansion, Monrovia, Liberia (Library of Congress)

The Liberian Senate, late nineteenth century (Library of Congress)

A Dei king and his family (Library of Congress)

Monrovia, Liberia, ca. 1900 (From Johnston, *Liberia*, vol. 1)

Ashmun Street, Monrovia, Liberia, ca. 1900
(From Johnston, *Liberia*, vol. 1)

ACS warehouse on Water Street, Monrovia (Library of Congress)

St. Paul's River, Liberia (From Johnston, *Liberia*, vol. 1)

Cape Palmas, Liberia (From Johnston, *Liberia*, vol. 1)

A sketch of Monrovia, ca. 1886 (From Stewart, *Liberia:
The Americo-African Republic*)

A drawing of the ACS ship, *Mary Caroline Stevens*
(From *Maryland Colonization Journal*, December 1856)

Immigrants at a bridge
near Arthington, Liberia
(Library of Congress)

Joseph C. Price, founder
and first president of Livingstone College (North
Carolina Collection, Uni-
versity of North Carolina
Library at Chapel Hill)

Shaw University, Raleigh, N.C. (From Whitted, *History
of the Negro Baptists of North Carolina*)

National seal of Liberia
(From Johnston, *Liberia*,
vol. 1)

Black North Carolinians
preparing to leave the
state, late nineteenth
century (From *Frank
Leslie's Illustrated Newspaper*, February 15, 1890)

FIVE. THE PRICE OF LIBERTY

ON FEBRUARY 12, 1831, a solar eclipse shaded the eastern seaboard of the United States. The phenomenon had been anxiously anticipated by doomsday fanatics, skeptics, and the curious in general, and it was a rare person who did not pause during his or her daily routine to witness this most mysterious of nature's spectacles. Yet despite the outlandish expectations of some, this lunar obscuring of the sun turned out to be rather disappointing, given the advance publicity it had received in almanacs, newspapers, and other media. The sky was not engulfed in impenetrable darkness as some had imagined it would be, nor was there any perceivable shift in the clockwork of the universe. Actually, if one had not known beforehand of the impending eclipse, he or she might have failed to notice it altogether. "The multitude have been sadly disappointed," one Boston editor concluded afterward. "They looked for darkness and the shades of light; they expected to drink horrors, and feed the power of superstition without its terrors or apprehension, they expected ... to see something that they might talk about now and hereafter—something to tell their children and grandchildren." The journalist was probably right in his assertion that the eclipse had been anticlimactic for most who observed it. However, at least one person had paid particularly close attention to this brief light show in the heavens. He had asked for it, indeed, prayed for it. Peering upward into the winter sky of Southampton County, Virginia, Nat Turner, a thirty-year-old slave preacher, saw nothing deficient in this ce-

Above: Southampton County, Va. (Photograph by author)

lestial event. To him, his destiny was linked to such forces of nature in ways that would soon become evident to all.[1]

Some would posit later that the Christian millenarianism and revolutionary abolitionism that inspired Turner's subsequent actions were scripted in antislavery newspapers and other literature that started seeping into southern states by the 1830s. Despite the absence of corroborating evidence, the preacher might possibly have heard of David Walker's *Appeal* or William Lloyd Garrison's *Liberator*, which went into publication a month before the eclipse. Yet, he need not have. A life in slavery had exposed him to many of the institution's evils and humiliations, which could not be captured by either the righteous fury of Walker or the abrasive broadsides of Garrison. Anyway, according to Turner, he had had visions of insurrection as early as 1825, long before these writers emerged as voices of the new abolitionism. In that year, the preacher had a revelation of "white spirits and black spirits engaged in battle" before an obscured sun and streams of blood. Furthermore, he claimed to have encountered "the Spirit" on May 12, 1828, which mandated that he "fight against the Serpent, for the time was fast approaching when the first should be last and the last should be first." By the time the eclipse appeared, Turner had already prepared himself for the work of destroying local slaveholders "with their own weapons." When he and his small band of followers commenced killing whites in Southampton on August 21, he understood his work to be divinely ordained and eminently just. To him, the eclipse had revealed all: white power and mastery completely engulfed by blackness. As it was in the heavens for that brief moment, he determined so shall it be on earth.[2]

News that Nat Turner and his compatriots had struck a lethal blow for liberty, which ultimately claimed sixty white lives, quickly crossed the border into North Carolina. Instantly alloyed with false rumors and hysterical fantasies, information about the revolt had a unique impact on the South. At no other time had so few black men killed so many white people in so little time. Predictably, as white officials, militiamen, and vigilantes mobilized to suppress the rebellion, the reprisal promised to be more monstrous than any in recent memory. With Nat Turner still at large, a sanguinary wave of white vengeance swept across eastern North Carolina. In Sampson County, Jim and Dave, two bondmen convicted of insurrection on the basis of coerced confessions, were seized from jail by a mob, shot, and beheaded. Eight days later in Wilmington, which had been rumored to be a target of uncaptured rebels, four blacks were whipped until they offered confessions. They were then hanged, and their severed heads were stuck on poles for public display. In Pasquotank County during late September, two white men who, according to John Ehringhaus, "were far from being *sober*" entered a black man's

THE PRICE OF LIBERTY

home and murdered him. One of the culprits escaped, but the other was caught and confined in the local jail. Despite the heinous nature of the crime, Ehringhaus believed that the "present excitement" in the county over the Southampton rebellion made it unlikely that a jury would convict the detained man of murder.[3]

Until Turner's capture on October 30, the search for rebels and sympathizers took on the appearance of a classic witch hunt, with all the attendant irrationalities. Those blacks who offered confessions, whether truthful or otherwise, and implicated others were routinely sentenced to death. Those who were genuinely innocent but were unwilling to offer false admissions of complicity or to drop the names of others were also killed. Notably, many blacks were spared by white marauders but terrorized nonetheless. The experience of Mrs. Colman Freeman, a freeborn woman who lived in northeastern North Carolina, was probably repeated numerous times during the early stages of the repression. After armed white men entered her residence in search of weapons, she was assailed by one of the intruders who pressed a pistol against her breast and threatened to kill her if she protested. At the time, she and her mother, who was also present, were unaware of the Southampton revolt and could only wonder about the cause of this sudden invasion of their home. Soon after the attack, she resolved "not to remain in that country" and migrated to Ohio and then to Canada. Mrs. Freeman was very lucky, as she surely realized once news of the arbitrary murder of African Americans circulated throughout the region. In the end, as many as two hundred blacks in Virginia and North Carolina, the majority of whom took no part in the insurrection, lost their lives in a killing spree fueled by white lust for revenge and a longing to restore a sense of security which was forever lost.[4]

Some of the worst repression in North Carolina took place in the northeastern county of Halifax. The ingredients for an antiblack pogrom had been coalescing there for years. In 1802, an insurrection scare shook the county, an episode which did not entirely fade from public consciousness. Further, the area's heavy reliance upon slave labor for cultivating cotton, tobacco, corn, and other products shaped its racial demography in a manner that could only increase white fears of future unrest. The 1830 census revealed that Halifax had the state's largest free black community, consisting of 2,079 persons, and an enslaved population of 9,790, which was nearly twice the tally of white residents, who numbered only 5,870. When news of the Turner rebellion riveted the county and its seat of the same name on August 23, nearly the entire white population took up arms. Guided by justices of the peace who had alerted the citizenry that "the spirit of insubordination and insurrection may extend among the larger body of slaves immediately around us," deputized whites rounded up male slaves in the town of Halifax and incarcerated them in the local jail. An arsenal was established at the courthouse, and a well-armed garrison fortified the town's defenses. During the week following the Turner revolt, the hunt for suspected rebels began in earnest with all of the usual random terror. A free black man passing through Halifax was shot dead in an encounter that ultimately ended with the man's head impaled on a pole. Similarly, a slave driving his female master and her children into the town was gunned down as their carriage reached its destination. Well into September, it seemed that no black man could enter Halifax without drawing suspicion and often gunfire.[5]

In the neighboring town of Enfield, the pattern of summary executions was much the same. One resident noted that even after the alarm over the Southampton insurrection had began to subside, African Americans were being "taken in different directions and executed every day." This included a free black man whom townspeople killed after failing to extract a confession from him. As the repression continued in Halifax County and elsewhere into the fall, it was clear that the white response to the panic had been shamefully excessive. In its August 25 edition, the *Raleigh Register* asserted that the threat of rebellion in Halifax and Northampton Counties "has probably been magnified." Even more telling, the *Carolina Observer* of Fayetteville reported on September 21 that "not a single party of negroes, nay, not a single individual" had been discovered in insurrectionary activities anywhere in the state. Governor Monfort Stokes, though alarmed by the Turner rebellion, recognized that the savagery that was being visited upon the state's black population had gotten quite out of hand. While the legislature itself, with its proscriptive laws of 1830, had set the tone for the antiblack lawlessness that enveloped the state, the governor seemed to rue, at least privately, the murderous brutality that was being inflicted upon black North Carolinians. "Nothing like a concerted or extensive plan has been discovered," he stated in a November letter to his South Carolina counterpart. "I am afraid, that among the negroes condemned and executed, some, who were innocent, have suffered."[6]

In this climate of racial turmoil, interest in colonization surfaced once again, just as it had during previous crises. Undoubtedly shaken by the shocking news from Southampton as well as by the bloody vengeance that was being carried out around him, Joseph Gray, a Halifax County slaveholder, wrote ACS secretary Gurley in early September 1831 to inquire about sending fourteen slaves to Liberia. Gray probably feared the emergence of a Nat Turner among his own bondmen or those of neighbors and thus took the preemptive step of freeing his slaves for removal to Liberia at the first opportunity. In addition to placing his enslaved people "at the disposal of the American Colonization Society," Gray also offered to pay twenty dollars toward the transportation expenses of each adult and ten dollars toward the cost of removing children between the ages of three and eleven. Beyond his interest in liberating his slaves for colonization, Gray also broached the subject to a number of free blacks in the vicinity. In the wake of shootings, beheadings, and other atrocities being inflicted upon local African Americans, he assured Gurley that "I have no doubt that a large number of them will be willing to emigrate if some trouble is taken to inform them correctly on the subject." In October, he confidently informed the ACS secretary that forty-nine "colored people" had applied for passage to Liberia and personally forwarded $150 to defray the cost of their deportation.[7]

Like Gray, ACS officials saw the bloody fallout from the Turner rebellion as a real opportunity to resuscitate the colonization movement in North Carolina and Virginia. Leaders of the organization were careful not to publicly express their hope that the ACS's program would thrive as a result of racial conflict, but their private correspondence left little doubt about their motives or intentions. "The effect of the troubles in Southampton County will be a general movement of the Free people of Colour from that & the neighboring counties," Norfolk agent John McPhail assured Gurley in late September. "Now is the Time that a cargo of from 150 to 200 Efficient emigrants can be obtained — Such as I am certain would prove the most valuable aquisition to the Colony that have yet emigrated." Ample proof of black suffering during the hellish repression that followed the Turner revolt arrived daily in the main office of the ACS in Washington. Much of the correspondence clearly illustrated that several counties in North Carolina and Virginia were experiencing refugee migrations as blacks fled white retribution. From Perquimans County, Caleb White inquired about the scheduling of the next emigrant expedition to Liberia, noting that blacks there "are so severely punished they had rather go any where than to stay where they are persecuted for innocency." Writing from neighboring Pasquotank County, Miles White told of how "the free blacks are badly & in many instances cruelly treated in this section of country." He estimated that well over fifty "respectable citizens" were willing to leave for Liberia as soon as possible, some having already sold their property in expectation of emigrating. In Wilmington, where the severed heads of suspected rebels had been displayed, Thomas Hunt penned a letter to Gurley on October 8, asking that a ship stop at that panic-stricken port. "I think that if it were known that she would stop here," he insisted, "we could furnish a number" of emigrants.[8]

Even before the Southampton insurrection and related refugee migrations materialized, the ACS had big plans for the year 1831. Although it had never sent out more than three expeditions in any given year, the organization's leaders hoped to outfit and launch six emigrant vessels during the twelve months beginning in July 1831. Unfortunately, ACS officials had hardly laid the appropriate groundwork in Liberia to accommodate such an exodus. Joseph Mechlin, the colonial agent, had previously been instructed to have a receptacle built in Monrovia to house one hundred emigrants. On hearing that the Washington-based leadership had such ambitious colonization plans for 1831–32, he informed Gurley that housing for 250 people was required in order to fulfill the organization's promise of six months of provisions and shelter for newly arrived immigrants. More ominously, the agent notified Gurley that the rainy season had been "unusually severe" and that contact with Millsburg and Caldwell had been "rendered difficult." Mechlin, perhaps more than anyone, knew the probable epidemiological consequences of sending so many people to Liberia without adequate housing and during a season when rain was "pouring down in torrents." As past experience had proven, malarial mortality in the capital, even during relatively salubrious times, could approach 25 percent among new colonists. Despite these well-known facts and the publication of Mechlin's letters of warning in the November issue of the *African Repository*, ships were chartered anyway, and a call for prospective emigrants was issued in earnest.[9]

In late October, John McPhail chartered the *James Perkins*, a 385-ton ship out of Boston, which he estimated could carry 300 immigrants to Liberia. As he had predicted earlier, the timing of the voyage could hardly have been better, given that the brutish persecution of blacks in North Carolina and Virginia had yet to cease, even as Nat Turner went to the gallows on November 11. Perhaps the majority of the 291 free African Americans who were fleeing Virginia originated in Southampton County. Along with this large company, 50 North Carolinians embarked at Norfolk, 30 having come from Pasquotank County, 1 from Halifax, and the remaining 19 from undocumented locales. While the ACS's organ characterized the group as "highly recommended for intelligence, morals, and industrious habits," this flattering description did not begin to capture the horrific experiences that had driven these people out of their homes. As they arrived in Norfolk, Nat Turner still cast a long shadow over the port city. White posses had roamed the streets for days after the rebellion, and into November local officials were indicting blacks by the dozen for allegedly residing in the city illegally. To the emigrants, Norfolk must have felt extremely uncomfortable and chaotic at this time, especially since local whites were both expelling free blacks and concurrently preparing for the peak season of the interstate slave trade.[10]

These refugees from Virginia and North Carolina comprised the largest emigrant party ever assembled for passage to Liberia. Initially, the *James Perkins*, packed with nearly 350 people, was prevented from sailing by port authorities, who claimed that it was overcrowded. An official survey of the vessel apparently negated this objection, but a coastal storm further delayed the ship's departure until December 9, when a steamboat finally towed it into Hampton Roads. When the emigrants arrived at Monrovia on January 14, the town was as unprepared for them as Mechlin had warned. The *James Perkins* had brought out some building frames that were erected as makeshift shelter, but this improvisation did little to rectify a housing shortage which "occasioned some embarrassment" for the colonial administration. Regardless of the inability of its colony to conveniently absorb new emigrants, the ACS sent more expeditions during the spring and summer of 1832. On May 9, the *Jupiter* set sail from Norfolk carrying 171 people from Virginia, Georgia, South Carolina, and North Carolina. Among the passengers from the latter state were the 14 manumitted slaves of Joseph Gray and 10 members of the freeborn Harwell family, all from Halifax County. It is worth noting that prior to this expedition, only one other liberated person—not including quasi-free blacks held by Quakers—had emigrated from North Carolina to Liberia since the voyage of the *Nautilus* in 1828.[11]

As had always been the case, the Society of Friends was instrumental to the coordination of the 1831–32 expeditions. Most of the African Americans who migrated from Pasquotank, Perquimans, and other counties with substantial Quaker populations were almost certainly assisted in some fashion by the church. Many of the emigrants had been in the custody of Friends for years, unable to enjoy anything more than a partial, de facto freedom due to restrictive state manumission laws. With several hundred blacks still in their care during the early 1830s, North Carolina Quakers, who had already sent hundreds of people to Liberia, Haiti, and the American Midwest, sought to complete the work of liberating themselves from slaveholding. In early June 1832 Friends chartered the *Julius Pringle* to transport ninety-two quasi-free blacks out of the state. Haiti was chosen as their initial destination, though that country had not received any North Carolina emigrants since 1826. For some reason, however, the party, under the supervision of Guilford Quaker George Swaim, set sail for Philadelphia instead of the West Indies. Friends in the former place had known of the planned expedition but had not encouraged their North Carolina brethren to ship more blacks to Pennsylvania. In fact, whites in that state were becoming increasingly hostile to the idea of Philadelphia serving as a haven for southern blacks. When the *Julius Pringle* arrived in Philadelphia harbor days later, even Friends were among those who were waiting to demonstrate how unwelcome its passengers were.

If Swaim was apprehensive about disembarking at Philadelphia, the African Americans aboard the *Julius Pringle* must have been terrified when they discovered that a mob had gathered along the harbor to prevent the ship from landing. According to Swaim, the angry throng had been riled by rumors that the vessel was carrying six hundred blacks who had participated in the killing of whites in Southampton County. Perhaps capturing the general sentiment, one "very influential friend" in the crowd predicted that the emigrants would share "the fate of Boston tea" if they attempted to come ashore. Unable to dock lest its passengers be assailed, the *Julius Pringle* simply floated in Philadelphia harbor, its crew unsure of its next course of action. After three sultry days of tensions, the stalemate was finally broken on June 17 when the ship was diverted to Burlington, New Jersey, where a committee of Friends received its passengers.

During the standoff in Philadelphia, many of the emigrants aboard the *Julius Pringle* had expressed a fervent desire to return to North Carolina where they at least still had family connections. When the possibility of immigrating to Liberia was posed, few exhibited any initial interest. However, by the time they were temporarily relocated to a farm in Red Bank, New Jersey, whatever resistance to being colonized in Africa that existed among the party had apparently waned. Undoubtedly, exhaustion, humiliation, and fear had been more responsible for this change of heart than any enthusiasm for frontier life in the distant colony. The board of managers of the ACS, which had approved of having the emigrants sent to Liberia while the *Julius Pringle* was initially en route to Philadelphia, arranged for the brig *American* to convey them from Norfolk. On July 15, eighty-nine North Carolinians, along with thirty-nine others from Virginia and Washington, D.C., set sail for Africa. Ironically, those blacks who had begun this migration with the help of North Carolina Friends ended up being refugees from both the Tar Heel State and the Quaker bastion of Philadelphia.[12]

With the departure of the *American*, the active participation of North Carolina Quakers in Liberian colonization ended. In financial terms, the Friends' responsiveness to the humanitarian crisis that was unfolding in the Chesapeake and eastern North Carolina was as admirable as ever, with London and Philadelphia Quakers contributing nearly five thousand dollars to defray the expenses of the *American* expedition. Yet, the benevolence of the Friends was not indicative of either an unqualified interest in the well-being of African Americans or an embrace of immediatist abolitionism. To be sure, the North Carolina Quakers and their brethren elsewhere had paid a substantial price for their manumission and colonization efforts. According to one Guilford Friend, an estimated one thousand blacks had been sent to "free governments" by 1834 at a cost of many thousands of dollars. When Quaker resources became depleted in the early 1830s and thus slowed the pace of colonization, a number of masters, who had previously transferred their slaves to the church for removal, filed lawsuits against the Friends to reacquire bondpeople who had not been sent to Liberia expeditiously. Moreover, even after the North Carolina Quakers stopped sending blacks in their custody to Africa, they still had five hundred legal slaves among them two years after the voyage of the *American.*

Aside from their relative moral progressiveness and financial sacrifices, the Quakers were not immune to either sectional influences or the values and sensibilities of other whites who had little use for abolitionism. In keeping with their corporatism, pacifism, and consensus mode of acting, many Friends found the uncompromising antislavery views of David Walker, William Garrison, and other "highly professional philanthropists" unnecessarily divisive and unproductive. One Piedmont Quaker, Jeremiah Hubbard, defended the gradualism inherent in the colonization movement as an unavoidable cost of ending slavery without alienating large segments of the society. Southerners had amply demonstrated that they would not entertain manumission without removal, and northerners, even Philadelphia Quakers, had erected legal and extralegal obstacles to block African American migration into free states. Thus, in the view of many Friends, Africa was the sole destination available, where emancipated blacks could truly live as free people, without triggering racial upheaval and sectional strife in America.

Pragmatic and persistent, Quaker colonizationists were no doubt animated by compassion and humanity regarding their efforts to liberate African Americans—and themselves—from slavery. Nonetheless, once many of them had sufficiently extricated themselves from the institution or had migrated to places that banned it, they tended to wash their hands of both bondage and blacks, just as many other whites were inclined to do. Generations of slaveholding and antislavery activities had linked blackness, in the minds of many Friends, to servitude, dependency, rebellion, immorality, and poverty. Furthermore, their abandonment of slaveholding did not alone necessarily free Quakers from the negative connotations that a black presence seemed to pose to their homogenous, insular communities and lifestyles. In this light, the violent aversion of Pennsylvania and Indiana Friends to having African Americans live among them is not surprising. To many Quakers, having blacks as neighbors was not too far removed from having them as slaves, or at least as unwanted, unassimilable dependents. One of the great draws of the ACS's program for many Friends, and countless others, had been that it aimed to permanently remove both slavery and blacks from the country, as well as all of the problems of discrimination, citizenship, and security related to their existence in America. In a context in which the Nat Turner revolt had made slavery, in the words of the *Greensborough Patriot,* "so dangerous . . . to write, think, or speak on," the natural inclination of the Quakers to seek a deliberated, conciliatory, and lasting resolution of their manumission dilemma meshed well with the claims of ACS spokesmen that free blacks had no real future in the United States.[13]

Regarding the emigrants themselves, a statistical profile of the 203 North Carolinians who departed for Liberia in five separate expeditions between July 1831 and January 1833 reveals commonalities as well as notable distinctions between these and earlier emigrants.[14] Most individuals traveled in family groups, with the *American* carrying the largest clans to Africa, including 29 Howards and 17 Sampsons. Most of the families that emigrated were listed as freeborn, with the exception of 14 Halifax County slaves and 2 others. Interestingly, 2 emigrants, Levina Overton of Perquimans, who departed in the *James Perkins*, and Thomas Hollister of Craven County, who left in the *Roanoke* in 1833, were recorded in the 1830 census as slaveholders, each owning a single slave. It is very probable that these two individuals had retained the legal title to loved ones whom they had purchased from others but could not conveniently emancipate. Given that North Carolina manumission laws made it prohibitively expensive to free slaves and required that liberated persons depart the state, Overton and Hollister undoubtedly found it simpler to keep these people in their legal, protective custody. Of the 165 of these people listed as freeborn in census and emigrant rolls, it is likely that some had known some form of servitude or quasi-freedom, particularly those from Quaker counties.[15]

The gender ratio of the individuals comprising the five expeditions was 1:1.20, with females making up 110 of the 203 emigrants. In regard to county of origin, 38 blacks came from Pasquotank, 25 from Halifax, 13 from Craven, 8 from Perquimans, and 7 from Randolph. Of the 112 individuals whose counties of origin were not chronicled, 88 sailed on the *American*, an observation suggestive of the duress under which this hasty migration was organized. As with past emigrant parties, age statistics indicate that the five expeditions of 1831–33 largely drew upon the youngest segment of the African American community of North Carolina, with children well represented on each ship. Accordingly, the average age of the 203 emigrants was 19.9 years, the median age was 16, and the modal age was 4, of which there were 11 instances.

In addition to these characteristics, the literacy rate among the emigrants was relatively high. Thirty-three percent (68) were listed as capable of reading or spelling, with all but ten of these departing on the *American*. In contrast, the group was occupationally unremarkable. Only twenty-three were listed as having one or more talents or skills, and eleven of these individuals, all males, also emigrated aboard the *American*. Among them were eleven farmers, four sawyers, two carpenters, two shoemakers, and a stone mason. Perhaps largely on the basis of their dearth of trades, colonial agent Joseph Mechlin found the *American* emigrants to be less than desirable as colonists.

"From such materials it is vain to expect that an industrious, intelligent and enterprising community can possibly be formed," he noted to his superiors in Washington. "They cannot but retard, instead of advancing the prosperity of the Colony" since they supposedly represented "the lowest and most abandoned of their class." The veracity of Mechlin's comments, which were reprinted in the *African Repository*, is difficult to evaluate, given that Philadelphia and New Jersey Quakers had previously praised the "orderly, temperate, industrious, and intelligent" demeanor of the *American*'s passengers. In any event, the agent discounted the circumstances that brought the company to Africa in the first place, as well as the fact that the colony was scarcely prepared to receive them.[16]

One thing that Mechlin had reported accurately was the impact of disease on the expeditions that landed in Liberia. As mentioned earlier, he had expressed reservations about the plan of the ACS leadership to send several shiploads of immigrants to Liberia before suitable accommodations could be constructed. Having seen the ravages of the *Anopheles* mosquito firsthand, his skepticism was hardly abated by the organization's published claim that "Men of color from the lower country of Virginia and North Carolina . . . may settle in Monrovia, without apprehension." According to Mechlin's calculations, the 649 emigrants who embarked for Liberia between July 1832 and March 1833 suffered a 21 percent malarial mortality. While people departing from northern states were affected worst by the disease, he reported that individuals of "no particular class, nor from no particular section of the United States, were exempt from the fatal effects of the fever." Like 1831, the year 1833 was an extremely unhealthy period, which was of no consolation to the record 796 emigrants who had arrived during the previous calendar year.[17]

Fortunately for the 203 North Carolinians who settled in the colony between 1831 and 1833, their aggregate malarial mortality was much lower than the general figure, though by no means negligible. Not wholly surprising, those who settled in Monrovia suffered the highest death rate. Of the 121 people who stayed in the capital, 20 (17 percent) died of fever as compared to only 4 (7 percent) of the 61 immigrants who were relocated to Caldwell. Remarkably, none of the 12 people who moved to Millsburg perished from malaria, and only three-year-old Lydia Richardson was lost among the 9 individuals who settled in New Georgia (an 11 percent mortality rate). Generally, the pattern of fever deaths for the five expeditions of 1831–33 resembled that of earlier times. For example, the very young and the elderly were most vulnerable to fatal bouts of malaria, and female victims (14) slightly outnumbered males (11). The average age of those who died of malaria was seventeen, and 72 percent of the deceased were under eighteen years of age. Altogether, the 203 North Carolina immigrants who arrived in the colony between 1831 and 1833 suffered a 12 percent malarial death rate. This figure compares favorably to the 18 percent mortality suffered by the 401 North Carolinians who immigrated to the colony between 1825 and 1830.

A few factors accounted for the improving chances of survival. Many immigrants arrived during the dry season, or the more salubrious months of the rainy season. Also, more of the damp foliage, especially mangrove, had been cleared by the early 1830s, though wet, low-lying vegetation was still abundant throughout the colony during this period. Furthermore, shorter stays in Monrovia for incoming expeditions and the establishment of settlements further inland definitely saved many lives, as did better housing, despite occasional overcrowding in receptacles. Undoubtedly, much was learned from local Africans regarding medicinal treatments for the disease, which still affected indigenous people though in less lethal ways. Ongoing exposure to and experiences with malaria produced a deepening reservoir of knowledge about the disease, which colonial officials and immigrants drew upon to enhance their immune responses. Over time, diets, housing, work routines, child rearing, and other aspects of their lifestyles were tailored to maximize their survival prospects. In these ways and many others, malarial morbidity and mortality, due to their ubiquitous impact on colonial life, became integral features of both emerging immigrant identities and the cultural meaning of Liberia, at home and abroad.[18]

With the departure of the *Roanoke*, which conveyed twenty blacks from Craven and Randolph Counties to Liberia in January 1833, the colonization movement in North Carolina slipped into dormancy. Without Quaker patronage, financial backing for emigrant expeditions was difficult to secure, and the migration of many Friends to the Midwest and elsewhere shattered organizational networks that had been vital to colonization efforts in the state. Most white North Carolinians had always been ignorant of the ACS and Liberia, and those who were knowledgeable tended to harbor sentiments that ranged from lukewarm acceptance or indifference to hostile opposition. Primarily due to the Quaker connection, many interpreted colonization as a mild form of abolitionism, and thus viewed the plan as unwelcome and potentially dangerous in a state with an unequivocal commitment to slavery. Ironically, the apprehensions that turned white North Carolinians off to black removal to Africa made Quaker-sponsored colonization appealing to African Americans, particularly those trapped in quasi-free status. While relatively few blacks, slave or free, left the state for Liberia, those who did go probably would not have been as willing if their removal had been coordinated by whites with less racially liberal reputations than the Friends. Not wholly coincidentally, black interest in Liberia tapered off as the Quakers withdrew from the colonization movement. Consequently, after the refugee expeditions of 1831–33, no black North Carolinians immigrated to Liberia until 1836.

The decline of colonizationist sentiment and organizational efforts in North Carolina was part of a larger trend that aversely affected the national movement. After sending seven ships to Liberia in 1832 carrying 796 emigrants—an all-time high for a single year—the ACS managed to cobble together only one expedition for 1834, composed of only 127 people. The following year 147 individuals departed for Africa under the organization's auspices, but in 1839 a mere 47 emigrants were sent out, the lowest number since the founding of the colony in 1822. A primary cause of the reversals that the ACS was suffering related to the debts that the voyages of 1831–33 had created. At their annual meeting in January 1834, ACS leaders reported obligations amounting to over forty thousand dollars. This "financial embarrassment" compelled the Washington headquarters to call on its auxiliaries for pecuniary relief and forced the ACS to limit expeditions until its debts were cleared. To their dismay, the organization's managers found that the state and local branches, two hundred in number in 1831, were strapped for both funds and members, including the North Carolina state society and ten local auxiliaries that had once seemed so promising. The fiscal malaise lasted well into the 1840s and was greatly exacerbated by the Panic of 1837 and subsequent depression. In addition to its arrears, other societal influences and historical circumstances were working against the ACS and its program, which cost the organization more political capital and good will than it had to spare.[19]

The ACS, and the idea of black removal in general, was wedged between countervailing ideologies, institutions, and forces that had become more polarized and combative during the 1830s. Colonizationists attempted to balance these opposing camps, or at least tread between them, but were finding that whatever middle ground existed was quickly disappearing. On the one hand, slavery and its proponents had become increasingly powerful and vocal regarding national affairs by this time. Much of this new vitality was defensive, whether in the guise of the nullification crisis, the congressional gag rule banning discussion of slavery, westward expansion of black bondage, or the frenzied southern assault on free African Americans. To many proslavery individuals, colonization reeked of abolitionism, albeit gradual and respectful of property rights. As northern branches of the ACS became more influential in its activities largely due to their financial contributions, removing blacks from the United States, especially those who were liberated expressly for that purpose, seemed more harmful to slavery than protective of the institution. The fact that some colonizationists openly depicted the ACS as a vehicle for slowly ending slavery was viewed by some as an indictment of slaveholding, an admission of its immorality and impermanence. In Upper South states, such as Maryland and Virginia, or among sects such as the Quakers, this abolitionist sentiment may have been tolerated, at least in times of relative calm. As bondage and cotton spread westward to conquer new lands, however, defenders of slavery brooked little dissent. Increasingly, colonization, with its promises of compromise and moderation, appeared subversive in many quarters.

On the opposite end of the political spectrum that the colonizationists were attempting to straddle stood antislavery forces in all their ideological shades and hues. Until the 1820s, colonization was not objectionable to many budding abolitionists who viewed it as both reformist and as offering a solution to black thralldom in America. However, by the 1830s, the ACS's program had advanced too slowly, was too expensive, and was too closely associated with slaveholders to have much appeal to antislavery activists or blacks, the putative beneficiaries of their efforts. Thus immediatist abolitionism, which called for the instantaneous emancipation of slaves without removal abroad or compensation for masters, was a retort to the low incidence of voluntary manumission in the South and the expansion of slavery in the West. It was also a product of the maturation of capitalism and free-labor ideology in northern states which, recently freed of slavery, were proving to themselves and others that economic prosperity and republicanism could exist without black bondage. Like few other developments, the emergence of abolitionism, with its hotbeds in Boston, Philadelphia, New York, and other northern cities, drew sectional battle lines that remained in place until the Civil War. But while the spokespersons and literature of the antislavery movement mostly emanated from above the Mason-Dixon line, the most fearsome abolitionism simmered in the South among the two million slaves who toiled there during the 1830s. The antislavery vision that so preoccupied Nat Turner as he looked to the heavens for divine confirmation was born not in the middle-class reformist circles of the urban North, but in the cornfields of Southampton County, Virginia. Subsequently, proslavery individuals dreaded abolitionism not only for what it advocated or from whence it came but for what it could become in the hands of malcontent slaves.[20]

With such antagonisms pulling the country in opposite directions, the ACS found that trying to stay at the center of an increasingly acrimonious national discourse over slavery and the future of African Americans gained it few friends. For many politically engaged Americans, the 1830s was a time for choosing sides, and the attempts of colonizationists to appear neutral on the most important question of the day appeared insincere and devoid of moral conviction. As its popularity and resources plummeted during this period, the ACS found it again necessary to reposition itself as a centrist friend of both North and South, proslavery and antislavery camps. At their annual meeting in 1835, ACS delegates unanimously passed a resolution denying that they were intent upon "interfering with the legal rights and obligations of slavery." They also reaffirmed their position that the organization's "operations would be productive of unmixed good to the colored population of our country and of Africa." Such declarations appear to have done little for the floundering credibility of the Society. Free blacks, in particular, continued to be alienated by the moral poverty of the ACS's position on slavery despite the organization's stated goal of doing them an "unmixed good."[21]

Throughout the antebellum period, ACS leaders consistently failed to appreciate that free African Americans, not white northern abolitionists or southern slaveholders, were the constituency that they primarily needed to convince. For the most part, white colonizationists, such as Kentucky slaveholder and politician Henry Clay, who became president of the ACS in 1837, exhibited little more than racist contempt toward free blacks on most occasions. From the beginning when the newly founded organization was searching for a site on which to establish a colony, ACS leaders failed to conceal their paternalistic arrogance toward African Americans, whose interests they claimed to champion. Instead of trying to come to a consensus with black leaders regarding plans for their removal, the organization's spokesmen announced unilaterally during its 1820 annual meeting that in selecting a site in West Africa, the "American [Colonization] Society have made this choice [of destinations] for them, after much inquiry and reflection." Ultimately, this insulting slight probably made little difference. Most free blacks thought of themselves as too deserving of American citizenship and civil rights and of the ACS's program as too fanciful and tainted by proslavery interests to lend it much support, especially given the haphazard nature of the colony's founding. Illustratively, during a convention in Philadelphia in June 1835, prominent African Americans made a strenuous effort to distance themselves from the plans of the ACS. Along with a denunciation of colonization which had become obligatory for such gatherings, the delegates also resolved "to remove the title of African from their institutions, the marble of churches, and etc." Of course, this resolution was a very important statement of who the conferees believed they were as a people and where they felt their rightful place of residence was. However, it was also a stark indication of the lengths they were prepared to take to utterly repudiate the ACS and its colony in West Africa.[22]

AS THE ACS DESCENDED into debt and disfavor during the 1830s, it became clear that its state and local branches were not politically synchronized on the issue of slavery, free blacks, or other matters. Generally, auxiliaries in northern states and a few in the Upper South tended to structure their activities within a gradual emancipationist framework, while those in the Gulf Coast states and the expanding cotton belt were more concerned about the removal of free blacks. Even within individual states, these disparate patterns existed. For example, in North Carolina, Quaker enclaves in Guilford and Pasquotank saw the ACS as an instrument for resolving their manumission problems. Others, in the wake of the Turner revolt in particular, hoped that deporting free African Americans would secure slavery. The regional loyalties and internal cultures of individual ACS branches made the national organization's guiding ideology and operations more complex and even contradictory than some would acknowledge, especially advocates and critics who chose to view it as a one-dimensional movement. With the declining revenue and activity of the ACS during the 1830s, tensions developed within the organization along both ideological and regional lines. In the wake of these crises, most auxiliaries continued to remain officially under the authority of the parent body based in Washington. However, a few state organizations attempted to make their own mark on colonization, subsequently becoming rivals of the national group. Inevitably, these independent actions resulted in a splintering of the movement during its weakest period.

The most dynamic and durable of the independent state auxiliaries was the Maryland State Colonization Society (MSCS) founded in February 1831. Like North Carolina, the state had recently passed legislation placing severe restrictions on free blacks and slaves. As part of a package of such bills, lawmakers appropriated funding for the removal of free African Americans amounting to as much as two hundred thousand dollars over a twenty-year period. The fund was to be controlled by a board of managers which included state officials and members of the MSCS. The new organization still styled itself as an auxiliary "exclusively directed . . . to aid the Parent Institution at Washington, in the colonization of free people of color of Maryland with their consent to the coast of Africa." However, after an expedition of 144 black Marylanders to Liberia in December 1832 experienced discouraging difficulties, including a 15 percent malarial mortality, John Latrobe and other white colonizationists in the state decided to found a separate colony at Cape Palmas, southeast of Monrovia.

The settlement, established the following year, advanced slowly due to poor agricultural lands, an imbalance in the gender ratio that favored females, and less than cordial relations with the surrounding Grebo people who were destined to have several wars with colonists. According to a census of the colony, only 624 immigrants resided there in 1842, including 329 females and 295 males. By necessity, the Maryland settlement, and its principal town of Harper, maintained close relations with Monrovia, and immigrants from the latter colony, including a number of North Carolinians, relocated to Cape Palmas throughout its existence as a separate entity. In 1836, the MSCS board of managers appointed James B. Russwurm, a black graduate of Bowdoin College and former editor of *Freedom's Journal*, to administer the colony as governor. In addition to the fact that Russwurm turned out to be an able steward, the symbolism of the appointment of an African American to lead the experiment was certainly not lost on supporters or adversaries of colonization. Nonetheless, no flood of black Marylanders entered the colony during his tenure, though the state had a free black population of 62,078 by 1840, the largest in the country.[23]

Inspired by the Maryland example and disappointed in the decelerating pace of black immigration to Liberia, northern colonizationists also embarked upon a separate colonial venture. In 1835, the New York City Colonization Society and the Young Men's Colonization Society of Pennsylvania consolidated their efforts and withdrew from the oversight of the parent organization. The latter body, broke and unable to intercede, reluctantly acquiesced to the secession and agreed to cease its fund-raising and recruitment activities in the two states in exchange for a portion of the annual collections of the auxiliaries. Bassa Cove, located approximately sixty miles southeast of Cape Mesurado, was selected as the site for a colony which was dubbed Port Cresson in honor of the secretary of the Pennsylvania auxiliary, Elliott Cresson. Even more than the founders of the ACS, these northern colonizationists hoped to create a utopian community in Africa, similar to some of the communitarian experiments forming in the United States, such as the Shakers, Mormons, and the Brook Farm cooperative of Massachusetts. Ideally, the first wave of colonists—including 110 liberated slaves from Rappahannock, Virginia—were to adhere to principles of temperance and pacifism, thus setting an example for future immigrants and local Africans.

As in the cases of other Liberian settlements, indigenous people were not very receptive of the newcomers, whose cultural predilections were often at variance with local values and practices. Within months of its establishment, Port Cresson was attacked by the forces of a neighboring monarch, King Joe Harris, who took full advantage of the colonists' lack of arms. Twenty of the immigrants were killed during the assault, and those who managed to flee, "under circumstances of extreme destitution," sought asylum in Monrovia. While a disheartening disaster for the New York and Pennsylvania colonization societies, the two auxiliaries decided to revive their experiment. During the latter part of 1835, their colonial agent surveyed and assigned town lots to returning immigrants, and by the following summer two hundred colonists had reportedly repopulated the coastal village. Similar to the Maryland colony, Port Cresson remained small throughout its short time as an independent settlement and was no less vulnerable to malaria. As late as 1843, it had only 124 residents, the second least populated village among all immigrant settlements in Liberia.[24]

Along with New York and Pennsylvania, a third state, Mississippi, founded a colony in Liberia during the 1830s patterned largely after the Maryland model. In June 1831, the Mississippi Colonization Society was organized for the express purpose of removing free blacks from the state. A burgeoning realm of black bondage and cotton production, Mississippi had a free black population proportionately smaller than that of any other state, numbering 519 in 1830, or .37 percent of the total population. Yet after Louisiana and South Carolina, the state had the highest ratio of slaves to whites, with bondpeople comprising 48 percent of the state's inhabitants. Although a numerically insignificant segment of the population, free African Americans were all the more conspicuous and unwanted in a state whose politics, economy, and social structure rested more on black slavery than on any other institution. Thus, the Mississippi state auxiliary charged itself with the primary responsibility of removing this population, though it was also open to deporting newly emancipated slaves to Africa as well. After sending sixty-nine blacks to Millsburg in 1835, many of whom were liberated slaves, the leaders of the Mississippi auxiliary decided to acquire territory along the Sinoe River, roughly halfway between Capes Mesurado and Palmas, for a separate colony. The settlement, known as "Mississippi in Africa," was technically subordinate to the colonial administration at Monrovia but had its own governor and principal town at Greenville, which was named after James Green, a Mississippi judge who had emancipated twenty-six of his slaves for colonization.

Similar to Port Cresson, Mississippi in Africa began and ended with misfortune. The site itself had been poorly selected as a sanctuary for American immigrants, proving to be as unhealthy as any along the Grain Coast. Illustratively, when an expedition of thirty-seven freedpeople arrived in July 1838, they immediately suffered a 30 percent malarial mortality, atrocious even by Liberian standards. While it was theoretically responsible for the settlement, the cash-strapped ACS provided very little assistance, financial or otherwise. To make matters worse, the state auxiliary sent few emigrants to the colony to replenish its dying population, and relations with neighboring Kru communities were generally unpleasant. The Louisiana Colonization Society, also formed in 1831, allied itself with the colony's sponsors and sent a few colonists to settle along the Sinoe but not enough to ease the isolation or negative demographic growth of the settlement. In September 1838, Robert Finley, the governor of Mississippi in Africa, was ambushed and killed by Africans as he traveled to Bassa Cove on business, an event that further drained the morale of the hapless immigrants. Subsequently, a war erupted between colonists and Africans in the region resulting in several casualties among the immigrants and the destruction of a number of houses. For several years after Finley's death, the colony continued to stagnate without a governor or any substantial influx of immigrants. In 1843, the population of Greenville stood at a paltry seventy-nine, making it by far the smallest immigrant village in Liberia.

Ambitious and short-lived, the separate colony of Mississippi in Africa was probably saved from complete collapse by the unification of Liberian settlements under the Commonwealth Constitution of 1839. This document made Monrovia the seat of a unitary colonial system but allowed constituent towns representation on the Council of Liberia, a new semi-autonomous legislative body. The Bassa Cove colony of the Pennsylvania and New York auxiliaries agreed to join the commonwealth in 1837, followed by the Mississippi settlement in 1841. Only the Maryland colony at Cape Palmas, relatively well-funded and slowly growing, chose to remain independent until it was nearly obliterated by a Grebo assault in 1856–57.[25]

Besides the state auxiliaries that attempted to establish separate colonies in Liberia, several others were active during this period, if less dramatically so. The colonization movement in Virginia was the most vibrant of all in regard to sending emigrants to Africa and would continue to be so into the second half of the nineteenth century. As mentioned in Chapter 1, the idea of black removal had a long history in the state and had attracted several prominent advocates who resided in the commonwealth, including Thomas Jefferson and James Madison. From the first voyage of emigrants to West Africa aboard the *Elizabeth* in 1820, Virginia seemed well-positioned ideologically and demographically for a central role in the program of the ACS. However, it was not until the early 1830s that the state clearly became a dominant force in the colonization movement. Since the beginning of emigrant expeditions from North Carolina in January 1825 through July 1831, the Tar Heel State and Virginia had sent roughly the same number of people to Liberia, 410 and 431, respectively. North Carolina actually sent more emigrants per voyage during this period, averaging 51 passengers per vessel to Virginia's 39. Nonetheless, following the Nat Turner revolt in August 1831, parity between the two states ended. From then onward, Virginia would consistently send more emigrants to Liberia than any other state during any comparable span of time before the Civil War.

In the aftermath of the Southampton insurrection, the Virginia legislature, fearful of a recurrence of antislavery violence among the state's nearly one-half million bondpeople, contemplated the feasibility of abolishing slavery. This discussion did not go far, for the state government, controlled by slaveholders, was too invested in the institution to end it and was not prepared to face the political or economic repercussions of such a momentous undertaking. Thus, after finding it "inexpedient" to do away with slavery, the legislature turned its attention to the removal of free blacks as an alternative solution for limiting the likelihood of future slave rebellions. The Virginia Colonization Society, formerly the Richmond auxiliary of the ACS, placed significant pressure on policymakers to pass measures mandating the deportation of free blacks. Run by tidewater and southern Piedmont planters, the state auxiliary itself had been dormant until shocked into action by the disturbing news from Southampton in the late summer of 1831. Legislative friends of colonization succeeded in convincing the House of Delegates and the Senate to formally take up the issue of removal in early 1832. After contentious debates and a series of close votes and amendments, the legislature approved "An Act, Providing for the Removal of Free Persons of Colour from this Commonwealth" in March 1832.

This legislation provided for the creation of a Central Board of Commissioners which was to supervise the process by which free African Americans would be transported to Liberia. The Board was to give priority to those blacks who voluntarily applied for removal but would secondarily commit itself to deporting free people of color who were in the state illegally. Last in preference were liberated slaves whose masters had not provided for their relocation. To finance these migrations and "subsequent temporary support" for immigrants in Africa, thirty-five thousand dollars was appropriated for the current year, and an additional fifty thousand dollars was earmarked for 1833.

Following Maryland's precedent of public financial support for colonization, Virginia surged well ahead of other states in the removal of free (and freed) blacks to Liberia. This accelerating influx of black Virginians into the colony allowed them to dominate much of the political and social life of Liberia. The first black governor and president, Joseph Jenkins Roberts, was a Virginian, as was a sizable portion of the merchant class. In the mid-nineteenth century, a settlement called New Virginia was even formed on the St. Paul's River, but it ended up being of minor importance. Despite this distinctive impact that black Virginians had on Liberia, there was never enough money, manumissions, or interest in the colonization program of the ACS or the legislature to make it a viable means of depleting the number of free African Americans in the state. Between 1830 and 1840, this segment of the population increased by 5 percent, and during the following decade it grew by 8 percent to 54,333, making Virginia second only to Maryland in the number of free blacks in a single state. With both the earliest and largest African American presence, Virginia remained riveted firmly to slavery. It would ultimately take civil war, not just colonization and slave revolts, to sever these ties.[26]

In Virginia's neighbor of Kentucky, which had grown exponentially due to migrations from coastal states, a state colonization society was founded in 1829. Senator Henry Clay, a founder of the ACS and its president by 1837, was a chief figure in the movement in Kentucky, lending credibility and political weight to the ambitions of both the state and national organizations. A Whig nationalist, Clay hoped to gradually abolish slavery through Liberian colonization, thus ridding the country of what he believed to be its prime evils: blacks (free and liberated), southern economic backwardness, and sectional conflict. To this end, he pushed for federal funding of the ACS, proposing in the aftermath of the Turner revolt that Congress set aside ten million dollars to colonize African Americans in Liberia. After a fellow congressman disabused him of the notion that such a measure had a chance of being passed, the senator proposed a Distribution Bill in 1832. This measure would have allowed individual states to use proceeds from the sale of public lands to finance a range of projects, including colonization. In arguing for the bill, Clay stressed the same themes that had become ideological cornerstones of the ACS. "The evil of a free black population is not restricted to particular States," he warned in a June 20 speech, "but extends to, and is felt by, all."

Skillfully shepherding the legislation through both houses of Congress, Clay could only watch in disappointment as the Distribution Bill was waylaid by a presidential veto. Andrew Jackson, who would defeat Clay in the presidential election later that year, was no friend of African colonization, though he had once been elected vice president of the ACS, a largely honorary position. As a Democrat, he had built his reputation upon states' rights and decentralized political power, as evidenced by his opposition to a national bank and internal improvements. Ironically, it was during his tenure in office that thousands of Native Americans were removed from their lands in the eastern states and forced to western territories. Still, his veto of the Distribution Bill signaled his distaste for grand governmental action and his loyalty to the slaveholding South which was generally suspicious of the colonization movement by this time. With this defeat, the possibility of federally funded free-black removal became more remote than ever. No future president or Congress would openly side with the cause of colonization again until the 1860s.

While Clay's crusade for a federally sponsored colonization movement failed, the Kentucky state auxiliary made the best of its slim resources and flagging popularity. In May 1833, 99 emigrants, mostly liberated slaves, were sent to Monrovia and Caldwell, where they suffered a malarial death rate of 32 percent. Subsequent expeditions fared somewhat better, but over the next decade only 133 black Kentuckians immigrated to Liberia. In 1845, colonizationists in the state attempted to raise five thousand dollars to purchase forty square miles of territory "within the bounds of Liberia." The settlement, to be named Kentucky, was intended to give "our free colored population . . . a country to emigrate to, and enjoy their freedom under an administration of their own color." Eventually, such a town was established but was of little consequence in size or influence.

As sectional tensions tightened during the 1850s, colonizationists lobbied the state legislature for funding for their program. In 1856, Kentucky lawmakers assented to their request and passed a measure that allotted five thousand dollars annually to the state colonization society "to be applied to the removal out of this State of negroes resident therein who are now free, and of such as may be born of them and be free." The act also appropriated seventy dollars to defray the cost of transporting, and maintaining for six months, each African American over the age of two who departed for Liberia. This financial backing was too late and civil war to close to make much difference regarding Kentucky's lackluster efforts to relocate its free black population, which numbered 10,684 in 1860, or .9 percent of the total population. The state's champion of colonization, Henry Clay, had died in 1852, and like every other region of the country, too few free blacks volunteered to emigrate, and too few masters were given to helping their slaves do so.[27]

In addition to the efforts of these individual state organizations, other colonization auxiliaries were involved in relocating free and liberated blacks to Liberia, albeit in more limited ways. In 1829, the Tennessee Colonization Society was founded in Nashville, and a trickle of emigrants from that state started arriving in the colony that year. While the state legislature offered the auxiliary financial support, it was not nearly as generous as its counterparts in Maryland, Virginia, and Kentucky. Only ten dollars was appropriated for each African American immigrating to Liberia, up to a maximum expenditure of five hundred dollars a year. Unsurprisingly, the Tennessee organization had sent only 726 people to Africa by 1860.

While the Tennessee organization received at least token support from the state, the colonization movement had been unwelcome in Georgia from the beginning. The state legislature passed resolutions as early as 1827 labeling as unconstitutional the ACS's plan to establish "an African Colony, at the distance of three thousand miles, on a barbarous and pestilential shore." As in its sister states of South Carolina and Alabama, no state colonization society materialized in Georgia, but a relatively substantial number of emigrants, both free and liberated, did migrate from the state to Liberia during the antebellum period. In 1860, Georgia ranked fourth among the states in the number of African Americans who had left for Liberia, its total of 1,147 emigrants placing it behind only Virginia, Maryland, and North Carolina. By the end of the century, the state would rank second—behind only Virginia—as the place of origin of Liberian emigrants.

Compared to the South, northern states, such as Vermont, Massachusetts, and Connecticut, sent few people to Liberia but made significant contributions to the treasury of the ACS. Midwestern states, such as Ohio, Illinois, and Indiana, contained auxiliary societies, though they, too, were more important as sources of revenue than as pools of prospective colonists. At some point during the nineteenth century, people in nearly every state in the Union east of the Mississippi River were engaged to some degree with the ACS or another sponsor of African colonization. In spite of this genuinely national appeal, colonizationist sentiment and activity were unevenly spread across the country and tended to wax and wane for a myriad of often unforeseen reasons.[28]

As mentioned earlier, the colonization movement in North Carolina turned dormant after the departure of five expeditions between 1831 and 1833 and the migration of a large number of Quakers out of the state at about the same time. The eleven auxiliaries, located in the eastern and Piedmont sections of the state, lost their vigor as the national organization fell into debt and disrepute. The North Carolina State Colonization Society continued to exist but was no more than an ineffectual advocacy group with little influence with the legislature or the public. Notwithstanding its fecklessness, the state auxiliary did meet in Raleigh during the summer of 1834 and unanimously passed a number of resolutions. Among them were promises to continue supporting the ACS, to reorganize the state branch, and to call upon local clergy to take up collections during the upcoming Fourth of July commemorations. In a May 1836 meeting, members of the auxiliary denounced the growing strength of the abolitionist movement, which had sapped much of the vitality and credibility of the ACS and its auxiliaries. "We cannot but consider," the conferees proclaimed from their meeting place in the office of the Secretary of State, "the Associations which have been formed at the North, for the Abolition of Slavery, as productive of nought but evil—pure, unmixed and dreadful evil—both to the bond and free, black and white, throughout all the slave-holding States." As had become typical of these gatherings, little concrete action followed such pronouncements and resolutions. Unable to coordinate or finance meaningful initiatives, the auxiliary's meetings became no more than therapeutic exercises designed to create an illusion of progress.

During this period and throughout the 1840s, North Carolina was all but cut off from the operations of the national organization. No individuals from the state attended the annual meetings of the ACS as delegates, and only Joseph Gales, the Raleigh editor, held a position in the Washington headquarters, which he resigned in January 1839. Few collections were raised in the state on behalf of the parent body, and subscriptions to the *African Repository* were rare. In an effort to be proactive, the state auxiliary society decided in May 1837 that it was "expedient to employ . . . a well qualified agent" to canvass the state for donations, something that the parent society had not done in years. However, without financial backing and African American willingness to emigrate, this resolution had little chance of breaking the stupor that had enervated the colonization movement since 1833. As it turned out, the future of the ACS's program in the state did not rest in the hands of fretting white men in Raleigh whose perfunctory meetings only confirmed their growing irrelevance. Instead, unfolding events in Bladen County, and in particular the force of character of a single black man, promised to provide the long awaited impetus that would rejuvenate, at least temporarily, the state's torpid colonization movement.[29]

IN THE 1830s, Bladen County looked like many other regions of eastern North Carolina. Located in the south central part of the state, the county was well sheltered by forests of oak, ash, and pine, which naturally made it a source of timber and naval stores. Several waterways and small lakes wound through the landscape, as did the Cape Fear River, which bisected the county as it flowed southeastward toward Wilmington and the ocean. Cypress swamps and alluvial deposits were concentrated near many of the streams, and much of the land was arable enough to produce a range of crops, including cotton, tobacco, corn, potatoes, and various fruits. Although the county seat of Elizabethtown was established along the banks of the Cape Fear River in 1773, the ruralness of Bladen was its most prominent characteristic. Even by North Carolina standards, the town was tiny and overshadowed by the neighboring urban areas of Wilmington and Fayetteville, which were themselves relatively unimpressive with populations of 3,791 and 2,868, respectively, in 1830. The most important developments in the county occurred on plantations and small farms, which checkered the fertile lands of the district. It was in these places, not Elizabethtown, where Bladen's political influence, economic strength, and cultural ethos were generated.[30]

Demographically, Bladen County was in the black belt of North Carolina, as were the adjacent counties of New Hanover, Brunswick, Cumberland, and Sampson, all of which had substantial African American populations. In 1830, the 3,122 slaves and 188 free blacks in Bladen accounted for 42 percent of its inhabitants, a proportion that rose to 48 percent by 1850. Black life in the county revolved around seasonal patterns of crop production, although slavery there, as elsewhere, was multifaceted and included many tasks that were not strictly agricultural, such as lumbering and domestic labor. For free African Americans as well, life in Bladen generally meant farm work and subordination to white authority. According to the 1840 census, only 245 of the county's 8,022 residents were involved in commerce, and no capital was in-

THE PRICE OF LIBERTY

vested in manufacturing in the district. Despite its lack of urban spaces and overwhelmingly agrarian atmosphere, Bladen County did produce a number of well-known personalities. John Owen, governor of the state from 1828 to 1830, was born there, as was James McKay, a planter who would represent the Wilmington area in the U.S. House of Representatives during the 1830s and 1840s. Prominent figures among the free black population of the county included Gooden Bowen who owned forty-four bondpeople in 1830, making him a rarity in both his occupation as a slave owner and the size of his holding. Perhaps the best known of Bladen blacks was Louis Sheridan, a successful merchant and entrepreneur of uncanny ability and ambition. From his humble origins as an emancipated slave in Elizabethtown, he eventually created a business and life that spanned two continents, leaving an unmistakable imprint on the course of the colonization movement in North Carolina.[31]

Born around 1793, Sheridan became involved in commercial pursuits early in life, perhaps influenced by local merchant Joseph R. Gautier, who was likely his former master and father. At some point, he was able to obtain a liberal education and subsequently took an interest in politics and the anti-slavery struggle. During the late 1820s, he became an agent for the abolitionist newspapers *Freedom's Journal* and the *Rights of All,* a vocation that became all the more dangerous once David Walker's *Appeal* infiltrated the neighboring port of Wilmington. Interestingly, given his work for these periodicals, Sheridan himself had a rather ambivalent relationship with African Americans and slavery. The 1810–30 censuses for Bladen County list him as white and by the latter year, he himself owned sixteen bondpeople, though the exact nature of his personal relationship with these individuals is unclear. A fair-skinned mulatto, Sheridan was acquainted with a number of white notables, including Governor John Owen, who highly recommended him to others, and Lewis Tappan, who encouraged him to liberate his slaves. In 1829, one white ACS correspondent in Raleigh even suggested that he be considered for an appointment as the colonial agent in Liberia, replacing the recently deceased Richard Randall.

Such respectability and connections, in addition to Sheridan's own talents and drive, helped him to establish far-flung business networks in Wilmington, Philadelphia, and New York. By the mid-1830s, he was estimated to be worth fifteen to twenty thousand dollars, exclusive of his property in slaves. For all his successes, the same world that had given Sheridan opportunities also restricted his ability to enjoy them in a dignified manner. The pile of anti-free-black bills passed by the state legislature in 1830 limited his mobility and personal security, not to mention his maritime commercial activities. Moreover, in 1835, a state constitutional convention stripped blacks of the right to vote in legislative elections, a prohibition that explicitly included

Sheridan and every other "free person of mixed blood, descended from negro ancestors to the fourth generation inclusive." This revocation of rights seems to have exasperated Sheridan to an unbearable degree, for it was around this time that he started seriously considering a course of action that he had previously been loath to entertain. In May 1836, he penned a letter to Joseph Gales of the national office of the ACS to request information about Liberia. Immediately, a correspondence began between the two men. Two months later, Sheridan informed Gales that though "500 others think it madness in me to leave N°Ca . . . I am Resolved."[32]

Given its financial malaise and damaged reputation, ACS officials viewed Sheridan's interest in Liberia as an opportunity to promote their program among free blacks and abolitionists. In their estimate, the Elizabethtown merchant, if courted properly, might serve as a recruitment tool for stirring interest in colonization among other well-heeled African Americans who had never considered migrating to Africa. To this end, Gales told Sheridan everything he believed the black man wanted to hear. When Sheridan informed him that he wanted to take boards, shingles, and other goods to Liberia, Gales assured him that a vessel large enough to carry such a load would be secured. When the merchant requested that a ship land at Wilmington to meet his party, the ACS official made the appropriate arrangements even though all previous North Carolina emigrants had been obliged to embark at Norfolk. So anxious were white colonizationists to prop up their sagging programs with Sheridan's notoriety that a rivalry erupted between the virtually independent Young Men's Colonization Society of Pennsylvania and the national organization in Washington. In a vaguely worded letter, Elliott Cresson of the Pennsylvania group suggested that Sheridan lead a company of one hundred emigrants to the colony at Bassa Cove, which had been nearly exterminated by Africans a year earlier. The Elizabethtown merchant, probably having read about the recent disaster, declined the offer and referred Cresson to Gales. Sheridan knew that a lot of risk was involved in immigrating to Liberia and resolved to take his chances with those who had been in the colonization business longest. In November, he reluctantly informed Gales that he would not be able to organize a party of forty emigrants as he had promised, for a number of those who had planned to go backed out as the departure date drew near. Still, he vowed in an almost heroic tone that "I shall go if I live & also . . . certain others will accompany me."[33]

Unfortunately for the ACS, efforts to get Sheridan to Africa under their auspices failed miserably. When the brig *Rondout* arrived at Wilmington on December 20, it was instantly apparent that it was too small to haul Sheridan's goods to Liberia, which amounted to "thirty-five tons of merchandise and 25,000 feet of lumber, besides the baggage, furniture, provisions and water of the company with him." After touring the ship, the merchant, incensed by the enormity of the ACS's miscalculation, refused to consider leaving in the brig without his cargo and immediately returned to Elizabethtown. The implications of the mistake were not lost on Francis Bacon, the coordinator of the expedition. After receiving a "beautifully written" letter from Sheridan declining a subsequent offer to visit the colony, Bacon warned Gales that "much injury" had been suffered by the ACS on account of its unfulfilled promise to transport the merchant and his goods to Liberia. In his opinion, Sheridan was "such a man as by his single weight can turn the scale for any part of Liberia to which he goes and against any part which has acquired his ill will." In particular, Bacon feared the likelihood that Sheridan, if his interest in Liberia remained strong, would be open to overtures from the Pennsylvania organization which had approached him earlier.

By the summer of 1837, Bacon's fears were clearly warranted. Sheridan, who had sold a substantial part of his estate in expectation of emigrating the previous year, returned to Wilmington with the balance of his property. In August, he notified Gales that he was still interested in emigrating, but his previous skepticism about "the Colonization scheme" had been revived by the intrigue between the ACS and the northern auxiliaries. In compelling prose, he offered Gales an ultimatum, demanding that "some *decided* measures be adopted for our Removal at the time I specify" or else "I shall surely change my destination to some other part of the world of which I have already some offers made me." Insolvent and outmaneuvered by rivals, the parent organization failed to act decisively on Sheridan's request, and the merchant finally accepted the invitation of the northern colonizationists to settle at Bassa Cove. On December 30, Sheridan and seventy-one others boarded the barque *Marine* at Wilmington and sailed for Liberia under the sponsorship of the New York and Pennsylvania auxiliaries.[34]

Louis Sheridan and his party arrived at the town of Edina, Bassa Cove, on February 8, 1838. Having sacrificed much to stand on "the soil of wretched Africa," the merchant was not pleased with what he found. Apparently, the New York and Pennsylvania auxiliaries had promised him "every accommodation and assistance," thus giving him the impression that he would be received in a manner commensurate with his achievements in North Carolina. Instead, he and his fellow immigrants discovered that they were expected to stay in pens of thatch and bamboo, to eat rotten corn meal, and to relocate to Bexley, a newly established settlement six miles up the St. John's River. To make matters worse, malaria overtook the immigrants within days of disembarkation, inflicting a 22 percent death rate before subsiding. Among the victims were Margaret Sheridan, the merchant's seventy-five-year-old mother, and John, a seven-year-old relative who was perhaps his son. Unaccustomed to such lack of control over his own affairs, Sheridan was infuriated by the nominal preparations that had been made for his arrival and the resultant inconveniences. He "utterly refused" to stay in the huts that had been erected for the party, preferring to rent housing from the residents of Edina at great expense to himself. Also, he found it prudent to pay for his own food, rather than rely upon the spoiled rations offered by the colonial storekeeper. Convinced that these tribulations threatened "to drive me to madness," Sheridan resolved to expose what was happening to him in Africa, employing his formidable literary talents to devastating effect.

In a December 1838 letter to New York abolitionist Lewis Tappan, Sheridan detailed the problems he and others had encountered in Africa. In addition to inadequate food and shelter, he criticized delays in the allotment of lands to his party, as well as their resettlement at Bexley, which placed him several miles from the main arteries of the coastal trade. Although his own access to oceanic commerce was restricted, Sheridan alleged that slave trading flourished "in sight of Monrovia . . . to a fearfully alarming degree." Not only had the colonial government failed to halt the immoral traffic but the colonists had proved unable or unwilling to exert much of an ameliorating influence on indigenous people, having converted only a few to Christianity.

In addition to these grievances, Sheridan was most perturbed by the undemocratic nature of the colonial administration of Bassa Cove. The humiliation he suffered due to the disfranchisement of North Carolina free blacks in 1835 was still a recent memory, and to find government by fiat in Liberia was distasteful to him. "I had come from the United States to be freed from the tyranny of the white man," he related to Tappan. "I shall not be easily brought again to submit to it." Convinced that the Bassa Cove governor, John Matthias, was guilty of ineptitude and malfeasance, Sheridan refused to take the oath of allegiance to the settlement's constitution and attempted to organize a petition drive to protest a colonial regime "accountable to nobody." Ultimately, his efforts failed to mobilize a substantial number of immigrants, and Sheridan was forced to acquiesce to his status as a colonial subject. Ironically, despite the misfortune that he had experienced in Liberia, the merchant declined to denounce colonization altogether as a remedy to the plight of free blacks in the United States. Even as he acclimated to Liberia under trying circumstances, he equivocated on the subject of black immigration to Africa. "I know not that our experiment will make for or against the colonization scheme," he told Tappan in late 1838. "I am not yet prepared to say, whether people ought to come here or not."[35]

If Sheridan was unsure of his final assessment of the colonization movement, Tappan was more than certain about how his unflattering letters could be used to damage the ACS and its colony in Africa. Probably with Sheridan's approval, the abolitionist had several pieces of his correspondence with the merchant published throughout the antislavery press, including the *Colored American* and the *Liberator*. Predictably, ACS officials were shocked by the scathing exposé of their program, though they could hardly have been surprised about the sources of Sheridan's bitterness. Much of what the merchant had said about the slave trade, the exorbitant prices of goods, and the undemocratic nature of Liberian governance could not be easily refuted. Aware that they were too far removed from the colony to address the particulars of Sheridan's letters, ACS leaders decided to have Governor Matthias and Reverend John Seys of the Methodist Episcopal mission in Liberia counter the charges in articles in the *African Repository*. Generally, their rebuttals read like the colonizationist propaganda that they were, hardly undoing Sheridan's damning critique. Unable to engage the merchant in any convincing fashion, ACS writers criticized him for going to Bassa Cove instead of Monrovia and tried to impugn his mental faculties. "It is impossible to account for some of the extraordinary statements in L. Sheridan's letter," an editorial in the February 1839 issue of the organization's periodical stated, "without supposing that he must have been under the influence of the fever which is so apt to attack emigrants on their first arrival on the African coast."[36]

This acrimonious exchange was the low point of the relationship between the ACS and Louis Sheridan. After these public recriminations, a symbiotic relationship of convenience developed. Before the merchant could do any further harm to its image, the organization allowed him to lease six hundred acres of land—an unprecedented concession—for an experimental plantation on which he employed one hundred laborers. He was also incorporated into the colonial apparatus through a series of appointments, including superintendent of commercial operations and public works at Bassa Cove, a position that paid an annual salary of twelve hundred dollars. As for Sheridan, his criticism of the ACS, which by 1839 administered Bassa Cove under the Commonwealth Constitution, was softened by his dependence upon the organization for imported goods and salaried employment. In subsequent letters to colonization officials, he seemed a bit embarrassed by his published tirade against Liberia and suggested that he and the ACS "turn over the leaf." While he seems to have pandered in some of his dispatches, Sheridan's correspondence generally reveals a complex man capable of grand visions and daring initiatives but also unbecoming pettiness and intrigue. In one instance, he might write how difficulties with corn or cassava crops had not extinguished his hope for black economic independence in Liberia. In another, he might discuss the depressing details of political infighting in the colony, colorfully describing his disdain for John Seys and others.

It is hard to tell whether Louis Sheridan ever found what he was looking for in Africa. He had certainly paid a hefty price to come to the colony. As late as 1842, he described himself as "an American Exiled," suggesting that his bonds with the land of his birth were still strong, though he never returned. Two years later, when he died of an enfeebling illness, perhaps malaria, he was more obscure in Liberia than he had been in his native North Carolina. Nonetheless, the ultimate meaning of migration to Africa for him was probably captured best in a statement he made back in 1836. "I would die tomorrow to be free today," he once wrote to Joseph Gales, perhaps the best testament to his triumphant and conflicted life.[37]

Despite their putative rapprochement, the ACS hardly acknowledged the merchant's death or contributions. To mark the occasion, the editor of the *African Repository* simply reprinted a letter that tersely noted, "Mr. Sheridan is dead." This coldness was primarily an indication that all had not been forgiven or forgotten. Sheridan's published condemnation of the ACS and Liberia had not been issued in a vacuum and had added more weight to the cumulative criticism that had been hampering the organization's activities since the early 1830s. In addition to Sheridan's reprinted letters to Lewis Tappan, another source of stress for colonizationists by this time was William Lloyd Garrison and his abolitionist mouthpiece, *Liberator*. In 1832, the Boston editor published a whole volume of anti-ACS essays, entitled *Thoughts on African Colonization*. In this work, he objected to the goals of the organization on a number of grounds, including its contention that "illiterate, degraded and irreligious" American blacks could Christianize Africa as well as its avowed respect for property rights in slaves. Garrison also held that colonization would deprive the country of the labor of free blacks, whose work in cities and plantations throughout the South "is indispensably necessary and extremely valuable." In an effort to authenticate his critique, the editor incorporated many of the observations of others and drew liberally on the literature of the ACS itself, including extensive quotes from the *African Repository* and the organization's annual reports. Some of these materials were taken out of context, and there was no effort to counterbalance the arguably negative features of the ACS's program and ideology with more positive elements, such as the early Quaker involvement. Still, as a four-hundred-page curse on the advocates of colonization, this volume had lasting value to the abolitionist cause, as did Garrison's routine denunciations of the ACS in the pages of his *Liberator*.[38]

Garrison's diatribes were not the only ones besieging the colonization movement, nor were they always the most damaging, since the Boston editor himself had been outlawed in many parts of the South, and his brand of immediatist abolitionism had alienated many northerners. Indeed, it was the occasional published stories of immigrants themselves, such as Louis Sheridan, and unimpressed visitors that marred the image of the ACS and its colony most. The *Colored American,* Samuel Cornish's newspaper, reveled in embarrassing the organization, sometimes publishing accounts that were hard to verify or refute. For example, one letter from Monrovia, written by J. R. Daily, described Liberia as "a nasty sickly 'nigger' colony, unfit for the residence of any respectable colored man." The author went on to depict the "sovereign power" that the ACS exercised over the territory as "the greatest despotism endured by any people of Christian denomination, upon the earth." In 1840, the *Colored American* published an article on the *Valador,* a former emigrant ship. This brig had carried forty-three North Carolinians to Liberia a decade earlier, but had since been converted into a slaver. In October the ship, renamed the *Scorpion* and then later the *Viper,* made perhaps the first of several runs between New Cess, near Bassa Cove, and Cuba, in one instance hauling 680 Africans into slavery. As late as 1844, it successfully eluded British and American cruisers, carrying three hundred more people into bondage. These widely reported episodes heaped more bad press on the ACS, which, of course, in its own published account did not mention that the *Valador* had once been in its employ.[39]

In a move to silence at least some of its critics and "for the better information of the public," the executive committee of the ACS decided to conduct a census of Liberia. They hoped that such a survey would illustrate that the colony was growing, prospering, and having a beneficial impact on the vast African population that surrounded it. A substantial part of the census was compiled from emigrant rolls, which listed names, ages, former status (free born or emancipated), literacy attainments, professions, initial places of disembarkation in Liberia, and relocation sites. The date and cause of death were also recorded when available, along with the health status of surviving immigrants, their towns of residence, and occupational pursuits as of 1843. The enumeration included a listing of properties owned by various immigrants, as well as crime statistics. Additionally, it documented the various religious organizations engaged in work in Liberia, along with the number of adherents of each.

In general, the demographic portrait was not inspiring. Of the 4,454 people who the ACS had reportedly sent to the colony since 1820, only 1,736 remained as of 1843. Over five hundred people had migrated out of Liberian settlements, some going to Sierra Leone and the Maryland colony at Cape Palmas. At least 108 returned to the United States, often with empty pockets and troubling stories. Significantly, 2,198, or nearly 50 percent, of the immigrants died during the first two decades of colonization. Discussed in further detail in Chapter 7, causes of death, as understood by ACS officials, ranged from consumption and anasarca to gynecological afflictions and old age. The most appalling feature of the mortality statistics related to the number of people who died of malaria, almost always within the first year after arrival. Twenty percent, or 874, of all immigrants died of "fever," making it the culprit in 40 percent of all deaths. Thus, it was not the existence of a number of prospering farmers or entrepreneurial traders in Liberia, or the 587 births that occurred in the colony between 1820 and 1843, that was the most salient statistic in the census. Instead, it was the dreadful malarial mortality that racked the colony year after year, sometimes consuming whole families, that captured the attention of most people who reviewed the population report. Altogether, the census, though a fascinating sociological study of the colony, made for unhappy reading and did little to spur interest in the languishing colonization movement.[40]

The ACS published only tidbits of the census in the *African Repository* and its annual reports and only those items which were least incriminating regarding the implications of the organizaiton's removal of African Americans to Liberia. Of the malarial death rate, the editor of the group's organ concluded that victims "mostly died through their own imprudence," in addition to a lack of appropriate medical attention. Notwithstanding ACS efforts to control access to the document, the census in its entirety did become available to the public to the chagrin of many colonizationists. Appended to a long report on American naval operations along the coast of Africa, the Senate published a copy of the demographic synopsis of Liberia, which turned out to be over 260 printed pages. For future researchers, the document became a valuable, even essential, tool for understanding the operational patterns and inner-workings of the colonization movement. Yet for ACS officials who initially thought publishing the census would provide an "unanswerable argument in favor of colonization," the report hardly fulfilled their purpose.

Many of the people who had supported the organization in the belief that its work was philanthropic in nature had serious misgivings after the census appeared. In 1845, Thomas Devereaux, a former vice president of the then defunct North Carolina State Colonization Society, told an ACS agent that the report "filled his mind with doubt" about the supposed humanitarian character of African American removal to Liberia. In an attempt to counter the depressing statistics contained in the census, the ACS published several articles offering information and advice about immigrating to Liberia. While it continued to extend free passage to the country and, theoretically, six months of provisions, the organization stressed that it was incumbent upon immigrants to bring numerous items to the colony, including tools, bedding, clothing, furniture, and especially money, which would enhance their comfort and chances of survival. Following a year in which it sent only fifty-one people to Liberia, the ACS frankly stated in its annual report of 1848 that people settling in the newly independent republic would not likely be as healthy as they had been in the United States. This was, of course, old news to anyone who had immigrated there over the past three decades.[41]

Throughout this period, the colonization movement in North Carolina was affected by many of the difficulties that were crippling the national organization. With the exception of the departure of the Sheridan party in 1837, colonization activism in the state continued to be moribund for a generation following the refugee expeditions that sailed in the aftermath of the Nat Turner revolt. Between 1838 and 1849, only sixty people migrated from North Carolina to Liberia. Moreover, only irregularly did an agent travel through the various counties to collect donations and prospective emigrants. To be sure, several individuals were commissioned to solicit contributions during this period. One diligent agent collected over three hundred dollars during a tour in late 1845. Still, itinerant officials rarely worked long before resigning, and many of their reports to their Washington superiors contained similar laments. For example, in March 1842, John Newlin informed then ACS secretary William McLain that slave rebelliousness in the state "makes the present time very unfavourable . . . to discuss the subject of colonization" in the vicinity of Orange County. Writing from Greensboro the following year, James Higgins complained to Ralph R. Gurley that he had found "poor encouragement" in North Carolina after a month of travels. In "presenting the claims of the Amer. C. Soc. before the people," he only netted thirty dollars during a week of solicitations in Raleigh. During the latter part of the decade, things were not much better for Henry Brown, who had been recently commissioned as the agent for North Carolina. "No one can more deeply regret my dear sir than myself," he confided to McLain in January 1849, "the little success that has [e]luded my Agency."

As with the national movement, colonization activities in North Carolina were sensitive to changes in both the political climate and the economic cycle. The Panic of 1837, the long depression of the 1840s, and the Mexican War did much to limit the ability of sympathizers to make donations to the ACS and its auxiliaries. Also, the continuing debt of the parent body, though greatly reduced by 1846, only worsened matters. Nonetheless, even if financial conditions had been propitious during this period, it is unclear whether the colonization movement would have fared appreciably better. The emergence of immediatist abolitionism and persistent reports of unpleasant happenings in Liberia, along with the retrenchment of slavery throughout the South, would still have hindered the ACS in many quarters. Additionally, the vast majority of free blacks continued to desire no part of colonization, even after a revival of emigrationist sentiment and activity during the 1850s. In March 1849, Henry Brown encountered such resistance among African Americans in Wilmington, the port of embarkation for two emigrant expeditions a decade earlier. One family in particular emphatically refused to entertain colonization due to, in the agent's estimate, "the great influence of Sheridan." Even in death, it seemed that the late merchant had had the last word in his duel with the ACS. In retrospect, he was perhaps singularly responsible for much of the antipathy that free blacks in southeastern North Carolina expressed toward colonization during this period.[42]

ONE OF THE MOST prominent motifs of this generation of colonization activity was the costs that various people were prepared to pay for freedom, however defined. Given that most of the period between 1830 and 1850 represented a long lull in ACS activity and African American emigration, it seems, at least on the surface, that not many individuals were affected by the colonization movement. Yet directly and indirectly, large segments of the population were engaged with the ACS and the implications of its program in ways that exacted a toll on nearly everyone involved.

Actually, the lessons of the period seem axiomatic. Whether in North Carolina, Liberia, or elsewhere, people almost always purchased liberty for themselves with the things most dear to them. Sometimes they gained their liberty through forfeiting the freedom, property, and lives of others. Thus, the price of liberty was rarely negligible or equitable. This was certainly the case with exiled African American emigrants such as Louis Sheridan, who gambled that their search for freedom in Liberia would not end in a fatal encounter with malaria. Similarly, Quakers, who had spent so many years removing quasi-free blacks to Liberia and other places, paid a heavy price for their spiritual and temporal liberation, whether measured in currency, time, lawsuits, or ultimately flight to the Midwest and elsewhere. Additionally, Africans, such as Kai Pa Brumley and the Dei, learned well the wages of colonization during their conflicts with the expanding Liberia colony which claimed their sovereignty, livelihood, and sometimes their lives. In a most dramatic fashion, Nat Turner paid the price of liberty in blood, his as well as others. Arguably, the state of North Carolina, too, was learning the cost of its freedom to hold African Americans in bondage during this period. Colonization, with its promises of sectional reconciliation and the gradual elimination of the divisive issue of slavery, may have helped obscure the mounting cost of states' rights and southern dependence upon bonded labor. In the end, though, civil war would be the price that the Tar Heel State would pay for the enslavement of African Americans, despite the efforts of colonizationists and others to avoid such a grim reckoning.

SIX. EMIGRATION RENAISSANCE

BY NORTH CAROLINA standards, New Bern was a metropolis in 1850. Situated at the confluence of the Neuse and Trent Rivers at the approximate center of Craven County, the town of 4,681 was readily accessible to the maritime traffic of the Pamlico Sound, though the long, winding Outer Banks substantially constricted passage into the wider Atlantic. During the colonial period, New Bern had been the seat of government; however, by the nineteenth century, its importance as both an administrative center and trading port was steadily eclipsed by Wilmington and other towns further inland. While small and partially tucked away in the state's contorted, serrated coastline, New Bern did have a number of attractions by midcentury, even if its infrastructure was of a minimalist sort. A theater and thespian society flourished at one time, and the legislature, beginning with an appropriation of fifty thousand dollars in 1815, poured significant resources into the Neuse River Navigation Company. Moreover, New Bern, despite its size, did experience occasional moments of excitement and turmoil. In 1828, a fire ravaged a number of homes on Middle Street, and conflagrations in 1835 and 1843 also inflicted heavy structural damage. Hurricanes blasted through New Bern in 1803, 1815, and 1821, and a particularly destructive storm deluged downtown streets in 1825. In the wake of the Nat Turner revolt of 1831, an artillery unit from Fort Monroe, Virginia, was stationed at the port, where rumors of insurrection had persisted for years. Notwithstanding these events, whatever

Above: Old plantation cotton press (William G. Reed Collection, Special Collections Library, Duke University, Durham, N.C.)

town life existed in New Bern at any given time was largely secondary to the oceanic world that had commercially and culturally engaged its inhabitants from its founding in 1723. Like its sister towns of Wilmington, Beaufort, and Elizabeth City, New Bern's history and future had always been waterborne, rising and falling with the waves of the Atlantic.[1]

Just as New Bern interfaced with oceanic realms, its African American community, forged over the course of generations, was also actively engaged with both town life and the vast currents of Atlantic commerce and cultures. In 1850, the population of Craven County was almost evenly divided between blacks and whites, with the former comprising 7,489 of its 14,409 inhabitants. Free African Americans numbered 1,538 in that year, representing 21 percent of the black population and 10 percent of all residents. Similar to those of their status elsewhere in the country, free blacks in Craven were largely common laborers, employed in farming, domestic production (especially as seamstresses and washerwomen), and other unskilled and semiskilled occupations. In New Bern, however, a number of African Americans established themselves as bakers, barbers, carpenters, tailors, nurses, and weavers by midcentury. Notably, Craven was second only to Halifax County in the number of free blacks living there. By 1860, this group accounted for almost 13 percent of New Bern's population, making it the largest community of free African Americans in any North Carolina town. On the eve of the Civil War, free blacks were the most urban of the county's social classes. While only 27 percent (2,360) of Craven's whites and 39 percent (2,383) of its enslaved population lived in New Bern in 1860, 52 percent (689) of the county's free African Americans resided in the town by this time.

Like free blacks—who were in some instances their relatives—slaves in Craven County lived in social and occupational spheres that produced a diversity of individual experiences within a generally oppressive environment. More numerous and rural than their free brethren, bondpeople were the principal labor force for the county's plantations and farms, and their condition as chattel property made their lot the least enviable of all the social classes of the region. Although life in the countryside often seemed more sedate than urban life, slaves were legally at the whim of their owners, whose daily decisions about their labors, relationships, and well-being could have profound consequences. To be sure, social spaces existed within Craven County slavery which allowed bondpeople a measure of control over their lives, albeit incomplete and often fleeting. On occasion, interplantation parties were held during which masters permitted their slaves to intermingle with others, a prime opportunity for young men and women to court. Even more significantly, slave watermen in particular lived highly mobile lives, dragnetting fish in the Lower Neuse River, stevedoring for visiting ships, and sometimes piloting vessels through the treacherous shoals and inlets of the Pamlico Sound. These mariners, with their agile lighters and entrepreneurial spirit, were the North Carolina equivalent of the Kru of Liberia. Some became highly skilled at different aspects of waterborne trade and travel, participating in a black maritime culture stretching from Canada to the Caribbean. Uniquely positioned by coastal geography and demand for their services and goods, these bondmen were able to negotiate a freedom of movement that most slaves would never know. Like the Kru, they made themselves indispensable to the survival and prosperity of both land dwellers and seafarers.

Despite such recreational and occupational outlets that encouraged slaves to measure life in personal, humanizing ways, their owners usually viewed them primarily as objects for their enrichment and convenience. The prerogatives of masters were, of course, most flagrantly demonstrated at the auction block, where the average slave commanded between six hundred and seven hundred dollars, but where a skilled bondmen might sell for up to fifteen hundred dollars. Children as young as four, underfed and poorly clothed, were sometimes sold hundreds of miles away, abruptly disconnecting them from kinship networks and familiar surroundings. According to William Singleton, who was enslaved in New Bern during the mid-nineteenth century, mounted patrols prowled the county nightly in search of blacks without permits, inflicting sound whippings upon those whose wanderings were unauthorized. As a boy, Singleton himself was beaten for allegedly opening a book, a reflection of white disdain for black literacy. Countless other manifestations of white power, privilege, and fear could be seen and felt on any given day, dramatizing the gross disparities in race relations. Predictably, there were always those bondpeople who sporadically reminded masters of the limits of their authority and control. As early as 1830, dozens of runaway slaves had set up camp in Dover Swamp in the western part of the county. Using both land and riverine networks, they established contact with several other fugitive cells, defiantly taking full advantage of the waterways that nourished the lands of their erstwhile owners.[2]

In common with swamp-based runaways, Andrew Dickinson was anxious to leave New Bern. At age forty-two, he had experienced and witnessed nearly a half-century of bondage along the waterfront and in the fields of Craven County and likely feared dying in the grasp of the institution if he did not soon act to improve his situation. Dickinson, though a slave, had not been enthralled in the rank servitude that many African Americans in the region endured. By 1849, he was a printer for the local paper, the *Newbernian*, which allowed him to acquire a skill that only a select number of blacks had opportunity to attain. Possibly, this occupation allowed him to achieve a certain level of literacy, though much of what he learned would probably have been self-taught. In addition to being part of the ever-changing maritime scene of New Bern, Dickinson was attuned to the social life of the local African American community. As an Episcopalian, he belonged to one of the local congregations which, according to one white observer, drew their members from the "Negro Elite" and were known for "perfectly astounding" displays of ceremony and dress. Dickinson's wife, Susan, a forty-five-year-old woman who had borne him two children (Julia, twelve, and Isaac, five), was Methodist but probably accompanied him to church, given that their daughter shared her father's denominational loyalties. Compared to many other enslaved families, the Dickinsons apparently were not accustomed to the worst cruelties that slavery had to offer. However, when Henry Brown, the North Carolina agent for the ACS, visited New Bern in February 1849, Andrew Dickinson made it a point to see him.[3]

The meeting was a poignant one. Brown found Dickinson to be "an intelligent, Shrewd and pious man," deeply interested in securing "for himself and family, the greatest earthly blessings." In his interview with the enslaved printer, the agent was so moved by the black man's story and plea for assistance that he could "barely refrain from tears." At the time, Dickinson was saving money to purchase his family's liberty, having nearly enough to redeem his wife and children Yet, he was three hundred dollars short of satisfying his master's asking price for his own freedom, which was set at four hundred dollars. In a letter to ACS secretary William McLain, Brown wondered if members of the Episcopal Church might help Dickinson cover the outstanding balance. He believed that one hundred dollars could be raised in New Bern, but the remainder would have to come from elsewhere. McLain, in accordance with the ACS constitution, informed Brown that he could not use the group's money to buy Dickinson's freedom, an act that would smack of abolitionism and thus compromise the organization's official position of neutrality in regard to slavery's morality and longevity. He did suggest that the printer could earn twenty-five to thirty dollars a month if he came to work in Washington, D.C., but recognized that this was an unworkable solution since, even if he had his owner's permission, "the Printer's association control the employers here & will not allow a Colored man to get work!"

McLain, unable to give Dickinson the money outright, remained intrigued by his case. Even though the volume of letters he received expressing interest in immigration to Liberia had increased markedly by the late 1840s, the ACS secretary continued to have a lively correspondence with Brown and others about possible solutions to Dickinson's dilemma. McLain felt that the North Carolinian would be a genuine asset to Liberia, especially since the Liberia Herald was currently looking for a printer. Undoubtedly, he was also aware that Dickinson could conceivably be a catalyst for reviving interest in colonization[4] in North Carolina, which had sent less than twenty-five emigrants to the colony-turned-republic over the last seven years.[5]

As McLain and others pondered his predicament hundreds of miles away in the nation's capital, Dickinson launched a fundraising offensive that he hoped would meet his master's asking price. Having already paid his owner seventy dollars from money he had earned working, the printer, assisted by his father-in-law, Mingo Croom, solicited subscriptions for the *African Repository*. By the end of February, he had gained six new readers. Croom turned out to be especially adept at handling such business. Although also enslaved, he was known for his interest in politics, as well as his "medical and dental knowledge." With the apparent acquiescence of his master, he succeeded in gaining the confidence of ACS officials in Washington to the extent that he collected and remitted subscriptions to the organization's organ through the 1850s. As Dickinson's efforts at securing contributions carried over into the summer months, he quietly purchased the liberty of his daughter, Julia. By July, he needed only fifty dollars for the freedom of his wife and son, which he felt sure that he could collect. Around this time, a benefactor in New York, apparently apprised of Dickinson's efforts by a local minister, offered one hundred dollars toward the printer's freedom. Now, only an unpaid balance of two hundred dollars was keeping him and his family from the docks of Norfolk, where emigrant ships were beginning to depart with increasing regularity.[6]

Despite his continuing solicitations and willingness to take on additional work in order to raise funds, Dickinson made no progress toward collecting the remaining two hundred dollars of his owner's asking price. Apparently, he found no supplemental employment through which to earn additional income nor a charitable propensity among either acquaintances or strangers, some of whom were likely approached more than once. Still actively interested in the printer's case, McLain pleaded with New York colonizationists for contributions to assist Dickinson. In the past, substantial collections had been raised among Quakers and others in northern states, and to the ACS secretary, Dickinson's situation seemed singularly compelling. Nonetheless, it was not until November that enough funds were forthcoming to cover the remaining cost of the North Carolinian's freedom. Reverend John B. Pinney of the New York Colonization Society was instrumental in gathering donations. In a November 24 letter to McLain, Dickinson expressed "unfeigned thanks" for the assistance of the ACS, extending his gratitude to Pinney as well. Given the fact that his master had been sympathetic to his fundraising and had asked for a relatively small price for his liberty, Dickinson likely voiced his appreciation to him as well, though his owner made it clear that he "would be offended" if his name appeared in print. More than likely, he feared being publicly associated with manumission and colonization, both subjects being taboo in many quarters of the state.

As he and his family made preparations for the journey to Liberia via Norfolk, Dickinson was ecstatic, as his letters clearly indicate. However, after such a protracted campaign for his freedom and that of his family, he became preoccupied, at least temporarily, with the question of reenslavement. In a letter to McLain, Reverend Daniel Stratton, a local white man who had diligently supported Dickinson's search for funds, informed the ACS secretary of the printer's concerns about the permanence of his liberty. "Can he get Free papers in Liberia," the clergyman inquired, "so that if at any future time, his children or descendants should ever return—they might not be alarmed[?]" It was, of course, a good question, but one that was academic. The United States had yet to recognize Liberia as an independent nation, and no embassy could represent or protect immigrants who returned to visit the country. Moreover, even if such documentation was provided by the government of the African republic, it would carry less weight in American courts than manumission papers issued by former masters. Still, Dickinson's concerns were solidly rooted in everything he had learned about slavery in Craven County. The racial injustices and white treachery that he had come to know firsthand over the past four decades seemed to shroud the future in troubling uncertainties.[7]

While the Dickinsons of New Bern were endeavoring to secure their liberty and passage to Liberia, a similar drama was being played out in Murfreesboro. Located within fifteen miles of the Virginia border, the small North Carolina town was the seat of the northeastern county of Hertford. Like Craven, slavery was firmly entrenched in this area of the state, having been nurtured by a climate favorable to the cultivation of tobacco, cotton, corn, and a number of other products. By 1850, slaves accounted for 46 percent of Hertford's inhabitants, and free blacks comprised another 11 percent of the total population. Throughout the antebellum period, white residents of the county were quite sensitive to their minority status, and every rumor about slave conspiracies rankled them. Unsurprisingly, when the Turner insurrection erupted just across the state line in 1831, a cavalry unit from Murfreesboro swiftly galloped to Southampton County and visited hellish reprisals upon blacks who were unfortunate enough to come into their view. In two days of unremitting carnage, the white horsemen slaughtered forty African Americans. Further, "as a warning to all who should undertake a similar plot," they decapitated fifteen slaves, placing their heads on poles for public display. As discussed earlier, Nat Turner and the retributive violence that followed his revolt cast a long shadow over eastern North Carolina, and race relations in Hertford were particularly affected by the violence of late 1831. On the eve of the Civil War, racial tension, suspicion, and hostility in the county could only have become more intense as blacks became an even greater percentage of the overall population.[8]

Although largely lukewarm and latent, interest in colonization had been present in Hertford since the 1820s when a branch of the ACS was founded in Murfreesboro. Few blacks from the county actually migrated to Liberia prior to 1850. Yet the colonization movement was familiar to many residents of Hertford, if only due to the county's proximity to others, such as Pasquotank, Perquimans, Northampton, and Wayne, from whence hundreds of blacks had emigrated over the past generation. When Murfreesboro slaveholder Tristram Capehart died in March 1849, his last will and testament again made colonization a topic of conversation in the small town. Capehart, whom one acquaintance described as "quiet, sensible, [and] ever peaceful," stipulated that upon his death the approximately sixty slaves whom he owned should be given the choice of either immigrating to Liberia or staying in bondage in Murfreesboro, to be parceled out among his descendants. For those who chose to leave, Capehart had ordered his estate to provide five dollars to each liberated slave over ten years of age, along with "plenty of good clothing and some farming implements." Since the slaves were needed to harvest the fall crop and to complete other tasks on three different farms, their manumission was delayed until late 1849. At that time, according to John W. Southall, Capehart's father-in-law and executor, they would "be in readiness, at least by December next" to embark upon their journey to Norfolk.[9]

Not uncommon among deceased masters who hoped to send emancipated slaves to Liberia during this period, Capehart had made no provision for defraying the cost of transporting his freed bondpeople to Liberia. Subsequently, Southall informed ACS officials that the expense of their relocation to Africa "will devolve entirely on the Colonization Society." In response, Secretary McLain notified Southall that his organization would cover the cost of sending the Capehart clan to Liberia in the emigrant expedition scheduled for December and would also arrange for them to receive the customary six months of support in Africa. McLain only asked that Southall commit to getting the freedpeople to Norfolk at his own expense. According to the secretary's estimate, the ACS would have to expend roughly three thousand dollars—fifty dollars per person—to finance the migration of the Capeharts to Liberia. These were resources that the organization did not have, however, given that the group was "at present very much pressed for funds to meet our engagements." As in the case of Andrew Dickinson, the ACS appealed to individuals friendly to the cause to help pay for the emigration of the Murfreesboro party. Advertisements appeared in Washington newspapers, and an article in the November issue of the *African Repository* pleaded for contributions to absorb the cost of sending "this large and interesting family" to Africa. By December, fourteen hundred dollars had been raised for this purpose. This fell short of the necessary amount, but McLain, recognizing the difficulty of raising such an amount so quickly, had already a month earlier committed the ACS to going into debt to cover whatever expenses donations did not offset. With the new departure date set for January, fifty-five members of the Capehart clan made preparations for the trip to Norfolk.[10]

Demographically, the Capehart people were a young, relatively homogeneous group. Males predominated among them, outnumbering females thirty-one to twenty-four. Of those listed with skills or occupations, there were fifteen farmers, two seamstresses, two washerwomen, a shoemaker, and a cook. (Fourteen of the farmers were male, in addition to the shoemaker.) None of the Capeharts are listed in the emigrant roll as literate, suggestive of a formidable opposition to black literacy among whites in Hertford County. The four individuals (all female) listed as having religious affiliations were identified as Baptist, even though twenty of the Capeharts had biblical or Hebraic names or derivatives. The average age of the clan was 15.9 years, and the modal age was one, of which there were five instances. Thirty-six individuals were less than twenty years of age, and twenty-one were younger than ten. These age statistics, in particular, boded ill for the clan's future in Liberia, for young children and adolescents were most susceptible to fatal bouts of malaria during their first weeks of residence in West Africa. Only two people, Rozetta, fifty, and Coreana, sixty, could be considered as elderly among the Capeharts, and they, too, would ostensibly exhibit less resistance regarding an anopheline attack than young to middle-aged adults. Interestingly, two of the oldest Capeharts, Jacob, fifty-five, and Rosa, fifty-six, did not emigrate with the larger group in 1850. In fact, they did not depart for Liberia until the summer of the following year after relatives encouraged them, along with their eighteen-year-old son, Nelson, to join them in Africa. Perhaps their initial hesitancy had been partially a result of stories they had heard regarding the insalubrity of the black republic. After all, unpleasant tales of high morbidity and mortality in Liberia had been circulating in eastern North Carolina since the Quaker-sponsored emigrant voyages of the 1820s.[11]

If the Capeharts were ill-prepared, due to their general youthfulness, to cope with the disease environment that awaited them in Liberia, efforts were made to prepare them in other ways for life in Africa. Each of the emigrants was allowed to take items aboard ship amounting to "the bulk of two barrels," not including bedding. By early January, Southall had reportedly provided each of the Capeharts with a pair of flannel shirts and a hand mill, which was commonly used among Liberians to grind meal. He also hoped to acquire for them a rowboat, carpenter tools, and farm implements, all of which would ease the arduous tasks of clearing land, building homes, and raising crops once in Liberia. While it is unclear whether the Capeharts ever received these items, it is known that they arrived in Norfolk in the dead of winter and during the early phase of the seasonal interstate slave trade. Along with the Dickinsons, sixty-nine Virginians, and a Pennsylvanian, the Capeharts cleared Norfolk harbor on January 26 in the *Liberian Packet*, a barque which the ACS had built in 1846 at a cost of nineteen thousand dollars.

Among the North Carolinians, the voyage to Africa was apparently quite eventful for Andrew Dickinson, who became very ill during the passage. He spent his first days in Africa in a convalescent state, which was perhaps made somewhat more tolerable by a visit from Joseph J. Roberts, the president of the republic. As for the Capeharts, after an initial stop in Monrovia the clan ended up in an "asylum" in New Virginia, a settlement across the river from Millsburg. There they struggled with the fever, chills, and aches characteristic of malarial infection. Rather miraculously, only one of their number reportedly perished during this period, though five of the Virginians who sailed with them had succumbed to malaria by April. Meanwhile, back in New Bern, Reverend Daniel Stratton informed ACS secretary McLain that interest in emigration, in the wake of the departure of the Dickinsons, was still very much alive in the port town.[12]

As the Dickinsons and the Capeharts endured acclimation in Liberia, significant developments in the United States promised to make 1850 a pivotal year in American history as well as in the evolution of the colonization movement. It had been clear for over a generation that the fraying union between the northern and southern states was steadily unraveling as both sections began to perceive their political interests and futures as being tethered to developments in the western territories. The question of whether to admit California as a slave or free state greatly amplified existing tensions between black bondage in the South and a maturing free-labor ideology among northerners. Beginning with the Constitutional Convention of 1787, compromises of various sorts had temporarily patched festering sectional differences over slavery, but by 1850, the stakes appeared higher than ever over whether the institution should take root in midwestern and West Coast lands. On the California question, Congress determined that the territory should ban slavery, a sop to northern states and Free-Soil proponents. Additionally, an act to suppress slave trading within the District of Columbia was also passed. In response to these measures, southern congressmen and other increasingly vocal defenders of states' rights pressed hard for reassurances that slavery would be federally protected where it already existed. Subsequently on September 18, as part of a comprehensive compromise package, President Millard Fillmore signed the Fugitive Slave Law of 1850.

This measure was not the first of its kind. The federal Constitution (article 4, section 2) had recognized the right of slaveholders to cross state lines to reclaim runaways. The Fugitive Slave Law of 1793 reaffirmed this right, though it was embedded in a larger act designed to assist law officers in tracking down fugitives from justice. The Supreme Court, in one of its major antebellum rulings on the subject, determined in *Prigg v. Pennsylvania* (1842) that "the owner of a slave is clothed with entire authority in every State in the Union, to seize and recapture his slave." This decision, of course, presaged the tribunal's even more momentous ruling in the *Dred Scott* case of 1857. Building on these precedents, the ten articles of the Fugitive Slave Law of 1850 gave vast powers to masters and their agents to recapture runaway bondpeople. It placed the courts and law enforcement officials at their disposal, allowing "reasonable force or restraint" to be employed to return fugitives to their owners. The law deprived the suspected runaway of the right of habeas corpus and prohibited the intervention of "any court, judge, magistrate, or other person whomsoever" on behalf of the slave. Generally, proslavery interests were pleased with at least the wording and intent of the law, though its spotty enforcement in free states aroused the ire of many slaveholders.

Like few other acts of the period, the measure's comprehensiveness and susceptibility to abuse jolted free blacks to the extent that both those who were legally free and actual fugitives collectively experienced a personal insecurity without recent precedent. Any individual could charge that any given black person was a runaway slave and would have to only convince a single judge or commissioner of the veracity of the charge in order to reduce the accused to slavery. The law was a recipe for dishonesty and mayhem and promised to disrupt many long-established communities of African Americans consisting of both the legally free and the recently escaped. Lethal black resistance to slave catchers in Christiana, Pennsylvania, in 1851 demonstrated that there were those intent upon remaining free at all costs. Additionally, violent defiance of the law flared in a number of other towns, necessitating the intervention of both local and federal authorities. Aside from these occasional conflicts, other patterns of resistance were more common and reliable indicators of just how resolute many African Americans were in their opposition to the new act. According to one estimate, as many as three thousand blacks fled to Canada within three months of the passage of the Fugitive Slave Law. Over the course of the 1850s, perhaps twenty thousand people sought refuge in that British territory, increasing its black population by 50 percent. The complete dimensions of the internal and international migrations inspired by the law are impossible to map, since many of the movements were enshrined in the secrecy of the Underground Railroad. Still, while the fugitive slave measure did sometimes have its intended effect, it often strained sectional tensions even more and encouraged a new vigilance among runaways.[13]

The Fugitive Slave Law of 1850 seemed to partially attenuate some southern fears, including the "deep concern and alarm" that the North Carolina General Assembly expressed a year earlier over "the constant aggressions on the rights of the slaveholder by certain reckless politicians of the North." However, white anxiety about slaves was eventually articulated through assaults of various sorts on free blacks, fomenting a hostility that expanded in scope and depth throughout the 1850s. In addition to its "deep concern" over the rights of slaveholders, the North Carolina legislature received reams of petitions from white citizens during this period, some calling for the removal of free African Americans to Liberia. Representative of this trend, whites in Beaufort County beseeched the General Assembly in 1850 to consider the "serious injury" suffered by white mechanics who had to compete with blacks. They lamented "the degradation" that these workers experienced, "being brought down side by side with negro labor." As a solution to this interracial competition for jobs, the petitioners requested that the state impose a tax upon African American mechanics "so as to guard more effectively against [their] increase." Furthermore, they called upon state legislators to tax free blacks as a group in order to raise a fund for sending them to Liberia.

During the same session, the General Assembly also received a petition from 77 Duplin County residents contending that the 345 free blacks of their district were abetting slave rebelliousness. Along with asking that the state government set aside a fund for transporting free African Americans to Liberia, the white petitioners suggested that the whole group in question "be compelled to go except those who prefer to be sold and become slaves." In endorsing these sentiments, the *North Carolina Whig*, a Charlotte newspaper, proposed a state-initiated program that would exile free blacks to Liberia. Similar to some strains of thought within the ACS, the editor asserted that such a policy would better secure the safety of slaveholders while rendering "our slaves more happy, contented, and tolerable."[14]

As colonization gained new adherents in some quarters of the white community, the ACS and the idea of black removal experienced a renaissance of national interest during the 1850s. A number of discernible factors were responsible for this new popularity. First, the Washington-based organization was simply in better financial shape. With the long economic expansion that followed the ending of the Mexican War, the group found it easier to garner contributions. Also, Liberian independence had relieved the ACS of the financial burden of financing a colonial administration thousands of miles away, thus freeing resources for other usages. Significantly, a limited number of blacks, both free and enslaved, began to find the idea of immigrating to Liberia more appealing than in previous years. Wider dissemination of information about the republic among increasingly literate African Americans both drew the attention of some and spurred others to inquire further. Actually, the voices of black North Carolinians began to come through in the voluminous correspondence of the ACS during the late 1840s, having, with the notable exception of Louis Sheridan, been conspicuously absent prior to this time. Although many African Americans in the Tar Heel State would continue to initiate dialogues with colonization officials through white surrogates, others began to directly establish contact with the ACS and its auxiliaries in this period.

Much of this new interest, of course, was related to the Fugitive Slave Law and other measures intended to both protect slavery and circumscribe the citizenship and opportunities of free African Americans. Moreover, the attractiveness of the ACS program to some was more a reflection of black frustration regarding the meager progress of the antislavery movement than an affinity for colonization. Twenty years of immediatist abolitionism had not brought general emancipation perceivably closer. If anything, it had served as a pretext for slave states to tighten the chains of bondage. This failure of a generation of William Lloyd Garrisons, Frederick Douglasses, and others to loosen the fetters of slavery definitely gave colonization a brighter aura.

Along with the entrenchment of slavery, free blacks were simply running out of options regarding their chances of living a dignified life on North American soil. Midwestern states, such as Ohio, Indiana, and Illinois, were beginning to pass new exclusionary laws banning the immigration of blacks. Northern states, never very welcoming of African American newcomers, fell squarely within the jurisdiction of the Fugitive Slave Law and thus were hardly safe havens for blacks of any status. Compounding these indignities, the Supreme Court's decision in the *Dred Scott* case (1857) deprived African Americans of citizenship altogether. Viewing this situation with great interest from the west coast of Africa, the editor of the *Liberia Herald* offered advice to African Americans cornered by hostile legislation and the expansion of slavery. "Better come to Liberia," he counseled with a tone of urgency. "Should Canada be annexed to the United States you will have to run for it again." At the time, his advice was not at all unreasonable.[15]

Just as they had in the wake of the Nat Turner revolt, ACS leaders saw an opportunity to greatly expand their operations in North Carolina during the anti-free-black onslaught of the 1850s. Indicative of their ambitions, the organization employed a new itinerant agent to solicit contributions and recruit emigrants throughout the state. Appointed in 1850, Jesse Rankin was a Presbyterian minister and former vice president of the Rowan County auxiliary society. In applying for the agency, he had informed William McLain that he did not only believe that removal to Liberia was advantageous to African Americans but also viewed it "as almost the only hope for the preservation of our union." Rankin, unlike most of his predecessors, turned out to be a tireless ACS operative. He regularly submitted long, tedious reports to the national office, outlining his weekly activities. More importantly, he collected over nineteen hundred dollars in contributions within a single year. Deeply familiar with the politics and social mores of the state, Rankin was able to gauge the prevalence of colonization sentiments in various regions and thus tailored his promotion of the ACS cause in ways that did not offend local sensibilities.

During his travels, the agent learned that many whites still conflated colonization with abolitionism, an association that originated in the era when Quakers dominated the state's colonization movement. Those who felt that the ACS was intent upon abolishing slavery simply did not give, especially at a time when some North Carolina blacks believed that Congress had actually freed them during its recent debates over slavery. On the other hand, he estimated that three-fourths of those who did donate money to the cause did so believing that colonization "is a process by which we will rid the country of free negroes." Rankin was probably not surprised to find that white support for the ACS's program fluctuated with the economic cycle. Depressed prices for cotton and tobacco in the western portion of the state during 1852 greatly impeded his ability to collect donations in the region and partially contributed to his decision to resign his agency in that year. Although his tenure was short, Rankin's efforts did much for the image of the movement in North Carolina and the coffers of its Washington headquarters. By 1855, there was even enough support for colonization in the state to warrant the reestablishment of the North Carolina State Colonization Society, which had been defunct since the mid-1830s.

While most North Carolina free blacks continued to keep their distance from the ACS, the records of the organization reveal a lively interest in Liberian emigration among African Americans in certain areas of the state. Consistent with past patterns, emigrationist sentiment among free blacks continued to be regional in concentration. As late as October 1850, Rankin still found that free African Americans in western North Carolina "have not as yet begun to think much of emigrating to Liberia." However, in the eastern agricultural and Piedmont counties where blacks were heavily concentrated, enthusiasm for emigration waxed like never before.

For example, after canvassing Elizabeth City in 1851, W. W. Kennedy reported to McLain, "Many of the free persons of Colour in this Town desire to emigrate to Liberia." During the 1850s, forty-one Pasquotank County blacks departed for the West African republic, including John Morris, a fifty-one-year-old, free-born "Hack-driver," who had become well known on the route between Elizabeth City and Norfolk. Similarly, in Raleigh, J. W. Lugenbeel sensed "quite a strong feeling in favor of emigration" during a recruitment visit in late 1852, a promising sign for colonizationists who hoped to gain the favor of the state legislature there. Months before Lugenbeel arrived in the town, Isaac Scott, a sixty-year-old black preacher and carpenter, had personally written McLain about his intention to emigrate. "After careful and mature deliberation upon my present state and my future prospects and those of my rising family," he resolved in lucid prose, "I have come to the conclusion to emigrate to the Republic of Liberia to spend the remainder of my life and rear my family." With his wife, Milly, and their five children, Scott departed for the African country in November 1852. In sharp contrast to the slow, lean years of the 1830s and 1840s, ACS secretary McLain found his Washington office flooded with letters from North Carolina. From Charlotte to New Bern and from Smithfield to Weldon, the inquiries indicate that perhaps thousands of black North Carolinians, free and enthralled, would have departed the state during the 1850s, if only the ACS could have afforded the cost of sending them to Africa.[16]

In 1852, one of the most riveting episodes in the history of the Liberian emigration movement took place among African Americans in Fayetteville. Second only to Wilmington and New Bern in population, the town of 4,646 was the seat of Cumberland County and established along the Cape Fear River. Like many other locales throughout the state, the county had been absorbed into the ever-widening dominion of King Cotton, which had displaced tobacco as the chief crop. In 1850, bondpeople comprised 35 percent of Cumberland's population of 20,610. Most of these slaves were farm workers, trapped in vast fields of cotton and tobacco, but a few served as blacksmiths, barbers, wagoners, and washerwomen. As in New Bern, a number of bondmen were employed as riverboat workers, pilots, and draymen along the Cape Fear River and other bodies of water. Notwithstanding variations in the manner in which Cumberland slaves experienced their oppression, there was a core consistency between their lot and that of slaves elsewhere.

As in many other places, slave patrols roamed the land in search of those who would dare be at large without authorization. A jail specifically designed to detain enslaved inmates existed in Fayetteville, and slave traders occasionally used the local papers to advertise their interest in purchasing black youths. Undoubtedly, slaves, along with the 946 free blacks who lived in Cumberland County in 1850, crafted values, institutions, and lives that both accommodated and resisted the ubiquitous racial prejudice and discrimination enmeshed in the region's culture. Still, frequent reminders of their subordinate status—such as the local tradition of blacks being responsible for the washing and shrouding of corpses—often conferred upon racial differences a rigidity common to caste systems.[17]

By 1849, Marshall Hooper knew Cumberland County quite well. Having spent perhaps all of his forty years in Fayetteville or its environs, he was intimately familiar with the trials and possibilities of black life in the area. Hooper had been a slave at one time, but by the late 1840s, had gained his freedom, perhaps having purchased it with wages he earned as a clerk. His wife, Rachel, was also free by this time, possibly having won her liberty in a similar fashion. Although the exact texture and meaning of the Hoopers' life experiences in Fayetteville are not known, they eventually found it expedient to depart the town—indeed, the country—for a new beginning elsewhere. In 1849, Marshall spent his last forty dollars on one-way fares to Monrovia, where he and his wife arrived on March 29. In material terms, Hooper seems to have done fairly well for a new immigrant in Liberia. Having survived the rainy season in the riverine town of New Virginia, he informed William McLain in November that "I am very well pleased with my new home." He was "off the public," meaning his six months of complimentary support had expired, but he still reported that "I am getting along pretty well."

Despite his glowing letter to the ACS secretary, Marshall Hooper was in heart-wrenching anguish. When he departed America aboard the *Liberian Packet*, he left nineteen of his children in slavery. None of them had been able to emigrate with him and his wife, and he did not have the funds necessary to free a single one of them. Ostensibly, Hooper had hoped to make enough money in Liberia to return to North Carolina to purchase the liberty of at least a few of his children. He made it a point to stay informed of their condition and whereabouts even though separated from them by the seemingly endless Atlantic. When a letter reached him in 1852 stating that three of his children were about to be sold, he was panic-stricken and immediately boarded a ship for Fayetteville. Frantic and desperate, he hoped to arrive in time to see if his offspring "might be purchased on fair terms" by him before others had a chance to acquire them.[18]

Arriving in Fayetteville during the summer, Marshall found that his former owner, "Mistress Hooper," had not disposed of his children through sale as he had feared. To his dismay, however, she left town on a trip shortly after his arrival, though she did agree to negotiate with him for his youngest child upon her return. In the meanwhile, Marshall, who had ventured back to North Carolina broke, attempted to raise enough money to free his sixteen-year-old daughter, Emily, who was owned by Sarah Mallett of Chapel Hill. In early August, Hooper convinced ACS secretary McLain to commission him as a recruitment agent, responsible for raising a company of one hundred emigrants from among blacks in Fayetteville and elsewhere. McLain promised

Hooper five dollars for every person whom he could persuade to embark for Liberia in the expedition scheduled for November. This arrangement gave Hooper three months to assemble what could potentially be the largest party of North Carolinians to emigrate since Louis Sheridan and his clan sailed for Bassa Cove twenty-five years earlier. Fortunately for Hooper, African American residents of the area voiced some interest in the prospect of starting anew in Africa. In late July, he reported to McLain that a few free blacks had indicated a willingness to emigrate. By the latter part of September, he was able to inform the secretary that he "had the promise of about 100 to go[,] mostly young people, and some of them of a superior class." To coordinate the migration, ACS officials in Washington dispatched J. W. Lugenbeel to North Carolina. A longtime white colonizationist, Lugenbeel arrived in Chapel Hill in early October, joining Hooper who was already in the area.[19]

Upon their first meeting and constantly reaffirmed during their subsequent journey to Fayetteville together, Lugenbeel became fully aware that Marshall Hooper's first priority was to secure the release of his daughter, Emily, from bondage. "He is very anxious to get her," he wrote McLain, "even if he cannot succeed (as I am satisfied he cannot) in getting any of the three younger children." In the same correspondence, Lugenbeel felt again compelled to stress that Hooper "seems to be bent on trying to get this girl." As the ACS agent learned, Mallett had agreed to free Emily for a payment of six hundred dollars, "a big price" in his estimate. Hooper informed Lugenbeel that he could raise approximately two hundred dollars toward this purpose, but hoped that the ACS would cover the outstanding balance. Lugenbeel made no promises beyond assuring Hooper that his organization would stand behind its agreement to pay him five dollars per emigrant recruited. He did, however, request that Mallett keep Hooper's daughter "in readiness to be delivered to her parents, at her price" by the time of the November expedition. Mallett, who departed for Fayetteville with Emily for a stay of several weeks, provisionally assented to doing so. Despite this small victory, Hooper was dismayed to learn that the six-hundred-dollar asking price, a virtual chasm separating his enslaved daughter from freedom in Liberia, was not negotiable. Making the situation worse, Lugenbeel found that Mrs. Hooper, Marshall's former owner, "hates him, but for his wife's sake, she may be willing to sell the youngest child." The agent believed that while the price was "not fixed," the child, a boy less than ten years of age, would not be granted his liberty for under four or five hundred dollars. To Lugenbeel, this amount seemed well beyond what Marshall could pay, given that he had not yet collected enough money to liberate Emily.[20]

Around November 10, Marshall Hooper handed Lugenbeel 198 dollars, all that he could raise to buy his daughter's freedom. Lugenbeel, who had recently spoken to Mallett about the enslaved girl, had decided to purchase her liberty and to arrange a plan of payment for the remaining balance due. In a startling illustration of his distrust of Hooper, the agent informed him that he intended to purchase Emily in his name, only transferring the title to her father once the family was actually aboard a ship destined for Liberia. Shocked by this scheme, Marshall, according to Lugenbeel, "exhibited one of those wild, significant looks, which seemed to be expressive of distrust and disappointment." In a letter to McLain, the agent conveyed his hope that "all will be right and honorable" and that Hooper and his daughter would emigrate forthrightly after final arrangements were made with Mallet. However, he assured the ACS secretary that "should he [Marshall] attempt to play any trick, so that she shall not go, I shall certainly advertise her as my slave."

Even given the official fence-straddling, amoral position of the ACS regarding slavery, Lugenbeel's proposed method of coercing the emigration of the Hoopers was unconscionable. His contingency plan disclosed both an unqualified contempt for Marshall Hooper and a willingness to callously manipulate the lives of blacks to advance the agenda of the colonization movement. It is unclear what William McLain or other ACS officials thought of Lugenbeel's tactics, though the organization's records reveal no outcry against his machinations. One can only imagine that Marshall Hooper boarded the ACS-chartered ship, *Joseph Maxwell*, with a less than flattering impression of Lugenbeel and his organization. Whatever the case, he and Emily sailed from Wilmington on November 22 for their new home along the St. Paul's River, along with sixty-nine other Fayetteville blacks whom Hooper had convinced to emigrate. At this point, Lugenbeel, Fayetteville, and America in general perhaps appeared less significant to Hooper than the fact that his mission to North Carolina to free his daughter had been successful. As his efforts in this instance—along with another futile attempt to free his young son during a return trip to Fayetteville in 1855—unmistakably demonstrated, nothing was more important to this father than his love for his children.[21]

PERHAPS NO IMMIGRANT settlement in modern times has had more conflicting reports circulated regarding its salubrity, inhabitability, and purpose than Liberia. The observations of immigrants, colonial officials, missionaries, and naval officers substantially crafted the image of the country as an actual geographic entity. Nonetheless, the cultural, political, and popular meaning of Liberia was primarily a product of philosophical sparring between abolitionist, proslavery, and colonizationist ideologues in the United States. For the ACS, the creation of the West African colony was from the very beginning an exercise in propaganda dissemination. Over the course of four de-

cades, the organization became quite adept at highlighting those developments that made Liberia appealing to potential emigrants and supporters
and dismissing reports that raised questions about the advisability of colonization. Concurrently, colonizationists developed a formidable body of literature supporting black removal, replete with decades of cumulative information on Liberia, free blacks, the slave trade, public opinion, and government
policy. These resources were constantly refined to take into account the changing political climate, economic conditions, organizational demography, and
other factors bearing upon the ACS's work. Consequently, by the 1850s, this
readily accessible knowledge base allowed for the further institutionalization
of the ACS as a self-proclaimed alternative to either immediate abolition or
permanent black bondage.

Arguably, this store of knowledge and language of self-justification ade-
quately served the needs of colonizationists during the politically raucous
decade of the 1850s. On many fronts of its propaganda war against critics,
ACS officials had erected standard retorts which, if rarely convincing to their
opposition, did not alienate their often fragile, shifting pool of sympathizers.
For example, when faced with charges of being proslavery or at least hampering immediate emancipation, colonizationists publicized instances of slaveholders freeing bondpeople for removal to Liberia as well as the country's increasingly significant role as a sanctuary for recaptives during the late 1850s.
Similarly, when adversaries pointed out that Liberia had been established on
the lands of dispossessed Africans, the *African Repository* was quick to reprint treaties purporting to show that indigenous monarchs had voluntarily
ceded their domains to the republic. Perhaps not fully conscious of the contradiction, the editors of the ACS organ seemed to delight in publishing highly
sensationalized accounts of battles between immigrants and neighboring
peoples, which almost always followed Monrovia's annexation of African
lands. In addition to these lines of attack, a common abolitionist tactic was
to portray the ACS as an organization of slaveholders seeking to rid the United
States of free blacks by dumping them in Liberia, which was itself dictatori-
ally run by whites as a sort of vast plantation. Liberian independence in 1847
and the election of Joseph J. Roberts as president made this criticism less potent, though some believed that Roberts's mulatto heritage made him more
palatable to southern proslavery interests within the ACS.

If there was an area in which the ACS routinely faltered when pressed by
opponents for credible answers, it was in regard to a circumstance over which
it had the least amount of control; that is, the omnipresent malarial scourge
that preyed upon every emigrant expedition that landed in Liberia. For years,
colonizationists had publicly downplayed the destructiveness of the anopheline plague in the African country, arguing that black American immigrants

had fared better than English colonists in seventeenth-century Virginia. Those advancing this line of reasoning also tended to maintain that the mortality faced by African Americans relocating to Liberia was an acceptable price to pay for the corresponding benefit of reducing their numbers in the United States. Without question, this position was untenable in most quarters of the free black community, which had come to expect such a dismissive attitude from colonization spokesmen regarding their well-being and future. Moreover, the publication of the 1843 census of the colony, which quantified the ravages of the *Anopheles* mosquito, provided the ACS with no defense against the indictment that relocation to Liberia had been a death sentence for hundreds of African American immigrants. Confronted with such charges, organizational officials could do little, besides suppress as thoroughly as possible the incriminating letters and reports that reached America detailing the ongoing malarial suffering. Unsurprisingly, after the publication of the appalling mortality statistics of the 1843 census, neither the ACS nor the Liberian government ever again disseminated information regarding immigrant death rates. Possibly, they stopped keeping such records altogether.

In part due to the malarial situation in Liberia and its own waffling on the issue of slavery, the ACS continued to be in bad odor with people of various political persuasions, notwithstanding the emigrationist revival of the 1850s. Disapproval came from both high and low places, but the general substance and tenor of the criticism was not in itself new; only the intensity and widespread publication of it was novel. In addition to the incessant reproach the ACS endured in the pages of Garrison's *Liberator*, Frederick Douglass, a former Maryland bondman who had become the most prominent black voice in the antislavery struggle, lambasted the group's program and motives at nearly every opportunity. He reveled in ridiculing ACS president Henry Clay, and in an 1851 speech in Rochester, New York, he labeled the organization "the arch enemy of the free colored citizens of the United States." So distasteful had the colonization movement become among some African Americans that even those who began to favor emigration were careful not to endorse Liberia.

Martin R. Delany, a leader of the budding black separatist movement in the United States, roundly denounced the African country in his nationalistic book, *The Condition, Elevation, Emigration and Destiny of the Colored People of the United States* (1852). Along with being unhealthy, Delany charged that Liberia "originated in a deep laid scheme of the slaveholders . . . to *exterminate* the free colored of the American continent." Not even political independence had made it deserving "of any respectful consideration from us," since in his view the country was "a poor *miserable mockery—a burlesque* on a government—a pitiful dependency on the American Colonizationists." If his criticism was brutal in this instance, many subsequent assessments were no kinder, such as when he exaggeratingly wrote in 1855 that "the whole country of Liberia is daily overflooded," requiring residents "to confine themselves to the few hill-points which border the sea-coast." Only after a visit in 1859 did Delany moderate his opinion of the republic. Even then, however, he could not bring himself to endorse immigration to the country.[22]

While writers for the *Liberia Herald* dismissed Delany's critique as suggestive of his "consummate ignorance" of the country, they likely found it more difficult to counter the unfavorable critiques published by former residents of the republic. Hostile letters from disaffected immigrants had occasionally appeared in the abolitionist press since the 1830s. Yet by midcentury, whole books were being devoted to denouncing Liberian emigration and all who were associated with it. William Nesbit, a free black from Pennsylvania who migrated to the republic in 1853, authored one of the most vituperative diatribes ever written about the country. In his *Four Months in Liberia: or African Colonization Exposed* (1855), Nesbit characterized colonization as "a scheme of the most consummate villainy ever enacted," having "enlisted in its cause as agents, some of the most unscrupulous men, white and colored, to be found anywhere." He charged further, in words similar to Delany's, that the black republic was "a burlesque on a free country." In his view, Liberia, "conceived as it was in sin, and having no great work to do, no high destiny to fulfill, it must irresistibly fall." Nesbit portrayed nearly every feature of the African country in negative terms, from climatic and agricultural conditions to the motives of the ACS and the customs of indigenous peoples. Arguably, his eighty-two-page polemic was an inadvert admission of his own inability to adjust to the rigors of tropical life in a poor country. Nonetheless, *Four Months in Liberia*, filled with both glaring inaccuracies and troubling truths, inflamed African American opposition to the idea of their removal to Africa.[23]

Partially in response to Nesbit's disparaging book, Samuel Williams, a clergyman who had lived in Liberia for four years, published a less damning appraisal of the black republic in 1857. His autobiographical *Four Years in Liberia* affirmed Nesbit's contention that the African country suffered from a number of dire shortcomings, such as a lack of fencing and beasts of burden, but his assessment of the prospects of Liberia was much more encouraging. Some of Williams's points assume a refutative tone, such as his denials that missionaries peddled rum in the republic or that mortality there was higher than in other countries established under similar circumstances. Moreover, a certain sentimentalism accents the work, including the last page where the author reassures his readers that "Liberia is my home and I expect to end my days in it." Notwithstanding his more positive impressions of the republic,

Williams, too, stressed the difficulties that new immigrants faced there. "My advice," he counseled them, "is to take every thing you possibly can, as every thing is difficult to be obtained in Africa." Furniture and kitchen utensils "are very high," he warned, and all who were determined to live in Liberia should take with them all necessary items, including various foodstuffs and "shoes enough for one year." Even though he believed that the country's development had been "steady and sure," he had seen enough deprivation in Liberia to convince him that no family should come to the republic with less than two hundred dollars.[24]

It is unknown whether works such as those of Nesbit or Williams found a wide audience among North Carolinians. Chances are they did not, given their northern origin and the intensifying censure in the South of any literature that even remotely hinted of abolition. Still, sentiments expressed in these publications were not alien to blacks in the Tar Heel State, and the same facts, inaccuracies, and outright fantasies that were shaping Liberia's image among northerners were also at work among southerners. Similar to themes in Williams's book, some letters by black North Carolinians, written both stateside and from Liberia, exhibited an optimistic view of the republic by the 1850s. For example, writing to William McLain in January 1851, Cledwell Whitted, a slave in Hillsboro, asserted that "there is no place in the World I should like to go to as much as to Leberra." Although he proved unable to save enough money to free himself and his wife, "a first rate dress-Maker," from slavery, Whitted hoped in earnest "that God in his kind providence might remove me to my dear Country." Striking similar chords of longing and destiny, Horace Day of Mill Creek, Person County, informed the ACS secretary that "my object in wishing to go to Africa is to try to do some good for the race of my ancestors." Not unlike the romantic emigrationism and Pan-Africanism being espoused by Martin R. Delany, Edward Blyden, and others, Day presumed he shared a timeless kinship with Africans that neither distance nor slavery had wholly disrupted. Additionally, one Raleigh man, David Matthews, told an ACS agent that he was convinced that he had been "called as were the Apostles to preach in Liberia." Despite his religious conviction, however, Matthews was ultimately unable to secure a passage to Africa for himself, his wife, and their three children.[25]

Coursing through these and other letters of prospective emigrants is the idea that the authors, and African Americans in general, were in diaspora. Moreover, a salient consciousness of uprootedness and a desire to return to some pristine black origin, some site of ancestral provenance, frame the writers' understanding of Africa, and the meaning they associate with Liberia's role as a homeland for African American emigrants. The notion of a transcendent connectedness between people of African descent in the Americas, based upon their loosely shared history, culture, enslavement, and perceived destiny, had been around since the beginning of the transatlantic slave trade. While developments such as Haitian independence and the emergence of the international abolitionist movement dramatized the similarities in condition and aspirations among blacks in the Western world, the sense of exile, of being displaced and in diaspora, predated these historical phenomena. Thus, Cledwell Whitted's reference to Liberia as "my dear Country" has to be understood as more than just a rhetorical device, emphasizing his desire to emigrate. Likewise, the intention of Horace Day to migrate to Africa "to do some good for the race of my ancestors" has a significance that goes beyond simply a will to pursue charitable work in the tropics. Indeed, their words and the sentiments that they evoked were part of an idiom of racial and self-identification that prospective Liberian emigrants employed to locate the history of American blacks and its meaning within a larger, transoceanic African experience. Certainly, this sense of black kindredness across space and time was an imagined community, subject to the same paradoxes, sentimentalism, and manipulation that complicate and confound all such essentialist ideas of race and ethnic origins. At any rate, for some black North Carolinians, Liberia proved a potent foil for imagining their identities in manners that connected them politically and psychically to Africa and its far-flung diasporic progeny.

While many individuals, including Whitted, Day, and Matthews, never reached the shores of Liberia, others who did emigrate expressed a similar affinity for the African republic in their letters to correspondents in the United States. Susan Capehart, one of the freed slaves who migrated from Murfreesboro in 1850, confided in a Chapel Hill acquaintance that though she was unmarried and "farming on the smalls" in New Virginia, "the longer I live in Africa, the better I like it." Significantly, she was in good health, and her daughter, Harriet, was attending school in Millsburg, which would have been an impossible pursuit if the Capeharts had remained in North Carolina. In the case of Henry Chavers Jr., who migrated in 1857, it was only after landing in Grand Cape Mount that he could inform a Lewisburg friend that "I now begin to enjoy life as a man should do." To him, his notions of masculinity, liberty, and racial identity were allowed fuller expression through migration to Liberia. Writing to an American acquaintance in 1860, George L. Seymour, a literate farmer who migrated to Bassa Cove in 1841, recorded a similar reaction to the country. Having ventured further inland than most other immigrants, Seymour concluded that "Africa is the black mans home."

Richard McMorine, a forty-three-year-old ex-slave from Elizabeth City who settled in Bassa Cove in 1854, also discerned greater opportunities for black men to experience a less constricted sense of manhood and responsibility in Liberia. In an 1858 letter to a white correspondent in North Carolina, he noted the poverty that pervaded the republic and the difficult adjustments being made by former slaves who had been used to being provided for by their masters. "It is a new Country," he reflected, adding "it is hard to live in all new Countrys at first." In spite of the rough lessons that he and others were learning about frontier life in the tropics, McMorine found enough to admire about Liberia "to hope that people will not say anymore that we cannot Live in Africa." In his letter, the ex-slave did ask for assistance in financing the construction of a house but still held that "God did not make a Country for the man of collor where he could not live."[26]

Here, it is worthwhile to note that the content and style of these and other letters written by Liberian emigrants were typically affected by the perceived views and expectations of the intended audience. Notwithstanding that the professed satisfaction of Capehart, Chaver, and McMorine with Liberia seems genuine, their correspondence must be examined and understood within the historical and sociocultural context in which they were written. Generally, ACS officials and their white supporters received letters from Liberian residents that were kind to the colonization cause. Many, if not most, letters from the African country were addressed to ACS officials and were thus tailored to be sensitive to their ideological leanings and emigration agenda. If a letter contained a request for aid of some sort, the writer sometimes went out of his way to portray the black republic in appealing terms, though the request itself disclosed the inability of the author to comfortably subsist on the resources available to him in Liberia. Interestingly, some missives addressed to former masters and other whites occasionally exhibited a striking degree of honesty about life in Liberia but tended to be deferential, especially when assistance was being solicited. In the case of Daniel Williams, a liberated slave from New Bern, his 1857 letter to his former owner opened with the salutation "Dear Master" and ended with a carefully worded request for "provisions and goods," a literary technique that many ex-slave immigrants employed to win aid. Again using language that he hoped would resonate with his former master, Williams promised to repay the favor "on the honor of a North Carolina gentlemen."[27]

Rather predictably, immigrant letters to blacks and abolitionists were more likely to offer candid, and often less pleasant, depictions of conditions in the country. Disgruntled individuals in particular fed damaging reports to the antislavery press as a way of both lashing out at the ACS and publicizing the disappointments they encountered in Liberia. Unfortunately, few letters penned by immigrants to North Carolinians have been preserved, and even more rare is correspondence written directly to black relatives and friends still in the state. Given these observations, the letters of Henry Chavers, Susan

Capehart, and others become that much more important as sources of information about Liberia; however, the substance of these letters, as well as their stylistic qualities, cannot always be taken wholly at face value. Consequently, immigrant writings must be considered against the backdrop of North Carolina race relations, the relationship between the writers and their intended audiences, and the purpose of the letters themselves before their value as credible documentation of life in Liberia can be confidently ascertained.

If Liberia enjoyed an alluring, liberating image among some black North Carolinians on both sides of the Atlantic, the country's reputation, along with that of the ACS, was hardly enviable in other quarters. Since the advent of the colonization movement, rumors of all sorts had crisscrossed North Carolina, with some—such as the poverty and malarial mortality of Liberia—eventually carrying more weight than others. Tales such as the one spread by a North Carolina congressman that portrayed many Liberian immigrants as "extensive slave owners" probably bothered fewer whites than stories alleging that the ACS provided sanctuary for fugitive American slaves in Liberia. Conversely, documented evidence of the racial biases of colonization officials certainly grabbed the attention of African Americans more readily than whatever emancipationist tendencies may have existed in the organization's program.

On this score, efforts by ACS leaders to appease southern supporters, not to mention nonabolitionist northern and midwestern constituencies, almost never failed to bare their disdain for blacks, which, of course, repelled many of the subjects of their putative philanthropy. Indeed, if one was looking for public expressions of racial prejudice among colonizationists, he or she did not have to look any further than ACS publications and meeting records. Thus, when Frederic Stanton, an ACS vice president from Tennessee, characterized African Americans as "an inferior race" deficient "in activity, intellect, and enterprize" at the 1852 annual meeting, he was not saying anything that had not already been said at several previous ACS functions. And while such insults did not inspire many blacks to heed the group's subsequent calls for more emigrant expeditions, they did reveal that the ACS was willing, time and again, to trade potential black support for the goodwill of whites. Especially during a decade when the typical emigrant was a liberated slave emancipated expressly for removal—as in the case of the Capeharts—free black opinion seemed to matter less to ACS leaders than the sensitivities of slaveholders or, conversely, the invectives of abolitionists.

Much of the antiblack sentiment that motivated some colonization officials never became public knowledge, such as the penchant of William Starr, the ACS agent at Norfolk, to refer to emigrant parties as "darkies" in his letters to his superiors in Washington. Even the explicit racial discrimination that took place aboard the *Sophia Walker*, which was chartered to take 252 emigrants (including fifteen North Carolinians) to Liberia in May 1854, eluded public disclosure. Regarding this voyage, one black passenger complained to William McLain that the company had been "completely, successfully and outrageously humbugged" by the ship's white crewmen, who "obliged [the blacks] to *wait outside the cabin* while they [the crew] are eating their meals." This episode was probably less the fault of the ACS than reflective of the racial mores of the white sailors involved. Nevertheless, this observation was probably lost on those who had actually experienced these indignities at the hands of ACS employees. Affected by both perception and reality, the organization's reputation as a humanitarian outfit suffered great harm during the 1850s, and many black North Carolinians undoubtedly noted each publicized instance in which racism seemed to undergird the group's agenda and activities.[28]

On the eve of the Civil War, the Liberian emigration movement in North Carolina suffered perhaps its greatest public relations setback in over three decades of activity in the state. A single embarrassing development tarnished even further its self-styled philanthropic image. Emily Hooper, who had accompanied her father, Marshall, to Africa in 1852, ended up disliking Liberia. Apparently, she found the hardships of life in New Virginia much more discomforting than bondage in North Carolina, where, according to her former master, Sarah Mallett, she "had never been accustomed to hardwork." In response to a letter from Emily, Mallet wrote Secretary McLain in September 1858 requesting assistance in bringing the young woman back to Chapel Hill. Concurrently, she successfully appealed to the House of Commons to pass "A Bill for the Relief of Emily Hooper of Liberia." The act allowed "That Emily Hooper a negro, and citizen of Liberia, be and she is hereby permitted, voluntarily, to return into a state of slavery, as slave of her former owner, Miss Sarah Mallet of Chapel Hill." In Washington, McLain, chagrined by the young woman's desire to return to bondage, either ignored Mallett's inquiry altogether or offered only surreptitious assistance, since there is no record of him having acted formally upon her request. In contrast to the ACS's official silence on the matter, the proslavery press of the state predictably made much of this proposed reverse migration. In January, the *Western Democrat* of Charlotte crowed that "Emily . . . is sick of freedom and prefers living with her mistress in the Old North State than to being fleeced by abolition friends in Liberia." In another article, the paper deemed the ACS "a nuisance, whose operations in the Southern States should be abated by law."

It is unclear whether Emily ever returned to North Carolina. The matter received no further mention in ACS records beyond Mallett's initial correspondence. Whatever the case, Emily's father, Marshall Hooper, who had struggled so tenaciously to secure her liberty and that of her siblings, could only have been distraught by his twenty-two-year-old daughter's decision to return to slavery. Despite the drubbing that the ACS received in the North Carolina press over this peculiar set of circumstances, the organization's embarrassment hardly measured up to the trauma endured by this family torn between American bondage and Liberian freedom.[29]

ALTHOUGH THE STATED primary purpose of the ACS was to rid the country of free blacks, the Liberian emigration movement in North Carolina was an instrument of emancipation from the beginning. In the hands of Quakers, colonization had always been coupled with the manumission of quasi-free blacks, whom state laws had made it near impossible to liberate. By the 1830s, other slaveholders had began sending freed slaves to Liberia, and by the 1850s, most of the North Carolinians migrating to Africa would be liberated bondpeople. Several reasons account for the increasing willingness of slave owners to emancipate slaves, particularly as part of their wills, for removal to Africa. Persistent fears of slave rebelliousness in the years following the Turner revolt encouraged some masters to part with their slaves. Exhausted soils and mounting debts forced the hands of others, as well as a glutted market for slaves in North Carolina. In addition to these considerations, some masters sent bondpeople to Liberia because they simply saw no opportunity for them to live dignified, independent lives in North Carolina. Like Lucy Peobles, a slaveholder in Northampton County, they bequeathed their bondpeople to the ACS, hoping that they could "be sent to Liberia or some other free state where they can enjoy their freedom."

Scruples about chattel bondage influenced a number of slaveholders to liberate slaves for removal. As in the case of William S. Andres of Bladen County, some conscience-stricken testators expressed a moral indignation over slavery reminiscent of Quaker colonizationists of an earlier day. Having received requested information from the ACS about Liberia, Andres wrote in 1845 that he was "convinced it [colonization] is the only practicable method of eradicating, safely, a most serious evil, & of conferring any lasting advantages to that most abject set of beings, which an inscrutable Providence has placed among us." In these cases, emancipating wills aimed to reconcile the self-centered, temporal, and economic needs of owners with their moral convictions and spiritual aspirations. Some deathbed conversions to abolitionism were definitely motivated by fear of the wrath of a just God. Also, a few emancipating masters surely recognized the abrasive sectional bitterness that slavery had spawned and discerned the future possibility of civil strife over the institution. Many slave owners, however, repudiated black bondage less on moral grounds than as part of a series of politically expedient and economically driven transactions designed to ensure the well-being of themselves and their heirs.[30]

North Carolina masters who died testate provided an assortment of instructions for the relocation of slaves to Liberia. On occasion, the will of the deceased mandated that existing financial resources of the estate be used to settle liberated slaves in Africa. In other instances, some of the properties comprising the estate were sold for the purpose of raising the money necessary to defray the cost of emigration. In her 1836 will, Mary Bissell of Chowan County ordered that two pieces of real estate in Edenton be sold so that the ACS "may be at no expense" in sending her nine bondpeople to Liberia. Similarly, John Rex of Raleigh stipulated that his lands, tanyard, "all my crop, stock of every kind, plantation tools and carriages, implements for tanning and currying, household and kitchen furniture" be liquidated to pay "for the establishment of said slaves" in Liberia. Far more common than these relatively generous provisions, however, was the practice of hiring out slaves until they earned enough wages to finance their removal to Africa. Illustratively, Thomas Russell, a slaveholder of Franklin County, instructed his executors to "bind out" two youths, Dick and William, to create an emigration fund. Both of the boys were to depart for Africa upon the twentieth birthday of the oldest, William. Although Russell's will was drafted in 1834, it was not until January 1850 that the two young men embarked in the *Liberian Packet* for Monrovia. In the case of the aforementioned William Andres, five hundred dollars was bequeathed to the ACS to cover the expense of removing his slaves to Liberia. In addition to this amount, the will stated that should this allotment prove insufficient to defray the complete cost of relocating the bondpeople, the executor of the estate was charged with hiring the slaves out "at public auction till the [needed] amount shall be collected." The monies accruing from the hire of the bondpeople was to be distributed equally among them "at the time of their departure for said colony."[31]

As one might imagine, the slaves whose lives were affected most by such wills and codicils were not always in agreement with the terms of their proposed emancipation. A variety of attitudes toward Liberia existed among North Carolinians, and bondpeople were often no less informed about the country's conditions than others. Anticipating resistance to emigration among at least some of their slaves, masters routinely included clauses in their wills that added a degree of coercion to their offers of manumission and removal. For example, John Rex, intent upon disposing of all of his enthralled property, instructed his executors to sell bondpeople who refused to embark for Liberia and to apply the proceeds toward transporting those who agreed to emigrate. William Andres's will stipulated that those among his slaves who preferred to remain in North Carolina would be given ten dollars each. Following this gesture, they were to be promptly exposed to sale. Maria Gordon of Perquimans County resolved not to traffic slaves who declined being turned over to the ACS, instead choosing to transfer them to the ownership of her daughter. Twelve of her slaves chose immigration to Liberia over this arrangement, departing for the country in 1856. Of those slaves owned by Lucy Peobles who might elect to remain in the state, the testatrix desired "that they be allowed to choose their own masters." Even though she offered the assistance of her executors to help them make "a good choice," twenty-three of her erstwhile slaves instead seized the opportunity to embark for Africa in 1858. In all of these instances, emancipation was less an option offered to bondpeople than an ultimatum. State laws hostile to manumission were at least partially responsible for the clauses in these wills that fused liberty with banishment. However, the willingness of many of these masters to send slaves to the auction block, and thus possibly separate families, diminished and made more dubious whatever magnanimity testators believed they were displaying by offering this form of emancipation.[32]

Unsurprisingly, judicial rulings played a very significant role in many of these deportationist manumissions. Legislative acts primarily set the tone of the government's attitude toward the issue of slave emancipation, but the courts, particularly the state Supreme Court, interpreted and ruled on individual cases of contested wills, which set precedents for the treatment of future disputes. From the 1830s to the Civil War, the North Carolina Supreme Court generally ruled in favor of masters whose wills provided for the manumission and removal of slaves to Liberia. The court usually upheld the original intent of the will, especially in cases in which legal technicalities did not obscure the lawfulness and meaning of a will to the extent that the document's purpose became indecipherable. Given that thousands of dollars in property were often at stake, legal challenges to emancipating provisions, often initiated by relatives of the testator, had an important impact upon the culture of slaveholding in the state and the fortunes of the colonization movement.

While several such contested wills reached the state Supreme Court during the antebellum period, a few representative cases highlight the evolution of legal theory regarding slave emancipation and removal. In 1841, the court ruled in *Cameron v. Commissioners* that John Rex's will, which mandated the selling of his various properties to finance the colonization of his slaves in Liberia, was legally constructed. "It is the declared policy of the State," the justices determined, "to . . . encourage their emancipation, so that they may be but removed . . . without the State." In *Cox v. Williams* (1845), the court decided that the will of Mary Bissell validly established a trust for the relocation of her slaves to Liberia, authorizing the ACS to receive both the funds and the emigrating freedpeople. The court asserted that state law was designed to limit the number of free blacks residing in the state, not to prohibit manumission entirely. The ruling went further to offer a commentary on the desirability of removing free blacks from the state. "It was, indeed, early found in this State . . . that the third class of free negroes was burdensome as a charge on the community," the ruling declared, "and, from its general characteristics of idleness and dishonesty, a common nuisance."[33]

In *Hogg v. Capehart* (1857), involving the estate of James Bryan, the court upheld the practice of hiring out emancipated slaves until their accumulated earnings were sufficient to defray the expense of their removal to Liberia. Significantly, this ruling also established that "liberty cannot be forced upon any of the slaves who are of age to choose for themselves." Emancipated children younger than fourteen were obliged to emigrate with their parents. Those minors whose guardians did not choose to embark for Liberia were to be given the option of emigrating upon reaching the age of majority. In a case indicative of the extent to which relatives would go to claim the emancipated bondpeople of a deceased master, the family of Wiley Nelson of New Bern filed suit charging, among other things, that the testator could not leave his slaves to what he termed the "collisination society." Insofar as no such organization existed, they claimed that the will was invalid. Discounting the legal significance of Nelson's poor spelling and allegations regarding his mental incompetence, the court ruled that the scrutable intent of his will called for the bequeathment of his thirty-three slaves to the American Colonization Society for the purpose of removal. As a legally executable provision of his will, the justices upheld what they believed to be Nelson's original intent, allowing his freed slaves to sail for Grand Cape Mount, Liberia, in May 1858.[34]

As a general policy, the ACS avoided formally becoming a party to legal cases such as the Nelson suit, fearing the potential costs of protracted litigation. The organization's leaders were probably also mindful that some might interpret their involvement as promoting abolitionism at the expense of the financial well-being of slaveholders' families. Despite this reluctance to become embroiled in judicial matters, such cases, including the Nelson proceedings, had the potential of transferring thousands of dollars to the ACS from testators' estates, not to mention a steady stream of emigrants for shipment to Liberia. Principally for these reasons, the organization, if not a formal party to a given case, participated as a discreet partner in several probate proceedings that promised to deliver both freed bondpeople and funds into its custody. Actually, of the $16,280.13 collected in North Carolina by the ACS and its agents between 1850 and 1860, almost 80 percent ($12,883.64) of this amount was derived from wills. Viewed in broader perspective, money bequeathed to the organization in wills comprised over half of the $23,439.53 that it collected in the state from 1825—when the *Hunter* took the first North Carolini-ans to Liberia—to 1860. Of all such collections, the single largest amount came from the estate of James Iver McKay, whose will also exceeded all oth-ers in the number of North Carolina slaves it sought to transfer to the ACS.[35]

In addition to being a wealthy slaveholder, James McKay was a well-known political personality in the state during the antebellum period. Born in Bladen County and thus a contemporary of Louis Sheridan, he periodically served in the state Senate between 1815 and 1830 and barely lost the gubernatorial election, decided by the General Assembly, of the latter year. From 1831 to 1849, McKay served in the U.S. Congress as the representative of the Wilmington district, retiring from politics two years after the death of his wife, Ann, in 1847. As a politician, John Quincy Adams found McKay to be "smooth as oil in outward form, and fetid as a polecat in inward savor." In appearance, the for-mer president described the congressman in 1841 as "a plain, mean-looking man, with a blacksmith air, and as careless of dress as myself." Days before his retirement, McKay angrily walked out of a meeting with President James K. Polk, who felt compelled to comment on the episode in his diary. "I knew he was a man of peculiar temperament and manner," the chief executive wrote, which was probably a reasonable assessment of the North Carolinian. When McKay died in Goldsboro in September 1853, his will, written twenty years earlier, disclosed that he had left his estate, Belfont, to Bladen County for use as a farm and orphanage. The document also revealed that he had instructed his executors to turn over to "the direction and patronage of the Colonization Society" thirty to forty of his slaves, a rather eccentric request for that day.[36]

Upon McKay's death, the provision of his will mandating the removal of slaves to Liberia was legally challenged by the politician's legatees. Several questions were raised regarding how McKay's will was to be interpreted. The main point of contention, however, was whether the will applied to the over one hundred slaves whom McKay owned at the time of his death or just the thirty to forty bondpeople he possessed when the document was composed in 1833. Specifically, the legatees argued that the sixty to seventy-five children born to slaves of McKay after the will was drafted were not covered by the emancipation and removal provision. Therefore, this younger generation of bondpeople, in the plaintiffs' view, was ineligible for migration to Africa, as they were still property of the estate and legally subject to division among the congressman's heirs.

To counter this construction of the will's meaning, ACS secretary William McLain hired C. G. Wright, a Fayetteville attorney, to argue for a liberal in-terpretation of the document. McLain hoped that the state Supreme Court could be convinced to render a verdict that would allow all of the slaves in McKay's possession at his death to migrate to Liberia. Initially, Wright expressed skepticism regarding whether the justices would rule in favor of the ACS. It was only after he had conducted further research into recent precedents that he felt confident enough to inform McLain that the "increase" of McKay slaves would likely be freed, the children taking the status of their emancipated mothers. Meanwhile, as the two litigating parties vied for advantage in the case, the McKay bondpeople were hired out in early 1855 for twenty thousand dollars. This arrangement obligated them to labor in slavery for at least one more year before any plan for their emigration could be effected.[37]

In February 1856, the state Supreme Court ruled in favor of the ACS, declaring that all of McKay's slaves were eligible for manumission and removal as provided by the original 1833 will. This was, of course, a welcome victory for McLain, though his jubilance was dampened by news that the McKay clan had once again been hired out and would not be able to emigrate until February of the following year. After the elapse of this hiring period, William Starr, the Norfolk agent, was dispatched to Bladen County to make arrangements with James Robeson, the administrator of the McKay estate. During his visit, Starr met a few of the newly freed bondpeople and discovered that they were not enthused about the prospect of going to Africa. "They have been shrewdly tampered with by somebody," the agent complained to McLain, "to prejudice them against Liberia." Notwithstanding this alleged tampering, Starr assured the ACS secretary that the whole group would likely assent to emigrating. His positive assessment of the willingness of the McKays to quit North Carolina was based substantially on his awareness that "they have no choice in the matter." Most if not all of the clan also recognized their lack of options, even though one of the liberated slaves reportedly told the agent that he wanted to emigrate because "Master knew it was for our good to go *there*." After the ACS's attorney visited the McKays in April, he informed McLain that "the largest majority are anxious to be transported." Nonetheless, two or three girls made their disinclination to emigrate known, despite the fact that their freedom was incumbent upon their exile to Africa.[38]

In demographic terms, the McKays were very similar to the Capehart family that had departed for Liberia seven years earlier. Of the 106 members of the clan who eventually emigrated, the gender of 104 individuals is known, revealing that at least 58 percent (60) of the liberated slaves were male. The McKays were a youthful group, but their average age of 22.8 years was statistically close to the mean age of all North Carolina slaves, which was 21.35 years in 1850. Sixty-four percent (68) of the freed bondpeople were younger than 24 years of age and thus represented the "increase" that had been born after 1833, when James McKay drafted his will. The oldest of the group was Jack McKay; at 90, he had been alive since the colonial period. The youngest was 3-month-old Liberia McKay, upon whose symbolic first name the family perhaps placed much hope.

Like the Capeharts, none of the McKays are listed in the ACS emigrant rolls as literate. However, this depiction of the educational attainments of the family was inaccurate, for at least a few of the McKays would write several letters to ACS officials once the group migrated to Africa. In contrast to many other emigrant parties, no member of the clan is listed as proficient in any trade or task. For a group of this size, it is very unlikely that none of the 106 McKays had any training as blacksmiths, carpenters, weavers, or farmers. Even in overwhelmingly rural Bladen County, an estate as large as James McKay's would have either required some skilled labor or provided opportunities for ambitious and talented slaves to learn various trades. The absence of recorded occupational and literacy data for the McKays was almost certainly due to an oversight on the part of the compiler of the emigrant roll, who may have largely relied upon the limited information provided by the administrator of the estate. Whatever the case, the McKays were a seemingly unremarkable group in relation to other emigrant parties. Still, their sheer number, along with qualities that could not be quantified in emigrant listings, promised to facilitate their adjustment to life in Liberia as a communal unit.[39]

Accompanied by Robeson, the estate administrator, the McKays left Bladen County on the steamer *Magnolia*, reaching Wilmington by way of the Cape Fear River on May 21, 1857. From there, the party was conveyed by railroad to Norfolk where they met McLain two days later. Robeson paid the ACS secretary an initial $4,025 toward defraying the expense of outfitting the McKays —who needed clothing and shoes, among other items—and transporting them to Liberia. The ship aboard which they were to travel, the *Mary Caroline Stevens*, arrived from Baltimore shortly afterward. A roomy 713-ton vessel, the *Stevens* had recently been built for the express purpose of conveying people to the African republic. While the McKays comprised the majority of the passengers, they were accompanied by emigrants from Kentucky, Virginia, and Tennessee, as well as cargo consisting of construction materials, a sugar mill, and "a universal assortment & variety of freight." The expedition set sail on May 28, beginning a journey that would end off the coast of Grand Cape Mount, Liberia, thirty-two days later.[40]

If this voyage of the *Stevens* was similar to other, better-documented emigrant expeditions of the late 1850s, then a number of tentative observations can be made regarding the McKays' transatlantic journey. On a typical day aboard ship, passengers were divided into "messes" at meal time, each with a head who was responsible for distributing both breakfast and dinner rations to their charges. Among the literate, some schooling of children took place during the day, as others engaged in sewing, gossiping, and deck-pacing.

After dinner, scenes of merriment were common, and dances, hymn singing, and "fun and frolic" often lasted well beyond sunset. Many emigrants retired to their quarters at nine o'clock, with bedtime coming earlier each week as the ship moved eastward toward Liberia. On temperate evenings, a few of the passengers remained on deck, even after most others disappeared below. Sometimes lovers, amidst moonlight and shadows, shared secret whispers in the night air, losing themselves in each other and the sensuality of the nocturnal Atlantic.

On a day with a good wind, the *Stevens* was capable of sailing over three hundred miles. But even at this speed, the ship could not outrace the effects of its own movement upon its passengers or the dreaded fear of the spread of contagious disease among them. Seasickness afflicted nearly every emigrant expedition, with the McKay party almost certainly being no exception. Describing the first voyage of the *Stevens* in December 1856 which carried thirteen North Carolinians to Liberia, one white traveler chronicled how ghastly the effects of motion sickness could be. "Some dropped on deck, some slid below, some groaned, some tried to brave it out with a laugh," he observed. "But all joined in a general regurgitation" that made it "almost impossible to keep the between decks in a tolerable condition." Despite its ubiquity among emigrant parties, seasickness was rarely fatal, and most individuals overcame their reactions to the nauseating sway of the ship within days. However, outbreaks of other ailments were quite serious matters, as the passengers of the *Elvira Owen* discovered. Sailing from Hampton Roads in June 1856, the company of this vessel, including forty North Carolinians, was afflicted by measles, diarrhea (perhaps dysentery), and other illnesses that ultimately claimed twenty-one lives during an unusually long passage of fifty days. Undoubtedly, many of the three hundred survivors arrived in Monrovia in a weakened state, poorly prepared to face the malarial hazards of the rainy season. Fortunately for the McKays, none of their number perished aboard the *Stevens*, all 106 arriving at the new settlement of Robertsport, Grand Cape Mount, on July 3, 1857. In a real sense, life began anew for them as they stepped onto African soil, the only place they had ever known freedom.[41]

Shortly after the McKays departed for Africa, the North Carolina legislature attempted to launch another assault on African Americans, especially those only marginally free. A number of recent national developments had aroused this new antiblack offensive, although local animosity toward African Americans always figured into these attacks. In 1857, the U.S. Supreme Court fortified the Fugitive Slave Law of 1850 with its decision in the *Dred Scott* case, which both deprived blacks of citizenship and prohibited Congress from regulating slavery in the territories. If this decision positively encouraged North Carolina lawmakers to more firmly fasten the chains of bondage upon the enslaved population, two other events frightened state politicians into more extreme actions. The aborted 1859 raid of John Brown and his abolitionist crusaders on the federal arsenal at Harpers Ferry, Virginia, served as a stark reminder of how bitter the sectional crisis over slavery had become. Additionally, the presidential campaign of Republican candidate Abraham Lincoln, a moderate Free-Soiler, promised to both reverse *Dred Scott* and greatly restrict the western migration of slavery.

In response to these and other developments, the North Carolina legislature, during its 1858–59 session, contemplated a bill that made it unlawful for free blacks to enter the state. The proposed measure also included a section that required free African Americans already residing in the state to depart within two years, lest they be apprehended and sold into slavery as of January 1, 1860. Despite its popularity among some white North Carolinians, the expulsion bill failed to pass the General Assembly. Nonetheless, a bill prohibiting posthumous manumissions "by will, deed, or any other writing, which is not to take effect in the life-time of the owner" did become law in 1860, banning the kind of emancipation provisions that had freed the Capeharts, McKays, and others. The willingness of the North Carolina legislature to make manumission nearly impossible reflected both the national and local conditions that were shaping its political ethos as well as the demographic configuration of the body itself. As of 1860, 85 percent of the General Assembly was composed of slaveholders—a higher percentage than any other state legislature—and over a third of these lawmakers owned at least 20 bondpeople. Ultimately, this overrepresentation of slaveholders in North Carolina government, among other factors, guaranteed that black bondage would not be legislated out of existence in the Tar Heel State. Indeed, on May 20, 1861, North Carolina political leaders decided to cast their lot with the secessionist Confederate States of America, hoping to place slavery beyond federal reproach once and for all.[42]

WHATEVER PROMISE Liberian emigration offered as a solution to slavery and the resultant sectional divide dissipated with the beginning of the American Civil War. The conflict turned the attention of the public away from most matters that were not tied directly to the war's progress and outcome, and economic crises in the South and elsewhere constrained the ability of the average person to contribute to organizations such as the ACS. Moreover, communication networks between sections—even within individual states —were disrupted by irregular mail delivery, hampering the ability of agents to coordinate emigrant expeditions. Further, an effective Union blockade of Confederate ports, including Norfolk and Wilmington, greatly reduced southern access to maritime commerce and travel. Perhaps more important than these circumstances, most free blacks, if they were not actively supporting the Union war effort, took a wait-and-see attitude toward the conflict. Never very fond of the colonizationist agenda, most were in no rush to leave the country before the conclusion of the war. Slaves had even fewer options, for their masters, not to mention the Confederate government, were in no mood to make provisions for their freedom, even in Liberia, during a war being fought to ensure their perpetual servitude. All together, these conditions forced the ACS into an unprecedented dormancy. During the four years of war, only one southerner immigrated to Liberia under the organization's auspices, and fewer individuals embarked for the country during this period than during any comparable span of years since the sailing of the *Elizabeth* in 1820.

Interestingly, there were those who were slow to concede that the Civil War had derailed the colonization movement. Abraham Lincoln, the newly elected president, continued to have dreams of a black exodus from the United States well after the opening hostilities at Fort Sumter. Inspired by both his Free-Soil vision and a conciliatory attitude toward the South, he offered, as part of his Preliminary Emancipation Proclamation of September 1862, financial assistance to states that desired to end slavery and colonize their black populations "with their consent upon this continent or elsewhere." Ironically, this unparalleled commitment of the federal government to colonization, supported by a congressional appropriation of six hundred thousand dollars, seemed to spawn the wildest schemes. For example, Lincoln flirted with sending blacks to remote areas of Texas, Florida, and Central America. An ill-fated expedition to Île a'Vache, off the Haitian coast, ended in a disaster that required the U.S. navy to retrieve survivors. During this flurry of colonization activity, the only worthwhile objective that the president achieved was the recognition of Liberian and Haitian independence and the establishment of diplomatic relations with the two countries. By 1863, Lincoln, a consummate politician, found it expedient to tone down his advocacy of colonization as a Union victory seemed more imminent and general emancipation increasingly imaginable. Although he hoped for a military and political victory that would ease the South back into the republic as quickly and amicably as possible, he ultimately repudiated the idea that the liberation of blacks required their subsequent removal.[43]

Unlike Lincoln, whose brief wartime dalliance with colonization had been wholly disappointing, the ACS entered the 1860s after having experienced its most active decade of Liberian emigration ever. Of the 9,807 people the organization transported to Africa between 1820 and 1860, 45 percent (4,455) emigrated during the decade preceding the Civil War. Most of those departing for Liberia before 1861 were freed slaves, liberated for the express purpose of their removal to Africa, and the 1850s was a decade that witnessed a significant increase in such deportationist manumissions. While most of the 1,363 North Carolinians who emigrated between 1820 and 1860 (and whose prior status is known) were free, 53 percent (323) of those embarking for Liberia during the 1850s were newly liberated slaves, reflecting a significant shift in the pattern and meaning of the emigration movement. Measured solely in figures, the number of people relocating to Liberia at midcentury seemed to imply a growing ability of the ACS to convince masters to free their slaves for removal. Even though the number of bondpeople emigrating during the 1850s represented a mere one-tenth of a percent of the number of African Americans enumerated in the 1860 census, colonizationists could rightly argue that they had freed more blacks from slavery during that decade than had a generation of immediatist abolitionism. The 1850s was certainly a pivotal decade for the ACS; actually, the period was the golden age of the organization. But the demographic dimensions of this burgeoning emigration movement and events in Liberia itself would have a dramatic impact on the republic's uncertain future.

As noted earlier, emigrant rolls and census records were not always accurate in chronicling the characteristics of migrating parties. Nonetheless, as an approximate set of descriptors of emigrants, the data in these records do delineate important features and patterns among various expeditions. Accordingly, of the 323 ex-slaves who departed North Carolina for Liberia during the 1850s, only 4 percent (13) are listed in emigrant rolls as being capable of reading. Only one liberated person was recorded as knowing how to spell, and supposedly none, with the known exceptions of a few McKays, could write. Among the 278 free people who emigrated from the state, 13 percent (36) could read, and 7 of these individuals could read and write. Additionally, free African Americans from North Carolina were almost four times more likely to have skilled occupations outside of farming (such as blacksmithing, carpentry, bricklaying, milling, and plastering) than their liberated counterparts, who were seven times more likely to be cultivators. As had been the case in North Carolina for many, literate free blacks with proficiency in some trade were better prepared to take advantage of limited opportunities in Liberia than illiterate, ex-slave field hands. Most of the republic's principal figures in politics, commerce, and religious life were both free born (or free long before migrating) and had at least a rudimentary education. Among North Carolina emigrants and Liberians in general, Louis Sheridans were rare, but his literate, entrepreneurial background was typical of the thin strata of people who fared relatively well in the African country.

The higher percentage of illiterate, unskilled, and penurious ex-slaves who

TABLE 1. Counties of Origin and Prior Status of North Carolina Emigrants, 1825–1860

County of Origin	Previously Free Emigrants	Liberated Emigrants	Unknown Prior Status	Total Emigrants from County
Bertie	17	0	0	17
Bladen	0	122	0	122
Cabarrus	5	1	0	6
Camden	15	1	0	16
Chowan	8	0	0	8
Craven	58	38	0	96
Cumberland	66	4	2	72
Guilford	0	7	0	7
Halifax	8	39	3	50
Hertford	0	72	1	73
Iredell	10	0	0	10
Mecklenburg	0	10	0	10
New Hanover	45	1	0	46
Northampton	13	73	33	119
Orange	13	4	0	17
Pasquotank	198	3	46	247
Perquimans	26	26	4	56
Stokes	0	25	0	25
Wake	62	18	0	80
Wayne	0	0	47	47
Other	120	31	88	239
Total	664	475	224	1,363

Source: Based on emigrant rolls, census records, and other sources.

arrived in Liberia from North Carolina and other states during the 1850s exacerbated the poverty already prevalent in the country, which could no longer rely upon the shallow coffers of the ACS as it had during the colonial period. Compounded by an explosion in the recaptive population during the late 1850s and 1860s that caused much social dislocation, economic misery, and political turmoil, the golden age of the ACS turned out to be Liberia's era of despair. Thus, while the organization was transporting to Africa those with perhaps the greatest thirst for freedom, it was also landing on the republic's shores people most lacking the resources to fully take advantage of their newly found liberty. Letters by immigrants themselves tell the story most poignantly. Writing to William McLain in July 1858 from Robertsport, the McKays informed him that "we hav arived [here] a year and can not support our selves." Sadly, they stated that "their is many of the McKay family are suffered to death," unable to eke out a living from their rocky plots on Grand Cape Mount. Having already endured the loss of eight of their number, the survivors could only sorrowfully conclude that "Liberia is a dark dark place," a realization that had now haunted two generations of North Carolina immigrants.[44]

Rather than lament how poorly equipped or unprepared many emigrants were for life in Liberia, ACS officials bemoaned the wartime lull in their enterprise. Elected in 1855, the new ACS president, John H. B. Latrobe of Maryland, understood many of the reasons for the hiatus in his organization's activities. At the 1864 annual meeting, he cited as the chief causes of the group's seeming irrelevance the "hesitation of the free negro to emigrate at this time" and the manner in which the war "has entirely cut us off from our usual supply of slaves, emancipated by southern masters." Latrobe was, of course, stating the obvious, but his subsequent contention that emancipation would not abate white hostility toward blacks presaged the postwar order. "The mere increase of the number of the free negroes . . . will not operate to remove or lessen the obstacles which now effectively exclude them from social equality with the whites," he assured his audience. For this reason, he was convinced that the ACS, though deprived of emigrants and dominated by northerners, would live on, since African Americans would eventually have "no alternative to extirpation but emigration." Echoing Latrobe's predictions, the *African Repository* rhapsodized in its August edition, "When races contend no longer with races for domination, and the world is no longer the theatre of human ambition, then will Colonization end, and not till then." Slavery was dying, but the mission of the ACS would fall away "when the world ends, not before." These were lofty words, indeed, for 1864, a year in which the organization sent only twenty-three people to Liberia, the fewest ever.[45]

SEVEN. TO LIVE AND DIE IN LIBERIA

ON THE CAROLINA COAST, morning unfurls from the Atlantic horizon. One faces the surging tides eastward to witness the dawn light up American skies. Standing atop Grand Cape Mount in Liberia, it is over land that daylight first moves, arching westward until the evening sun dissolves in fading brilliance over the shimmering ocean. As one of the continent's great natural wonders, the main promontory of the cape rises like an immense pyramid into the clouds, its apex some one thousand feet above sea level. At its base, foamy surf glides over tan beaches, which give way to the ascending supergrowth of mangrove forests. The lands of the three-mile-long cape are largely rocky, though interspersed with red clay, loam, and rivulets. Similar to Mesurado approximately fifty miles southeast, the soils and creeks of the cape are much less striking, or visible, to an approaching ship than the dense swamps that wind uninterrupted up hills and along the waterfront. It is this teeming, tangled luxuriance that commands the attention of observers more than anything else, even when the sultry haze of the dry season or the pale mist of morning dulls its evergreen splendor.[1]

Since perhaps the late fifteenth century, Grand Cape Mount had been inhabited by the Vai, a Mande-speaking people from modern-day Guinea. Their initial migration to the coast was probably motivated by the desire to participate in the salt trade, salt being an essential commodity in the tropics. In common with other ethnic groups of the region, the Vai eventually came under the

Above: Robertsport, Liberia (From Johnston, *Liberia*, vol. 1)

hegemony of the Mandingo, who had successfully projected their political power and economic prowess westward from their inland capital of Bopolu. Mandingo traders subsequently spawned significant trade networks over the cape, which opened markets for their kola nuts, ivory, cloth, and slaves. While most of the Vai continued to embrace indigenous religious systems well into the nineteenth century, a minority of them, especially those with commercial ties to Mandingo Muslims, converted to Islam, thus advancing the economic and cultural integration of the region's peoples. As in other areas of the Grain Coast, the suzerainty of Bopolu over the Vai was unevenly felt over the breadth of the cape and, over the course of generations swelled and receded. As a testament to their ingenuity and independence, the Vai had invented their own alphabet by the time the first African American colonists settled along the coast, an achievement that one Liberian president cited as proof of their intellectual superiority over many of his immigrant countrymen. Further, as evidence of their economic opportunism, the Vai created profitable trade relations with European newcomers by the late seventeenth century, exchanging gold, camwood, rice, fruit, and fish for cloth, kettles, beads, and guns. Ultimately, the increasing demand for slave labor in the Americas would transform Vai-European commerce, making Grand Cape Mount an important exporter of bonded Africans.[2]

By the mid-nineteenth century, the cape was engulfed in violence as Vai and Gola warlords, among others, struggled for advantage in the slave trade and other matters. Contiguous to the infamous slave market at Gallinas to the north, the region was incessantly brutalized by raids, kidnappings, counterattacks, and refugee migrations. Fueling the hostilities, slave ships bound for the Americas sometimes set sail with their cargoes within sight of British naval patrols ostensibly committed to ending the traffic. During a guerrilla war in the region in 1855, a report in the *African Repository* exasperatingly asserted that "only supernatural agency; the influence of the gospel" could end the bloodshed and chaos, for no other means had proven effective. Ironically, Methodist missionaries had abandoned this idea a decade earlier, conceding that their proselytizing activities at the cape had been "an entire and hopeless failure" which had necessitated their withdrawal from the area. After "purchasing" the territory in 1849, the Liberian government negotiated a temporary halt to the fighting, hoping to establish immigrant settlements along the coast. Unfortunately for Monrovia, the involvement of a few "renegade Colonists" in slave trading with local rulers did nothing toward strengthening its credibility as a peace broker.[3]

Unable to wholly resolve the political and social turmoil at Grand Cape Mount, the Liberian government decided in 1855 to proceed with plans for establishing a new town in the area. Named Robertsport in honor of the republic's first president, the proposed settlement on the stony soils of the cape was surveyed into lots, and a two-story receptacle for newly arrived immigrants was erected at an expense of sixty-five hundred dollars. It was in this building that the McKay clan of Bladen County spent its first months in Africa, enduring the debilitating effects of malaria as torrents of rain drenched the landscape. Although the ACS provided them with free food, medical attention, and shelter for six months, the family's first years in Africa were distressing.

Many of the letters written by the McKays disclose their unpreparedness for the deprivation they would experience in Liberia as well as a steady attrition of their number. Additionally, their missives to William McLain usually included requests for a range of goods, along with pleas for money that the estate of James McKay had earmarked for their benefit. Typical of these entreaties, Hugh McKay, writing to the ACS secretary in August 1857, asked that two hogsheads of tobacco, "1 keg of Powder 1 Bag of Buck shot 1 Box of Cloth for Pantaloons and . . . umbrellas" be sent to him. Edward McKay solicited McLain for "1 Box Red Flannell cloth, 1 Gun, 1 Box of Mens shoes No 8 . . . 9 . . . 10 . . . 1 Plough of Coulters make," and other items, along with whatever remained of the money bequeathed to him by his former master "in gold or silver." Washington McKay asked for similar things in September, but he, like the others, was obliged to wait until the summer of 1858 before McLain could inform them that he had received additional funds from the estate of their former owner.[4]

As the ACS secretary arranged to send the residue of the McKay estate to Liberia, the situation at Robertsport became more desperate. Writing in July 1858, one McKay complained to McLain, "they give us lots upon rocks and i can not get the hoe to the ground for rocks." This individual also reported that at least one woman with several children was allotted only a quarter of an acre of land to subsist upon. Moreover, corn would not grow well at the cape, and other foodstuffs, such as flour and butter, were too expensive to buy. "Mr. Mc Clain our true friend," the writer pleaded, "pleas send us Provision that will give us a start." A note sent by John McKay and others reiterated that the family had come to Liberia "quite un Prepared for a . . . Country Like this." In response to these letters, McLain sent $1,280.20 that he had collected from the McKay estate in October 1859. Although this payment only partially relieved the ex-slaves' plight, Nip McKay informed the ACS secretary in February 1861 that "we all geting on tolible well at the present," suggesting that the clan was adjusting to at least some of the hardships of life in Robertsport. By 1864, two of the immigrants, Samuel and July McKay, would even serve as justice of the peace and constable, respectively, for the town. Nonetheless, Nip alerted McLain that only 96 of the original 106 members of the family were still alive as of 1861, many of the deceased likely victims of malaria.[5]

If there were any success stories among the McKays, the experience of Diana McKay Sheridan perhaps came closest to demonstrating how a few did prosper moderately in Robertsport. Diana was fifty years old when the *Stevens* landed her at Grand Cape Mount in July 1857. Arriving with six children, four of whom were between fifteen and twenty-two years of age, she already had a plan for herself and her dependents. She declined a town lot in Robertsport, aware that her future was an agrarian one. Instead, she and her children, after recuperating from malaria in the receptacle, proceeded to clear land in the countryside, slashing and burning trees until they had created an open field. Despite the fact that she found her four-acre lot to be a mixture of clay and sand, Diana and her children planted a variety of crops, including cassava, sweet potatoes, beans, plantain, and American corn. Concurrently, the family built a two-room log cabin on land overlooking the Atlantic and promptly moved into it once their six months of free subsistence expired at the receptacle. With an eye to the future, Diana reserved a barrel of corn for the next planting season and grew enough other crops to be in a position to offer McLain samples of the cotton, peppers, and ginger she had grown herself. While she occasionally wrote the ACS secretary for items such as hoes, axes, garden seed, and coffee, she self-consciously attempted to illustrate her ability to live on her own resources in Liberia, hoping "to give to my children habits of industry."

Diana was a rarity among the McKays and, indeed, Liberian immigrants in general. An ex-slave, single mother of six, and yeoman farmer, she had carved out a life for herself and her family where nothing had existed but dense forest and poor soil. However, like so many others, part of her identity was still in America, and her life as a free woman in Robertsport remained tied to the site of her former bondage. Her husband, Alfred Miller, was unable to accompany her to Africa, for his apparent enslavement in Wilmington precluded him from emigrating with his family. Like Marshall Hooper, she attempted to maintain a relationship with her spouse, though thousands of miles of ocean separated them. In a March 1859 letter, she asked McLain to write Miller to inform him "that his children have grown up finely," including their fifteen-year-old son, Dallas, who was "doing pretty well" in school. She longed to hear from her husband and hoped "to know how he is getting on & [to] tell him we are all living comfortably & doing pretty well." What happened to this marriage is unknown; Diana's subsequent letters to McLain make no further references to Miller. Whatever the case, Diana McKay Sheridan persevered in Liberia and seemed to adapt well to her role as head of her household. In an 1860 letter to the ACS secretary, she reminded him that "I

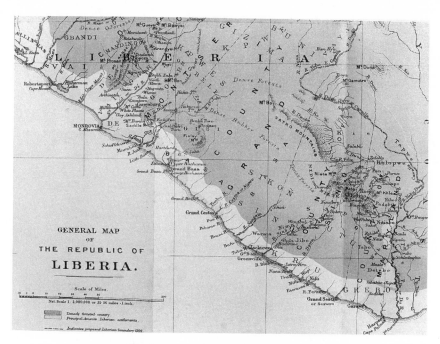

MAP 3. Liberia, ca. 1906 (From Johnston, *Liberia*, vol. 1)

write for myself and 5 children," alluding to both the weight of her parental responsibilities and her formidable strength of character.[6]

Fortunately, the extant letters of the McKays allow for at least a sketchy reconstruction of their saga at Robertsport. From Diana's longing for her husband to Edward's bid for the "gold or silver" of his former master, this correspondence offers glimpses into the quality of life, expectations, and possibilities of North Carolina immigrants in midcentury Liberia. The literacy of a few of the McKays provided them with a historical voice, no matter how limited, and likely opened up opportunities for a select number of them that would have been largely unavailable to illiterates. Relative to other immigrants from their home state, the lettered McKays were the exceptions to the rule when compared to both the previously free and the recently liberated. Illustratively, less then 10 percent (59) of the 602 people who arrived in Liberia from North Carolina between 1850 and 1860 were listed in emigrant roles as literate in any fashion, and only 12 percent (170) of the 1,363 individuals who left the state between 1825 and 1860 were lettered. Additionally, at least 87 percent (148) of these literate individuals migrating during the antebellum period were free before relocating to Liberia, and a little over half (89) were male. As mentioned earlier, the prevalence of literacy among North Carolina emigrants was underestimated in emigrant rolls, which failed to record the read-

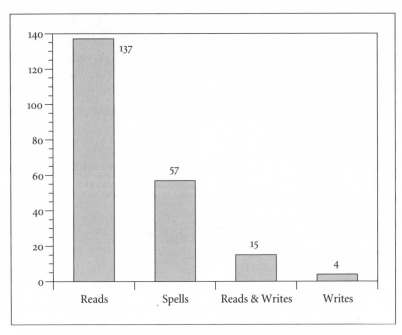

FIGURE 1. Literacy Attainments among 2,030 North Carolina Emigrants, 1825–1893
Sources: Based on emigrant rolls, census records, and other sources.

ing, writing, and spelling abilities of the McKays and others. Nonetheless, as an approximation of the educational attainments of migrating North Carolinians, these records were probably reliable overall. Consequently, when Diana McKay Sheridan brought to McLain's attention that "I write for myself and 5 children," she was probably aware that this was no small matter.[7]

While the experiences of the McKays at Robertsport are better documented than those of most other North Carolina settlers, an influx of people from the Tar Heel State also shaped the coastal communities of Bassa Cove, located southeast of Monrovia. Bexley, six miles from the mouth of the St. John's River, had been established by Louis Sheridan and his party in 1837. Divided into an upper and lower district, the town stretched four miles along the river's high banks and was home to 135 residents by 1843. A Methodist and a Baptist church operated in the area, along with day and Sabbath schools. At one time, Bexley farmers produced significant quantities of coffee, ginger, sweet potatoes, arrowroot, and cassava. Even cattle, always scarce in Liberia, were known to have grazed local lands, and some fowl, sheep, and goats were kept. In spite of these hopeful signs, Bexley was destined to be a minor settlement in a backwater region.

Following a tour of the area in the mid-1840s, then governor Joseph J. Roberts was shocked by the "shamefully neglected" farms he saw. He was particularly dismayed to learn that a number of immigrants had abandoned agricultural pursuits altogether, preferring "an itinerant traffic with the natives in this country." Undoubtedly, a desire to "grow rich more speedily" through trade was partially responsible for the neglected fields that Roberts encountered during his tour. Yet perhaps more important, Bexley, like other Liberian towns, was in desperate need of labor, and neighboring African communities were apparently not anxious to satisfy demand. "We are in want of Men of the right [stuff]," George Seymour, a North Carolina immigrant, notified an ACS official in 1854, "as our men are thinned by removal & death." Despite this plea, few immigrants arrived in the town after 1845, and only twelve North Carolinians disembarked there after the Sheridan company.[8]

As immigration to Bexley tapered off and its farms succumbed to weeds, the new town of Buchanan, situated between the St. John's and Benson Rivers, experienced a notable degree of growth at midcentury. Between 1851 and 1854, ninety-six North Carolinians, largely from Pasquotank, Wake, and Bladen Counties, arrived in the settlement. Two-thirds of these newcomers were free born, 54 percent were male, and the average age of the group was twenty-one. According to emigrant rolls, the vast majority of these individuals were ostensibly illiterate and unskilled, although among them were three farmers, two blacksmiths, two bricklayers, a carpenter, a printer, a cook, and a washerwoman. Buchanan, like Bexley, was divided into upper and lower districts. The soils of the area were unremarkable, mainly sand, and the streets were overgrown with vegetation. While there were no oxen in the settlement as of the late 1850s, a small number of cattle, sheep, hogs, and goats were kept. The two mules in the town were reserved for transportation purposes only, apparently viewed as too precious to pull a plow. By this time, Buchanan had become an important port in the coastal trade, with $71,623 in camwood, palm oil, ivory, and coffee passing through it in 1854 alone.

Notwithstanding its rather lively commercial life, most of the 350 people residing in Upper Buchanan in 1858 lived simple lives. They drank water from wells, lived in unadorned houses, and sent their children to the three local schools. Occasionally, excitement stirred the community, such as when a tornado swept away the emigrant receptacle in the fall of 1855. Furthermore, as with all Liberian settlements, fighting between townspeople and local Africans could break out at anytime, and the strategic placement of nine cannon around Buchanan only underscored ongoing tensions. Still, the basic routines of life offered little unpredictability. Only the very real prospect of an early death seemed to interrupt the social and agricultural patterns of the town in decisive ways. Not unlike other new settlements, Buchanan struggled to reverse its negative population growth rate during the 1850s, with little success outside of the replenishing effect of continual immigration. Subsequently, as the village celebrated eighteen births in 1857, it was forced to mourn the passing of thirty-one of its number.[9]

During the 1850s, immigrant mortality at Buchanan actually scandalized both the republic and the ACS, neither of which had made adequate plans for the settlement of newcomers in Grand Bassa County, the official name of the region. Insofar as the ACS and the Liberian government refrained from publishing mortality statistics after the embàrrassing census of 1843, it is impossible to determine the extent of the ravages of malaria and other ailments. However, anecdotal information from a number of sources suggests that the death rate at Buchanan was horrendous during the mid-nineteenth century. For example, one resident estimated that over 60 of the 149 emigrants of the *Morgan Dix* expedition of 1851—which included 13 North Carolinians—perished in Buchanan. "Whole families have died," he informed a confidant in a June 1852 letter. A year later, a group of Monrovians lamented the practice of landing emigrants in insalubrious regions of the country, guessing that as much as 90 percent of some parties had died after arriving in Grand Bassa County. "Why did not the agent cut their throats before they left," they rhetorically stated in a letter to an ACS official. "He would have had less sin to answer for, at the Bar of God And they would have had a far easier death." Some believed that emigrants were coerced into settling in Buchanan by ship owners and merchants who hoped to profit from transporting them to the town. Others, such as George Seymour, simply asked William McLain to halt further expeditions to Buchanan, "for I have been made sick at the thought of the loss of shuch valuable lives."[10]

If the weight of these tragic reports alone were not enough to deter the ACS from sending more immigrants to Buchanan, public exposure in the American press surely made colonizationists in Washington reconsider their operations. During the early 1850s, the *New York Tribune* printed at least two letters by a Liberian immigrant who rebuked the ACS for the disaster at Grand Bassa. Under the pen name A. W., the writer charged the organization with being responsible for "the murderous work" of landing the emigrants of the *Morgan Dix* in a deadly environment where they were confined to "old, rickety, thatched houses," given insufficient food and medical attention, and buried in "old gun-boxes." The author asserted that the expedition suffered a 90 percent mortality rate, perhaps the highest ever endured by an emigrant party. Of the 261 emigrants aboard the *Banshee*—including 4 North Carolinians—who settled along the St. Paul's River in December 1853, A. W. estimated that a third had died within a year, a catastrophe that left local residents "all in controversy about it." The mortality figures cited in these articles are impossible to accurately confirm, though the independent observations of others tend to support the contention that an unusually high immigrant death rate prevailed at Buchanan and along the St. Paul's River at this time.

Unable to wholly suppress news of these calamities, the ACS sporadically printed abbreviated lists of deceased immigrants which, as shown below, illustrated how the very young and the elderly continued to be most at risk regarding fatal bouts of malaria. As printed in the June 1853 edition of the *African Repository*, North Carolinians who sailed aboard the *Joseph Maxwell* and the *Linda Stewart* in November 1852 only to die on the banks of the St. Paul's included:

> *Patsy Boon*, aged 55, from Chapel Hill, N.C., *William Johnson*, aged 34, *Mary Johnson*, aged 26, *William Wright*, aged 65, *Robin Waddel*, aged 90, *Patsy Waddel*, aged 75, *William Young*, aged 8, *Andrew Young*, aged 6, *Thomas Young*, aged 2, *Elbert James*, aged 2, and *Sarah Hagan*, aged 6 months, all from Fayetteville, N.C.

Having thus partially, if inadvertently, confessed its culpability in these costly debacles by printing such obituaries, the ACS abruptly stopped sending expeditions to Grand Bassa County following public disclosure of the upsurge in immigrant deaths. North Carolinians and others were subsequently directed to places such as Robertsport and Careysburg which proved to be less affected by the anopheline plague. This decision spared colonizationists further embarrassment that they could ill afford as the Panic of 1857 rattled their coffers. More important, this change of plan saved the lives of numerous future emigrants, including the industrious Diana McKay Sheridan and many of her relatives who landed at Grand Cape Mount.[11]

Amidst the horrific scenes of suffering and death in Grand Bassa, a few immigrants fared well in the county, at least relatively speaking. In Bexley, Louis Sheridan became a local notable through his mercantile entrepreneurship and agribusiness pursuits. Although he died in 1843, the colonial census of that year discloses that he was one of the most affluent men in Liberia. Among his properties were two wooden houses, 570 acres of land, six sheep and goats, and $2,000 in "stock employed in trade." Of the forty-five acres of land that he actually had under cultivation, ten were devoted to a cassava crop, four produced potatoes and yams, and much of the remaining acreage was planted with six thousand coffee trees. At his death, Sheridan owned three thousand dollars in real estate and personal property, enough to qualify him as one of the "merchant princes" of the colony. Along with these substantial holdings, he served in public office, though he never fully overcame his self-image as "an American Exiled."[12]

George Seymour, who beseeched ACS secretary McLain in 1853 to stop sending emigrants to Buchanan, was personally spared many of the tragedies that he witnessed along the St. John's River and succeeded in making a life for his family of four in Bexley. A literate farmer who migrated to Bassa Cove in 1841, Seymour established a modest twenty-acre farm in Bexley, consisting of cassava, potatoes and yams, and thirty coffee trees. Over the next decade, he pursued public office, first serving as a high sheriff and justice of the peace before being elected in 1853 to represent Grand Bassa County in the Liberian legislature. Aside from politics and farming, Seymour's real passion lay in exploration. Wanderlust, curiosity, and a touch of missionary zeal led him deep into the hinterland of the republic where he conducted a kind of ethnographic survey of the Pessay people during the 1850s. Among this African group, Seymour found "a kind and peaceable race, industrious and ingenious, hospitable to strangers." He was impressed by the fact that the Pessay made their own iron, cotton, pottery, and medicines, and cultivated "farms of many acres." However, he had less praise for their slave trading and polygamous relationships. To Seymour, the Pessay were "savages," a common view of Africans among Liberian immigrants. Even though he found facets of their culture praiseworthy, the explorer was glad to find that members of the group sought to have their children learn English and noted approvingly that the Pessay way of life was "very favorable to the spread of the Gospel." Seymour would become one of the few Liberians to record for posterity his peregrinations among indigenous Africans. And while his writings were influenced by the cultural arrogance and ethnic chauvinism so prevalent among Liberians, they are valuable for both the information they provide about indigenous people and for what they suggest about the nature of immigrant-African relations.[13]

In addition to the new settlements at Grand Cape Mount and Grand Bassa, older Liberian towns along the St. Paul's River continued to exist at midcentury but with declining vitality. Caldwell remained almost as rural as it had been at its founding, though it stretched for a mile and a half along the southern bank of the river into lower and upper districts. Houses were generally one hundred yards to a quarter-mile apart and ranged in variety from two-story brick structures worth over twelve hundred dollars to dilapidated dwellings on unkempt lots that had reverted back to government ownership. Caldwell residents had struggled to claim and reclaim land from the creeping fecundity of local underbrush for a generation with only mixed results. In the late 1850s, the settlement had 303 town lots and 76 farm lots surveyed, the latter producing sugar, coffee, yams, groundnuts, bananas, oranges, and other crops. By this time, cleared lands along the river could sell for forty to fifty dollars an acre, particularly those areas that were said to be as fertile as "the best sugar lands in Brazil." Despite the fact that a number of farmers did well in Caldwell, the town was still very much a small clearing in a vast tropical forest. Compounding both its rurality and isolation, the settlement lacked horses, and no cattle lived in its lower district. Most lands, even in town limits, were uncultivated, and the majority of what was produced never reached markets beyond Monrovia. As always, malaria continued to drain Caldwell at midcentury, though surviving residents had acquired some resistance to the disease over years of exposure. According to a report in the *Liberia Herald* in 1842, the lower district proved to be "the grave of nearly all the residents" settled there, undoubtedly a primary reason for the town's small immigrant population of 306 in 1854.[14]

Upriver from Caldwell on the northern bank, Millsburg remained an unremarkable agricultural settlement at midcentury. Farther from the coast than any other Liberian settlement, this town was also divided into upper and lower sections, though most of its 190 town lots had been abandoned. In 1841, Millsburg farmers cultivated twenty-five acres of cassava, twenty-three acres of potatoes, nine acres of sugar cane, and five acres of rice. One hundred and fifty coffee trees covered the landscape, and numerous hogs, sheep, and fowl were kept. Along the "main street" of the town itself, the staple institutions common to nearly all Liberian settlements—two churches (a Baptist and a Methodist), two schools (a day and a Sabbath), and a militia with a ready supply of cannon and shot—existed by the late 1850s. Particularly noteworthy was the Female Academy that the Methodist Episcopal church had established in the town by this time. Aside from these social structures, Millsburg, largely disconnected from coastal trade, still remained the quintessential boondocks community of Liberia. Seasonal flooding of its lower district guaranteed an agricultural backwardness, as did the poverty of its residents and the endemic presence of *Anopheles* mosquitoes. Similar to many of its sister settlements, Millsburg probably never managed to grow naturally, and in 1841 deaths in the town outnumbered births twenty-two to eleven. One observer who visited Millsburg in the 1880s found only "a graveyard," the last remnants of one of the ACS's most hopeful experiments in colonization.[15]

A principal reason for both the stagnation in Caldwell and the desolation that eventually fell over Millsburg was the lack of immigrants settling in these towns after 1840. As noted earlier, the numbers of African Americans arriving in the country was depressed during many of the years between 1833 and 1847. Moreover, when the emigration movement finally revived in the 1850s, the vast majority of the new arrivals settled in places such as Buchanan, Robertsport, Careysburg, and Monrovia, not Caldwell or Millsburg. Among North Carolina immigrants, 351 people settled in Caldwell between 1825 and 1839, and 115 individuals established residence in Millsburg between 1828 and 1837. One hundred and forty-eight others, mainly from Wake and Cumberland Counties, immigrated to towns along the St. Paul's River in 1853, but this was the last influx of North Carolinians into these older settlements for the

TABLE 2. Gender and Places of Settlement of North Carolina Emigrants, 1825–1893

Place of Settlement	Emigrants Known to Be Female	Emigrants Known to Be Male	Total Emigrants
Arthington and Brewerville	307	300	609
Bassa Cove	6	9	15
Bexley	37	46	84
Buchanan	38	45	83
Caldwell	179	169	351
Cape Palmas	16	19	35
Careysburg	7	17	25
Grand Cape Mount	10	8	18
Greenville	12	6	18
Marshall	1	1	2
Millsburg	55	60	115
Monrovia	207	194	406
New Georgia	5	4	9
Robertsport	44	61	107
St. Paul's River (unspecified town)	58	89	148
Other	2	3	5
Total	984	1,031	2,030

Source: Based on emigrant rolls, census records, and other sources.

rest of the century. Since migration to both Caldwell and Millsburg was concentrated in the two decades following their founding, the first generation of immigrants greatly shaped the life and culture of these towns. As noted in Chapter 4, North Carolinians made up a sizable minority of the population of these settlements, and they subsequently made significant contributions to the values and sense of community within these towns. A few even served in public office, such as Philip Pritchard of Pasquotank County, who was appointed justice of the peace in Caldwell, and Shedrick Kennedy of Wayne County, who occupied the position of town clerk in Millsburg. Yet like the typical American immigrant, most people from North Carolina cultivated farms or worked at trades, thus establishing the slow, agrarian tempo of the region.[16]

If most North Carolinians led undistinguished lives in the riverine settlements, the activities of several affected the towns in ways that were not appreciated by other residents. Of those immigrants from the state who committed crimes between 1828 to 1843, most lived in either Caldwell or Millsburg. The poverty of the area, combined with an underdeveloped law enforcement apparatus, perhaps influenced some to participate in illegal activities, especially property offenses. Whatever the case, a number of notable acts of criminality occurred during the formative years of the settlements, several involving North Carolinians. For example, one of the better known criminals of Caldwell was Diver Fletcher, a liberated slave from Perquimans County who had immigrated to Liberia in 1828. In 1838, the Court of Quarter Sessions convicted him of grand larceny and imposed a sentence of nine months imprisonment. Three years later, Fletcher received a twelve-month sentence for a stabbing. Priscilla Taylor of Camden County was also convicted of grand larceny in 1831, as was forty-five-year-old Essex Peele only two years after his arrival in Caldwell from Northampton County in 1827. In contrast to these cases, the most serious crime committed by a North Carolinian took place in Millsburg. Having arrived in the colony only weeks earlier, Venus Peele was convicted of second-degree murder in May 1828 and sentenced to three years in prison. Of the seven recorded homicides that took place in Liberia between 1828 and 1843, she was both the only woman and the only North Carolinian charged with perpetrating such a crime.

Without question, one of the most notorious lawbreakers to arrive in Liberia during the colonial period was James Parker of Pasquotank County. The twenty-two-year-old married farmer had initially been reluctant to emigrate, having told Quaker colonizationists that he was both in debt and "fearfull of crossing the ocean." Eventually, he decided to depart with the *Doris* expedition, landing in Monrovia in April 1827. After surviving the 23 percent malarial mortality that cut through his party as it settled in Caldwell, Parker retired to the countryside, perhaps having witnessed too much suffering and desirous of the solitude of the backwoods. This self-imposed withdrawal from community life did not last long, however. Over the next several years, the Pasquotank native would accumulate a criminal record that would make him well known among both Caldwell residents and law officers.

In October 1829, Parker was convicted of grand larceny and sentenced to thirty-nine lashes and three months of incarceration. Two years later, he and a man from Northampton County were fined twenty-three dollars for lewdness. In 1832, Parker was again at the whipping post for another count of grand larceny, which also earned him a year-long stint in prison. Unfortunately, neither time behind bars nor strokes from the lash deterred him for long, as he proved when he was again arrested for burglary and robbery in January 1835. For these offenses, he was sentenced to seven years in prison, the longest term of incarceration imposed upon any immigrant during this period. Whether this punishment made any difference regarding his propensity for criminal behavior is hard to tell. At any rate, James Parker's story ended in 1838 when census records listed him as having been shot to death, perhaps by his jailers or during the commission of yet another crime. While such serial criminality was not the norm among immigrants, Parker's lawlessness, and that of others, does suggest that some individuals experienced considerable difficulty adjusting to the civil society that the colonists had fashioned in the African tropics. Although the known details of his Liberian experience are largely limited to his extensive criminal record, Parker's short, infamous life does provide a window into the antisocial alternatives that were available to individuals who were either unwilling or unable to resist certain predatory temptations.[17]

In addition to the Venus Peeles and James Parkers who did nothing for the image of North Carolinians in early Liberia, other immigrants from the state pursued careers that were at least laudable in their intent, if not their impact. Among them were missionaries, such as Frederick James, who serviced congregations along the St. Paul's and farther inland. James had emigrated from Bertie County in 1826 at age eight. His family of nine settled in Caldwell, and he apparently became interested in the ministry some time afterward. In 1847, the Southern Baptist Convention (SBC) appointed him as a missionary "to labor among the destitute churches, in the vacinity of Monrovia," but he also became responsible for evangelizing neighboring indigenous people. In October, he reported to the SBC missionary board that he had visited Millsburg, New Georgia, and Monrovia in search of new converts and to fortify the faithful. In two African towns that he toured, he was less successful in his proselytizing activities, informing the board that his talks had yet to have an "effect upon their hearts." James ultimately settled in New Virginia, across the river from Millsburg, and established separate day schools for immigrant and African children.

Despite his fervent efforts, James was poorly supported by the SBC. His teaching duties, in his estimate, suffered because the board did not hire an assistant instructor. Moreover, his family waited indefinitely in Monrovia for him to establish a residence in New Virginia that would be comfortable enough to house them. In the midst of an increasingly desperate situation, James died rather suddenly in 1848, only a year after his appointment. While the SBC passed a resolution in 1849 to provide forty dollars per year to his family, James's widow, Priscilla, wrote the board in 1851 to remind them that "I have not received the first cent." She continued to correspond with the SBC for several years regarding the matter. In the meanwhile, the Baptist mission in Liberia sputtered for lack of missionaries. Even though it would continue to be the chief denomination among North Carolinians, by the late nineteenth century it would lose much ground to the more vibrant recruitment initiatives of the Methodists.[18]

The first Methodist Episcopal mission was founded in the colony in 1833. From the beginning, the Methodist Conference in the United States relied heavily upon black missionaries to spread the gospel among both settlers and indigenous Africans in the colony. Their employment of African American missionaries was predicated on the prevailing belief among the Methodists and other denominations that blacks were better suited physiologically than whites for work in Liberia. Erroneously, the Conference assumed that both skin color and ancestral origin imparted to black missionaries natural immunities, which would protect them from malaria and other deadly diseases endemic to tropical Africa. Also, as part of a "providential design," the Methodists, and many black missionaries, believed that God had meant for African Americans, tutored in the gospel in the West, to go to Africa and spread Christianity to their supposedly benighted brethren. Actually, black missionaries did tend to live longer in Liberia than their white counterparts. However, this had more to do with their status as permanent immigrants who had been in Liberia long enough to acquire an immune response to malaria, than any biological assumptions based on race. Thus, whereas 74 percent of black Methodist missionaries appointed in Liberia between 1833 and 1875 lived for at least ten years after entering missionary service, 88 percent of white missionaries sent out either withdrew from the field or died within the first nineteen months of service. Thus, the spread of Methodism in the country was largely left up to black emigrants from America.[19]

Of the seventy-three African American immigrants who served as Methodist missionaries, at least four were from North Carolina. Of this number, Samuel F. Williams, who emigrated from New Bern in 1850, served the mission longest, laboring from 1857 to 1861 before withdrawing from the field. Henry Capehart, an ex-slave from Murfreesboro who also emigrated in 1850, worked in the mission for two years (1871–73) before withdrawing. Similarly, William Hagan, a free-born emigrant from Fayetteville, served for roughly a year (1874–75) before abandoning missionary work in Liberia. The brevity of the service of black missionaries from North Carolina suggests that their contribution to the spread of Methodism in Liberia was minimal, especially given that 60 percent of all American-born black Methodist missionaries served at least ten years. While in most instances it is difficult to know exactly what drove North Carolina missionaries from the field, at least one case, that of William P. Kennedy, suggests that mission work required a discipline and sense of commitment that was not easily found among North Carolinians drawn to this profession.[20]

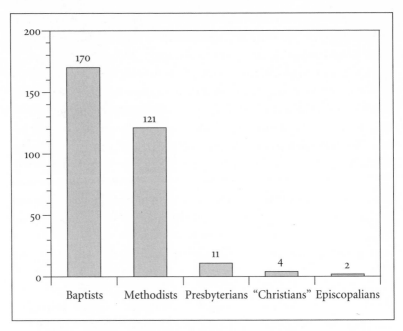

FIGURE 2. Religious Affiliations of North Carolina Emigrants, 1825–1893
Sources: Based on emigrant rolls, census records, and other sources.

Kennedy had emigrated from Wayne County, North Carolina, in 1828 at age eight. He settled, along with his family, in Millsburg and took up carpentry as a trade. Kennedy became a member of the Methodist Conference in 1843, beginning a career in missionary work that same year. In its effort to convert Africans, the church assigned him to the Morrisburgh mission, which was established among the Gola people. However, after only a year, the Conference had determined that the mission was "almost a failure," especially since Kennedy was away from his post "during a greater part of the year." Kennedy remained officially associated with the mission for two more years before his service was "discontinued" in 1846. Of the Methodist missionaries from North Carolina, he served the second longest term, though his work was apparently undistinguished.[21]

Beyond missionary activity, an institutionalized Methodist church emerged in Liberia as early as the 1830s. Available sources do not reveal the number of North Carolina immigrants who were affiliated with the various Christian congregations, but anecdotal evidence suggests that those arriving during the first generation of the colony's existence were as likely to be Methodist as any other creed. In Caldwell, Millsburg, and Monrovia, Methodism was the dominant Christian denomination among American immigrants. According to the 1843 census of the colony, the largest Christian church structure was a sixty-by-forty-foot Methodist meeting house in Monrovia which had a membership of 238 people, including 212 immigrants and 18 converted Africans. Methodist churches in Caldwell and Millsburg had 87 and 68 members, respectively, and other places where North Carolinians had settled, such as Bexley and New Georgia, had Methodist congregations as well.[22]

Along with churches, the Methodists also established schools throughout the colony. Like the Baptists and others, they believed that literacy in English, along with Christianity, was a hallmark of modern Western civilization and thus was instrumental in combating what they viewed as superstition and ignorance among Africans. Eventually, by the time of Liberian independence in 1847, Methodist educational institutions were being founded in most of the settlements. In the following decade, observers reported the existence of a Methodist-run academy in Monrovia and a day school in Millsburg. It is impossible to know the exact impact of these schools on the culture of literacy in Liberia beyond noting that children born in immigrant towns often learned to read and write. Interestingly, among Africans living in and around Liberian settlements, Western education and Christian instruction in general were often viewed in utilitarian ways. At least some indigenous communities accommodated missionaries for the primary purpose of learning English, ostensibly to facilitate trade and diplomacy between themselves and the increasingly immigrant-dominated coastline. Still, overall, Methodism and other Christian denominations made very slow inroads among Africans. The 1843 census found only 353 indigenous Christian converts in Liberia with the great majority of these (293) being Methodists.[23]

Besides the mission work of the Baptists and the Methodists, other denominations vied for influence in Liberia but with even less success. An Episcopal church was founded in the Maryland colony at Cape Palmas in 1849, with segregated ministries and schools for colonists and the neighboring Grebo people. In the 1860s, Reverend Alexander Crummell, a Liberian scholar and statesman, established St. Stephen's Church in Caldwell but attracted largely indigent, widowed women. Of North Carolina immigrants, only Andrew Dickinson of New Bern and his daughter, Julia, were identified in emigrant rolls as Episcopalians. While this church made little headway outside of Cape Palmas, other sects fared even worse. The General Synod of the Evangelical Lutheran Church of the United States announced ambitious plans in June 1855 to train African Americans for mission work in Liberia. Particularly, the church hoped to recruit black orphans and "youthful liberated slaves" to carry the gospel to the African republic. Nothing seems to have come of their vision, which could only have been blurred by the outbreak of the American Civil War six years later.

Curiously, though hundreds of North Carolina immigrants had lived amongst Quakers for years before departing for Liberia, none were listed in census records or emigrant rolls as members of the Society of Friends. Similarly, no individuals with past affiliations with other sects—such as the twenty-five Stokes County immigrants who were freed by Moravian masters in 1836—were reported as adherents of these denominations. The communal insularity of these religious groups, along with their discriminatory treatment of African Americans under their control, was partially responsible for this lack of immigrant identification with Quakers, Moravians, and others. Yet as noted earlier, censuses and other period records were subject to inaccuracies of various sorts, and immigrants themselves often offered no more information than was required of them.[24]

By midcentury, North Carolinians, both the farmer and the craftsman, the missionary and the criminal, were settled throughout Liberia, with substantial communities at Grand Cape Mount and along the St. Paul's and St. John's Rivers. Yet it was Monrovia that attracted the largest number of immigrants from the state, and it was here that their experiences were most varied. Changes in Monrovia from its founding in 1822 to the 1850s were largely in degree rather than kind, and the town remained chiefly a country village resting on the rocky slope of Cape Mesurado. In approaching the town from the mouth of Stockton Creek, visitors still had to walk uphill along winding paths, bypassing stone warehouses and thick vegetation before finally stepping onto the grassy streets of Monrovia. Although the capital was linked to the busy commercial life of the West African littoral, one observer noted in 1859 that no buoy existed to mark the shoal, no pier to service ships, nor "a respectable wharfage for canoes and lighters." At the apex of the cape, a lighthouse provided a beacon for incoming vessels, but Monrovia still remained difficult to access from the ocean.

The town itself was a mix of the urban and the rural. Three hundred houses on quarter-acre lots lined broad, unpaved roads. Some were impressive two-story brick structures; others were old wooden frame shacks, badly damaged by rain and the tropical sun as well as by termite infestations. Banana, lemon, and coffee trees shaded nearly every yard, although agriculture in general had never taken hold in the ferruginous soil on which the town was erected. The seat of government was here, and the principal public buildings—including the two-story brick presidential mansion—were clustered together near Broad Street. Still, there was little that was stately or impersonal about the town of two thousand people. Residents were known for their hospitality to strangers, and the community made good use of its several churches and schools. The town was a relatively quiet place to reside, insofar as few vehicles of any sort passed through, notwithstanding an occasional heavy cart. Overgrown walkways gave the settlement a decidedly rustic appearance, even if snakes and leopards were known to lurk beneath the underbrush. In common with its sister villages, Monrovia had little success in reversing its negative population growth, and residents, according to one visitor, were "very anxious to encourage immigration." In 1841, two decades after its founding, the town witnessed nineteen births and thirty-four deaths, the third-worst ratio among Liberian settlements.

For Monrovia, business and commerce were the lifeblood of its economy. In addition to its trade links to the maritime world, a proliferation of small retail shops highlighted the town's preoccupation with entrepreneurial pursuits. The concentration of professional talents around the seat of government gave the village a character distinct from the agrarian, riverine settlements. In 1858, the capital boasted five lawyers, twenty-six carpenters, eighteen masons, three shipbuilders, and several blacksmiths, tailors, shoemakers, and coopers. Moreover, nine schools and at least three churches were in operation, along with "a good assortment of places for hot pies and cakes, and beer." The assessed value of property in the town was two hundred thousand dollars in 1857, and one hundred people owned assets between five hundred and ten thousand dollars in worth.

Predictably, as the oldest and largest immigrant town, Monrovia attracted a disproportionate number of craftsmen and other skilled workers. Among the 2,030 North Carolinians who immigrated to the country (via ACS ships) between 1825 and 1893, 113 had occupations outside of farming, and 22 percent (25) of these individuals settled in the capital. Among them were four carpenters, three shoemakers, two seamstresses, two ministers, a caulker, a teacher, and a clerk. Several North Carolinians were identified in census records and emigrant rolls as proficient in at least two trades, and many others likely had multiple talents that were undocumented or underreported. Most individuals trained in carpentry, sawyering, masonry, and other fields were generalists, capable of working on many different projects. Thus, a cooper might also have expertise in cabinetmaking, and sawyers, who often worked in teams, might also be adept at plastering. Some craftsmen took on African American and African youths as apprentices; this practice allowed many North Carolinians, both free born and liberated, to learn trades prior to emigrating. A few individuals, such as Christian Outland, a farmer from Wayne County, even found it possible to give up the hoe for professional opportunities available in the capital. Having initially settled in Millsburg, Outland had become a magistrate for Mesurado County by the early 1850s.[25]

At midcentury, Hull Anderson of Washington, North Carolina, was among the most successful residents of Monrovia. Unlike most immigrants, he had amassed considerable property in his home state, including a shipyard and other properties, from which he continued to receive rent after embarking

TABLE 3. Known Occupations of North Carolina Emigrants, 1825–1893

Occupation	Males	Females	Total
Blacksmith	8	0	8
Bricklayer	3	0	3
Cabinetmaker	1	0	1
Carpenter	24	0	24
Caulker	1	0	1
Clerk	1	0	1
Coachman	1	0	1
Cook	0	2	2
Cooper	4	0	4
Domestic	0	1	1
Engineer	2	0	2
Farmer	219	4	223
Fisherman	1	0	1
Gardener	1	0	1
General work	0	1	1
House painter	1	0	1
Laborer	1	0	1
Machinist	1	0	1
Mason	2	0	2
Midwife	0	1	1
Minister	5	0	5
Plasterer	3	0	3
Printer	1	0	1
Sailmaker	1	0	1
Sawyer	7	0	7
Seaman	3	0	3
Seamstress	0	2	2
Shinglemaker	1	0	1
Shoemaker	10	0	10
Spinster	0	2	2
Tanner	5	0	5
Teacher	3	2	5
Washerwoman	0	3	3
Weaver	0	4	4
Wheelwright	4	0	4
Total	314	22	336

Source: Based on emigrant rolls, census records, and other sources.

for Liberia in 1841. Anderson was a caulker by trade but became a grocer and farmer after arriving in Monrovia. By 1843, he owned ten acres of land in the capital town upon which he grew cassava, potatoes, yams, and coffee. Among his other properties were wooden and stone buildings and fifteen hundred dollars of "stock employed in trade." While Anderson's net worth was set at three thousand dollars in that year, his fortunes apparently soured over the next decade. In an 1851 letter to an ACS official, he stated that he found Liberia "to be a very hard country." Having failed to receive the complimentary six months of provisions when he arrived in the colony ten years earlier, he requested a late payment of "these favours." His appeal for assistance was made the more urgent by the plundering of his corn and cassava crop by "the country people." Although ACS records do not disclose how Anderson's request for aid was handled, the grocer probably did not descend into penury, regardless of what provisions were or were not given to him. However, his situation does illustrate that even the more prosperous immigrants could experience financial difficulties in a town where food prices, especially for meat and dairy products, could be obscenely high and where the vagaries of coastal and domestic trade could quickly deplete individual assets.[26]

As in other settlements, penury was no stranger to Monrovia. As one observer noted in 1857, the capital never created enough jobs to employ all of the people who wandered its streets, nor did it produce enough of a harvest from its rocky soils to satisfy the hunger of the indigent. This situation was made more acute by the fact that most immigrants, including 85 percent of North Carolinians, arrived first in Monrovia before being relocated to other settlements. A plurality (20 percent) of people from the Tar Heel State actually established residence in the capital rather than moving to other towns. After exhausting their six months of free provisions, many individuals, having brought few resources to Liberia, found it inadvisable to relocate to the St. Paul's River or Grand Bassa, where uncleared land and underdeveloped facilities awaited them. Especially in the case of widowed women whose husbands were often victims of malaria, staying in Monrovia was sometimes preferable to migrating to one of the agricultural towns without a spouse and usually with small children in tow. Men who found themselves in the same predicament were perhaps more likely to leave Monrovia for another settlement, given that they could more easily find work elsewhere and might be better prepared for the arduous task of clearing land and establishing a residence. Women, however, were less apt to do so, particularly those who could not afford to hire laborers. As a result of these evolving migratory and demographic patterns, the problem of impoverished single women and dependent children in the capital emerged early after the colony's founding.

The colonial government and ACS officials tried to address this dilemma with a number of edicts. In February 1834, the colonial council passed an act to establish a public farm, hoping to make poor people less reliant upon charity. The following year, the ACS board of managers issued a resolution calling for the "removal of unemployed women and children, and others, living at the expense of the agency at Monrovia, to Caldwell," where they would supposedly "earn their own maintenance." The board also sought to limit the number of elderly and "unprotected women and children" entering the colony. Furthermore, to combat bastardy and its attendant social and economic implications for single women, an 1838 law attempted to hold suspected fathers financially responsible for their illegitimate offspring by threatening them with imprisonment.

Along with these policies aimed at addressing public morality and fiscal concerns, other statutes seemed more progressive in their treatment of female immigrants. For example, single women were entitled to land grants just as male heads of household were. Several North Carolina women, including Mary Mulberry of Chowan County and Matilda White of Pasquotank, received lots in Monrovia during the colonial period, and a few, such as Diana Sheridan McKay of Robertsport, distinguished themselves as able freeholders and matriarchs. The 1847 constitution even protected the property of women from the creditors of their spouses. Nonetheless, despite the appearance of liberalism regarding gender, the constitution barred women from voting, and divorces could only be granted by an act of the (all-male) legislature. Rather surprisingly, no established law or legal precedent defining rape was codified before 1898, when the Court of Quarter Sessions and Common Pleas of Mesurado County was obliged to draw on Anglo-American common law in order to adjudicate a case. Tellingly, between 1828 and 1843, no immigrant was ever convicted of a sex crime, although at least three Africans were.[27]

In regard to North Carolinians, male and female immigrants shared many characteristics yet, in some ways, experienced migration and settlement in Liberia differently. Statistical profiles of the two populations reveal many similarities. For example, of the 2,030 North Carolinians whom the ACS transported to Liberia during the nineteenth century, 48 percent (984) are known to have been female. The age distribution of emigrants at the time of their departure from the United States tended to be consistent along gender lines. Overall, the North Carolina emigrant population was a young one (see Figure 3).[28] One in three female emigrants was under ten years old, and 56 percent were under twenty, compared to 55 percent of male emigrants in this age range. Among emigrants fifty years of age or older, women and men were nearly equally represented, both in number and as percentages of their respective populations. The average age of female emigrants was 20.5 years, consistent with the North Carolina average of 20.6, and the median age was

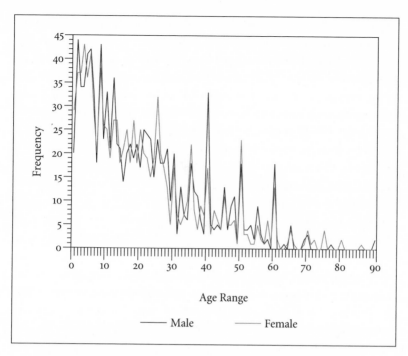

FIGURE 3. Age Distribution of 2,030 North Carolina Emigrants, 1825–1893
Sources: Based on emigrant rolls, census records, and other sources.

seventeen. The female modal age was three (43 instances), compared to five (83 instances) for all emigrants leaving the state. As these figures illustrate, a sizable portion of the North Carolina female population was in its prime productive and reproductive years, which boded well for an immigrant population that was expected to increase naturally over time. Almost 41 percent of the females were of child-bearing age, assuming that an age range of fifteen to forty years was optimal for child bearing during this period. Also, most emigrants traveled to Liberia as families, which accounts for the nearly even gender ratio.[29]

Of the total number of known female emigrants who migrated between 1825 and 1893, 95 (9.6 percent) were listed as capable of reading, writing, or spelling, compared to 117 (11.3 percent) males. Only 2 female and 13 male emigrants liberated expressly for colonization are listed as literate in any fashion. These figures suggest that access to literacy among previously free or freeborn emigrants from North Carolina was not substantially determined by gender—an observation that does not hold true for the relatively few literate ex-slaves freed solely for removal to Africa. Regardless of these cultural dynamics, female literacy in the Tar Heel State and in Liberia did not bring women corresponding career opportunities. Of the 984 emigrants known to be female, only 22 (2.2 percent) are listed in emigrant rolls as having occupations (see Table 3). As with literacy, many of these emigrants likely had some sort of skill or talent which, for whatever reason—the information was not offered by the individuals or solicited by the compilers of emigrant rolls —was simply not recorded. Furthermore, since the vast majority of female emigrants from North Carolina were from the eastern agricultural counties, a sizable number of them were familiar with some sort of agricultural work, including tobacco, corn, and cotton cultivation. Thus, like males, many women could have been justifiably labeled as farmers in emigrant rolls. Yet given that the female emigrant population was such a young group on average, most would have been fairly new to any occupation that they may have had and perhaps were less likely to claim expertise in any particular area. Additionally, ideas about femininity and patriarchy among blacks, and within society in general, may have further discouraged many from identifying themselves with occupations, such as farming, that were perceived to be masculine pursuits.

In relation to religious affiliation, male and female emigrants were almost equally represented among four denominations, but unevenly associated with a fifth church. According to emigrant rolls, 58 males and 66 females identified themselves as Methodists, and seven males were Presbyterians, as compared to four females. Among those identifying themselves as Episcopalians or simply as "Christians," males and females were equally represented in both groups. However, among Baptists, women outnumbered men 103 to 66, a difference that is difficult to explain. Perhaps this denomination had a gender-oriented appeal in parts of North Carolina, or male believers were grossly undercounted in emigration records. Another way to speculate about this imbalance is to consider the manner in which people incorporated religion into their identities. For instance, naming patterns among both males and females were heavily influenced by biblical and Hebraic nomenclature, indicative of the Western acculturation of black North Carolinians and, by extension, Liberian emigrants. The adoption of these names was not a reliable indicator of the prevalence of the Christian faith among emigrants from the state. Nonetheless, the fact that free and literate blacks chose to bestow such names upon their offspring does seem to intimate that these names carried a religious significance among at least some black North Carolinians by the nineteenth century. Among female emigrants, the five most common first names, along with their frequency, were:

1. Mary (95) and the derivatives Maria (29) and Marianna (1)
2. Elizabeth (23) and the derivatives Eliza (32) and Betsey/Betsy (13)
3. Sarah (41) and the derivative Sally (8)

4. Ann (39) and the derivatives Nancy (32) and Anna (9)

5. Jane (25)

Altogether, approximately 40 percent of female emigrants had biblical or Hebraic names, which may have had implications regarding their propensity for church membership. As shown above, 1 in 10 of these individuals was named Mary, and 64 percent (61) of those named after the biblical matron would settle along the St. Paul's River—religious symbolism that was perhaps not lost on many of them.

While biblical or Hebraic names were also popular among male emigrants from North Carolina, English or German names were just as common, and only a quarter of men and boys leaving the state for Liberia bore names derived from the Bible. Among males, the most common names were:

1. John (78) and the derivative Jack (5)

2. William (68) and the derivatives Will (1), Willis (6), Willie (1), Bill (2), and Billy (2)

3. Henry (50)

4. James (41) and the derivative Jim (2)

5. George (32)

When not taken from scripture, names given to black North Carolinians were typically adopted from broader naming trends that were popular at any given time. Like surnames, first names were often passed down through generations, usually from males to their descendants, but in some cases from older women to female infants. In addition to these patterns, emigrant rolls and census records list several names of Greco-Roman origin, such as Minerva, Venus, Nero, and Caesar. Moreover, males tended to be named after contemporary public figures more often than females, with names such as Napoleon Peobles, John Q. Adams Jones, and Jesse James Johnson bestowed upon several youths. In contrast, very few names appear to have had African roots, and the rare one that might have originated from that continent was always paired with a non-African surname, as in Sally Ogon Hollister and Abijah Holt. Notwithstanding these variations, naming practices among North Carolinians were remarkable for their consistency over the course of the nineteenth century rather than their variety or originality.[30]

As with any group, names were important markers of male and female identities among black North Carolinians. This kind of cultural evidence drawn from emigrant records, along with other statistical data, illustrate the ways in which the backgrounds and migratory experiences of men and women both overlapped and diverged. Yet for all their utility, these sources do not sup-

plant the power and significance of firsthand accounts of immigrants themselves, which are so necessary for filling in the many gaps that census tabulations and other sketches leave blank. The correspondence of female North
Carolinians in Liberia, in particular, adds both historical context and social
texture to their lives in their new country. Their letters are the cultural pas-
sageways through which their identities, their private struggles, flow, and
they are the most useful means for accessing their personal experiences.

Many missives of immigrant women speak of poverty and deprivation,
common themes in letters from Liberia. For example, Lavinia Nelson, a twenty-
two-year-old liberated slave who migrated from New Bern in 1858, echoed a
perennial complaint when she informed William McLain about her hardships in Careysburg, located approximately thirty miles east of Monrovia. "I
am not able to seporte myself without some healpe," she wrote in September
1861. "My littel log hut wants repairing but I have not the means to do it with
& the peopel is so harde hirted that they do not want to do the leas thing for
a widdow." Martha Nelson, a relative of Lavinia's, offered similar observations in an 1863 letter to an ACS official, stressing the vulnerability and economic distress experienced by single women with children. "I am a lone woman
and no husband to support me," she lamented, "and this is the place persons
oblige to have means to support themselves, as things is hard to get in this
our ancestors country." To be sure, the motifs of poverty and helplessness
that course through such letters were not always unrelieved by small plea-
sures and triumphs. Although on her own, Martha Nelson still found a time
and purpose for a black silk dress that she ordered through McLain, and other
immigrant women, such as Susan Capehart, boasted about the educational
opportunities available in Liberia. Still, for many, hardship was more of a
constant in Liberia than anything else, and some women suffered grievously
from the lack of basic necessities.

Sometimes certain personal decisions made life more difficult. This was
definitely the case with Julia Peele, a liberated slave from Northampton County.
After migrating in 1828 and surviving an anopheline attack that killed 25 percent of her shipmates, she settled in Millsburg only to end up having two illegitimate children by different men. Widespread matrifocal family networks
among African American slaves and West Africans perhaps served as models for her adjustment to single motherhood. Still, women with dependent
children almost always found poverty inescapable in the backwoods of Liberia. On many occasions, it was not the women whose bad choices doomed
them to a precarious existence. Instead, the actions and shortsightedness of
others determined their situation, including masters who sent newly liberated slaves to Africa with little or no resources and ACS officials who shipped
boatloads of paupers across the Atlantic year after year. For female immi-

grants especially, the ongoing demographic crisis caused by malaria and other afflictions multiplied the burdens they carried as mothers, widows, toilers, and second-class citizens. Actually, the abundance of sickness and death in the country directly or indirectly affected the lives of all.[31]

SOME CALLED MALARIA "country fever," ague, or simply "the chills." Others, employing the scientific language of the day, labeled it bilious intermittent, malignant, or miasmatic fever, the former designation based on the theory that imbalances in one or more of the four bodily fluids—blood, phlegm, yellow bile, and black bile—were responsible for the febrile condition. Often conflated with other ailments, such as typhoid or yellow fever, nineteenth-century medical theorists and practitioners held that malaria resulted from putrid effluvium emitted by decaying vegetation and stagnant water, or what the Italians called *mala aria* ("bad air"). *Anopheles* mosquitoes, which were attracted to such marshy, wet environments, had yet to be isolated as the vectors of the disease, which was passed to humans through the injection of parasitic plasmodia into their bodies by the winged carriers. Among Liberian immigrants and colonizationists, illness caused by *Plasmodium falciparum*, which would eventually be responsible for hundreds of deaths, was generally known as "African fever," though some, such as Daniel Rhodes of Guilford County, still referred to it as "that Monster" as late as the 1850s.

Keen observers of the disease had learned that malaria was often a seasonal and geographic phenomena with a high incidence of infection during warm, wet periods and lower frequency in cooler, elevated areas. Scientists had even determined that the disease progressed in predictable ways, with symptoms often recurring at intervals. Accordingly, intermittent fevers were labeled as having quotidian, tertian, quartan, or quintan cycles, depending on whether the chills, febrile condition, or perspiring recurred every day, every other day, every fourth day, and so forth. Remittent fevers abated for a time, perhaps for weeks or months, but could flare up again without warning. In midcentury North Carolina, physicians had yet to understand that distinctions in the lethality and symptomatic qualities of the disease resulted from different plasmodia carried by their mosquito vectors. Thus, *vivax* malaria, a rarely fatal variant endemic to parts of the state, was only distinguishable from *falciparum* malaria, the most lethal strain, by its symptoms, not by the presence of certain vectors. Subsequently, in the federal census of 1850, enumerators lumped the two types of malaria together with other illnesses with febrile symptoms, recording 839 people as having died of "unclassified" fevers during the previous year, a number that represented 8.3 percent of all deaths in the state. Similarly, in Liberia and other parts of West Africa, the *malariae* variety of the disease was distinguished from the more dominant *falciparum* strain by the more dramatic symptoms and higher mortality resulting from the latter, not through an understanding of the disease's etiology and transmission or a knowledge of specific causal parasites.[32]

As hundreds of immigrants came to learn, a bout of *falciparum* malaria was quite a serious matter. Observers noted that each individual afflicted with the illness experienced it in unique ways, some exhibiting few symptoms and recovering quickly while others were drastically affected by the disease for a protracted period of time. Yet despite variations in the refractoriness of victims, general patterns of symptoms and reactions could be readily discerned in most cases. After being injected with *Plasmodium falciparum* by anopheline vectors, the victim was usually stricken within days or a few weeks with fever accompanied by a severe headache, dry throat, sore limbs, and sometimes diarrhea and vomiting. Drowsiness and listlessness set in, often punctuated with moments of delirium and violent paroxysms. The liver and spleen, attempting to filter out the parasites, swelled in size, an effect which could sometimes be seen externally as a protrusion in the abdominal region. Further, jaundice occasionally appeared as hepatic dysfunction became extreme. In fatal cases, the red corpuscles, overwhelmed by the sheer density and magnitude of the parasitic attack, erupted and released the poisonous plasmodia into the blood stream, clogging arteries responsible for supplying blood to the brain and other vital organs. Once the victim lapsed into coma, death was usually near. Surviving the illness meant that an individual's immune system was able to marshal enough white blood cells to contain the parasitic invasion, and that vital organs, such as the liver and spleen, were not rendered inoperable during the attack. While sometimes spared the anemia, swelling, acute diarrhea, or stomach hemorrhaging of the less fortunate, survivors were often permanently weakened by their first and subsequent malarial infections, never fully recovering their former vitality.[33]

Since few American immigrants arrived in Liberia with formidable innate or acquired immune defenses against *falciparum* malaria, the vast majority experienced at least some of the symptoms of anopheline infection if not ultimately death. Even individuals from southern states where *falciparum* malaria was better known would find it difficult to adjust to the relatively stable temperatures and abundant rain that made the disease hyperendemic year-round along the African coast as opposed to its seasonal appearance in the American South. Into the nineteenth century, a substantial number of African Americans still carried the sickle-cell trait, glucose-6-phosphate dehydrogenase deficiency, and other natural protections against *Plasmodium falciparum*. However, these biological defenses had been greatly weakened among those who had not been constantly exposed to malarial environments or whose West African genetic structure had been altered by admixture with Caucasian genes. Thus, with the exception of some African recaptives, it was a rare immigrant who enjoyed a resistance to malaria comparable to that of the Kru, Dei, and other indigenous peoples.

In addition to these considerations, other variables affected malarial mortality and morbidity rates. Diet, clothing, hygiene, and housing conditions influenced one's chances of survival, as did geographical location and season of arrival in Liberia. As these factors became better understood over time, preventive measures aimed at reducing the likelihood of infection became enmeshed in the cultural practices of the immigrant population. Where the local ecology could not be changed to lessen anopheline infestations, people learned to psychologically and physically accommodate the ever-present threat of malarial infection. For example, newcomers were encouraged to avoid overexertion, to refrain from consuming certain foods believed to lower resistance, and to establish homes outside of wet, low-lying wooded areas where "miasmas" were thought to flow. In concert with these adjustments, ACS officials gradually decided to avoid sending emigrants to the country during certain unhealthy times. Moreover, by midcentury the organization sent medicines to the colony, such as "sulphate of quinia," which promised to lower malarial mortality. Consistent with contemporary beliefs in the curative power of bloodletting, blistering, and purging, the ACS also supplied Liberian physicians with "Blistering ointment" and diaphoretics, which were questionable febrifuges though still reputable in many scientific circles.

In the end, it was less these precautions and treatments that substantially lessened individual susceptibility to Liberian malaria than the biological immunity that one slowly acquired after surviving several bouts of the disease. Successfully enduring the first infection was most crucial, for the vast majority of terminal cases of malaria among North Carolina immigrants and others occurred within the first year of arrival in Liberia. After recovering from the initial affliction, the chances of subsequent attacks being fatal were notably reduced. This lessened risk did not mean that a person was able to avoid infection altogether but that the victim had acquired the immunological ability to produce enough antibodies to limit the number of parasites in the bloodstream. Such defenses against malaria were never absolute regardless of frequency of exposure and successful recovery. Parasites remained in the bodies of ostensibly healthy people, and the less mature or older a person's immune system, the higher the possibility of a terminal case of malaria. Thus, the death rates among both young children and the elderly were higher than those of young to middle-aged adults. Finally, immunity to malaria depended upon constant exposure to infection. Once a person left an environment where the disease was endemic, acquired defenses declined. As a consequence, this loss of refractoriness made re-entering anopheline areas more hazardous in proportion to the duration of the absence.[34]

The disease experience of North Carolinians in Liberia was consistent with the dominant trends among African American immigrants in general, and certain variables affected their ability to survive *falciparum* malaria once they settled in the country. Unfortunately, reliable quantified information on mortality in nineteenth-century Liberia is limited to the ACS-sponsored census of 1843 which surveyed the colony over a twenty-three-year period. One can assume that certain morbidity and mortality trends continued beyond that year in both abated and enhanced forms. However, only the figures for the first generation of colonization are extant, and thus only these years can be examined. The available data reveals that malarial mortality was shaped by several important factors, but age and gender were among the most salient.

The malarial mortality curve of North Carolinians rose highest among the youngest and oldest immigrants, whose immune systems were least prepared to fight off anopheline infection. Among the 741 North Carolinians who migrated to Liberia between 1825 and 1843, children less than ten years of age accounted for 74 (60 percent) of the 124 individuals known to have died of "fever," the common designation for Liberian malaria. This age group suffered a 30 percent malarial mortality, almost twice as high as the overall North Carolina death rate of 17 percent and significantly higher than the aggregate immigrant figure of 20 percent. Unsurprisingly, infants under one year of age were most susceptible to fever, with one half of them dying following their arrival in Liberia. As the smallest segment of emigrants from the state, individuals over forty-four years of age endured a 17 percent mortality rate compared to only a 9 percent death rate among those age ten to forty-four, the largest age grouping. The average age of North Carolinians who died of malaria was 13.8 years old, and the modal age was three (11 instances). For young children especially, immigration to Liberia entailed huge risks, and factors such as place of settlement, adequate housing, sufficient nourishment, access to medicinal treatments, and parental care had a significant impact on their survival rates. In addition, their chances of overcoming an initial bout of malaria would have been reduced by pre-existing conditions, such as roundworms, measles, rickets, and teething difficulties, which were known to afflict children in particular.[35]

Along with age, gender was an important determinant of one's susceptibility to terminal malaria. On the surface, male and female North Carolinians experienced the disease in similar ways. Between 1825 and 1843, the average age of female victims was 13.8 years compared to the male average of 13.3 years, and largely the very young and the very old of both genders were most lethally affected by the disease. However, while fever was the recorded cause

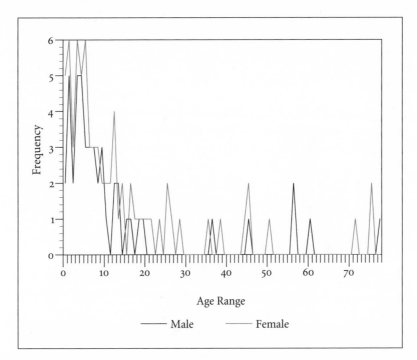

FIGURE 4. Malarial Mortality among North Carolina Emigrants, by Age and Gender
Sources: Based on emigrant rolls, census records, and other sources.

of death for 39 percent of North Carolinians for whom a cause of death is known, 64 percent more females (74) than males (48) died of fever. Possible causes of this discrepancy were reduced immune resistance to malaria on the part of females due to pregnancy; more sedentary lives as housewives and thus less exercise; and pre-existing, complicating conditions, especially of a respiratory nature, which were more common among women. Also, discriminatory distribution of medicinal treatments, which would have favored male heads of household and the financially well off (who also tended to be male), likely increased female vulnerability. In some instances, malaria was the secondary cause of death for women since it weakened the immune system, making individuals less refractory regarding other illnesses. While no statistics exist to corroborate this point, it is quite likely that the birthrate in Liberia was depressed by not only the incidence of malarial deaths among young women but also by the enhanced risk of death that pregnant women and their fetuses faced when stung by *Anopheles* mosquitoes. The 74 births that occurred among North Carolinians between 1825 and 1843 hardly offset the 340 known deaths, and malaria among women of child-bearing age was certainly a major cause of the negative population growth. Relatedly, malarial fevers also would have elevated the scrotal temperature of men which might

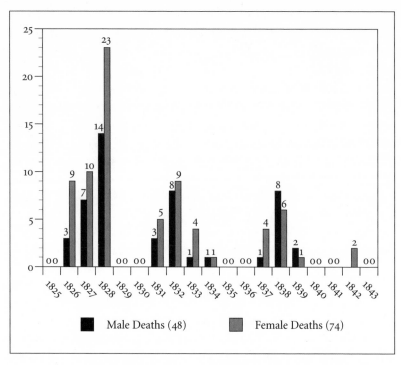

FIGURE 5. Malarial Mortality among North Carolina Emigrants, by Gender and Year
Sources: Based on emigrant rolls, census records, and other sources.

have diminished their sperm counts, not to mention sex drives, perhaps further reducing the birthrate.

In this important way, female North Carolinians again experienced migration and settlement in Liberia very differently than males. Not only was malarial mortality gendered in reference to who died from the disease but also in relation to who would be expected to provide care for the afflicted. Immigrant women, when not prostrated by ailments themselves, were largely responsible for comforting those suffering from malaria. Women pushed into widowhood by the disease's ravages often found themselves solely responsible for the well-being of young children who were the most vulnerable to fatal anopheline infections. Interestingly, among Africans as well, women were traditionally assigned the task of providing for the sick and impaired, and women often applied medical treatments for a range of illnesses. "Fever teas" and other herbal remedies were almost certainly produced mainly by African women, and Liberian immigrants, perhaps primarily females, had resorted to these local febrifuges by midcentury. Undoubtedly, gender shaped both the ways that women experienced morbidity and mortality in Liberia and how diseases and suspected causes of death were culturally interpreted in the country. Malaria, along with other illnesses, was particularly associated with gender in regard to individual susceptibility, and over time Liberians might have come to associate it with other diseases believed to be peculiar to females.[36]

In addition to fever, other causes of death listed for deceased North Carolina immigrants in the 1843 census included respiratory illnesses (consumption, diseased lungs, and pleurisy), anasarca, anasarca exanthem, female disease, diseased brain, drowning, decline, and old age. It should be noted that these rather broad categories for defining illnesses were not exact and, indeed, illustrate the limitations of the knowledge of the ACS and colonial officials as well as the rudimentary nature of nineteenth-century Western diagnostic medicine in general. The recorded causes of death were often based on symptoms, as opposed to an empirical or scientific understanding of the etiology and nature of particular diseases. Since autopsies were uncommon before midcentury, determining the causal factor(s) behind any particular death was often a guessing game, based on the behavioral patterns, appearance, and other observed external conditions of the afflicted. While accurate diagnoses of primary causes of death were made in some cases, many illnesses, which would have required a careful examination of the victim's internal organs to accurately categorize them, were often misdiagnosed and thus inaccurately recorded in censuses and other records. In light of these observations, the mortality tables and statistics of the 1843 census do offer pertinent information about the epidemiological environments that emigrants left in North Carolina and found in Liberia. Nonetheless, these tabulations raise as many questions as they answer, especially regarding the boundaries of nineteenth-century medical knowledge.

Second only to fever, respiratory illnesses were a major cause of death among North Carolina immigrants. Consumption alone was listed as being responsible for 13 percent (44) of the 340 deaths that occurred among immigrants from the state by 1843. In most instances, this cause of death was likely diagnosed accurately as tuberculosis since nineteenth-century Americans and others would have been quite familiar with its symptoms. Yet on occasion, this suspected illness could have actually been emphysema, lung cancer, asthma, or a variety—or combination—of other ailments. Slaves and free blacks living in poorly ventilated housing, working in wet weather, wearing inadequate clothing, malnourished, or suffering from other illnesses would have been most susceptible to tuberculosis while in America. According to the federal census of 1850, respiratory illnesses, including tuberculosis, were the primary killers of North Carolinians during the prior year, accounting for 20 percent of known causes of death. In some cases, the voyage to Liberia may have facilitated the spread of tuberculosis among emigrants, particularly if they were

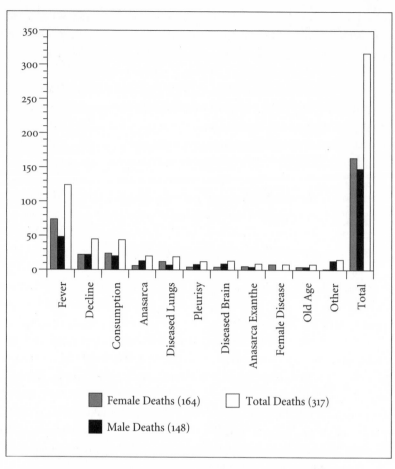

FIGURE 6. Recorded Causes of Death for North Carolina Emigrants, 1825–1843
Sources: Based on emigrant rolls, census records, and other sources.

housed in close quarters while aboard ship. Additionally, pre-existing tuber-
cular conditions were undoubtedly exacerbated in Africa by malaria, tobacco
consumption, seasonal rains, insufficient housing, and other factors. As with
fever, women were slightly overrepresented in this cause-of-death category
(see Figure 6). This gender discrepancy can be attributed to several likely
causes, including the more sedentary, indoor lives of most women; the traditional role of females as caregivers for the sick, which sometimes exposed
them to contagious diseases; reduced immune resistance because of pregnancy; and cooking responsibilities, which often exposed women to open fires
that emitted carcinogens.

For many of the reasons cited above, women were also overrepresented
among the nineteen North Carolinians who were listed as having died of dis-

eased lungs. As a catchall term for respiratory illnesses, this alleged cause of death—diagnosed mainly through observed behavior and external symptoms—could have referred to a number of conditions, including cancer, emphysema, bronchitis, diphtheria, and influenza. In contrast to malaria, individuals in their prime productive and reproductive years were more likely to perish from these respiratory ailments than children. Among North Carolina immigrants, the average age of victims recorded as having died of diseased lungs was 25.7 years compared to 31.3 years for those who were believed to have succumbed to tuberculosis. Regarding the gendered nature of these ailments, only pleurisy, documented as a separate respiratory disease in Liberia, seems to have affected men in a notably disproportionate manner. Characterized by inflammation of the parietal pleura of the lungs, pleurisy was suspected as the primary terminal illness in twice as many male North Carolinians as females (4 versus 8), though it was sometimes likely confused with tuberculosis, pneumonia, and other diseases. Overall, respiratory illnesses were putatively responsible for 24 percent of deaths among North Carolinians in Liberia between 1825 and 1843.[37]

Along with fever and respiratory ailments, other less prevalent causes of death were also gender differentiated. Among North Carolina immigrants, "female diseases" were listed in the 1843 colonial census as the reason for the deaths of eight individuals. Each of the females recorded as having died of this cause was free born, five were from Pasquotank County, all were under thirty-three years of age (except one fifty-year-old), and with one possible exception, all immigrated to Caldwell in 1826 or 1832. The average age of the victims was 24.8 years, and the youngest was ten. This demographic sketch suggests that this cause of death was almost solely restricted to females of child-bearing age, and further intimates that most of these immigrants died due to pregnancy or postpartum complications. Also, it is possible that vaginal infections, ovarian cancer, and menstrual ailments were among these "female diseases." As with other ailments, most of the gender-specific illnesses suffered by women would have been worsened by malaria and other afflictions, as well as malnutrition, exposure, poor housing, inadequate medical attention, and so forth. Given that few autopsies were performed before mid-century, colonial officials, physicians, and others would have concluded largely through observation that such a person had died primarily as a result of a "female disease."

As in the case of female immigrants, certain ailments and causes of death were known to primarily affect males. Diseased brain was one such condition chronicled in the colonial census. Of the thirteen people who died of this alleged affliction, nine were male. The average age of both male and female victims was nineteen, and the youngest was eight-year-old Harris Taylor of Camden County. Proof of this cause of death would have been largely based on the observed behavior of the sufferer. Suspected neurological ab-normalities were sometimes attributable to brain cancers or tumors but were probably just as often symptomatic of other conditions, such as typhoid fever, encephalitis, or syphilis. In addition to diseased brain, male immigrants from North Carolina also died in disproportionate numbers from anasarca (gen-eralized, massive edema), though the sexes perished in similar numbers from anasarca exanthem, which was probably an eruptive version of anasarca ac-companied by fever and a rash. Altogether, seventeen males succumbed to these ailments, compared to nine females, and the average age for all victims was twenty-three. Finally, a few men lost their lives in ways that females were able to wholly avoid. Five North Carolina males drowned between 1825 and 1843, suggesting that they were less sedentary and more seafaring than women. Similarly, five were killed in conflicts with Africans and European slave traders, perennial hazards of colonial frontier life in Liberia.[38]

Of all recorded reasons for mortality among North Carolina immigrants, "decline" and old age were the causes of death least skewed by gender consid-erations. Like diseased lungs, decline was a vague diagnosis which covered everything from cancer and diabetes to malnutrition and African sleeping sickness. Degenerative illnesses of various sorts also would have been included under this rubric, as would ailments that appeared to affect mostly older members of the population, such as heart disease and stroke. Males and fe-males were equally victimized by this collection of unnamed afflictions, and the average age of those perishing from decline was 44. Predictably, deaths attributed to old age were also evenly divided between males and females. Four women (average age of 71.3 years) and four men (average age of 63.8 years) were listed as dying from this cause. Six of the eight (three men and three women) were free born, suggesting that even in Liberia, former status influenced life expectancy. Old age as a mortality category, of course, ob-scured other causes of death and, like decline, would have encompassed a range of infirmities associated with elderly populations. If not primary pre-cipitants of death, malaria, respiratory ailments, and other maladies were often secondary and tertiary factors in the demise of the elderly, complicat-ing pre-existing terminal conditions.[39]

As a study of the colonial population of Liberia, the 1843 census offers a wealth of information about the texture and contours of life among the first generation of immigrants. In particular, the mortality statistics disclose a formidable disease environment, varied in content and impact, with critical implications for the ways in which people experienced childhood, old age, gender differences, settlement patterns, climatic and geographical condi-tions, and much more. In addition to the information that the census contains, interesting and glaring omissions in the mortality schedule reveal both the intellectual limitations of its compilers and the politics of ACS census-taking. For example, no one is listed as dying of dysentery, smallpox, measles, pneumonia, influenza, or diphtheria, all specific causes of death that were recognizable by the mid-nineteenth century. Certain illnesses, such as sea-sickness and cholera, may have been purposefully expunged from census records to protect the reputation and program of the ACS. In some cases, these unnamed causes of death were simply subsumed under more vague designations, such as diseased brain and decline. In other instances, unique descriptions of fatalities may have masked other issues. This observation may have been especially applicable to the death of Matilda White. Emigrating from Pasquotank County in 1831 at age eighteen, she was listed as having died of "grief from family loss" in 1843, perhaps a euphemism for suicide.

Along with causes of death that were discernible at midcentury, many sources of morbidity and mortality would have perhaps been harder to define during that period. Such was the case in deaths resulting from intestinal worms (especially among children), pellagra, hepatitis, tetanus (especially among field workers), ulcers (which were sometimes complained about), venereal diseases, trypanosomiasis (sleeping sickness), and Sudden Infant Death Syndrome. Disease exchanges between immigrants and neighboring Africans also eluded census enumerators. Children produced by relationships between male colonists and indigenous women would definitely have reconfigured the genetic makeup and immunological terrain of the country's population. Likewise, African youths residing among immigrant families were surely exposed to contagions for which they had few defenses. As another element of these exchanges, indigenous medicinal treatments probably helped staunch the incessant malarial hemorrhaging of the colony. However, the concurrent flow of large quantities of alcohol and tobacco into the region weakened African and immigrant immune responses to a host of diseases. Unconcerned with such issues, the mortality statistics of the 1843 census were an imperfect instrument for examining the demographic qualities of the colonial population over time. Nonetheless, despite its omissions, vagueness, and conceptual limitations, the study is still a valuable framework for understanding the quality—and brevity—of life among North Carolinians and others in early Liberia.[40]

OF THE NORTH CAROLINIANS who risked death in going to Liberia, Bennett Demery was a survivor. Born free, he had been a sailmaker and carpenter in Edenton where he and his wife, Sally, raised two children, Ann Eliza and Warren. The specific conditions and circumstances that encouraged them to depart in the ACS-chartered ship, *Indian Chief,* are unfortunately unknown. Whatever the case, the family took up residence in the new settlement of Caldwell after arriving in Liberia in March 1826. While their North Carolina shipmates immediately suffered a 10 percent malarial mortality, the Demerys were spared this kind of grief until Sally died of consumption in 1832 at age thirty-six. Over the next several years, Ann Eliza became an apprentice in Monrovia and continued to enjoy good health as late as 1843, according to the colonial census of that year. Her younger brother, Warren, was apparently still alive at that time, but beyond his initial arrival in Caldwell, his experiences were unchronicled. Bennett, widowed and in search of work, moved to the mission station at Heddington, upriver from Millsburg, where his talents as a carpenter gained him employment as an assistant. Working alongside Sion Harris, a farmer from Tennessee, Bennett helped construct the mission buildings which were intended to facilitate the spread of Christianity among neighboring Africans. That he and the handful of immigrants with whom he lived and worked would one day have to defend their religious commune from the very people they hoped to proselytize was an irony that surely was not lost on him.[41]

Indigenous communities in the vicinity of Heddington had not been pleased to see yet another colonial settlement established in their midst along the St. Paul's River. One local satrap in particular, Gotorah, did not care to witness more foreign encroachment upon African lands and in early 1840 made his distaste for the new mission known. At daybreak on a March morning, the leader led a multiethnic army of as many as four hundred into Heddington, ostensibly to destroy the mission. According to Harris, two of the attackers came within eight yards of the front door of the head missionary's home before being met by a volley of one ounce balls and buckshot. Demery, "an Elegant marksman" in Harris's estimate, joined the Tennessean in holding off the advance elements of the army until both men ran out of ammunition. Falling back as Gotorah personally moved toward him brandishing a large knife, Harris fortuitously spotted and seized a loaded rifle belonging to one of the four Africans who were defending the mission. Taking "deliberate aim" at the approaching commander, he discharged the weapon's contents, and Gotorah, mortally wounded, fell before him.

Demoralized and in disarray, the defeated army scrambled to collect the bodies of twenty-two of their comrades, along with their fallen chief, before retreating from the scene. Harris reported later that four of the dead were left behind "and the wood[s] stank in places where the wounded had died." When news of the assault on Heddington reached Monrovia, governor Thomas Buchanan, assuming that a second attack was imminent, ordered a preemptive strike against the town of Gotorah's ally, Gay Toombay. After a brief battle, a colonial force captured and burned the village but failed to apprehend its ruler. Hoping to make a "terrible example" of him, Buchanan offered a bounty for the capture of Gay Toombay, who had allegedly killed two messengers, including Willis Peele, an ex-slave from Northampton County. Ultimately, Gay Toombay was never captured, and no reward was collected, but the governor did receive a macabre trophy from the earlier fighting. African enemies of the late Gotorah found it fitting to send Buchanan his severed head, confirmation of the deeds of Harris and Demery.[42]

By the time Buchanan received his ghastly souvenir, the recurrent patterns of immigrant intrusion, African resistance, and colonial counterresponse had become a central motif of the relations between the two groups. While significant, Heddington in itself was not unique but part of a continuum of conflict between Africans and the newcomers. Arguably, battles at Cape Mesurado in the 1820s, along the St. Paul's River in the 1830s, and in Grand Bassa, Sinoe, and Cape Palmas in the 1850s were all part of a single, ongoing war over African lands and trade, not discreet, unrelated hostilities. As with the earliest fighting at Cape Mesurado, these attempts by colonists to cauterize indigenous opposition with gunshot and treaties generally proved to be illusory remedies. Nonetheless, in very real ways, conflicts with Africans over land and sovereignty helped forge immigrant identity. Heddington became yet another site where the tragic birth pains of the Liberian colony and an emergent national consciousness were acted out. In the view of ACS officials and many immigrants, each subsequent battle further defined the colony as a besieged Christian experiment in civilization which was providentially protected from the relentless nemesis of civilized progress, the "savage."

These cultural and psychic elements of Liberian colonial and national identity operated on deeper levels. Even among many African Americans who had migrated in hope of finding an inclusive expression of black nationality and identity in Africa, their particularist cultural baggage limited the potential for a cosmopolitan, tolerant Liberia. In the United States, many fissures in African American communities had been obscured by the homogenizing power of white racism and racialized slavery which defined blacks in collective terms and which conditioned their responses to oppression in a similarly corporatist manner. However, outside of the context of American slavery and white supremacy, these divisions, whether in regard to religious affiliation, socioeconomic class, educational attainments, gender, or color, starkly emerged and displayed themselves in Liberia in a range of attitudes, prejudices, interests, and practices. These transformations of consciousness illustrated that the identities of immigrants, as with other people, were transitory, fluid, and elastic, molded by their interpretation of different environments and their possibilities and limitations.

Perhaps it was inevitable that these particularisms and antagonisms would surface in a place where blackness alone rarely took on any generalized meaning and was too superficial a social construct to sustain a unified Liberian identity flexible and integrative enough to include Africans. Once removed from the American cultural context, notions of race among many immigrants shifted and relocated away from black/white, slave/free dichotomies that were prevalent in the United States to settler/native, Christian/heathen, civilized/uncivilized, and other divisions and imaginings of self and others that embodied self-interests, expediency, and even fantasy in Africa. At bottom, no Liberian identity could exist without Africans or America, and no "natives," "heathens," or "savages" could exist without settlers and their psychological need for self-justification. Conflict, especially violence that could be portrayed as preemptive or defensive, validated in the eyes of many colonists and ACS officials the expropriations, exploitative practices, and very existence of the immigrant population of Liberia. Consequently, there could hardly be a Liberian colonial or national ethos that was not shaped and compromised by the fact that war, dispossession, and exclusionary cultural practices were the very means through which this refugee society had been invented along the West African coast.

Predictably, the architects of the Liberian state revealed no hesitancy in proclaiming their values and sense of mission to the world following independence. In his first inaugural address in 1848, newly elected president Joseph J. Roberts consciously evoked the self-serving narrative of colonial triumph over native savagery to commemorate the occasion. He reminisced about "a time, when . . . a mere handful of isolated christian pilgrims, . . . surrounded by savage and warlike tribes bent upon their ruin and total annihilation . . . determined in the name of the 'Lord of Hosts' to stand their ground and defend themselves to the last extremity against their powerful adversary." In his view, the survival of immigrant communities was predicated on "tokens of providential favor" as well as an inspired destiny that would eventually uplift Africans from their putative barbarism. The settlement of "civilized" African American Christians along the Liberian coast made possible "the redemption of Africa from the deep degradation, superstition, and idolatry in which she has so long been involved." Moreover, these colonies of immigrants were uniquely positioned to introduce "civilization and religion among the barbarous nations of this country."

In characterizing Liberian history in this fashion, Roberts was publicly performing rituals of cultural chauvinism and ethnic supremacy that were common to the self-rationalizing ethos of colonizing powers. Mixing the language of paternalism with the lexicon of coercion, the president sought to assure several audiences—including immigrants, Africans, the ACS, and the

Western world generally—that the creation of Liberia had benefited all in some manner and promised to confer further benefits in the future. Rather than deny that the colonists had gained a foothold in Africa to the disadvantage of indigenous peoples, Roberts celebrated the colony's territorial acquisitions as divinely ordained. He even intimated that there was a certain moral efficacy to the violence that had been used to wrench lands from Africans, given that the dispossessed would ultimately profit from contact with the advanced civilization and Christianity of the immigrants.[43]

Although Roberts and other African American immigrants may have actually convinced themselves that their fortunes in Africa were divinely determined, they were nonetheless still aware that the fate of their new republic rested on its ability to marshal a critical mass of violence in the face of African resistance. The ACS regime of the colonial era had known this well, and Roberts, the last colonial governor and first president, was a crucial transitional figure in the maintenance of patterns of immigrant political domination. On the eve of Liberian independence, he appreciated the potential for African revolts well enough to request U.S. naval ships to patrol the coast as he pressed local rulers into relinquishing "the native tittle to all the lands lying between Cape Palmas and Cape Mount." In his annual message of 1853, Roberts skillfully evoked the siege mentality that underpinned Liberian national consciousness, reminding his audience that "savage tribes who delight in war" had only been held at bay by "a knowledge of the readiness and power of the government to punish their temerity." Couching his language in an increasingly romanticized construction of the colonial past, Roberts appealed to the formidable gun culture that had taken root in Liberia in order to bolster a sense of esprit de corps among immigrant communities. "Our citizens should be thoroughly trained in the use of arms," he counseled in his 1853 speech, "and for acting together if called into the field."

Roberts's frequent reference to laager imagery disclosed his awareness that Liberian nationality was not only based on restrictive definitions of citizenship and civil society but also on a fragmented political vision that pitted a scattered network of "remote and weak" immigrant towns against vast indigenous communities. To be fair, Roberts had not created the dilemma that he found himself presiding over during the 1840s and 1850s. The cumulative weight of past African-immigrant belligerency had poisoned relations between the two groups long before he became governor or president. However, his failure to rethink the limits of the ideology and practices that had soured these relations during the ACS's colonial regime did reveal a lack of political imagination and moral fortitude. Indeed, his often unreflective willingness to emulate the paradigm of domination that his erstwhile superiors had institutionalized was the biggest flaw of his statecraft.[44]

Notwithstanding the many crises that characterized African-immigrant relations, interactions between the two groups did not always result in bloodshed. As discussed in Chapter 4, many opportunities existed within the boundaries and along the fringes of Liberian society for cross-cultural exchanges, collaborations, and alliances of different sorts. For example, trade links connecting coastal and riverine towns to inland African communities bound the newcomers and indigenous peoples together economically. Africans continued to trade camwood, palm oil, cassava, rice, and various other items with immigrants in exchange for tobacco, cotton goods, rum, and beads. Similarly, indigenous pharmacological knowledge, as mentioned earlier, probably saved many immigrants from the worst effects of malaria and other illnesses. Beyond these interactions and exchanges, a few settlers even adopted the lifestyles and values of neighboring communities though instances of African American settlers "going native" were largely anecdotal and difficult to quantify. In general, it may have been easier for immigrants to win acceptance among Africans than vice versa. However, the degree of social distance and political alienation that characterized relations between the two groups should not be discounted. Illustratively, despite an 1841 act that offered citizenship to Africans who "abandoned all the forms, customs, and superstitions of heathenism" and embraced "the forms, customs and habits of civilized life," few indigenous people were granted equal rights within Liberian society. According to one estimate, only fifteen of the several thousand Africans residing in Grand Bassa County had been extended citizenship in the republic as late as 1858, a clear indication of their general exclusion from civic life.[45]

In some cases, very personal, even intimate, relationships did develop between immigrants and indigenous people, which slightly blurred cultural and ethnic lines. From the founding of the colony, African children served as apprentices and servants among families in Monrovia and elsewhere, often becoming emotionally attached to their hosts. Especially in instances where consanguineous ties existed between immigrant and indigenous families, some of these relationships could be quite affectionate and respectful. As late as the 1870s, one visitor to the country admiringly noted that African parents voluntarily placed their children with immigrant families. In these new settings, the youths were reportedly "clothed, fed, learned reading, writing, Christianity and her handmaid Civilization." The placement of indigenous children in settler households did establish meaningful dialogues between Africans and immigrants which may have minimized conflicts between various settlements and adjacent villages. Still, aside from these observations, a number of these arrangements were probably versions of pawning, which parents had assented to under legal or economic duress.

Young and impressionable, many of these African children were undoubtedly exposed to the ethnic prejudices of their immigrant custodians who believed that their contact with American-born blacks offered them a chance to become "civilized" Christians. Exemplary of this view, Edward C. Peele, an immigrant from Northampton County and a Baptist missionary, felt that incorporating African youths into settler households was the best way to "wean" them from the spiritual values of their parents. Along with such religious motivations, these relationships were usually paternalistic and economic in tone, arranged along terms most beneficial to immigrants. As American diplomat John H. Smyth noted in 1879, African wards were commonly exploited as menial laborers by their immigrant guardians, and "[t]heir scholastic training was entirely neglected." Many indigenous youths, in spite of long years of residence with Liberian families, often learned nothing more than how to "understand and speak English imperfectly." More troubling, tales of egregious treatment of African apprentices and other servants, even outright enslavement, continued to circulate beyond the shores of Liberia with a frequency that virtually confirmed their basic veracity. Considering the imbalances in power between Africans and immigrants, these dependent relationships further undermined the ability of the former to challenge the territorial and cultural encroachment of the latter. According to Smyth, indigenous communities, such as the Vai, came to "uniformly" detest immigrants for their abuse of the apprenticeship system and readily disclosed "their absence of any love for the Liberians."[46]

As with most interactions between immigrants and Africans, boundaries were often erected by the former to ensure their political and cultural dominion over the latter. These boundaries were porous, but served the purpose of demarcating power relations between the two groups. This discriminatory tendency was perhaps most lucid in regard to intermarriage. Early on, observers commented on the reluctance of immigrants to formally choose Africans as partners. Diana Skipwith, a Virginia immigrant residing in Monrovia during the 1830s, may have expressed a common attitude among colonists when she informed an acquaintance that "there is not a Native that i have see that i think that i could make myself hapy with." Writing in 1854, one disgruntled immigrant who returned to America regretted that a significant number of female colonists "have even been reduced to the extremity of marrying, or taking up with naked native men." Furthermore, into the late nineteenth century, travelers continued to recognize a "spirit of distinction" that undergirded immigrant interactions with Africans, despite the fact that numerous Liberian men participated in sexual unions with indigenous women and sometimes sired children by them. "A marriage or an illicit union between an Americo Liberian man and a native woman . . . was looked upon as a shameful occurrence," remarked one visitor at the turn of the century, "an episode to be kept in the shade as much as possible."[47]

Unfortunately, it is unclear how much of the disinclination of immigrants to intermarry with Africans was cultural as opposed to racial though the two perspectives are not mutually exclusive. Whatever the reason, substantial evidence does strongly imply that skin color played a significant role in Liberian culture. Throughout the nineteenth century, many individuals commented on the presence of mulattoes among the immigrant population, suggesting that their numbers were not negligible. Specifically, visitors and others often noted that mixed-race people, such as Joseph J. Roberts, James S. Payne, John Day, Reginald A. Sherman, and Louis Sheridan, tended to dominate the public affairs of the country, ranging from the presidency and municipal offices to the military and business institutions. Several possible reasons may explain this trend. Compared to the slave population, a disproportionate number of free African Americans were mulatto as defined by the 1860 United States census. Since free people, as opposed to liberated slaves, were overrepresented among individuals departing for Liberia, mulattoes would have been a disproportionate percentage of the immigrant population, compared to their percentage of the overall African American population of the United States. In North Carolina, 71.6 percent of the free black population of 30,463 was recorded as mulatto by census enumerators in 1860 while only 6.9 percent of the state's 331,059 slaves were categorized as such. Considering that at least 49 percent of those who left North Carolina for Liberia between 1825 and 1860 were previously free, mixed race people were almost certainly well represented among the immigrants. Moreover, the tendency of the ACS, Quaker colonizationists, and others to describe the putative beneficiaries of their programs as the *free people of color* was perhaps in recognition of the hybrid racial heritage of many free African Americans who were viewed as potential emigrants and who actually migrated.[48]

Free people who migrated from North Carolina and other states to Liberia tended to be more literate and skilled in various occupations than liberated slaves. Differences in social status, education, occupational training, and complexion had spawned color distinctions and prejudices in the United States among people of African descent which were transferred and played out in various ways in Liberia. These class differences created a social strata of privilege in Monrovia and other settlements, which favored more literate, skilled, and resourceful mulattoes. Also, at least a few mixed-race individuals maintained alliances with whites, particularly within the ACS, that further secured for them a measure of influence in the colony, and later the republic, that was generally unavailable to darker, recently liberated immigrants. Conceivably, some in this group would have been less likely to marry those well beneath their social standing in Liberian society, especially Africans. This observation does not mean that darker-skinned, newly emancipated immigrants were eager to partner with indigenous people or that no mixed-race settlers ever did. Instead, it is only meant to suggest that, in a society in which immigrants found it politically and culturally expedient to stress their differences vis-à-vis the indigenous population, color biases, along with religion, language, and dress, were yet another means of dramatizing such distinctions.

Aside from these sociocultural dynamics, a major development that complicated all ideas about race and identity in Liberia at midcentury was the sudden influx of a substantial number of recaptured Africans into the country. Originally, the colony had been established by the U.S. government as a settlement for people being illegally imported from Africa as slaves. Yet the vast majority of individuals who actually migrated to Liberia were American-born blacks, many of whom had never been in bondage. Recaptives trickled in sporadically during the colonial period, but it was not until the late 1850s, when cheap prices for slaves revitalized the traffic, that a significant wave of these displaced Africans reached Liberia. Between 1858 and 1861, about a dozen slavers bound for Cuba and other places were intercepted and diverted to Monrovia. A few, such as the *Erie* and the *Bonito*, disgorged nearly a thousand Africans upon Liberian shores, and by late 1860, over thirty-six hundred recaptives had arrived in the republic in just two years. Dejected, emaciated, and wracked by "aggravated dysentery," scurvy, and other afflictions, these rescued individuals—or "Congoes" as they were called—overwhelmed the resources and immigrant population of Liberia, which numbered only about seventy-six hundred in 1858. John Seys, the U.S. agent for recaptives at Monrovia, struggled to secure clothing and blankets for the new arrivals and tried to place many of them with families in various settlements. However, scores died shortly after arriving in the country, unable to recuperate from their horrific experiences below the crowded, putrid decks of transatlantic slavers.[49]

The "Congo Question" reconfigured Liberia's ethnic and cultural tapestry in important ways. Even more so than in the past, recaptives formed an intermediate zone between the worlds of African American immigrants and indigenous peoples. Like local Africans, they were exploited by settlers who eagerly solicited John Seys for recaptive laborers to serve in their homes and on their farms. However, over time, their "Congo towns" were integrated into immigrant communities more thoroughly than Dei, Kru, Grebo, and Vai villages would ever be. In addition to shifting ethnic and cultural boundaries, the rapid arrival of so many young, naked, poor people into the country stretched its meager resources in ways that intensified cycles of poverty and deprivation already existing among immigrants. To be sure, the labor of recaptives was largely responsible for the boom in coffee exports and other commodities that Liberia enjoyed during the 1850s and 1860s. Nonetheless, hard times were much more frequent and pervasive than economic expansions, and Liberian agriculture and all associated with it suffered in the wake of subsequent foreign competition and declining prices. In some cases, recaptives became known for preying upon various settlements, scavenging for food and other items. Lavinia Nelson, the Careysburg widow who arrived from New Bern in 1858, complained to William McLain that hungry recaptives "Stold all peopel things tha could get thar hands upon." As a result, even those like herself "who had a little mad[e] out quite bad indeed."[50]

Just as important as these consequences, this influx of thousands of Africans, mainly from the Congo River region, darkened the immigrant population, as did the arrival of hundreds of liberated American slaves during the 1850s. These demographic trends would have implications for existing color prejudices and patterns of mulatto privilege. By the 1870s, electoral politics in the country would become notably color coded as would the culture and operation of other institutions. Perhaps some of the ethnic labels and epithets that had become part of the often hostile dialogue between American immigrants and indigenous people were even altered or took on new meanings once thousands of recaptives rearranged the social landscape of Liberia. On this score, it would be interesting to know if indigenous peoples referred to the new arrivals as "merica man" as they sometimes called immigrants from the United States. Similarly, it would be telling to learn whether African American settlers labeled recaptives "Guinea niggers" or reserved such derogatory terms solely for the Dei and other local peoples. Whatever the case, indigenous Africans had their own ways of retorting to such labels though their cultural and political frames of reference were also affected by the dramatic surge in the recaptive population. According to one visitor writing in the late 1870s, the Kru in particular "are very proud of having never been slaves, and frequently twit the Liberians with the fact, when a quarrel occurs." It is very likely that they "twitted" recaptives in this fashion as well.[51]

Despite the many changes that boatloads of recaptives precipitated in Liberia, American immigrants still stressed distinctions between themselves and their "uncivilized" neighbors. From their insatiable appetite for American foods to their frame houses and Christian arrogance, many Liberians self-consciously defined themselves as Westerners or, at least, non-Africans. Even in the heat of the tropics, immigrant men clung to their top hats and frock coats as markers of their cultural refinement. Similarly, women could be seen as late as the 1880s paddling canoes along the St. Paul's, their "jaunty bonnets" and muslin dresses immediately disclosing their "civilized" character. Interestingly, though they were in Africa, many immigrants were still psychologically in diaspora, not quite at home in Liberia but no longer simply American refugees. While some imagined their migration to the continent as a return to ancestral roots, their consciousness was still filtered through a diasporic frame of reference, which was often quite Western centered. Their dietary habits, clothing, naming practices, political values, social rituals, and immunological systems were largely products of their experiences among the hybrid cultures of the Atlantic world where their African heritage had been blended with and diluted by countless other influences. For many, the realization that they were not Africans in any essentialist sense was only clear when they encountered Africa itself, usually first in the guise of Kru stevedores. Only then did their Americanness, juxtaposed with their utter unfamiliarity with Africa and Africans, seem most natural, even valuable. Only then did many come to know who they really were or, at least, desired to be.[52]

AS HAD ALWAYS BEEN THE CASE, Liberia continued to mean different things to different people. Those who had come from America looking for liberty sometimes found a semblance of what they sought, but very few discovered absolute freedoms untempered by hardships and sacrifice. For some, freedom came to mean dropping the hoe in favor of trade, attending churches of one's choosing, and attaining the rudiments of literacy in makeshift schools. For others, it meant having one's womenfolk beyond the predatory grasp of the slave master and raising families not subject to separation through sale or probate proceedings. Freedom was land, a farm, and independent, if drudging, subsistence. It was also living on the doorstep of the roaring Atlantic and watching one's children play carefree along sandy shores named after liberty itself. Particularly for ex-slaves, freedom meant legalized personhood, civil rights, and a documented existence. In essence, it was the unfettered ability to create one's own familial, communal, and civic relations in a land beyond the overbearing control of white people.

Whatever it meant to specific individuals, liberty usually carried a price. One's freedom could be inextricably tied to the happiness of others but could sometimes be at their expense. Immigrant homesteads, institutions, and legal rights were carved from African lands in a fashion that dispossessed thousands of indigenous people of millions of acres of territory. African American liberty in Liberia, therefore, meant African loss of independence, property, and lives, a steep price to pay for the enfranchisement of foreigners. Further, immigrant settlements along the coast disrupted African access to oceanic trade with port of entry laws and other mechanisms that injected Liberians as middlemen in commercial transactions between Africans and Europeans. Additionally, well-armed missions—such as the one at Heddington —and the apprenticing of indigenous children could only have eroded traditional religious and kinship systems. Ultimately, the overall costs of colonization for Africans is incalculable. One can hardly measure simply the psychological ramifications of this sustained assault against their dignity, sovereignty, and hopes for posterity, much less the totality of this multifaceted tragedy.[53]

Along with Africans, however, others paid a price for liberty as well. Marshall Hooper paid it in separation from his children. Similarly, Diana McKay Sheridan experienced the costs in terms of the rupturing of her marriage and the trials of single motherhood atop rocky Grand Cape Mount. For at least one in six North Carolina immigrants, freedom in Liberia was to be a brief experience, truncated by the depredations of *Anopheles* mosquitoes. For survivors, it was often a long, agonizing ordeal, mired in poverty, sickness, and perennial warfare. For recaptives, liberty meant living, for at least a while, in limbo between two worlds while experiencing alienation from both. For many of these displaced people, it meant imitating the "civilized" ways of African American immigrants even though one's cultural frame of reference and very appearance resembled those of local Africans, whom the settlers routinely derided as "savages." Such were the various benefits, costs, and meanings of freedom in Liberia. Such was the timeless truism that freedom was never truly free.

EIGHT. THE LAST WAVE

BY NINETEENTH-CENTURY standards, Alonzo Hoggard, at age forty-seven, was an old man when he resolved in 1868 to spend his last days in Liberia. During his many years of enslavement and his brief experience with freedom, he had witnessed a myriad of developments unfold in the northeastern county of Bertie which ultimately led him to imagine a life beyond North Carolina shores. Economically dependent upon slaves and cotton, the county had a black majority in 1860, with bondpeople comprising 57 percent (8,185) of its population of 14,310. The outbreak of the Civil War polarized the county into Unionist and Confederate camps though slavery, geography, and cotton virtually assured that its prominent men would succumb to secession. Four years of hostilities wrought unprecedented changes in life in Bertie. Runaway slaves by the hundreds took up arms for the Union, and scores of white yeomen retreated to the woods to avoid Confederate conscription patrols. Despite the fact that the small county seat of Windsor served as a supply depot for the rebel government, the prices of every marketable commodity rose exponentially as the federal blockade and battlefield victories took their toll. Some slaveholders, hoping to cash in on the hyperinflation, reaped handsome rewards from the sale of slaves, with field hands going for as much as twenty-five hundred dollars by July 1863. Others lost their bondpeople to Union naval forces plying the Chowan River; such forces made no secret of their willingness to recruit fugitives for military service. When the guns of

Above: Windsor, Bertie County, N.C. (Photograph by author)

war finally fell silent in the spring of 1865, the transformative nature of the conflict was starkly apparent to all. Forty thousand North Carolinians had lost their lives fighting for secession, a figure unmatched by any other southern state. Quite significantly, approximately a third of a million slaves were suddenly untethered from generations of bondage, making the grave sacrifices and grand promise of the war seem all the more apocalyptic.

As one of the thousands of African Americans liberated from slavery in Bertie County, Alonzo Hoggard stood at the twilight of a new age that was still obscured by the fog of the ever-present past and an inscrutable future. At least initially, emancipation and the continuing federal occupation seemed to promise new, more hopeful possibilities for black lives in North Carolina. Beyond a legislative enactment that "forever prohibited [slavery] within the State" as of October 1865, a full-blown constitutional convention three years later fundamentally challenged the planter aristocracy that had governed the state since the eighteenth century. The new constitution called for the enfranchisement of all male citizens twenty-one years of age or older as well as the abrogation of property requirements for gubernatorial and legislative candidates. Very importantly, judges and county officials were to be popularly elected, making them directly accountable to local constituents. State support for education was codified in article IX, section 2, of the constitution, which mandated "a general and uniform system of public schools, wherein tuition shall be free of charge to all the children of the State between the ages of six and twenty-one years." Other policy changes at the county and municipal level further eroded patterns of privilege that had defined North Carolina society and politics for decades. Reinforced by amendments to the federal Constitution which abolished slavery, guaranteed due process and equal protection of the laws, and deracialized male suffrage, political and legal equality for blacks appeared more imaginable in 1868 than at any other time in the nation's history.[1]

Notwithstanding this legislative enlightenment, the forces of reaction in the South were legion after Confederate defeat and slave emancipation, casting a long shadow over the postwar fortunes of African Americans and the region in general. Many southern whites, especially conservative elites, emerged from the war with a palpable longing for the old order and made strenuous efforts to reinvent the world that the Union army and congressional statutes had trampled. To this end, North Carolina, like most other former Confederate states, enacted Black Codes to restrict African American freedom. Passed in 1866, the North Carolina code, entitled "An Act Concerning Negroes and Persons of Color or Mixed Blood," closely resembled the slave codes that had existed prior to the war. One section of the act criminalized unemployment, or vagrancy, as a misdemeanor, making those "with no apparent means of subsistence" subject to arrest. Moreover, the code allowed for the apprenticing of black children, apparently against their will in some instances, and gave the former master, "in preference to other persons," the first opportunity to claim apprenticed youths. In an attempt to recover some of the mystique of white supremacy lost during the war and emancipation, the code nullified and criminalized interracial marriages. It further dictated that "an assault with an intent to commit rape upon the body of a white female" was to be considered a capital crime when perpetrated by "any person of color."

Once Republicans came to power in North Carolina in 1868, the flagrantly discriminatory sections of the Black Code were repealed. However, where such laws failed to safeguard white supremacy, the terroristic vigilantism of the Ku Klux Klan and other violent hate groups demonstrated that conservative, Democratic, and antiblack forces were not adverse to employing extralegal means to demolish the egalitarian experiments of the reconstructed state. Widespread Klan violence against blacks, white Republicans, and others reached crisis proportions by the end of the decade as hundreds of people were whipped, robbed, exiled, and murdered due to their race or political leanings. According to a congressional report of the early 1870s, at least 260 Klan "visitations" had occurred in twenty North Carolina counties by that time, with 174 of such episodes directed against African Americans. Complementing the election fraud, bribery, economic intimidation, and other means that white supremacists used to diminish black freedom, Klan violence did great harm to the infrastructure of the state's Republican Party. Although the group's excesses did eventually arouse both a state and federal campaign to suppress the lawlessness, the activities of the Klan and other such groups did ultimately impair the willingness of the national government to intervene in southern states for the purpose of protecting African American rights and lives.[2]

As Republicans ascended to power in North Carolina and Klan outrages became increasingly common, Alonzo Hoggard decided to solicit the ACS for aid in relocating to Liberia. As with so many others who had immigrated to Africa before him, the exact causes of his disaffection with North Carolina can only be speculated about. In 1868, the appearance of a man claiming to be a Liberian native stirred much interest in emigration among Bertie blacks. According to one observer, his advocacy of African American removal to Liberia was potent enough to make many of his listeners contemplate crossing the Atlantic "in boats of not more than ten ton burden." While Hoggard was perhaps one of the individuals who "place[d] the most implicit confidence" in this intriguing itinerant, his decision to emigrate was almost certainly shaped by other factors.

To be sure, Hoggard was not among the most oppressed and desperate blacks in the state. At some point, he had learned to read and write and had become affiliated with the local Baptist church. Neighbors thought highly of him, and his employer, John Tayloe, knew him as "a man of high moral character." Despite these observations, Hoggard's life as a poor tenant farmer in the cotton fields of Bertie County was hardly fulfilling for him and scarcely provided enough income to support his wife, Nancy, and their five children, all under twenty years of age. Even as the franchise and civil rights were being extended to African Americans, their ongoing landlessness, lack of educational facilities, and physical insecurity could only have dampened Hoggard's desire to remain in the state. Having initially notified the ACS of his intention to emigrate in 1868, the tenant farmer and his family were unable to make the expedition scheduled for that year for reasons unspecified in correspondence. However, in May of the following year, Hoggard, facing a cotton crop threatened by frost damage, requested that John S. Shepperd, a local white acquaintance, inform ACS secretary William Coppinger that he and his family would "sertinly be reddy" to depart in the near future.[3]

Hoggard's eagerness to go to Liberia was well received in the Washington office of the ACS. Having survived the lean years of the early 1860s, the organization resumed its emigration program immediately following the Confederate surrender, sending over sixteen hundred blacks to Liberia between 1865 and 1868. Tumultuous postwar race relations were largely responsible for the thousands of applications for passage to Africa that flooded into the ACS headquarters. No longer were agents needed to scrounge up emigrant parties; the Klan, Black Codes, poverty, and other problems had created a ready pool of prospective voyagers. The ACS's continuing generosity with African lands also encouraged this burgeoning interest in emigration though it deepened the enmity already existing between immigrants and indigenous people in Liberia. In conjunction with the Liberian government, the group now offered twenty-five acres of land to migrating families of "worthy people of color" along with free transportation to the republic, six months of complimentary support, and shelter in a receptacle. These "free gifts" were more than enough to entice thousands of people to consider refuge in Liberia, including the Hoggards of Bertie. In 1866, the ACS was confident enough in its future prospects to purchase the *Golconda*, a refurbished 1,016-ton ship capable of conveying as many as six hundred people to Africa at once. Between May 1867 and May 1868 alone, the thirteen-year-old *Golconda* carried, in three voyages, 1,086 emigrants to Liberia, the most in any twelve-month period since the refugee migrations of 1831–32.

During the pivotal decade of the 1860s, little had changed regarding the guiding ideology and basic operation of the ACS. Although it no longer straddled the slavery debate, the belief that blacks and whites were doomed to a perpetual state of antagonism in which one of the races would naturally seek mastery over the other still served as the foundational premise undergirding the work of colonizationists. Emancipation, in the view of one spokesman, had only underscored the incompatibility of the races since most African Americans were "not fit for citizenship in such a Republic as ours." Reminiscent of antebellum colonizationists of the Free-Soil variety, ACS president John Latrobe candidly asserted at the 1868 annual meeting that "a homogenous population of white men will one day prevail in America." Always dependent upon the goodwill of sympathetic donors, the decades-old message of the ACS still resonated in some quarters of the society, at least enough to raise the money needed to outfit its annual expeditions. With renewed vigor, the organization's leadership made ambitious plans for both a major expedition in the fall of 1869 and the establishment of two new settlements along the St. Paul's River. Funded by British philanthropist Robert Arthington and a bequest of the late Charles Brewer, administered by the Pennsylvania Colonization Society, the proposed settlements promised to be the most significant enterprise the ACS would undertake during the postwar period.[4]

In agreeing to give the ACS one thousand pounds sterling to send emigrants to Africa, Robert Arthington instructed the organization to establish an inland settlement "consisting as much as possible of men of Missionary spirit, and deeply and prayerfully interested in the moral redemption of all Africa." He, like ACS officials, believed that the well-applied capital of philanthropists and industrialists, along with the "civilizing" influence of Christian African American immigrants, would produce monumental cultural and material improvements in Liberian life. Arthington's windy letters to William Coppinger were saturated with a zealous, if paternalistic, preoccupation with Africa, which the ACS secretary, dutifully deferential to a major benefactor, replicated in his responses. Typical of Arthington's flourishes, he announced to Coppinger in an August 1868 missive, "*We must have universal elementary education in Liberia,*" as if he personally had a stake in such a proposition. Similarly, in a November letter, he reminded the secretary that "I am set for the redemption,—the deliverance from the curse of slavery, and the evangelization, *of Africa!*" Coppinger, with Arthington's money in hand and piles of applications on his desk, looked to North Carolina for the "men of Missionary spirit" whom the Englishman had requested be sent to Liberia. He hoped to satisfy Arthington's crusading passion for African "redemption" with a boatload of poor tenant farmers from the cotton fields of the Tar Heel State.[5]

Traveling by "horse and waggon," Coppinger arrived in Windsor on August 25, 1869, and met with Alonzo Hoggard the following day. He was much impressed by the high regard in which the tenant farmer was held by local people and further pleased to find that he was settling his affairs in prepara-

tion for embarkation. Despite Hoggard's enthusiasm, Coppinger was cognizant of the fact that opposition to Liberian emigration was formidable in
Bertie. John Shepperd, a local white man who was assisting in the organization of the expedition, had warned the ACS secretary in July that many African Americans would not countenance migration for fear of being sold into
Cuban slavery. In addition to these apprehensions, other rumors maintained
that colonizationists hoped "to get [black] republican voters out of the country so that the democrats may get into power." In a second trip to the area the
following year, Coppinger learned that self-interested politicians, landlords,
and merchants were among the most vocal critics of black removal to Liberia. Many of these individuals charged that the ACS divided families and
forced emigrants to repay, with interest, the cost of their passage to Africa.
Such anti-emigration propaganda certainly undercut the organization's popularity in Bertie and other counties, particularly given that unfavorable reports concerning living conditions in Liberia had circulated through eastern
North Carolina for years. Yet aside from such opposition, Coppinger's visit to
the county in the late summer of 1869 did succeed in generating enough interest in emigration to warrant designating Alonzo Hoggard's party, which
came to number several dozen, the Arthington Company. In neighboring
Martin County, a similar dynamic was at work that resulted in the organization of the Brewer Company, named after the late Pennsylvania benefactor.[6]

After Coppinger returned to Washington, emigration fever struck hard in
Bertie and Martin Counties as the cold of winter approached. On November
1, scores of prospective emigrants, including sixty from Jamesville in Martin
County, showed up at Shepperd's home in Windsor expecting to depart for
Liberia that day. Surprised and unprepared for the crowd, Shepperd made
arrangements for housing his "much disappointed" guests, who were obliged
to stay a few more days in Windsor. On November 5, the steamer *Isadore* carried seventy-nine Bertie blacks—including fifteen Hoggards—and forty-
four people from Martin County to Norfolk, where they awaited the arrival
of the *Golconda* from Baltimore.

Unlike every other party of North Carolina emigrants who had passed
through the Virginia port en route to Africa, this group was not forced to
witness the seasonal routine of interstate slave-trafficking that had made
Norfolk a notorious site of black dehumanization. Unfortunately, the party
did have to cope with an icy cold front that blasted through the city the day
after their arrival. The climatic change was compounded by scheduling problems, common to ACS expeditions, that delayed the appearance of the *Golconda* until November 10. In a letter to William McLain, Coppinger reported
that the frigid weather caused notable suffering among women and children,
"making a few talk of returning to the 'fleshpots of Egypt.'" In the end, no

MAP 4. Northeastern North Carolina, ca. 1880

one trekked back to North Carolina even though the massive *Golconda* did not sail through Hampton Roads on course to Liberia until November 15. Writing to Robert Arthington eleven days later, Coppinger apprised him of how well his money had been spent, a prelude to future requests for aid. Anticipating the Englishman's missionary interest in the expedition, the ACS secretary assured him the North Carolinians "have the highest welfare of Africa at heart."[7]

Following this expedition, the fifth—and last—voyage of the *Golconda* in November 1870 would take an additional 196 North Carolinians to Liberia, 112 of whom would be from Bertie County. With the beginning of the new decade, postwar emigration reached its high point, tapering off precipitously as the country plunged into a depression triggered by the Panic of 1873. Between 1871 and 1893, only 348 North Carolinians would embark for Liberia under the auspices of the ACS, an average of 16 per year, the lowest for any comparable span of years since the beginning of the movement. In relative terms, North Carolina continued to be a major source of Liberian emigrants during the postwar period, second only to Georgia in the number of people departing on ACS ships after 1865. But compared to the heydays of the 1820s and 1850s, the last decades of the nineteenth century marked the final decline of Liberian emigration.

Lack of funding was largely responsible for the sudden drop in expeditions, notwithstanding that conditions continued to exist in North Carolina and elsewhere that prolonged black interest in migration. For instance, a Democratic-controlled convention rewrote the state's constitution in 1875 to include articles mandating school segregation, the leasing of convicts, and the prohibition of interracial marriage "forever." The Landlord and Tenant Act of 1877 gave land owners near absolute control over the crops produced by tenants and other agricultural workers. Moreover, a Common Road Law requiring males between the ages of eighteen and forty-five to labor on road construction without remuneration operated to the detriment of black men, who were disproportionately called upon for such work. Tumbling prices for cotton and tobacco exacerbated the despair that many African Americans experienced by the end of the decade as did the Republican Party's abandonment of its role as a defender of black civil rights following the 1876 presidential election. Although these developments resulted in an outburst of interest in Liberian emigration among North Carolina blacks, less than 10 percent of those who expressed a desire to go to Africa in the 1870s and 1880s were actually transported due to the meager resources of the ACS. Unable to stand life in the Tar Heel State following the collapse of Reconstruction, some African Americans turned westward for a refuge, paying train fares that proved more affordable than passage to Africa. Subsequently, as many as three thousand North Carolina blacks migrated to Indiana during 1879 and 1880 alone, more than the total number (2,030) who immigrated to Liberia during the entire nineteenth century.[8]

The letters received during this period by the ACS headquarters, which was moved to New York City in 1877, offer a unique glimpse into both African American life in North Carolina as well as the ways in which blacks conceived of Liberia and the meaning of migration. The postwar years marked the unraveling of the Liberian emigration movement, but this era was also characterized by a rising incidence of literacy among blacks as reflected in the number and quality of letters of inquiry that they sent to the ACS. Beyond emigration societies that were organized in places such as Currituck County, Charlotte, and Elizabeth City, scores of individual African Americans corresponded with ACS officials more regularly and openly than ever before. Each of their letters contained its own unique mix of motifs, solicitations, desires, and literary techniques, but common themes course through many of them. Generally, the letters of prospective emigrants reveal that larger societal forces, macrohistorical trends, and communal aspirations substantially shaped their lives in North Carolina and informed their interest in Liberia.[9]

An enduring theme that emerged from many letters was the notion that Liberia, and Africa in general, was the natural home of black people. This idea, of course, had been salient in African American correspondence with the ACS as early as the 1850s and continued to be prominent through the turn of the century. However articulated in individual letters, the theme of a collective consciousness among black North Carolinians stressed that they were not only related in some culturally, even biologically, essentialist manner to each other but shared ties of history, lineage, and destiny with the continent of Africa and its people. Typical of these correspondents, A. W. Power of Jamesville, writing in December 1869, informed an ACS official that "we all here waunts to go to liberia for we know it is ower home and the only home for the Poor B[l]ack man to live." Miles A. Bright of Camden County also conceived of emigration as a return to ancestral roots when he wrote in 1877, "We believe that our ancestors come from there and we desire to return back." In even more rapturous language, Harry Roberts of New Bern notified Coppinger that many people desired to immigrate to "our god Blessed country" in late 1879. "Oh! Sweet torrid zone," he waxed poetically, "may we all go back home." Some blacks asserted that a sense of obligation to Africa motivated their interest in emigration, suggesting a sort of selfless, missionary devotion to the well-being of the continent and its people. "It is not for my personal benefit that calls me to my native country," Peter Mountain of Windsor disclosed to the ACS secretary in an October 1870 letter, "but a duty which I owe my race." Whatever the stated motivation for emigrating, these romanticized imaginings of transoceanic black kinship and common interests often wilted once immigrants arrived in Liberia and learned that their cultural mores and practices, material interests, and political assumptions were very different from those of Africans. Notwithstanding these subsequent realizations, prospective emigrants, from the vantage point of North Carolina, dreamed of Liberia in largely idyllic ways, as revealed in their many vivid letters to the ACS.[10]

By the 1870s, when formal black membership in Protestant denominations rose dramatically due primarily to emancipation and active church recruitment, religious themes became commonplace in many of the letters sent to the ACS. Undoubtedly, some writers employed Christian imagery and missionary language to ingratiate themselves to their audience, hoping that the latter would be impressed enough to entirely defray the cost of passage to Liberia, which the organization could no longer afford to do by 1877. Still, it can be assumed that the sentiments of many correspondents were sincere, given that Methodist and Baptist congregations could be found in almost every black community of any size by this time. Accordingly, R. S. Lewis of Clinton stressed in an 1877 letter to Coppinger that "I want to go where I can Educate my children and where I can become a man." In emphasizing his lack of interest in personal aggrandizement, he held that "it is not so much for my eating or drinking that I want to go to Liberia, it is because I want to try & do that race some good in the name of God." The following year, Jerry Jones of Rosedale conveyed a similar—if more patronizing—sense of obligation to Africa when he noted to Coppinger, "i feel it my duty to Preach to a Lost and Benighted Continent as afria." Likewise, Cain Gibbs, an Enfield minister, told William McLain that he simply wanted "to go there and labor in the Gospel for that people." Unfortunately for them, Lewis, Jones, and Gibbs never reached Liberia, and thus their missionary zeal and religious ambitions were never tested. However, for Reverend John Wilkins of Currituck County, who migrated in 1878, life in Africa probably did much to temper the idealism that he had expressed in a November 1877 letter. "We believe that Africa is Heaven," he once fantasized, "and we ar a try hard to get Home."[11]

Not unrelated to the religious sentiments expressed by some would-be emigrants, church interest in evangelizing Africa peaked during the late nineteenth century. In North Carolina, Livingstone College in Salisbury, founded by the African Methodist Episcopal Zion (AMEZ) denomination in 1879, trained students for mission work in Africa. Additionally, several Africans attended the college by the 1890s, including James Aggrey of the Gold Coast. In 1884, the General Conference of the AMEZ church appointed Andrew Cartwright as their missionary representative in Liberia. Cartwright, who had originally emigrated from Pasquotank County in 1876, was given the authority to ordain preachers and organize annual church conferences in Liberia. In 1887, his young wife, Caroline, joined him in the St. Paul's River settlement of Brewerville, where she established a school sponsored by the AMEZ board. By March of the following year, she could report that 174 people—including thirteen Africans—attended her day and Sunday schools.[12]

Along with the Methodists, Baptists also exhibited interests in Liberia as a mission field. Shaw University of Raleigh, a black Baptist-affiliated school incorporated in 1875, trained several students for work in Africa, among them Sherwood Capps and James O. Hayes. In 1877, Capps served as secretary of the North Carolina Freedmen's Emigration Aid Society, a pro-Liberia group that had been originally organized in Elizabeth City six years earlier. In January 1878, he embarked for Monrovia at the age of twenty-six, hoping to redeem some "of the 200 000 000 of Heathen in Africa." A year later, he secured employment in an ACS-sponsored school at Brewerville, where he also founded a "Manual Laboring School" for local boys. A contemporary of Capps, Hayes, too, felt destined to be "an instrument in the redemption of the african race of which I am a member." While at Shaw, he pursued theological training, a popular course of study on a campus where two-thirds of the population allegedly favored work in Liberia. When he immigrated to Brewerville during the summer of 1881, Hayes found, perhaps to his surprise, a country inundated by seasonal rains and perennial poverty. Certainly to his dismay, he also found family members who had emigrated years earlier unable to plow fields for lack of oxen, to make bread for want of a grist mill, or to live "comfittable" in thatch houses that could not be substantially improved despite "all that may be don to them." Such was the life awaiting the young minister when he stepped onto the banks of the St. Paul's River "with the love of Sauls in my heart & . . . [the] gospel in my hand."[13]

Interestingly, while the thought of immigrating to Liberia generated evangelical fervor among some North Carolinians, others damned the idea with a commensurate amount of zeal. For example, Bishop James W. Hood of the AMEZ church lambasted emigration schemes in fiery speeches, as did several "leading colored men" at a meeting in Raleigh in October 1877. Reverend Joseph C. Price, president of Livingstone College, also dismissed Liberia as a refuge for African Americans though he supported mission work in Africa. When offered the position of U.S. minister to Liberia in 1888, he politely declined, maintaining that his primary calling was "the education of Negroes, and the bringing about of a better state of things in the South generally." If the opposition of prominent black spokesmen did not significantly diminish enthusiasm for emigration, the fate of the *Azor*, a ship independently chartered to take 252 South Carolina emigrants to Liberia in 1878, did much to tarnish the allure of the black republic among North Carolinians. Having lost twenty-three shipmates during the voyage to Monrovia, returning survivors brought back well-publicized tales of disease, misery, and death. Their stories, along with existing opposition to Liberian emigration, may have been partially responsible for the growing appeal of westward migration among black Carolinians the following year. Unsurprisingly, the *Azor* disaster was deftly used by prominent critics of emigration to cool Liberia fever in various parts of the Tar Heel State.[14]

Beyond black opposition to their departure for Africa, prospective emigrants also endured formidable white hostility to their efforts to leave the country. Some of the opposition was political; white (and black) Republican officials were dependent upon African American voters and thus did not desire a decline in their numbers. Others, especially planters and merchants, wished to see no siphoning off of black laborers and customers from whom they largely derived their income. In Woodville, Isaac Skinner reported in 1877 that white opposition to black emigration was so staunch in that northeastern town that landowners withheld wages in order to discourage the departure of their workers. In 1870, William Coppinger had personally witnessed law officers attempting to impede the embarkation of blacks from Windsor and Plymouth, the whites there using "every conceivable device . . . to prevent emigration." In one particularly harrowing episode, Jerry Johnson, a thirty-two-year-old Methodist farmer from Rosedale, tried to leave the state in December 1877 with a young girl whom he had raised for the past three years. A constable, alerted of Johnson's intention by the girl's mother who opposed her leaving for Liberia, caught up with the two on a boat en route to Norfolk and returned the child to Rosedale.

In response to such cases and the upsurge in black migration to the Midwest, the North Carolina legislature passed a law in 1881 that levied a fine against anyone who encouraged blacks to leave the state. The measure also penalized African Americans who left North Carolina in violation of labor contracts. Predictably, the law did not end outmigration, for by the end of the decade tens of thousands of blacks, facing low wages, disfranchisement, and lynchings, had quit the state for Arkansas, Oklahoma, Texas, and other destinations. Consequently, by 1890, 116,400 African Americans native to North Carolina lived in other states, compared to only 93,390 in 1880. While most people anxious to leave the Tar Heel State looked westward during these years, a few continued to gaze to the East. That sunny, distant shore on the other side of the Atlantic still seemed to beckon them.[15]

ARRIVING AT MONROVIA on December 19, 1869, Alonzo Hoggard hoped to begin life anew in Liberia. As the proposed founders of the Arthington settlement, his company was a pioneering one, which by definition meant at least some initial hardships. The selected site of the town was in the hilly, uneven, but picturesque lands located four miles northeast of Millsburg along the northern bank of the St. Paul's River. It was a good area for growing coffee and a variety of other crops and apparently somewhat shielded from malarial exposure by its elevation. With no receptacle or other immigrant dwellings, the men of the Arthington company were obliged to spend much of their first months in Liberia clearing lands and building cabins at the new site. Concurrently, women and children stayed in Monrovia, roughly twenty miles downriver, until this work was completed. This arrangement was not wholly agreeable to most of the newcomers. Hoggard later suggested to one ACS official that a receptacle be constructed at Arthington so that future immigrants would not have to bear such separation while their houses were

THE LAST WAVE

being built. For the time being, however, male immigrants labored steadily until May 1870, when enough dwellings had been prepared to house family members staying in Monrovia. In a letter to Coppinger, Hoggard informed him that "with the Exception of chills" the company was "much pleased with our location and our prospects." They had been well treated by Henry W. Dennis, the ACS agent whom they regarded as a sort of father figure in "a straing land."

By his own account, Alonzo Hoggard fared well in Liberia, at least better than he had in Bertie County. After building a thirteen-by-fifteen-foot log cabin on his allotted land, he immediately began cultivating rice, potatoes, corn, peas, cucumbers, mustard greens, and ginger, with plans for a cotton crop the next year. By the following May, he boasted that he had two thousand coffee plants growing on his farm. "The men in Arthington exspect to go largely in Coffee an in Cotton and in ginger and in corn and in cane," Hoggard predicted in an 1873 letter to Coppinger. "In a few years we want to be able to Ship Coffee and cotton and ginger over to you to Sell for us." Outside of his ambitious agricultural pursuits, Hoggard's letters reveal a simple, diligent man, satisfied with the slow, rural life of backwoods Liberia, but ever trying to improve his lot. The laziness of some of his fellow immigrants bristled him, and their lack of appreciation for the settlement's possibilities sometimes aroused his scorn. A forward-looking man, he helped raise a Baptist church from the clay and gravel of Arthington and required that all of his children attend the local school. He never lost sight of the larger context in which he lived and hoped that a line of steamers would eventually visit the St. Paul's on a monthly basis. Above all, he remained grateful to be out of Bertie County and in Africa since "she has made me free."

Despite his affable personality and hard-working ways, Hoggard was a settler, an identity he shared with all immigrants, who by this time generally thought of themselves as Americo-Liberians. His "civilized" nature and Christian character were now social and political commodities in a country that still maintained exclusionary boundaries between the civilized and the savage, the believer and the heathen. Sometimes, Hoggard's cultural biases were almost comical, such as when he informed Coppinger, "I has got one of the [African] kings to waring clothen Britches and shert." In other instances, his myopia could have serious implications, as when he asserted in 1871 that it was necessary to "whip" Africans militarily in order to end slavery among them. On occasion, Hoggard could be endearing toward indigenous people though his condescending views conditioned his interactions with Africans. In an 1873 letter, he reported approvingly that Arthingtonians hoped "to civilize and Crisianize" an indigenous man currently living among them. Arguably, Hoggard's paternalism was both a product of the inequitable African-immigrant relationship that had evolved over the past fifty years and a function of his role as founder and communal elder of Arthington. When he died at age sixty in June 1880, one neighbor remembered him in paternal terms, eulogizing him simply as "the father & leader of this place."[16]

As in other settlements, life in Arthington was lived in routines and slow rhythms, accented with occasional unexpected events and twists of fate. Not all experienced freedom along the St. Paul's River with the same satisfaction as Alonzo Hoggard. In 1871, several single women were reported "to get a long badly" for lack of husbands and land, a common theme of Liberian life. Immigrants such as John B. Roulhac and Peter Mountain, both of Bertie County, craved meat, still a luxury item in Liberia. Roulhac even claimed that some individuals were actually "suffering for want of meat" and requested that Coppinger send dogs to Liberia to facilitate the hunting of deer. As in the past, the struggle against the environment was the major preoccupation of Arthington residents. While malarial mortality there did not approach the epidemic proportions that it had in earlier years, tales of chills, sores, and other ailments were regularly chronicled in correspondence. Unfortunately, the heavy rains of the early 1870s could only have increased the sickliness of the region. As late as 1886, Arthington, which had not experienced any further immigration for over a decade, had a population of only 293, revealing that the community, consisting primarily of North and South Carolinians, was slowly dying. In common with its sister towns, the settlement had quickly become an odd mix of beauty and tragedy. Standing on a hillside, one could not help but be impressed by the long columns of coffee trees dipping into valleys and reaching over adjacent hills as far as the eye could wander. At the same time, death frequently menaced this rolling, scenic landscape and was simply part of life in Arthington.[17]

Brewerville, established on the north bank of the St. Paul's River, shared similar patterns of development with Arthington. Located approximately ten miles from Monrovia, the town was founded by Jamesville immigrants in 1869 and continued to receive newcomers from North Carolina into the 1880s. John B. Munden, a forty-five-year-old literate farmer from Jamesville, was a founder of the settlement, filling a leadership role similar to Alonzo Hoggard's position among Arthington settlers. His relatively successful farming operations in Brewerville resembled those of the tenant farmer from Bertie and were extensive enough to produce five hundred pounds of coffee in 1876. Like Hoggard, Munden despised the idleness of immigrants, and some of his letters revealed a judgmental temperament. When people from Concord, North Carolina, returned to the state in 1883, he noted to one acquaintance that the dissatisfied immigrants had been "too lasey to wash their face or hands [and] too lasey to comb their head here." When he was not sizing up his neighbors,

Munden lived a simple life in a small log cabin among coffee trees, apparently satisfied with such an existence. However, he was definitely one of the residents of Brewerville who occasionally made life there eventful.[18]

In 1871, a dramatic constitutional crisis in Monrovia briefly drew Munden into national politics. Elected in 1869, President Edward J. Roye triggered a political imbroglio when he sought to stay in office beyond the statutory limit of two years. Roye ignored an election in May 1871 which resulted in the re-election of Joseph J. Roberts and proceeded to make himself even more unpopular by securing an ill-advised public loan from British financiers. Opponents of the chief executive managed to remove him from office on October 26, 1871, but not before he declared martial law. Aware of where his remaining political strength lay, Roye appealed to the upriver settlements for aid in combating his foes in Monrovia. According to ACS agent Henry W. Dennis, Munden and others in Brewerville became "vehement supporters" of the president, some even arming themselves for civil war. As it turned out, Roye was arrested before any widespread violence took place, but his drowning under ambiguous circumstances following a jail break in February 1872 only heightened political tensions in the country.

One element of this episode that attracted the attention of Munden and others was the issue of color. Roye, a dark-skinned man, had been elected by a coalition of recaptives, upriver Americo-Liberians, and others who desired to challenge the political supremacy of the Republican Party, which had historically been led by mulattoes like Joseph J. Roberts. Issues of class, region, and policy priorities were, of course, also responsible for the cleavages between the Republicans and Roye's True Whig Party. However, the topics of caste prejudice and mulatto privilege were notable features of the political terrain of the period. As the constitutional crisis unfolded, the issue of color proved to be more potent, complex, and contradictory than one may have otherwise imagined.

Edward Blyden, the Liberian intellectual and clergyman, had been quite vocal in the assault on what he believed to be a mulatto monopoly on positions of power and authority in the republic. In letters to Coppinger, he opposed further immigration of mixed-race people to Liberia, which would supposedly strengthen the "mongrel clique" that ruled the country. To his chagrin, his own credibility was publicly called into question when rumors of an alleged affair between Blyden and Mrs. Roye, the president's wife, circulated. Ironically, a group of black men nearly lynched him on the streets of Monrovia for his purported sexual indiscretion, a most embarrassing spectacle that was probably engineered by Blyden's erstwhile ally, Edward J. Roye.

If this incident revealed the conflictual and mercenary nature of Liberian politics, it also focused attention on the question of color privilege. For John

Munden, it fortified his political convictions and lessened his tolerance of color discrimination. In 1881, he told Coppinger, as Blyden had done earlier, not to send "molatters" to Brewerville. According to him, Sherwood Capps, the Shaw-trained teacher from Raleigh, had discriminated against darker-skinned pupils in the local school, causing bitter divisions among residents. "Send to us the *Negro* who do not think themselves better than they are," he beseeched the ACS secretary. "Please keep them [mulattoes] on that side" of the Atlantic.[19]

While an important theme in the overall evolution of Liberian society, the color issue was, at best, of secondary importance to many in Brewerville. Survival was a much more immediate concern and, to some extent, a more pressing matter than it was in Arthington. Unlike John Munden, numerous residents of Brewerville found much to complain about, and their letters disclosed a multifaceted degree of deprivation and suffering reminiscent of earlier times. For example, in a pitiful 1875 letter, Samuel S. Hardy of Plymouth begged ACS agent Dennis for more food. "Pleas for god sake . . . give us a little more provision," he pleaded, "for we are realy starving." Alexander Hays, brother of the Shaw-educated minister James O. Hayes, also informed colonization officials of the desperate poverty of Brewerville and requested a long list of items, including a steam mill, a portable engine, and blacksmith tools. As in Arthington, the themes of sickness and death framed much of the correspondence coming out of Brewerville though the latter settlement appears to have been the less salubrious of the two. Illustratively, having been ill since his arrival in 1878, William Harvey inquired in 1881 whether Coppinger could arrange to get him and his family back to the United States. "I come hear with 7 Children and they all have been sick ever since they have been hear [and] one have died," he noted to the ACS secretary. "We all . . . been down crawling on our hands and knees with ulcers and sores and one [not] able to take care of the other."

Of all the dismal experiences of North Carolinians in Brewerville, the plight of the Browne family may have been the worst. The clan of twelve emigrated from Littleton in 1879 just as migration to the Midwest was pulling African Americans in the opposite direction. Over the next four years, seven members of the family died. Compounding their misery, unremitting sickness and abject penury forced the remaining Brownes to sell their clothes, an extraordinary measure even for the most indigent of immigrants. Norfleet Browne, in an 1883 letter, shared their tragic story with Coppinger, adding that "I beg and pray that the Society will [assist] . . . as much as in her funds to do." Even in a country where suffering was abundant, the appalling misfortunes of this family must have shocked their friends and neighbors.[20]

In the vast majority of cases, the ACS did nothing to alleviate the desperation of individual families in Liberia. Its limited funds and abdication of moral responsibility for the country's quality of life left many immigrants in the lurch once they set foot on the republic's impoverished, malarial shores. Judging from the scarcity of copies of response letters in ACS records, most of the pleadings of immigrants went unanswered. Ever protective of its reputation, the ACS enthusiastically reprinted good news from Liberia, and the letters of optimistic survivors such as Alonzo Hoggard and John Munden regularly appeared in the *African Repository* and annual reports. The organization also made it a point to publicize certain statistics, such as the fact that it—along with state auxiliaries—had transported, at a total cost of almost $3 million, over 15,000 blacks to Liberia by 1886. However, bad news, such as that contained in Norfleet Browne's letter, was thoroughly suppressed and never appeared in ACS publications. Moreover, unpleasant statistics, such as mortality and morbidity tallies, continued to go unrecorded by organizational officials, many of whom still remembered the controversy that the 1843 colonial census had provoked.[21]

In regard to the 667 North Carolinians who arrived in the country between 1869 and 1893, demographically they were much like their predecessors. Half of the emigrants were female, reflecting that people traveled in family groups. The average and modal ages of both sexes were twenty-one and one, respectively. Nearly twice as many of the emigrants identified themselves as Baptists as opposed to Methodists (157 vs. 84), and only 43, or 6.4 percent, were listed as capable of reading or writing. Occupationally, of the 139 individuals listed with a vocation, 108 were farmers. Among the remainder were nine carpenters, five teachers, four ministers, three blacksmiths, and three coopers. One in every two emigrants was from the northeastern counties of Bertie (196), Washington (101), and Currituck (84) though dozens of people migrated from Mecklenburg, Pasquotank, Craven, and other counties. If there was anything that notably distinguished North Carolina emigrants leaving the state following the Civil War from those who departed between 1825 and 1860, it was their settlement in primarily two adjacent towns, Arthington and Brewerville. Ninety-one percent (or 609) of the 667 individuals arriving in the country after 1860 were located to these towns—indeed, they were instrumental in the founding of both. Accordingly, by the 1890s, the chain of settlements along the St. Paul's River, including Caldwell, Millsburg, Arthington, and Brewerville, was indelibly imprinted with the culture, labor, hopes, and tragedies of North Carolinians, more so than by people from any other state. Their decades-long search for freedom in this place had produced a history and lore rich in triumphs and possibilities, but also replete with catastrophes and unsatisfied yearnings.[22]

At the turn of the century, the prospects for Liberia, as an experiment in

TABLE 4. Counties of Origin of North Carolina Emigrants, 1869–1893

County of Origin	Total Emigrants from County
Bertie	196
Cabarrus	35
Camden	2
Craven	55
Currituck	84
Duplin	12
Halifax	4
Martin	44
Mecklenburg	38
Pasquotank	34
Perquimans	10
Sampson	1
Tyrrell	7
Wake	8
Warren	34
Washington	101
Wayne	1
Other	1
Total	667

Source: Based on emigrant rolls, census records, and other sources.

both philanthropy and nation-building, were not very favorable. The continuing decline of the price of its chief export, coffee, boded ill for the future, as did the perennial dearth of beasts of burden, farm implements, readily accessible transportation networks, and capital. Likewise, the slowing trickle of emigrants from the United States failed to reverse overall population decline. By 1900, there were only an estimated twelve thousand Americo-Liberians in the country, despite the fact that sixteen thousand American immigrants had migrated there over the course of the nineteenth century. Without the constant addition of new arrivals to its scattered communities, the settler republic faced the real possibility of simply fading away.

Meanwhile, as the economy and population stagnated and declined, immigrant relations with Africans continued to be exploitative and adversarial. Token representation of indigenous groups in the Liberian legislature and loudly celebrated instances of the rare intermarriage did not obscure the political dominance of immigrants or the general exclusion of Africans from

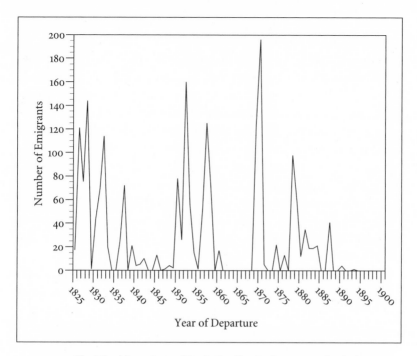

FIGURE 7. The Migration of 2,030 North Carolina Emigrants to Liberia, by Year
Sources: Based on emigrant rolls, census records, and other sources.

Liberian life. The great uprising of the Grebo in 1875–76 only confirmed the existence of these realities, as would a similar rebellion of the Kru in 1915. To be sure, there were countervailing voices that stressed the need for one Liberia with immigrant and indigenous communities merged into a single nation, thus destroying the colonial paradigm once and for all. Border disputes with European imperial powers actually encouraged this sort of unification if only to protect Americo-Liberians from foreign subjugation. Nonetheless, a meaningful reordering of power relations between immigrants and Africans was not to be, at least not yet, and like its new European neighbors, Monrovia entered the twentieth century a colonial regime of the settler variety.[23]

JULIUS STEVENS WAS THE last North Carolinian to be sent to Liberia by the ACS during the nineteenth century. Hailing from Goldsboro, the thirty-nine-year-old teacher had accepted an appointment as the organization's agent in Liberia and planned to establish a permanent residence in the country. Stevens's position in the African republic was highly atypical of North Carolinians, who almost never served in any notable positions of authority. There had been exceptions, such as Louis Sheridan and Moore T. Worrell, an emigrant from Hertford County who served as Secretary of the Treasury during the 1880s. Additionally, three North Carolinians—Moses A. Hopkins, Ezekiel E. Smith, and Owen L. W. Smith—filled the post of U.S. minister to Liberia during the late nineteenth century, though none of their terms were particularly noteworthy. Notwithstanding these instances, Stevens was rather unique among emigrants from the state insofar as he would be closely associated with the upper echelons of the Americo-Liberian government at Monrovia.[24]

When he embarked for Liberia on April 5, 1893, the new agent sailed between worlds in transition. The dawn of American empire and overseas expansion was on the horizon as the country would reach for colonies from the Philippines to Puerto Rico. Concurrently, Europeans were completing their conquest of Africa, and hardly a square mile of the continent had not been the object of their ambitions. Even North Carolina, still overwhelming rural and poor, was undergoing changes. Populist farmers and Fusionist politicians were challenging the Democratic hold on the state with unprecedented success though race relations continued to deteriorate with the emergence of segregation, disfranchisement, and lynch law. Disaffected black Tar Heels still migrated to havens in the Midwest and elsewhere but not in such numbers as would leave in the wake of the Great Migration of the World War I period. For most, the New South turned out to be the Old South in different clothing. Gone were the whips, slave codes, and anti-free-black persecutions of the antebellum period. Nevertheless, restrictive tenancy laws, grandfather clauses, and racist violence—such as the Wilmington race riot of 1898—provided a certain continuity between antebellum and postwar North Carolina.

Regarding the ACS, the country's oldest organization dedicated to colonizing Africa, its glory days were entirely over. Trumped by the midwestern migrations, the depression of 1893, and other developments, the group had virtually stopped sending any emigrants to Liberia by the turn of the century. At the 1903 annual meeting, the committee on emigration reported that "contributions made to the Society are more for the purpose of education as it is now regarded as chimerical to attempt to send the entire mass of Negroes back to their native land." Such was the eulogy for an organization that had denied the fantastical nature of its objectives for almost a century. Interestingly, it was not until six decades later that the group finally closed its doors. In a quiet transaction of business, five directors passed "Articles of Dissolution," formally terminating the ACS on March 22, 1963. The following year, the remainder of the organization's treasury was transferred to the Phelps-Stokes Fund of New York, a philanthropic institution. Somewhat fittingly, its voluminous records, chronicling over a century of its activities, were deposited in the Library of Congress, not far from where a group of prominent white men had met 147 years earlier to create "the American Society for Colonizing the Free People of Color in the United States."[25]

By the time Julius Stevens landed at Monrovia in mid-1893, a most remarkable history of colonization had been played out in the rural districts of his home state and upon the shores of his new country. Over the course of the nineteenth century, the notion of removing blacks to Africa had engaged presidents and Quakers, slaveholders and Free Soilers, and a wide range of others. Free blacks had both embraced it and shunned it. Some slaves had longed for the freedom that it promised while others were cruelly victimized by the deportation clauses of their masters' wills, which doomed them to familial separation, hardship, and death. As the 2,030 North Carolinians who emigrated between 1825 and 1893 came to realize, the costs of colonization could be as high as its benefits. In the eyes of some, Liberia offered lands for the landless, liberty for the bonded, and nationality for the exile. It was the black race's second republic, a sanctuary for refugees from the world's largest democracy. Liberia, in all its cultural hybridity, allowed for the unfurling of the fantasies of white men and black men alike—the former wishing to remake his world solely in his own image, the latter hoping to fashion an image in his new world. An invention, Liberia was freedom in all its idiosyncratic, contradictory, and selfish manifestations. It was an idea that each individual immigrant endowed with personalized meanings.

Aside from whatever benefits it seemed to offer, Liberia was an expensive proposition. Black American immigration to the west coast of Africa meant war, dispossession, and oppression. There was no equitable way to take the land of others, even when self-serving treaties announced that expropriation had been a mutually agreeable process. For the Dei, Gola, and others, African Americans seeking freedom in Liberia did not become Africans but rather foreigners whose "civilized" identity and exaggerated sense of self-worth were born as soon as the first loin-clothed Kru mariner approached their incoming ships. For recaptives, freedom meant assimilation and denying the past. An option not available to the vast majority of indigenous people, joining "civilized" Americo-Liberian society ultimately meant rejecting a part of one's self.

Beyond being an idea and experience, Liberia was an actual place with its own flora and fauna, rivers and promontories, seasons and histories. Etched on rocky capes, along winding waterways, and in lush forests, immigrant towns became part of the meaning of Liberia, though only in a dialectical way as settlers incessantly struggled with the tenacious forces of nature and the resistance of the dispossessed. For many, the cost of freedom was often less connected to the seen than the unseen, or at least the misunderstood. This was certainly the case regarding the *Anopheles* mosquito, which waged its own covert war against the newly arrived and unacclimated. Sometimes, the price of liberty meant no liberty at all, for poverty, sickness, conflict, exile, and death were their own prisons. Indeed, Liberian colonization was expensive to many on both sides of the Atlantic, and no single person or group—neither Quaker, free black, slave, African, nor colonizationist—seemed to enjoy freedom without paying a price for it, or causing others to do so.

EPILOGUE. EVERYTHING IS UPSIDE DOWN

DURING THE PREDAWN HOURS of April 12, 1980, seventeen noncommis-
sioned officers of the Liberian army entered the Executive Mansion, home of
President William Tolbert. Led by Samuel Doe, a twenty-eight-year-old master sergeant of Krahn background, the intruders proceeded to kill twenty-
seven people within the building, including Tolbert, whom they shot and
skewered with bayonets. Having disposed of the head of state and his security detail, the junta seized control of the government radio station and proclaimed, "the Tolbert government is no more." Following this announcement,
the junior officers, all of indigenous African descent, organized themselves
into the People's Redemption Council, with Doe as chairman. To both punish members of the deposed government and to forestall a countercoup, the
junta rounded up ninety Tolbert officials and jailed them at the Barclay Training Center. On April 22, thirteen of the prisoners, mostly cabinet officials,
were taken to a nearby beach, tied to posts, and executed before a group of
invited journalists. As for Tolbert and his retinue killed ten days earlier, their
bodies were carted through the streets of Monrovia for all to see. To the cheers
of a crowd, the corpses were irreverently dumped in a swamp across from the
Palm Grove Cemetery.[1]

Four years before his assassination, William Tolbert said that "sectionalism
and tribalism, favouritism and nepotism are cancerous proclivities that can
only sap the springs of national vitality and dry the wells of peace and plenty."
Undoubtedly, he was correct in his reading of Liberian history but too late in
deciding whether to abide by his own words of wisdom. The African soldiers
who overthrew the aging president claimed to have been motivated by the
dire necessity to save the country from the Americo-Liberian elite that had
enriched itself at the expense of the vast majority of the population. Notwithstanding this rationale, the coup did not signal the beginning of a far-reach-
ing social revolution as many had hoped. Instead, Doe and his compatriots
simply replaced a self-indulgent settler aristocracy—which had quite remarkably survived a century and a half of such crises—with their own cor-

rupt, ethnocentric regime. Thus, while many people in Monrovia and elsewhere in the country greeted the news of the coup with spontaneous jubilation, their initial celebrations would be tempered by the disappointments of coming days.

Aside from conciliatory gestures toward various groups, Doe, poorly educated and lacking vision, proved to be little better than his predecessors. Like Tolbert, he parceled out government jobs to members of his ethnic group, harassed the political opposition, and enriched himself at the expense of the public. Much of the aid received from foreign countries—over five hundred million dollars from the United States alone—was squandered, and the international community subsequently distanced itself from Doe's abuses. When a rebellion broke out against his increasingly tyrannical rule in the eastern province of Nimba in December 1989, government troops visited appalling brutality upon both insurgent and civilian alike. Eventually forced to barricade himself in the Executive Mansion to avoid encroaching enemies, Doe remained adamant in his refusal to resign the presidency, reportedly telling one foreign diplomat, "Tough times never last. Tough people do." The former master sergeant's time ran out on September 9, 1990, when a rebel group, led by Prince Johnson, started a gunfight with his security forces in Monrovia. During the battle, sixty of Doe's men were killed, and the president himself, wounded in both legs, was taken into custody by Johnson. Interrogated and tortured, Doe died at the hands of his captors the following day. His mangled body, like that of Tolbert, was displayed at a local hospital, making for a gruesome spectacle.[2]

Although Doe was captured and killed by Johnson's forces, the man most responsible for the collapse of his regime was Charles Taylor, an American-trained economist of Americo-Liberian and Gola heritage. During the 1980s, Taylor had actually served in the Doe government but fled back to the United States after being accused of embezzlement. To avoid extradition, he secretly returned to Africa where he organized a small force and invaded Liberia through Côte d'Ivoire on December 24, 1989. While Taylor managed to gain control over much of the countryside, the death of Doe did not resolve the widespread chaos caused by the war. During the 1990s, rebel factions, in their ongoing struggle for the capital and political supremacy, turned on each other with a ferocity that horrified many observers. Ultimately, an estimated two hundred thousand people died as a result of the conflict. Underscoring the tragedy, hundreds of thousands of others fled the country, creating a Liberian diaspora that stretched around the world.

Taylor's National Patriotic Front turned out to be the most resourceful—and ruthless—of the insurgents. To outfit his forces, the rebel leader exported timber and other products from the provinces that he controlled. To outmaneuver rival armies, he invaded the massive 120,000-acre rubber plantation of Bridgestone Firestone, an American tire company whose capital and influence had deeply penetrated Liberian political and economic life since the 1920s. When his insurgency needed recruits, Taylor's lieutenants armed children with AK-47 and other Kalashnikov assault rifles, eventually impressing thousands of boys under age fifteen into their fold. Despite its grisly nature, the fighting was not constant, and periods of truce and exhaustion temporarily halted hostilities. However, it was not until the elections of 1997 that the war appreciably subsided. Partially out of weariness from years of combat and out of fear that Taylor would resume fighting if he lost, the rebel leader was elected president by a landslide, winning 75 percent of the vote. Having virtually destroyed the country in his effort to master it, Taylor found himself presiding over a people disfigured by civil strife, disease, poverty, and illiteracy. Over the next four years, he fulfilled few of his promises to improve the quality of life of Liberians. As one resident of Monrovia put it, "He brought the war in this country and destroyed the water system, the electricity, the sewer, telecommunications. . . . Everything is upside down."[3]

If he was long on promises and short on achievements, Taylor did manage to resuscitate one element of the old order—the Americo-Liberian elite. Several top officials of his administration, including the maritime commissioner and the commerce minister, descended from settler families. In 2001, Professor Moore T. Worrell, the namesake of a North Carolina immigrant and former Secretary of the Treasury, served as Vice President for Administration at the University of Liberia. Additionally, a number of other Americo-Liberians were incorporated into Taylor's inner circle. To be sure, no wholesale revival of settler dominance occurred. Many who could trace their ancestry back to American immigrants chose to remain in exile following the 1980 coup and subsequent civil war. Nonetheless, government officials and business people with Americo-Liberian names and backgrounds became increasingly common in Liberian spheres of power by the early years of the presidency of Charles Taylor. This development was not wholly surprising given that the president himself, born in Arthington, was more than likely a descendant of the Tayloe family that emigrated from Bertie County, North Carolina, in 1870.[4]

In further regard to the contemporary North Carolina connection, a July 1999 talk given by Liberian Ambassador Rachel Gbenyon-Diggs in Winston-Salem seemed to bring full circle a number of themes and developments that had distinctively shaped the African country's history for almost two centuries. The talk itself was part of a lobbying effort to raise local awareness of the need for U.S. assistance in rebuilding Liberia. The ambassador had given the speech many times before, but in this context it offered meanings of which she was probably not fully aware. To start with, the location of her talk was not too far from where North Carolina Quakers had pondered generations earlier the best place to send their de facto emancipated slaves. Moreover, her audience was largely composed of members of the Liberian Organization of the Piedmont, a group consisting primarily of exiles whose very presence in central North Carolina promised to revitalize the historical links between the Tar Heel State and Liberia. Most interesting was the language of the presentation, which had a definite historical resonance. "The past is the past," she asserted at one point. "But the future can be glorious if we do it together." Ironically, her words were eerily similar to something Samuel Doe had said in the wake of the bloody coup that brought him to power in 1980. "We are prepared to let the past go quickly into history," he stated in a national address, two days after killing William Tolbert and dozens of others. As Gbenyon-Diggs's boss, Charles Taylor, would (re)discover four years later, it was not so easy to consign the past to history. With his government bogged down in a war against dissidents and crippled by United Nations sanctions, the rebel-turned-president was forced to resign and flee into exile in Nigeria in August 2003.

Moses Z. Blah, Taylor's vice-president, was inaugurated as head of state in the wake of the former chief executive's departure. Days before his elevation to this transitional role, Blah had again sounded the all-too-familiar refrain, "Let bygones be bygones." Whether Blah's successor, Charles Gyude Bryant, a Liberian businessman and head of a national reconciliation government, can manage this shattered country until planned elections can be held in 2005 remains to be seen. As of November 2003, fighting was still flaring in the countryside, and international peacekeepers had yet to arrive in substantial numbers. What is clear, however, is that the past was not truly the past, but very much the present state of things in Liberia.[5]

NOTES

Much of the statistical data used to describe the North Carolina emigrant population in this book is derived from the North Carolina Emigrant Roster. Compiled by the author, this source is a listing of the 2,030 emigrants who left North Carolina for Liberia during the nineteenth century. It is based on the emigrant rolls in the Records of the American Colonization Society (microfilm reel 314); *African Repository*, 1825–92; and Senate, *Roll of Emigrants That Have Been Sent to the Colony of Liberia*, 28th Cong., 2d sess., 1844, S.Rept. 150, 152–414. The North Carolina Emigrant Roster and a computerized database of North Carolina emigrants are in the possession of the author. This roster is abbreviated below as NCER.

ABBREVIATIONS USED IN THE NOTES

FHC   Friends Historical Collection, Hege Library, Guilford College, Greensboro, N.C.
NACPM   National Archives II, College Park, Md.
NCER   North Carolina Emigrant Roster
NCSA   North Carolina State Archives, Raleigh
RACS   Records of the American Colonication Society, Library of Congress, Washington, D.C.
SHC   Southern Historical Collection, University of North Carolina, Chapel Hill
SHP   Svend Holsoe Papers, Archive of Traditional Music, Indiana University, Bloomington

INTRODUCTION

1. Parramore, *Norfolk*, 160, 187–89; Buckingham, *The Slave States of America*, 451–53; North Carolina Emigrant Roster (compiled by the author from emigrant rolls in the Records of the American Colonization Society, Library of Congress, Washington, D.C. [microfilm reel 314]; *African Repository*, 1825–92; U.S. Senate, *Roll of Emigrants That Have Been Sent to the Colony of Liberia . . .*, 28th Cong., 2d sess., 1844, S. Rept. 150, 152–414).

2. Bogger, *Free Blacks in Norfolk*, 2–3, 39, 53–54; American Colonization Society, *Eighth Annual Report of the American Colonization Society* (1825), reprinted in *The Annual Reports of the American Society for Colonizing the Free People of Colour of the United States*, vols. 1–91 (New York: Negro Universities Press, 1969), 45–46.

3. Tadman, *Speculators and Slaves*, 5, 7, 70; Drew, *The Refugee*, 204; Buckingham, *The Slave States of America*, 485–86; *American Slavery as It Is*, 183; "Marine News," *Norfolk Herald*, February 26, 1827.

CHAPTER ONE

1. Stoesen, *Guilford County*, 1–2, 6; Hilty, *New Garden Friends Meeting*, 6; Arnett, *Greensboro*, 4, 7.

2. Northern Quakers probably migrated southward, and not westward, during the mid-1700s because French and Indian conflicts discouraged them from settling in the Ohio River Valley. Seth B. Hinshaw, *The Carolina Quaker Experience*, 19; Arnett, *Greensboro*, 10–13; Weeks, *Southern Quakers and Slavery*, 105–9; Hilty, *New Garden Friends Meeting*, 1–25; Stoesen, *Guilford County*, 2; White, "The Quakers of Perquimans," 278–81.

3. Cone, *The History of Guilford County*, 57; Hilty, *New Garden Friends Meeting*, 12–13; Stoesen, *Guilford County*, 9; Arnett, *Greensboro*, 21, 25.

4. Beeth, "Between Friends," 118; Hinshaw, *The Carolina Quaker Experience*, 40; Wiggins, *Captain Paul Cuffe's Logs and Letters*, 132.

5. Hilty, *New Garden Friends Meeting*, 12, 18–20.

6. Butler and Watson, *The North Carolina Experience*, 194–99; Crow, Escott, and Hatley, *A History of African Americans*, 3–4; Kay and Cary, *Slavery in North Carolina*, 10–51.

7. *The Federal and State Constitutions*, 1408; Clark, "Aspects of the North Carolina Slave Code," 150–59; Crow, Escott, and Hatley, *A History of African Americans*, 3; "United States Historical Census Data Browser," ‹http://fisher.lib.Virginia.edu/census/›.

8. Drake, *Quakers and Slavery in America*, 4, 9–10; Davis, *The Problem of Slavery in Western Culture*, 304–6; Aptheker, "The Quakers and Negro Slavery," 331–32, 340–41; Higginbotham, *In the Matter of Color*, 267–310.

9. Drake, *Quakers and Slavery in America*, 68; Hickey, "'Let Not Thy Left Hand Know,'" 6; Davis, *The Problem of Slavery in Western Culture*, 292, 299, 306–8, 328–30.

10. Davis, *The Problem of Slavery in Western Culture*, 304–6, 313; Higginbotham, *In the Matter of Color*, 295.

11. Bruns, *Am I Not a Man and a Brother?*, 3–4; Weeks, *Southern Quakers*, 198–99; Higginbotham, *In the Matter of Color*, 295; Davis, *The Problem of Slavery in Western Culture*, 330–31; Haskell, "Capitalism and the Origins of the Humanitarian Sensibility," 357–58.

12. Beeth, "Between Friends," 108–9; Wiggins, *Captain Paul Cuffe's Logs and Letters*, 54–55; Winks, *The Blacks in Canada*, 54; McKiever, *Slavery and the Emigration of North Carolina Friends*, 13–17; Sowle, "The North Carolina Manumission Society," 47–48; Hinshaw, "Friends Culture in Colonial North Carolina," 43, 53–55; Higginbotham, *In the Matter of Color*, 299.

13. Weeks, *Southern Quakers*, 218; Clark, *The State Records of North Carolina*, 328; Hinshaw, *The Carolina Quaker Experience*, 50; Crow, Escott, and Hatley, *A History of African Americans*, 42.

14. Sherrill, "The Quakers and the North Carolina Manumission Society," 32; Crow, "Slave Rebelliousness and Social Control in North Carolina," 92.

15. Weeks, *Southern Quakers*, 220–23; Taylor, "The Free Negro in North Carolina," 8.

16. Cadbury, "Negro Membership in the Society of Friends," 156, 177.

17. Weeks, *Southern Quakers*, 224–26.

18. Taylor, "Slaveholding in North Carolina," 9; Lefler and Newsome, *North Carolina*, 305–6.

19. Lefler and Newsome, *North Carolina*, 301–7; U.S. Bureau of the Census, *Fourth Decennial Census, Table 5: Population of the 61 Urban Places, 1820*, ‹http://www.census.gov/population/documentation/twps0027/tab05.txt›.

20. "United States Historical Census Data Browser," ‹http://fisher.lib.Virginia.edu/census/›.

21. Ibid.

22. Emphasis in original Jefferson quote. In 1790, Virginian Ferdinando Fairfax proposed that Congress establish an African-American émigré settlement, asserting that "the seat of this colony should be in Africa, their native climate." Anticipating future arguments in favor of African colonization, he suggested that such an establishment would supposedly bring Christianity and civilization to "ignorant" Africans, "and, after some time, . . . [should] become an independent nation." Ferdinando Fairfax, "Plan for Liberating the Negroes within the United States," *American Museum*, 8.6 (December 1790), 285–86; Slaughter, *The Virginian History of African Colonization*, 1–7; Ford, *The Writings of Thomas Jefferson*, 8:103–7, 153–55, 161–65; Jefferson, *Notes on the State of Virginia*, 137–43; Alexander, *A History of Colonization*, 59–73; Jordan, *White Over Black*, 546–69; Saillant, "The American Enlightenment in Africa," 261–82; Freehling, *The Reintegration of American History*, 145.

23. Aptheker, *A Documentary History*, 1:7–8; Brooks, "The Providence African Society's Sierra Leone Emigration Scheme," 183–202; Dixon, *African America and Haiti*, 32.

24. Harris, *Paul Cuffe*, 13–72; Thomas, *Rise to Be a People*.

25. Thomas, *Rise to Be a People*, 38, 46–47; Harris, *Paul Cuffe*, 29; Sherwood, "Paul Cuffe," 160, 170.

26. Thomas, *Rise to Be a People*, 13–29.

27. Sherwood, "Paul Cuffe," 170, 181–93; Harris, *Paul Cuffe*, 38–55; Wilson, *The Loyal Blacks*.

28. Thomas, *Rise to Be a People*, 98–100, 115–19; Sherwood, "Paul Cuffe," 198, 203; Paul Cuffe to Samuel J. Mills, January 6, 1817, reprinted in Harris, *Paul Cuffe*, 234–36.

29. Harris, *Paul Cuffe*, 70–71; Sherwood, "Early Negro Deportation Projects," 492–95; Thomas, *Rise to Be a People*, 118; Drake, *Quakers and Slavery in America*, 126.

30. Wagstaff, "Minutes of the N.C. Manumission Society," 13–15, 36–43.

31. Ibid., 15–20.

CHAPTER TWO

1. Brown, *Biography of the Rev. Robert Finley*, 103–5; Garraty and Sternstein, *Encyclopedia of American Biography*, 209–11.

2. Brown, *Biography of the Rev. Robert Finley*, 106–13.

3. Ibid., 113–14; Garraty and Sternstein, *Encyclopedia of American Biography*, 915–16.

4. Bushrod Washington was the nephew of President George Washington. Brown, *Biography of the Rev. Robert Finley*, 116–18; Garraty and Sternstein, *Encyclopedia of American Biography*, 643, 1103–4.

5. In 1820, Lower South states had the following numbers of free blacks and (/) slaves: Alabama, 633/47,449; Georgia, 1,763/149,656; Louisiana, 10,897/69,064; and Mississippi, 458/32,814. "United States Historical Census Data Browser," ‹http://fisher. lib.Virginia.edu/census/›; ACS, *Eighth Annual Report* (1825), 38–42; Alexander, *A History of Colonization*, 41, 239; Murray, *Wake*, 165; ACS, *Third Annual Report* (1820), 139.

6. Fredrickson, *The Black Image*, 6.

7. For references to Africa as an asylum for free blacks, see ACS, *Third Annual Report* (1820), 22; ACS, *Eighth Annual Report* (1825), 13. Jordan, *Black over White*, 436–40; Egerton, "Averting a Crisis," 142–56; Egerton, *Charles Fenton Mercer*; Peterson, *The Great Triumvirate*, 284–86.

8. ACS, *Eighth Annual Report* (1825), 13; ACS, *Ninth Annual Report* (1826), 6; ACS, *Tenth Annual Report* (1827), 21–22; Ashmun, *Memoir of the Life and Character of the Rev. Samuel Bacon*, 229; Aptheker, *A Documentary History*, 1:71–72; Horton and Horton, *In Hope of Liberty*, 187–88.

9. ACS, *First Annual Report* (1818), 5; ACS, *Second Annual Report* (1819), 9; ACS, *Sixth Annual Report* (1823), 7.

10. "An Act in Addition to the Acts Prohibiting the Slave Trade," reprinted in ACS, *Third Annual Report* (1820), 43–46; Egerton, *Charles Fenton Mercer*, 169–73.

11. Samuel J. Mills to Paul Cuffe, December 26, 1816; Paul Cuffe to Samuel J. Mills, January 6, 1817; and Samuel J. Mills to Paul Cuffe, July 14, 1817, reprinted in Harris, *Paul Cuffe*, 233–36, 255; ACS, *First Annual Report* (1818), 11–13; ACS, *Second Annual Report* (1819), 4, 19–67; ACS, *Fourth Annual Report* (1821), 22; Huberich, *The Political and Legislative History of Liberia*, 1:70–79; Staudenraus, *The African Colonization Movement*, 47.

12. ACS, *Third Annual Report* (1820), 19; ACS, *Fourth Annual Report* (1821), 4–16, 22.

13. ACS, *Fourth Annual Report* (1821), 7; U.S. Senate, *Roll of Emigrants*, 155–56; ACS, *Fifth Annual Report* (1822), 55–67; Staudenraus, *The African Colonization Movement*, 58–67; Alexander, *A History of Colonization*, 113–77; Ashmun, *History of the American Colony in Liberia*, 3–42.

14. Probably in imitation of the American Society for Colonizing the Free People of Color in the United States, the MCS changed its name to the Manumission and Colonizing Society of North Carolina during an April 28, 1817, meeting, but changed the name back to the Manumission and Colonization Society of North Carolina three months later. Wagstaff, "Minutes of the N.C. Manumission Society," 19–22, 210, 215, and 218–19; Proceedings of the Board of Managers of the American Colonization Society, September 19, 1817, and May 30, 1820, reel 289; and George Swain to Elias Cald-

well, November 18, 1819, reel 177B, RACS; Minutes of the N.C. Yearly Meeting, November 10, 1819, FHC; Cone, *The History of Guilford County*, 54–57; Hickey, "'Let Not Thy Left Hand Know,'" 3–10; Hinshaw, *Encyclopedia of American Quaker Genealogy*, 788.

15. Fredrickson, *The Black Image*, 6; Extract from the Minutes of the Presbytery of Fayetteville, October 4, 1819, reel 177B, RACS; "Address from the Presbytery of North Carolina," (Hillsborough), April 18, 1818, and "Resolution of the Methodist Conference of Virginia and North Carolina," (Oxford, N.C.), February 28, 1825, both reprinted in U.S. House Report, 21st Cong., 1st sess., 1830, H. Rept. 348, pp. 248, 250.

16. Johnson, *Ante-bellum North Carolina*, 569–70; Murray, *Wake*, 165; ACS, *Third Annual Report* (1820), 139–42; ACS, *Fourth Annual Report* (1821), 72.

17. "Colonization Society," *Raleigh Register*, May 3, 1825, 3; ACS, *Eighth Annual Report* (1825), 67; Escott, *Many Excellent People*, 62; *African Repository*, May 1825, 90; ACS, *Ninth Annual Report* (1826), 61.

18. Minutes of the N.C. Yearly Meeting, November 3, 1817, November 3, 1818, and November 15, 1821, FHC.

19. Challenged in court, Thomas Wright's transfer of slaves to the Society of Friends was declared illegal in 1831. Referring to the bequest as "qualified emancipation," the North Carolina Supreme Court declared, "A stern necessity arising out of the safety of the commonwealth forbids it." *Redmond v. Coffin*, 2 Dev. Eq. 437, June 1831 and December 1833, in Catterall, *Judicial Cases*, 2:62, 69.

20. Minutes of the N.C. Yearly Meeting, November 11, 1819, November 9, 1820, November 7, 1822, and December 11, 1824, FHC; Wagstaff, "Minutes of the N.C. Manumission Society," 24–25; Weeks, *Southern Quakers*, 224–27.

21. Drew, *The Refugee*, 251–52; Minutes of the N.C. Yearly Meeting, November 3, 1818, FHC; ACS, *Ninth Annual Report* (1826), 61.

22. Coffin, *Reminiscences of Levi Coffin*, 20; Beal, "The Underground Railroad in Guilford County," 20–24; Arnett, *Greensboro*, 27–28; Gara, *The Liberty Line*, 78–83; Cecil-Fronsman, *Common Whites*, 75.

23. Wagstaff, "Minutes of the N.C. Manumission Society," 75–79, 88–93.

24. Coffin, *Reminiscences of Levi Coffin*, 75–76.

25. Ibid., 75–76; Minutes of the N.C. Yearly Meeting, November 4, 1823, FHC.

26. Dixon, *African America and Haiti*, 32–34; Griggs, *Thomas Clarkson*, 133–34.

27. Montague, *Haiti and the United States*, 47–52; Blackburn, *The Overthrow of Colonial Slavery*, 480; Logan, *The Diplomatic Relations*, 185–200.

28. According to the 1820 census, there were 13,028 whites, 1,611 slaves, and 208 free blacks in Guilford County. "United States Historical Census Data Browser," ⟨http://fisher.lib.Virginia.edu/census/⟩; Baur, "Mulatto Machiavelli," 325–26; Griggs and Prator, *Henry Christophe & Thomas Clarkson*, 249.

29. Wagstaff, "Minutes of the N.C. Manumission Society," 83–84; Minutes of the N.C. Yearly Meeting, November 8, 1824, FHC; "North Carolina—Important," *Genius of Universal Emancipation*, December 1824, 1.

30. Wagstaff, "Minutes of the N.C. Manumission Society," 57–60.

31. Ibid., 88, 97–107; "Communication from N. Carolina," *Genius of Universal Emancipation*, December 1826, 90–91.

32. The poll was conducted in Wayne, Northampton, Pasquotank, Perquimans, and

Carteret Counties. Some sources list 317 blacks as willing to immigrate to Liberia. "Account of the People of Colour under the Care of Friends," Manumission Society Papers, SHC; Minutes of the Meeting for Sufferings, May 19, 1826, FHC; "Manumission," *Elizabeth-City Star and North Carolina Eastern Intelligencer*, June 17, 1826, 2.

33. Hilty, *New Garden Friends Meeting*, 30–31; Minutes of the N.C. Yearly Meeting, November 9, 1825, FHC.

34. Reputed to have owned as many as one hundred bondpeople at once, George C. Mendenhall began secretly emancipating his remaining slaves during the 1850s, sending a number to Ohio to live as free people. Love, "Registration of Free Blacks in Ohio," 38–47; Cone, *The History of Guilford County*, 55–56; Hickey, "'Let Not Thy Left Hand Know,'" 3–24; George C. Mendenhall to Richard Mendenhall, March 27, 1826; Charles Outland to Richard Mendenhall, April 1826; Minutes of the Meeting for Sufferings, May 20, 1826; and "A List of the Names . . . ," June 10, 1826, Manumission Society Papers, SHC; "Removal of Slaves from N. Carolina," *Genius of Universal Emancipation*, January 1826, 164–65; "Mr. George C. Mendenhall," *African Repository*, August 1857, 252; Dillon, *Benjamin Lundy*, 23–24; Baur, "Mulatto Machiavelli," 326–27.

35. Minutes of the Sufferings, May 20, 1826; "Report and Manifest of the Cargo Laden at the Port of Beaufort"; and Report of George Swain to Meeting for Sufferings, July 8, 1826, Manumission Society Papers, SHC; Minutes of the Meeting for Sufferings, May 19, 1826, FHC-GC; "Letter to the Editor," *Genius of Universal Emancipation and Baltimore Courier*, June 24, 1826, 342–43; Weeks, *Southern Quakers*, 230.

36. Report of George Swain to Meeting for Sufferings, July 8, 1826, Manumission Society Papers, SHC; "Letter to the Editor," *Genius of Universal Emancipation and Baltimore Courier*, June 24, 1826, 342–43.

37. Phineas Nixon to George Swain, July 13, 1826, Manumission Society Papers, SHC.

38. Report of George Swain to Meeting for Sufferings, July 8, 1826, Manumission Society Papers, SHC; Minutes of the Meeting for Sufferings, May 19, 1826, FHC.

39. Montague, *Haiti and the United States*, 71; Alexander, *A History of Colonization*, 263; Baur, "Mulatto Machiavelli," 326–27.

40. Wagstaff, "Minutes of the N.C. Manumission Society," 103–4; Minutes of the Meeting for Sufferings, December 5, 1825, FHC; and ACS, *Eighth Annual Report* (1825), 44.

41. ACS, *Third Annual Report* (1820), 26–27.

42. NCER.

43. ACS, *Seventh Annual Report* (1824), 5–6; Fox, *A Memoir of the Rev. C. Colden Hoffman*, 205–6; Brown, *Biography of the Rev. Robert Finley*, 300; Brooks, *Yankee Traders*, 224–25; Dow, *Slave Ships and Slaving*, 325; Morison, "*Old Bruin*," 68.

CHAPTER THREE

1. N.C. Department of Agriculture, *North Carolina and Its Resources*, 379–80; Corbitt, *The Formation of the North Carolina Counties*, 171–72.

2. Corbitt, *The Formation of the North Carolina Counties*, 380; Griffin, *Ante-bellum Elizabeth City*, 51–52, 71.

3. In regard to this expedition and subsequent ones, the terms *family* and *clan* are

used loosely to describe people sharing the same surname and place of origin. The author recognizes that individuals who shared the same last names, home counties, and even former masters were not necessarily related consanguineously or through marriage and that people with different surnames were, indeed, sometimes related. "United States Historical Census Data Browser," ‹http://fisher.lib.Virginia.edu/census/›; Griffin, *Ante-bellum Elizabeth City*, 51–52, 69, 124; Kay and Cary, *Slavery in North Carolina*, 80–81, 113–14, 154, 199.

4. Herbert Aptheker, "Maroons within the Present Limits of the United States," in Price, ed., *Maroon Societies*, 152, 154; Hadden, *Slave Patrols*, 129, 142; R. H. Taylor, "Slave Conspiracies in North Carolina," 24–25.

5. Watson, *Perquimans County*, 25, 59; Winslow, *Perquimans County History*, 8–9; Northampton County Bicentennial Committee, *Footprints in Northampton*, 9–10; Kay and Cary, *Slavery in North Carolina*, 202–3; Caleb White to R. R. Gurley, June 26, 1827, reel 1, RACS.

6. Minutes of the N.C. Yearly Meeting, November 9, 1825, FHC.

7. NCER.

8. Ibid.; "A List of Emancipated Blacks," in *American State Papers*, 1:165.

9. *Raleigh Register*, February 28, 1826, 3; Wilkeson, *A Concise History*, 26; Gurley, *Life of Jehudi Ashmun*, 309; ACS, *Fiftieth Annual Report* (1867), 56; "Latest from Liberia," *African Repository*, August 1826, 184; NCER.

10. An ad appearing in the August 16, 1827, edition of the Raleigh *Star* described the exploits of a slave named Ephraim who, traveling under the alias of John Artis and carrying a "badly executed" pass, trekked roughly a hundred miles from Waynesboro to Guilford County in wintry January in order to join blacks migrating to Indiana. Whether he was successful in eluding those who were offering a twenty-five-dollar reward for his capture is unknown. "Account of the People of Colour under the care of Friends," 1826, Manumission Society Papers, SHC; *The Star* (Raleigh), August 16, 1827, reprinted in Parker, *Stealing a Little Freedom*, 482.

11. Weeks, *Southern Quakers*, 232–33; Thornbrough, *The Negro in Indiana before 1900*, 55–58; "N. Carolina Yearly Meeting," *Genius of Universal Emancipation*, December 16, 1826, 94; ACS, *Fiftieth Annual Report* (1867), 56–64.

12. Opper, "North Carolina Quakers," 49; "Negroes—1826," Manumission Society Papers, SHC.

13. John Ehringhaus to R. R. Gurley, September 30, 1826; Nathan Mendenhall to R. R. Gurley, September 29, 1826, reel 1, RACS; Minutes of the N.C. Yearly Meeting, November 7, 1826, FHC; "Emigration to Liberia," *African Repository*, January 1827, 351.

14. John Ehringhaus to R. R. Gurley, September 30, 1826; David Lindsay to Joseph Johnston, December 11, 1826; Mary Mendenhall to R. R. Gurley, March 17, 1827, reel 1, RACS; "N. Carolina Yearly Meeting," *Genius of Universal Emancipation*, December 16, 1826, 94; "Manumissions," *African Repository*, March 1827, 27.

15. Unsigned to R. R. Gurley, January 3, 1827; Joseph Gales to R. R. Gurley, September 11, 1826; John W. Norwood to R. R. Gurley, September 1826; John Kennedy to R. R. Gurley, January 17, 1827; and John Kennedy to R. R. Gurley, January 22, 1827, reel 1, RACS.

16. The sex of two one-year-old infants of the White family was not recorded. NCER.

17. Ibid.

18. *Elizabeth-City Star and North Carolina Eastern Intelligencer,* October 7, 1826, 3; John Kennedy to R. R. Gurley, January 17 and 22, 1827, reel 1, RACS.

19. *Raleigh Register,* March 16, 1827, 3; "Latest from Liberia," *African Repository,* September 1827, 208–9; Kennedy to [Gurley?], February 1, 1827, and John Kennedy to R. R. Gurley, February 19, 1827, reel 1, RACS; ACS, *Fiftieth Annual Report* (1867), 56.

20. Emphasis in original Ashmun quote. NCER; ACS, *Eleventh Annual Report* (1828), 8–13, 32, and 41–42; "Latest from Liberia," *African Repository,* September 1827, 208–9.

21. ACS, *Tenth Annual Report* (1827), 22; Wagstaff, "Minutes of the N.C. Manumission Society," 148–58.

22. Nathan Mendenhall to R. R. Gurley, August 13 and October 9, 1827, reel 2; James Nourse to R. R. Gurley, November 3, November 30, December 11, 1827, January 18 and 28, 1828, reel 3, RACS; "Formation of Auxiliary Societies," *African Repository,* February 1828, 377–78; ACS, *Eleventh Annual Report,* (1828), 118–19.

23. ACS branches organized in Rowan and Randolph Counties voted to make themselves auxiliary to the North Carolina state organization in February 1828. "Formation of Auxiliary Societies," *African Repository,* February 1828, 377–78; "North Carolina Colonization Society," *African Repository,* January 1828, 349; "Greensborough, N.C. Auxiliary Society," *African Repository,* October 1826, 260; "Extract of a Letter Dated, Stokes County, (N.C.) Feb. 19, 1826," *Genius of Universal Emancipation and Baltimore Courier,* March 4, 1826, 211; "Captions," *Greensboro Patriot,* February 24, 1827, 1; Franklin, *The Free Negro,* 24.

24. ACS, *Eleventh Annual Report* (1828), 101; James Nourse to R. R. Gurley, December 29, 1827, reel 3, RACS.

25. John McPhail to R. R. Gurley, November 11, November 28, and December [?], 1827; Nathan Mendenhall to R. R. Gurley, December 9, 1827, and January 15, 1828, reel 3; Jehudi Ashmun's letter, March 6, 1828; John McPhail to R. R. Gurley, May 12, 1828; John McPhail to John Kennedy, May 13, 1828, reel 4, RACS; NCER; ACS, *Twelfth Annual Report* (1829), 6; "Departure of the Nautilus," *African Repository,* December 1827, 317–18.

26. NCER; "United States Historical Census Data Browser," ⟨http://fisher.lib.Virginia.edu/census/⟩; "Manumission," *African Repository,* January 1827, 352.

27. NCER.

28. Ibid.; U.S. Senate, *Roll of Emigrants,* 152–306; Nathan Mendenhall to R. R. Gurley, December 1827, reel 3, RACS.

29. Emphasis in original quote regarding a mulatto colony. John C. Ehringhaus to R. R. Gurley, January 1, 1827, reel 1; James Nourse to R. R. Gurley, November 30, 1827; Nathan Mendenhall to R. R. Gurley, December 9, 1827, reel 3; James Nourse to R. R. Gurley, October 27, 1828; Nathan Mendenhall to Richard Smith, November 1, 1828, reel 4; Nathan Mendenhall to Richard Smith, December 8, 1829, reel 7A; John Kennedy to R. R. Gurley, March 13, 1830, reel 7B; Josiah Polk to R. R. Gurley, September 15, 1830, reel 9; Isaac Overman to R. R. Gurley, August 1, 1827, reel 2; and Arch. Smith to R. R. Gurley, March 3, 1828, reel 3, RACS.

30. "The 4th of July," *Raleigh Register,* June 18, 1824, 3; Allen, "The Racial Thought,"

57; ACS, *Seventeenth Annual Report* (1834), xxvi; "Liberia," *Freedom's Journal*, February 14, 1829, 362; "Experience," *Rights of All*, September 18, 1829, 34.

31. Emphasis in original Walker quote. Hinks, *David Walker's Appeal*; Hinks, *To Awaken My Afflicted Brethren*, 1–115.

32. Hinks, *David Walker's Appeal*, 58, 67.

33. Franklin, *The Free Negro*, 66–67.

34. "United States Historical Census Data Browser," ‹http://fisher.lib.Virginia.edu/ census/›; Josiah Polk to R. R. Gurley, September 20, 1830; and Miles White to R. R. Gurley, September 28, 1830, reel 9, RACS.

35. Butler and Watson, *The North Carolina Experience*, 209–10; "Intelligence," *African Repository*, January 1831, 343; Hamer, "Great Britain, the United States, and the Negro Seamen Acts," 16; Franklin, *The Free Negro*, 69–70; Clark, "Aspects of the North Carolina Slave Code," 157–58.

36. Forty-three emigrants from North Carolina ultimately traveled to Liberia on the *Valador*. Josiah Polk to R. R. Gurley, September 20, 1830; Caleb White to R. R. Gurley, September 24, 1830; Miles White to R. R. Gurley, September 28, 1830, reel 9; Miles White to R. R. Gurley, October 9, 1830, November 2, 1830; John Wheeler to John McPhail, October 29, 1830; Josiah Polk to R. R. Gurley, October 30, 1830, reel 10; and John Kennedy to R. R. Gurley, April 16, 1831, reel 11, RACS; NCER.

37. Sandy Peele is listed as Alexander Peele in the emigrant roll. NCER; John Wheeler to John McPhail, October 29, 1830, reel 10; and John Kennedy to R. R. Gurley, April 16, 1831, reel 11, RACS.

38. Former governor James Iredell was a delegate to the ACS annual meeting of January 1831. He, along with a General Barringer, would be the first North Carolinians ever listed in ACS records as participating in their yearly conference in Washington, D.C. U.S. House Report, 19th Cong., H. Rept. 160, pp. 5–7; U.S. Senate Document, 20th Cong., S. Doc. 178, pp. 1–15; "A bill to raise a fund for the removal of free persons of colour from the State to Liberia," reprinted in *African Repository*, January 1831, 341–42; *Journal of the Senate of the General Assembly of the State of North Carolina* (1831), iii.

39. Weeks, *Southern Slavery*, 228, Memorial of the Society of Friends, December 13, 1831, Sessions Records, "Petitions" folder, box 6, NCSA; "Intelligence," *African Repository*, December 1830, 19; "Interesting Intelligence," *African Repository*, May 1829, 94; ACS, *Thirteenth Annual Report* (1830), 14.

40. Wagstaff, "Minutes of the N.C. Manumission Society," 189, 199, 205, 208; John Ehringhaus to R. R. Gurley, September 29, 1831, reel 12; and John Ehringhaus to R. R. Gurley, September 1, 1832, reel 15, RACS.

CHAPTER FOUR

1. Dow, *Slave Ships and Slaving*, 325; Lugenbeel, *Sketches of Liberia*, 6; J. W. Lugenbeel to R. R. Gurley, January 17, 1844, reprinted in *African Repository*, May 1844, 146; Morison, "*Old Bruin*," 68; Brooks, "A. A. Adee's Journal," 58; Brown, *Biography of the Rev. Robert Finley*, 300; Fox, *A Memoir of the Rev. C. Colden Hoffman*, 205–6; Williams, *The Liberian Exodus*, 26–27, 38; "Letter from Captain Bell," *African Reposi-*

tory, Oct. 1, 1840, 294–95; Cowan, *Liberia, as I Found It*, 14–15; Davis, *Ethnohistorical Studies on the Kru Coast*; Brooks, *The Kru Mariner*.

2. Brooks, *Yankee Traders*, 82–83, 224–25; Ashmun, *Memoir of the Life*, 251; J. Ashmun letter, May 15, 1823, reprinted in ACS, *Seventh Annual Report* (1824), 74.

3. Fox, *A Memoir of the Rev. C. Colden Hoffman*, 207–8; Ashmun, *History of the American Colony in Liberia*, 6–7; Williams, *The Liberian Exodus*, 38; Konneh, *Religion, Commerce, and the Integration of the Mandingo*, 6, 9–10.

4. Lugenbeel, *Sketches of Liberia*, 4–5, 25–27; Fox, *A Memoir of the Rev. C. Colden Hoffman*, 207–8; and "Latest from Liberia," *African Repository*, March 1828, 15.

5. Officer, *Western Africa*, 21–22; Williams, *The Liberian Exodus*, 57; Stewart, *Liberia*, 25–30; Lugenbeel, *Sketches of Liberia*, 10–13.

6. ACS, *Fifth Annual Report* (1822), 64–66; Ashmun, *History of the American Colony in Liberia*, 5–6; Lugenbeel, *Sketches of Liberia*, 6; "Latest from Liberia," *African Repository*, May 1826, 77–78.

7. Lugenbeel, *Sketches of Liberia*, 6; Gurley, *Life of Jehudi Ashmun*, 330; "American Colonization Society," *Missionary Herald*, September 1830, 292; Captain W. E. Sherman to Edward Hallowell, May 10, 1830, reprinted in ACS, *Thirteen Annual Report* (1830), 48; ACS, *Sixteenth Annual Report* (1833), 6–7; *Third Annual Report of the Ladies' Liberia School Association* (1835), 7; ACS, *Tenth Annual Report* (1827), 42.

8. ACS, *Tenth Annual Report* (1827), 42–43.

9. Alexander, *A History of Colonization*, 261–62; ACS, *Eleventh Annual Report* (1828), 36; "Latest from Liberia," *African Repository*, February 1827, 378; Syfert, "The Liberian Coasting Trade," 218–28; "Intelligence from Liberia," *African Repository*, November 1831, 259–60.

10. Captain W. E. Sherman to Edward Hallowell, May 10, 1830, reprinted in ACS, *Thirteenth Annual Report* (1830), 48; NCER; and Proceedings of the Board of Managers of the ACS, November 24, 1830, reel 289, RACS.

11. Alexander, *A History of Colonization*, 266; Lugenbeel, *Sketches of Liberia*, 5; ACS, *Ninth Annual Report* (1826), 42–43.

12. Gurley, *Life of Jehudi Ashmun*, 233–38; Alexander, *A History of Colonization*, 220–21; ACS, *Ninth Annual Report* (1826), 11; Brown, *Biography of the Rev. Robert Finley*, 106–13; Campbell, *Maryland in Africa*, 46.

13. "American Colonization Society," *Missionary Herald*, September 1830, 292; NCER; Williams, *The Liberian Exodus*, 48.

14. NCER.

15. "Digest of the Laws Now in Force in the Colony of Liberia, August 19th, 1824," ACS, *Eleventh Annual Report* (1828), 60; "Letter from the Secretary of the Society," *African Repository*, December 1827, 292–93; Gurley, *Life of Jehudi Ashmun*, 130, 312; "Latest from Liberia," *African Repository*, February 1827, 378.

16. Gurley, *Life of Jehudi Ashmun*, 361–62; Lugenbeel, *Sketches of Liberia*, 7; *Third Annual Report of the Ladies' Liberia School Association*, 4; Jesse and Mars Lucas to Albert Heaton, [December 29?], 1831; Mars Lucas to Townsend Heaton, June 19, 1830; Jesse Lucas to Albert Heaton, March 10, 1830, Lucas Brothers of Liberia Letters, University of Virginia Library, Charlottesville; Malinda Rex to Duncan Cameron, November 15, 1839, "Correspondence 1830–40" folder, box 185.1, Pattie Mordecai Papers;

Mitchell and Mitchell, "The Philanthropic Bequests of John Rex of Raleigh," part 1, 260–61, 269; "Latest from Liberia," *African Repository*, March 1828, 42; NCER.

17. On November 8, 1828, Lott Carey and eight others were accidentally killed while making cartridges near Monrovia. Apparently, a candle ignited some gunpowder, which resulted in a lethal explosion. "Death of the Rev. Lott Cary," *African Repository*, March 1829, 10–14; "From Liberia," *African Repository*, September 1828, 209–10; "OFFICERS, Civil and Military, of the Colony of Liberia, for the political year beginning September, 1826," *African Repository*, June 1827, 126.

18. Lugenbeel, *Sketches of Liberia*, 7; "Late from Liberia," *African Repository*, May 1828, 85; Jehudi Ashmun's letter, June 12, 1827, reprinted in *African Repository*, September 1827, 15; Gurley, *Life of Jehudi Ashmun*, 155, 382; NCER; U.S. Senate, *Roll of Emigrants*, 183–210; "American Colonization Society," *Missionary Herald*, September 1830, 292.

19. NCER.

20. According to colonial agent and physician Joseph Mechlin, Millsburg lacked a "suitable" receptacle in 1830, which undoubtedly had an impact on sanitation, the spread of disease, and the recuperative capacity of afflicted immigrants. Huberich, *The Political and Legislative History of Liberia*, 1:383–84; NCER; U.S. Senate, *Roll of Emigrants*, 183–210; Proceedings of the Board of Managers, May 14, 1832, reel 289, RACS; McDaniel, *Swing Low, Sweet Chariot*, 92; Humphreys, *Malaria*, 8–29; Kiple and King, *Another Dimension to the Black Diaspora*, 14–23, 50–57; Todd L. Savitt, "Black Health on the Plantation: Masters, Slaves, and Physicians," in Numbers and Savitt, *Science and Medicine*, 329–31; John Duffy, "The Impact of Malaria on the South," in Savitt and Young, *Disease and Distinctiveness*, 29–36.

21. U.S. Senate, *Roll of Emigrants*, 175–79; "Intelligence," *African Repository*, July 1827, 154; ACS, *Second Annual Report* (1819), 13–16; ACS, *Third Annual Report* (1820), 14–16; Proceedings of the Board of Managers, June 21, 1819, reel 289, RACS.

22. The Richardsons arrived in January 1832, the recaptives of the *Heroine* landed in March 1830, and the *Norfolk* emigrants from Georgia reached Monrovia in July 1827, around the time of the "middle dries." U.S. Senate, *Roll of Emigrants*, 175–79, 198–200, 210–20; NCER; Proceedings of the Board of Managers, May 14, 1832, reel 289, RACS; "American Colonization Society," *Missionary Herald*, September 1830, 292. New Georgia was originally named Careysburg, after Lott Carey. Huberich, *The Political and Legislative History of Liberia*, 1:631–32.

23. *Third Annual Report of the Ladies' Liberia School Association*, 8; "Latest from Liberia," *African Repository*, May 1826, 94; "Letter from Captain Bell," *African Repository*, October 1, 1840, 291; Kappel, Korte, and Mascher, *Liberia*, 126–27.

24. Brooks, "A. A. Adee's Journal," 60; "Latest from Liberia," *African Repository*, May 1826, 97–98; Burrowes, "Economic Relations within Pre-Liberian Societies," 83; "Letter from a Liberian Emigrant," *African Repository*, September 1855, 278; Shick, *Behold the Promised Land*, 100–101, Joseph Mechlin to R. R. Gurley, reprinted in *African Repository*, July 1832, 135–36; Brooks, *Landlords and Strangers*, 38–39, 137.

25. "Captain Kennedy's Letter," *African Repository*, July 1831, 154; Proceedings of the Board of Managers, November 1, 1831, reel 289, RACS; Louis Sheridan to Lewis Tappan, November 24, 1838, reprinted in *Colored American*, December 8, 1838, 165; ACS, *Ninth Annual Report* (1826), 19.

26. Crummell, *The Future of Africa*, 258–59; Inaugural Address of President Daniel B. Warner, January 4, 1864, and Inaugural Address of President Edward J. Roye, January 3, 1870, both reprinted in Guannu, *The Inaugural Addresses*, 42–54, 76–85; President Anthony W. Gardner, Message to the Liberian Legislature, December 10, 1879, in U.S. House, *Executive Documents*, 46th Cong., p. 697; "Letter from Captain Bell," *African Repository*, October 1, 1840, 291–92; ACS, *Twenty-Fourth Annual Report* (1841), 23; Lynch, ed., *Black Spokesman*, 28–29, 42–43, and 195–204; Edward W. Blyden to William Coppinger, July 20, 1871, reprinted in Lynch, *Selected Letters of Edward Wilmot Blyden*, 84–85.

27. Joseph Mechlin to R. R. Gurley, April 1832, reprinted in *African Repository*, July 1832, 135; "Letter from Mr. Latrobe," *African Repository*, September 1838, 9; NCER.

28. *Misericordia* means "mercy" in both Spanish and Portuguese. Later, the spelling *Montserrado* would become more common than *Mesurado*. Richardson, *Liberia's Past and Present*, 13–14; Johnston, *Liberia*, 1:40 (n. 9); Brooks, "A. A. Adee's Journal," 59 (n. 8); Stewart, *Liberia*, 17; Morison, "*Old Bruin*," 68; ACS, *Fifth Annual Report* (1823), 64–66.

29. "Constitution" and "Digest of the Laws," ACS, *Eleventh Annual Report* (1828), 54–61; Proceedings of the Board of Managers, November 8 and 24, 1830, reel 289, RACS; "The Colony of Liberia Slandered," *African Repository*, September 1833, 201–2; "Remarks," *African Repository*, May 1833, 66–68; "A New Attack on the Colonization Society," *African Repository*, August 1833, 181–82.

30. Jehudi Ashmun to Secretary of the Navy, December 7, 1823, reprinted in ACS, *Seventh Annual Report* (1824), 52; ACS, *Tenth Annual Report* (1827), 44; ACS, *Fourteenth Annual Report* (1831), 11; "Log of the Brig Gleaner, 1835–1836," in Bennett and Brooks, *New England Merchants in Africa*, 164; "Captain Kennedy's Letter," 155; Huberich, *The Political and Legislative History of Liberia*, 1:393; Proceedings of the Board of Managers, November 1, 1830, reel 289, RACS.

31. Emphasis in original Ashmun quotes. Gurley, *Life of Jehudi Ashmun*, 33–35, 128–30, 364; Alexander, *A History of Colonization*, 220; "Latest from Liberia," *Raleigh Register*, May 10, 1825, 2.

32. J. Mechlin Jr. to R. R. Gurley, January 1832, reprinted in *African Repository*, April 1832, 38; Ashmun, *History of the American Colony in Liberia*, 19–40; ACS, *Eleventh Annual Report* (1828), 63–64.

33. "Latest from Liberia," *African Repository*, February 1827, 378; "Latest from Liberia," *African Repository*, April 1830, 53; "From the Colony," *African Repository*, December 1831, 302–3.

34. Konneh, *Religion, Commerce, and the Integration of the Mandingo*, ix–x, 6–10, 13, 18; Corby, "Manding Traders and Clerics," 47–48; J. Ashmun to Rev. Dr. Blumhardt, April 23, 1826, reprinted in *African Repository*, November 1827, 261; Holsoe, "A Study of Relations," 334–35; written inset on Liberian map, *African Repository*, May 1832, 89.

35. Ashmun to Rev. Dr. Blumhardt, April 23, 1826, reprinted in *African Repository*, November 1827, 261; Burrowes, "Economic Relations within Pre-Liberian Societies," 81–83.

36. Burrowes, "Economic Relations within Pre-Liberian Societies," 83.

37. J. Mechlin to R. R. Gurley, April 1832, reprinted in *African Repository*, July 1832, 130; Holsoe, "A Study of Relations," 344–46.

38. J. Mechlin to R. R. Gurley, April 1832, reprinted in *African Repository*, July 1832, 130–31; Ashmun, *History of the American Colony in Liberia*, 11; ACS, *Eleventh Annual Report* (1828), 41.

39. J. Mechlin to R. R. Gurley, April 1832, reprinted in *African Repository*, July 1832, 130.

40. Ibid., 131–32; Joseph Mechlin to R. R. Gurley, December 14, 1831, reprinted in *African Repository*, April 1832, 35; Proceedings of the Board of Managers, April 9, 1832, reel 289, RACS.

41. NCER.

42. J. Mechlin to R. R. Gurley, April 1832, reprinted in *African Repository*, July 1832, 132–35; Joseph Mechlin to Board of Managers of the ACS, May 1, 1832, reprinted in *African Repository*, September 1832, 195.

43. "King Bromley," *Liberia Herald*, February 19, 1847, 35; "Expects to Be King," *Liberia Herald*, August 26, 1847; "The Meeting of the Dey Chiefs," *Liberia Herald*, September 3, 1847, 79; Holsoe, "A Study of Relations," 345–53.

CHAPTER FIVE

1. Masur, *1831*, 3–21, 217 (n. 5); Oates, *The Fires of Jubilee*; "The Confession of Nat Turner," reprinted in Frazier, *Afro-American History*, 36–47.

2. Oates, *The Fires of Jubilee*, 147–66; "The Confession of Nat Turner," 39–40, 46.

3. Emphasis in original Ehringhaus quote. John Ehringhaus to R. R. Gurley, September 29, 1831, reel 12, RACS; Grimsted, *American Mobbing*, 136–41.

4. Drew, *The Refugee*, 332; Oates, *The Fires of Jubilee*, 110–43.

5. Egerton, "'Fly Across the River,'" 87–110; "United States Historical Census Data Browser," ‹http://fisher.lib.Virginia.edu/census/›; Morris, "Panic and Reprisal," 34–36.

6. Morris, "Panic and Reprisal," 35–36; Elliott, "The Nat Turner Insurrection," 4–5, 12; Monfort Stokes to James Hamilton, November 14, 1831, reprinted in Foner, *Nat Turner*, 65.

7. Joseph Gray to R. R. Gurley, September 7, September 29, and October 22, 1831, reel 12, RACS.

8. John McPhail to R. R. Gurley, September 22, 1831; Caleb White to R. R. Gurley, September 7, 1831; Miles White to R. R. Gurley, October 1 and 24, 1831; Thomas Hunt to R. R. Gurley, October 8, 1831, reel 12, RACS.

9. "Intelligence from Liberia," *African Repository*, November 1831, 267, 271.

10. John McPhail to R. R. Gurley, October 28, 1831, reel 12, RACS; Oates, *The Fires of Jubilee*, 142–43; U.S. Senate, *Roll of Emigrants*, 210–20; NCER; "Departure of the James Perkins," *African Repository*, December 1831, 320; Bogger, *Free Blacks in Norfolk*, 41.

11. Seth Crowell to Louis M. Lane, November 29, 1831, reel 12; Proceedings of the Board of Managers, December 8, 1831, reel 289; and John McPhail to R. R. Gurley, December 7, 1831, reel 12, RACS; "Marine News," *Norfolk Herald*, December 9, 1831, 2; Wilkeson, *A Concise History*, 47; "Departure of the Jupiter," *African Repository*, May 1832, 94; NCER.

12. There is a discrepancy in the sources regarding the original number of emigrants who boarded the *Julius Pringle* (92) and the number of North Carolinians who left for Liberia in the *American* (89). Possibly the three missing emigrants could have abandoned the party in New Jersey or Norfolk. Opper, "North Carolina Quakers," 56–57; Hilty, *Toward Freedom for All*, 56–62; Hilty, *By Land and by Sea*, 58–62; Proceedings of the Board of Managers, June 6, 1832, reel 289, RACS; NCER; ACS, *Fiftieth Annual Report* (1867), 57; "Colonization Society," *Greensborough Patriot*, September 12, 1832, 2.

13. "Departure of the Brig American," *African Repository*, July 1832, 155; ACS, *Fifteenth Annual Report* (1832), 50; Jeremiah Hubbard's letter, reprinted in the *African Repository*, September 1834, 213–17; Drake, *Quakers and Slavery in America*, 126, 141–42; NCER; "Latest from Liberia," *Greensborough Patriot*, June 13, 1832, 2.

14. The five expeditions and their departure dates were the *Criterion* (July 30, 1831), the *James Perkins* (December 9, 1831), the *Jupiter* (May 9, 1832), the *American* (July 15, 1832), and the *Roanoke* (January 4, 1833).

15. NCER; Woodson, *Free Negro Owners of Slaves*, 24, 26.

16. In 1835, Mechlin's own moral character was called into question by a Virginia immigrant who accused the agent of becoming "criminally intimate" with his wife. In two letters to ACS secretary Gurley, the man charged Mechlin with "a most hanious depredation on the peace of family," which allegedly resulted in the birth of a mulatto child, whom the agent abandoned when he resigned his office and returned to the United States in 1833. Joseph Blake to R. R. Gurley, March 9 and May 13, 1835, reel 153, RACS; Hilty, *Toward Freedom for All*, 58; NCER; "Latest from Liberia," *African Repository*, December 1832, 298–99.

17. "Health of Liberia," *African Repository*, July 1831, 158; Wilkeson, *A Concise History*, 51–53; ACS, *Fiftieth Annual Report* (1867), 57.

18. NCER; Proceedings of the Board of Managers, May 14, 1832, reel 289, RACS.

19. ACS, *Fiftieth Annual Report* (1867), 56–58; ACS, *Seventeenth Annual Report* (1834), xvi–xvii; ACS, *Twenty-Second Annual Report* (1838), 4; "To the Auxiliary Societies of the American Colonization Society," *African Repository*, June 1834, 108–9; ACS, *Fourteenth Annual Report* (1831), 35–41.

20. Friedman, *Gregarious Saints*; Mayer, *All on Fire*; Rosen, "Abolition and Colonization," 177–92; Howard Temperley, "The Ideology of Antislavery," in Goodheart and Hugh Hawkins, *The Abolitionists*, 12–26.

21. ACS, *Eighteenth Annual Report* (1835), 15–17.

22. ACS, *Twenty-First Annual Report* (1837), 3; ACS, *Ninth Annual Report* (1826), 6; ACS, *Tenth Annual Report* (1827), 21–22; ACS, *Third Annual Report* (1820), 26–27; and Aptheker, *A Documentary History*, 1:159.

23. Campbell, *Maryland in Africa*, 18–53, 73, 87–91, 124, and 145–46; U.S. Senate, *Roll of Emigrants*, 235–40; Laughon, "Administrative Problems in Maryland in Liberia," 333; "Census of Maryland in Liberia," *African Repository*, November 1843, 341; NCER; "United States Historical Census Data Browser," ‹http://fisher.lib.Virginia.edu/census/›.

24. ACS, *Nineteenth Annual Report* (1835), 23–27; ACS, *Eighteenth Annual Report* (1835), 12, 26; Staudenraus, *The African Colonization Movement*, 234–36; ACS, *Twentieth Annual Report* (1836), 14, 16; U.S. Senate, *Roll of Emigrants*, 255–58, 376.

25. "United States Historical Census Data Browser," ‹http://fisher.lib.Virginia.edu/census/›; Sullivan, "Mississippi in Africa," 79–85; Poe, "A Look at Louisiana Colonization," 112–16; "Arrival of the Brig Mail," *African Repository*, March 1839, 80; ACS, *Twenty-Second Annual Report* (1838), 2, 12, 35; ACS, *Twenty-First Annual Report* (1837), 16–17; U.S. Senate, *Roll of Emigrants*, 259–61, 280–81, 376; ACS, *Twenty-Fifth Annual Report* (1842), 24.

26. Tyler-McGraw, "Richmond Free Blacks and African Colonization," 219–22; NCER; ACS, *Fiftieth Annual Report* (1867), 57–64; ACS, *Fifty-Fifth Annual Report* (1872), 47; ACS, *Sixty-First Annual Report* (1878), 22; ACS, *Sixty-Ninth Annual Report* (1887), 23; Slaughter, *The Virginian History*, 17–19, 49–51, 76; "Virginia in Africa," *African Repository*, September 1845, 270–71; "United States Historical Census Data Browser," ‹http://fisher.lib.Virginia.edu/census/›.

27. Garraty and Sternstein, *Encyclopedia of American Biography*, 209–11; ACS, *Twenty-First Annual Report* (1837), 3; Peterson, *The Great Triumvirate*, 284–86; Egerton, "Averting a Crisis," 142–56; Allen, "Did Southern Colonizationists Oppose Slavery?," 104; Staudenraus, *The African Colonization Movement*, 185–87; Fredrickson, *The Black Image*, 26–27; Turner, "Kentucky Slavery in the Last Ante Bellum Decade," 303–6; "Kentucky in Africa," *African Repository*, December 1845, 380; U.S. Senate, *Roll of Emigrants*, 245–50, 300–305; "United States Historical Census Data Browser," ‹http://fisher.lib.Virginia.edu/census/›.

28. Mooney, "Some Institutional and Statistical Aspects of Slavery in Tennessee," 204–5; *Resolutions of the Legislature of Georgia*, 7; Sims-Alvarado, "The African Colonization Movement in Georgia"; "United States Historical Census Data Browser," ‹http://fisher.lib.Virginia.edu/census/›; ACS, *Fiftieth Annual Report* (1867), 56–64.

29. Joseph Gales served as the treasurer of the ACS during the 1830s. ACS, *Twenty-Second Annual Report* (1838), 9; "North Carolina State Colonization Society," *African Repository*, July 1834, 149–50; "North Carolina State Colonization Society," *African Repository*, June 1835, 191–92; *African Repository*, June 1837, 175.

30. N.C. Department of Agriculture, *North Carolina and Its Resources*, 308; Corbitt, *The Formation of the North Carolina Counties*, 27; Sprunt, *Chronicles of the Cape Fear River*, 682; Bureau of the Census, *Fifth Decennial Census, Table 6: Population of the 90 Urban Places, 1830*, ‹http://www.census.gov/population/documentation/twps0027/tab06.txt›.

31. "United States Historical Census Data Browser," ‹http://fisher.lib.Virginia.edu/census/›; Powell, *Dictionary of North Carolina Biography*, 4:154, 5:332–33; Franklin, *The Free Negro*, 161.

32. Gatewood, " 'To Be Truly Free,' " 333–34; "Authorized Agents," *Rights of All*, September 18, 1829, 40; Huberich, *The Political and Legislative History of Liberia*, 1:516; "Expedition to Bassa Cove," *African Repository*, February 1838, 55; "Important Intelligence for Liberia," *Colored American*, December 8, 1838, 165; Thomas Hunt to R. R. Gurley, September 3, 1829, reel 6, RACS; *The Federal and State Constitutions*, 1416; Louis Sheridan to Joseph Gales, May 20, 1836, reel 26, RACS.

33. Louis Sheridan to Joseph Gales, May 20, 1836; and Louis Sheridan to Joseph Gales, May 27, July 22, October 5, and November 1, 1836, reel 26, RACS.

34. Among those who emigrated with Sheridan were seven of his recently emancipated slaves. "Expedition to Bassa Cove," *African Repository*, February 1838, 55; Hall

McRae & Co. to Joseph Gales, December 21, 1836; Francis Bacon to Joseph Gales, December 21 and 24, 1836, reel 26; and Louis Sheridan to Joseph Gales, May 15, August 7 and 18, 1837, reel 28, RACS; NCER.

35. After he later witnessed Bibles and other religious literature decaying in a colonial warehouse, Sheridan warned one ACS official to stop sending such items to Africa unless they were specifically requested. NCER; Louis Sheridan to Lewis Tappan, November 24, 1838, reprinted in the *Colored American*, December 8, 1838, 165–66; Louis Sheridan to Samuel Wilkeson, October 22, 1839; and Louis Sheridan to Benjamin Coates, June 22, 1839, reel 154, RACS; Wilkeson, *A Concise History*, 74; Alexander, *A History of African Colonization*, 554.

36. Louis Sheridan to Lewis Tappan, November 24, 1838, reprinted in the *Colored American*, December 8, 1838, 165–66; Powell, *Dictionary of North Carolina Biography*, 5:333; "Louis Sheridan's Letter," *African Repository*, February 1839, 34.

37. Wilkeson, *A Concise History*, 74; ACS, *Twenty-Third Annual Report* (1839), 28–29; Louis Sheridan to Benjamin Coates, June 22, 1839; Louis Sheridan to Samuel Wilkeson, June 22, 1839; and Louis Sheridan to Executive Committee, January 24, 1842, reel 154, RACS; Gatewood, "'To Be Truly Free,'" 347; Louis Sheridan to Joseph Gales, November 1, 1836, reel 26, RACS.

38. J. N. Lewis to William McLain, September 9, 1844, reprinted in the *African Repository*, January 1845, 9; Garrison, *Thoughts on African Colonization*.

39. J. R. Daily to James M'Crummell, September 6, 1840, reprinted in the *Colored American*, December 5, 1840, 3; "Liberia," *Colored American*, December 26, 1840, 2; "Emigration Both Ways," *African Luminary*, September 18, 1840, 51; "Intelligence," *African Repository*, June 1844, 191.

40. ACS, *Twenty-Sixth Annual Report* (1843), 4; ACS, *Twenty-Eighth Annual Report* (1845), 17; U.S. Senate, *Roll of Emigrants*, 152–414.

41. U.S. Senate, *Roll of Emigrants*, 152–414; "The Long Anticipated Statistics," *African Repository*, June 1844, 161–62; "A View of the Past, Throws Light upon the Future," *African Repository*, January 1846, 5–6; "Moral Statistics of Liberia," *African Repository*, June 1847, 192–93; ACS, *Twenty-Eighth Annual Report* (1845), 17; "North Carolina State Colonization Society," *African Repository*, July 1834, 149–50; J. B. Pinney to William McLain, November 9, 1845, reel 48, RACS; ACS, *Thirty-First Annual Report* (1848), 18, 34–35.

42. NCER; "Receipts of the American Colonization Society" (North Carolina), *African Repository*, December 1845, 383; Proceedings of the Board of Managers, July 26, 1838, reel 290; R. W. Bailey to Samuel Wilkeson, February 27, 1840, reel 34; John Newlin to William McLain, March 25, 1831, reel 177B; James Higgins to R. R. Gurley, May 1842, reel 40; Henry Brown to William McLain, January 6 and February 2, 1849, reel 58; and Jesse Rankin to William McLain, March 26, 1851, reel 64, RACS; ACS, *Twenty-Ninth Annual Report* (1846), 8.

CHAPTER SIX

1. Singleton, *Recollections*, 5; Corbitt, *The Formation of the North Carolina Counties*, 74; Barnes, *North Carolina's Hurricane History*, 35; Andriot, *Population Abstract of the*

United States, 483; Sprunt, *Chronicles of the Cape Fear River*, 87; Watson, *A History of New Bern*, 270, 304, 312.

2. Singleton, *Recollections*, 7, 33–38, and 41–44; Cecelski, *The Waterman's Song*, 64–65, 128, 141; Watson, *A History of New Bern*, 156, 305–35; "United States Historical Census Data Browser," ‹http://fisher.lib.Virginia.edu/census/›.

3. Watson, *A History of New Bern*, 310–11; NCER; Henry Brown to William McLain, February 2, 1849, reel 58, RACS.

4. Although the migration and settlement of African Americans and others in Liberia technically became *emigration* (or *immigration*) after the independence of the republic in 1847, ACS officials and others continued to refer to this process as *colonization*, as well as emigration. Thus, the terms were often used interchangeably. Accordingly, the present author also uses these words synonymously to describe black migration and settlement in post-independence Liberia, both to reflect the language of the period and to stress that immigration to the republic still resembled colonization. New immigrants continued to found new towns in the country until the late 1800s, and dispossessed Africans continued to contest the legitimacy and existence of such settlements. Along with the impact of European encroachment upon lands claimed by the republic, these historical patterns ensured that Liberia's national boundaries and political influence would remain unstable beyond the turn of the century.

5. Initially, Brown mistakenly believed that Dickinson's master had requested one thousand dollars for his liberty, of which seven hundred dollars had already been paid by the black printer. Henry Brown to William McLain, February 2, 1849, reel 58; Daniel Stratton to William McLain, November 1, 1849, reel 60; and William McLain to Daniel Stratton, July 17 and 20, 1849, reel 189, RACS.

6. A. H. Dickinson to William McLain, February 28, 1849, reel 58; Daniel Stratton to William McLain, November 22, 1849, reel 60; Mingo Croom to William McLain, June 28, 1852, reel 67; Mingo Croom to William McLain, May 18, 1859, reel 87; and Daniel Stratton to William McLain, July 24, 1849, reel 59, RACS.

7. Daniel Stratton to William McLain, October 1, November 12 and 22, 1849, reel 60; William McLain to Daniel Stratton, November 9, 1849, reel 189; and A. H. Dickinson to William McLain, November 24, 1849, reel 60, RACS.

8. "United States Historical Census Data Browser," ‹http://fisher.lib.Virginia.edu/census/›; Oates, *The Fires of Jubilee*, 113; Stephenson, *Murfreesboro, North Carolina*, 9.

9. NCER; Tom Parramore, "A Passage to Monrovia," (unpublished paper delivered at Chowan College, Murfreesboro, N.C., 1973, and graciously provided to the present author); Moore, *Historical Sketches of Hertford County*, 71, 80; John W. Southall to James Corner & Sons, August 21, 1849; and John Southall to William McLain, November 5, 1849, reel 60, RACS.

10. John W. Southall to James Corner & Sons, August 21, 1849, reel 60; William McLain to John Southall, August 29 and November 9, 1849, reel 189; and John Southall to William McLain, November 5, 1849, reel 60, RACS; "Three Thousand Dollars Wanted in Thirty Days," *African Repository*, November 1849, 321; and "Late and Interesting from Liberia," *African Repository*, December 1849, 377.

11. The age statistics are based on the ages of the fifty-three Capeharts for whom an

age was entered on the emigrant roll. NCER; John Southall to William McLain, March 12, 1851, reel 64, RACS.

12. John Southall described the one Capehart death in Liberia as being caused by "imprudence." William McLain to John Southall, November 9, 1849, reel 189; John Southall to William McLain, January 7, 1850, reel 61; Daniel Stratton to William McLain, June 18, 1850, reel 62; and John Southall to William McLain, March 12, 1851, reel 64, RACS; ACS, *Thirtieth Annual Report* (1847), 13, 39–42; ACS, *Fiftieth Annual Report* (1867), 60; and H. J. Roberts to Rev. Mr. McLain, April 16, 1850, reprinted in *African Repository*, August 1850, 233.

13. According to the federal census, 1,011 slaves fled to free states during 1850. Campbell, *The Slave Catchers*, 5–12, 23–24; Quarles, *Black Abolitionists*, 211–12, 217; Landon, "The Negro Migration to Canada," 22–36.

14. U.S. House, *Miscellaneous Documents*, pp. 1–2; "Memorial," June 29, 1850, 1850–51 session records, "Petitions" folder (Nov. 1850–Jan. 1851), box 8, NCSA; Franklin, *The Free Negro*, 211–12; "Our Colored Population," *North Carolina Whig*, September 29, 1852, 2.

15. "Negro Law of Illinois" and "Negro Exclusion," *African Repository*, April 1853, 105–8, 110–11; *Liberia Herald*, May 21, 1851, 39.

16. William McLain to Jesse Rankin, January 8, 1850, reel 190; Jesse Rankin to William McLain, December 15, 1849, reel 60; Jesse Rankin to William McLain, June 12, 1851, reel 65; Jesse Rankin to William McLain, July 11, 1850, reel 62; Jesse Rankin to William McLain, January 14, 1852, reel 66B; Jesse Rankin to William McLain, October 8, 1850, reel 63; and Jesse Rankin to William McLain, March 26, 1852, reel 67, RACS; "Formation of Auxiliary Societies," *African Repository*, February 1828, 378; Jesse Rankin to William McLain, October 8, 1850, reel 63; Jesse Rankin to William McLain, March 26, 1852, reel 67; W. W. Kennedy to Secretary of the ACS, October 4, 1851, reel 66A; William Starr to William McLain, March 16 and 27, 1852, reel 67; William Starr to J. W. Lugenbeel, May 20, 1852, reel 67; J. W. Lugenbeel to William McLain, October 8, 1852, reel 68; and Isaac Scott to William McLain(?), May 25, 1852, reel 67, RACS; NCER.

17. The population figure for Fayetteville is based on the 1850 census of the town. Andriot, *Population Abstract of the United States*, 482; Parker, *Cumberland County*, 27, 40–44, 48–49, 53–59; Cecelski, *The Waterman's Song*, 50, 115; Sarah Louise Augustus interview, in Rawick, *The American Slave*, pt. 1, 52, 54; Nellie Smith interview, in Rawick, *The American Slave*, pt. 2, 287.

18. NCER; William H. Bayne to William McLain(?), January 15, 1849, reel 58; Marshall Hooper to (?), April 10, 1850, reel 154; Marshall Hooper to William McLain, August 1, 1852, reel 68; Marshall Hooper to William McLain, November 14, 1849, reel 154; J. W. Lugenbeel to William McLain, October 12, 1852, reel 68; and Marshall Hooper to William McLain, August 1, 1852, reel 68, RACS.

19. Marshall Hooper to William McLain, July 25 and August 1, 1852, reel 68; William McLain to Marshall Hooper, August 5, 1852; McLain letter, "To all whom it may concern," August 5, 1852, reel 193; Marshall Hooper to William McLain(?), September 20, 1852, reel 68; and J. W. Lugenbeel to William McLain, October 8 and 12, 1852, reel 68, RACS.

20. J. W. Lugenbeel to William McLain, October 12 and 14, November 10, 1852; J. W. Lugenbeel to William McLain(?), October 28, 1852, reel 68, RACS.

21. Marshall Hooper's return to North Carolina in 1855 to raise funds for the purpose of buying his son's freedom displeased ACS secretary William McLain. In a letter to an ACS agent, he stated, "We do not desire Mr. Hooper to stay any longer in the U. States. He came of his own free well—He has staid under the same—& he can leave at the same." J. W. Lugenbeel to William McLain, November 10, 1852, reel 68; Marshall Hooper to (?), October 15, 1855, reel 77; Marshall Hooper to J. W. Lugenbeel, March 15, 1853, reel 155; Marshall Hooper to William McLain, July 1854, reel 156; William McLain to John Latta, December 27, 1855, reel 197, RACS; NCER.

22. Emphasis in the original Delany quotes. Frederick Douglass speech, January 26, 1851, Rochester, New York, reprinted in Blassingame, *The Frederick Douglass Papers*, 2:300; Delany, *The Condition, Elevation, Emigration*, 170–71; Martin R. Delany, "Introduction" of Nesbit, *Four Months in Liberia*, 4, 8; Delany, *Official Report of the Niger Valley Exploring Party*, 47–67.

23. Edward Blyden, "A Brief Notice of Certain Statements," *Liberia Herald*, October 6, 1852, 17; "Martin Roberson Delany's Book," *Liberia Herald*, October 6, 1852, 19; "List of Emigrants," *African Repository*, March 1854, 88–89; and Nesbit, *Four Months in Liberia*, 10–11, 29, 53–54.

24. Nesbit and Williams both embarked for Liberia aboard the *Isla de Cuba* in November 1853. "List of Emigrants," *African Repository*, March 1854, 89; Williams, *Four Years in Liberia*, 12–17, 55–66.

25. Cledwell Whitted to William McLain, January 23, 1851, reel 64; Horace Day to William McLain, October 5, 1852, reel 68; and H. B. Hayes to William Starr, October 10, 1853, reel 71, RACS.

26. Susan Capart to John Kimberly, March 1, 1857, reprinted in Wiley, *Slaves No More*, 270–71; Henry Chavers Jr. to Ellis Malone, August 2, 1857, box 21-H (Correspondence, 1788–1859), Ellis Malone Papers; George L. Seymour to [?], January 25, 1860, reel 159, RACS; and Richard (Blount) McMorine to Johnston Pettigrew, June 1858, reel 13, Pettigrew Family Papers, SHC.

27. Daniel Williams to Amos Wade, August 16, 1857, reprinted in *Maryland Colonization Journal*, November 1857, 89–90; Miller, "*Dear Master*," 41–42.

28. Emphasis in original emigrant (Isaac Mouden) quote. Jesse Rankin to William McLain, December 12, 1850, reel 63; William Starr to J. W. Lugenbeel, May 26, 1852, reel 67; William Starr to William McLain, August 28, 1852, reel 68; William Starr to William McLain, April 14, 1853, reel 70; and Isaac H. Mouden to William McLain, May 28, 1854, reel 73, RACS; ACS, *Thirty-Fifth Annual Report* (1852), 15, 30; ACS, *Fiftieth Annual Report* (1867), 61.

29. Ms. S. Mallett to William McLain, September 30, 1858, reel 84; and James A. Dickson to William McLain, May 4, 1859, reel 86, RACS; Franklin, *The Free Negro*, 219; "Return to Slavery," *Western Democrat*, January 11, 1859, 3.

30. Between 1830 and 1840, the number of bondpeople in the state remained constant due largely to the export of North Carolina slaves to the Lower South and Midwest. "Extracts from the Last Will and Testament of Mrs. Lucy Peobles," reel 314, RACS; Mitchell, "Off to Africa," 267–68; NCER.

31. The Will of Mary Bissell, October 31, 1836, Chowan County; "Copy of the Last Will and Testament of William S. Andres, Deceased," November 1, 1857, reel 313; "Extract from the Will of John Rex of Raleigh," November 14, 1838; and The Will of Thomas Russell, October 3, 1834, Franklin County, reel 314, RACS; Catterall, *Judicial Cases*, 2:94–95, 115–16; Mitchell and Mitchell, "The Philanthropic Bequests of John Rex of Raleigh," pt. 1, 254–79; NCER.

32. Catterall, *Judicial Cases*, 2:94–95; "Copy of the Last Will and Testament of William S. Andres, Deceased"; "Will of Maria L. Gordon of Perquimans County," March 3, 1854; and "Extracts from the Last Will and Testament of Mrs. Lucy Peobles," reel 314, RACS.

33. Catterall, *Judicial Cases*, 2:94–95, 115–16, 208; Will of Mary Bissell; "Supreme Court, N. Carolina, December Term 1845," December 1845, reel 314, RACS.

34. Amos Wade to "Gentlemen," August 23, 1856, reel 80; and A. G. Hubbard to R. R. Gurley, March 19, 1858, reel 83, RACS; Singleton, *Recollections*, 8, 43–44.

35. ACS financial figures cited here are based on the compilation of North Carolina collections found in Franklin, *The Free Negro*, 238–46. William McLain to B. F. Moore, July 25, 1852, reel 195; and B. F. Moore to the Executive Comm. of the Amer. Col. Soc., July 18, 1853, reel 70, RACS.

36. While in the North Carolina Senate, James McKay served on a joint select committee that inquired into the advisability of establishing a state fund for financing the removal of free blacks to Liberia. As mentioned in Chapter 3, a subsequent bill authorizing such an expenditure was never passed by the legislature. *Journal of the Senate of the General Assembly of the State of North Carolina* (1831), 83; Powell, *Dictionary of North Carolina Biography*, 4:154; *Cyclopedia of Eminent and Representative Men*, 2:611; McKee, *Vital Records of Bladen County*, 21; Will of James I. McKay, November 26, 1833, reel 313; and C. G. Wright to William McLain, February 17, 1854, reel 72, RACS.

37. Mitchell, "Off to Africa," 274–76; Will of James I. McKay; C. G. Wright to William McLain, February 6 and 17, 1854, reel 72; C. G. Wright to William McLain, July 7, 1854, reel 73; and C. G. Wright to (?), March 22, 1855, reel 75, RACS.

38. C. G. Wright to William McLain, February 16 and 23, 1856, reel 78; William McLain to C. G. Wright, March 8, 1856, reel 199; William Starr to William McLain, February 6, 1857, reel 81; and C. G. Wright to McLain, April 5, 1857, reel 82, RACS (emphasis in original quote of McKay ex-slave).

39. NCER; De Bow, *Statistical View of the United States*, 103.

40. James Robeson to William McLain, April 1, 1857, reel 82; William McLain to C. G. Wright, April 7 (erroneously dated March 7), 1857, reel 200; C. G. Wright to William McLain, May 23, 1857, reel 82; William McLain to C. G. Wright, May 26 and June 4, 1857, reel 200; and William McLain to R. R. Gurley, May 26, 1857, reel 82, RACS; "Gen. J. J. McKay's Negroes," *Maryland Colonization Journal*, June 1857, 14; "Voyages of the Ship M. C. Stevens," *Maryland Colonization Journal*, November 1857, 81; Cowan, *Liberia, as I Found It*, 7–9; "The Ship M. C. Stevens," in ACS, *Fortieth Annual Report* (1857), 44–45; ACS, *Fiftieth Annual Report* (1867), 62; NCER.

41. James Hall, "Voyage to Liberia," *African Repository*, October 1857, 299; James Hall, "Voyage to Liberia," *African Repository*, September 1857, 270–74; John Seys to R. R. Gurley, August 10, 1856, reprinted in *African Repository*, October 1856, 306; Demp-

sey R. Fletcher to James Hall, October 28, 1856, reprinted in *Maryland Colonization Journal*, February 1857, 334; NCER; Robert McKay Sr. to [?], July 22, 1857, reel 157, RACS.

42. A petition by 114 citizens of Currituck County revealed that the proposed expulsion law had support in areas of the state. The signatories of this document assured lawmakers that they had "no qualms as to the right of the legislature either to expel [free blacks] from the State, or to reduce them to a condition of slavery." Hamilton, *The Papers of Thomas Ruffin*, 2:616–17; Franklin, *The Free Negro*, 214, 216–17; Taylor, "The Free Negro," 20; Catterall, *Judicial Cases*, 2:6; and Escott, *Many Excellent People*, 15.

43. ACS, *Fiftieth Annual Report* (1867), 56–63; Hunt, *The Essential Abraham Lincoln*, 279; Scheips, "Lincoln and the Chiriqui Colonization Project," 419; McPherson, *Ordeal by Fire*, 276–77; "President Lincoln as a Colonizationist," *African Repository*, April 1890, 48; "Bill Become a Law," *Congressional Globe*, 37th Cong., 2d sess., 2596.

44. The former legal status of 1 of the 602 North Carolinians who migrated to Liberia between 1850 and 1860 is unknown, and thus the literacy figures are based on 601 of the emigrants. ACS, *Fiftieth Annual Report* (1867), 56–63; NCER; McKay to William McLain, July 17, 1858, reel 158, RACS.

45. As had always been the case, no North Carolinians were among the 102 vice presidents of the organization as of 1861, nor had any served in high office since Joseph Gales retired as treasurer in 1839. ACS, *Twenty-Second Annual Report* (1838), 9; ACS, *Forty-Fourth Annual Report* (1861), 2; ACS, *Thirty-Eighth Annual Report* (1855), 3; ACS, *Forty-Seventh Annual Report* (1864), 21, 24; "No End of Colonization," *African Repository*, August 1864, 251–52.

CHAPTER SEVEN

1. U.S. Senate, *Executive Documents*, 92–93; Bennett and Brooks, *New England Merchants in Africa*, 108; Fox, *A Memoir of the Rev. C. Colden Hoffman*, 204; "From Liberia," *African Repository*, June 1827, 123–24; James Hall, "Grand Cape Mount," *Maryland Colonization Journal*, September 1857, 53.

2. Konneh, *Religion, Commerce, and the Integration of the Mandingo*, ix–x, 6, 12–13, 18; Corby, "Manding Traders and Clerics," 47–49; Singler, "Language in Liberia," 77; ACS, *Forty-First Annual Report* (1858), 15; Holsoe, "The Cassava-Leaf People."

3. "Guerilla in the Vey Country," *Liberian Herald*, August 22, 1855; J. J. Roberts to William McLain, January 24, 1845, reprinted in *African Repository*, April 1845, 116; *Twenty-Sixth Annual Report of the Missionary Society of the Methodist Episcopal Church* (1845), 22–23; J. J. Roberts to William McLain, September 22, 1849, reprinted in *African Repository*, December 1849, 377; James Hall, "Voyage to Liberia," *Maryland Colonization Journal*, October 1857, 65.

4. "Legislature of the Republic of Liberia," *African Repository*, July 1855, 206–8; Cowan, *Liberia, as I Found It*, 17, 29–30; Hugh McKay to William McLain, August 12, 1857; Edward McKay to William McLain, August 13, 1857; Washington McKay to William McLain, September 1, 1857, reel 157; William McLain to Washington McKay, October 29, 1857; and William McLain to McKay Family, July 26, 1858, reel 240, RACS.

5. McKay to William McLain, July 17, 1858; John McKay et al. to William McLain,

July 22, 1858, reel 158; William McLain to the McKay Family, October 29, 1859, reel 240; and Nip McKay et al. to William McLain, February 12, 1861, reel 160, RACS; Minutes of the Liberian Senate, February 22, 1864, box 4, SHP.

6. Cowan, *Liberia, as I Found It*, 29–30; Diana Sheridan to William McLain, March 1, 1859; and Diana Sheridan to William McLain, January 23, 1860, reel 159, RACS; NCER.

7. NCER; Diana Sheridan to William McLain, January 23, 1860, reel 159, RACS.

8. Bexley was named after Lord Bexley, the president of the British Colonization Society. Gatewood, " 'To Be Truly Free,' " 342; Lugenbeel, *Sketches of Liberia*, 8; Brown, *Biography of Finley*, 314; Cowan, *Liberia, as I Found It*, 100, 103; U.S. Senate, *Roll of Emigrants*, 376; NCER; J. J. Roberts to W. McLain, April 4, 1845, reel 172; and George Seymour to J. W. Lugenbeel, July 28, 1854, reel 156, RACS.

9. NCER; Cowan, *Liberia, as I Found It*, 98–99, 141–45, 167; Brown, *Biography of Finley*, 312.

10. John Smith to L. R. W. Bailey [?], June 23, 1852; Elie W. Stokes et al. to William Draper, June 8, 1853, reel 70; H. B. Hayes to William McLain, February 1, 1854, reel 72; and George L. Seymour to William McLain, January 4, 1853, reel 155, RACS.

11. The articles by A. W. originally appeared in the *New York Tribune* but were reprinted in *Frederick Douglass' Paper*, December 15, 1854, 1. They are quoted here from Kinshasa, *Emigration versus Assimilation*, 129–30. Also see ACS, *Fiftieth Annual Report* (1867), 61–62; NCER; "Late from Liberia," *African Repository*, June 1853, 182.

12. Gatewood, " 'To Be Truly Free,' " 347; U.S. Senate, *Roll of Emigrants*, 393, 395; ACS, *Twenty-Third Annual Report* (1839), 28–29; Louis Sheridan to Exec. Committee, January 24, 1842, reel 154, RACS.

13. NCER; U.S. Senate, *Roll of Emigrants*, 388, 394; Minutes of the Liberian Senate, February 8, 1848, and December 26, 1851, SHP; "Results of the Election," *African Repository*, September 1853, 286; Stockwell, *The Republic of Liberia*, 227–31.

14. Cowan, *Liberia, as I Found It*, 55–59; Slaughter, *The Virginian History*, 110; Brown, *Biography of Finley*, 305; and *Liberia Herald*, August 31, 1842, 38.

15. Cowan, *Liberia, as I Found It*, 89–90; Lugenbeel, *Sketches of Liberia*, 7; ACS, *Twenty-Fourth Annual Report* (1841), 36–37; J. J. Roberts to Rev. J. B. Pinney, May 11, 1842, reel 172, RACS; Stewart, *Liberia*, 88.

16. NCER; "Commonwealth Legislature Proceedings, 1839–1847" (folder), box 19, SHP.

17. NCER; U.S. Senate, *Roll of Emigrants*, 406–12; "Negroes—1826," Manumission Society Papers, SHC.

18. NCER; Stepp, "Interpreting a Forgotten Mission," 62, 69, 94, 102, 172–74, 186, 193.

19. Park, "Black and White American Methodist Missionaries," 49–56, 199–200; Stepp, "Interpreting a Forgotten Mission," 186; Williams, *Black Americans and the Evangelization*, 7.

20. Williams, *Black Americans and the Evangelization*; NCER.

21. NCER; U.S. Senate, *Roll of Emigrants*, 351; Park, "Black and White American Methodist Missionaries," 208, 237.

22. U.S. Senate, *Roll of Emigrants*, 405.

23. Cowan, *Liberia, as I Found It*, 34; Hendrix, "A Half Century of Americo-Liberian

Christianity," 257, 267; Park, "Black and White American Methodist Missionaries," 147; Tom W. Shick, "Rhetoric and Reality: Colonization and Afro-American Missionaries in Early Nineteenth-Century Liberia," in Jacobs, *Black Americans and the Missionary Movement*, 52–55; Hoff, *A Short History of Liberia College*, 49–50; U.S. Senate, *Roll of Emigrants*, 405.

24. Dunn, *A History of the Episcopal Church*, 81; Moses, *Alexander Crummell*, 165–69; NCER; Officer, *Western Africa, a Mission Field*, 42; Reichel, *The Moravians in North Carolina*, 140; Africa, "Slaveholding in the Salem Community," 271–307; Sensbach, *A Separate Canaan*.

25. Brown, *Biography of Finley*, 301–3; Fox, *A Memoir of the Rev. C. Colden Hoffman*, 205–6; Alexander, *A History of Colonization*, 513; Lugenbeel, *Sketches of Liberia*, 6; Nesbit, *Four Months in Liberia*, 12–13; Cowan, *Liberia, as I Found It*, 38–41, 80–81; Delany, *Official Report*, 59, 62–63; *Liberia Herald*, September 18, 1850, 15; George R. Ellis McDonogh to John McDonogh, May 14, 1844, reprinted in Wiley, *Slaves No More*, 133; "Intelligence," *African Repository*, July 1856, 217; J. J. Roberts to Rev. J. B. Pinney, May 11, 1842, reel 172, RACS; Minutes of the Liberian Senate, December 26, 1851, box 4, SHP; Bishir, "Black Builders," 423–61.

26. NCER; Cecelski, *The Waterman's Song*, 42; U.S. Senate, *Roll of Emigrants*, 375, 390, and 395; J. M. Sherwood to R. R. Gurley, November 26, 1858, reel 85; and Hull Anderson to [?], May 15, 1851, reel 155, RACS; Richard Judkins to William Blount Rodman, April 13, 1853, box 76.6, William Blount Rodman Papers, NCSA.

27. Cowan, *Liberia, as I Found It*, 40–41; Huberich, *The Political and Legislative History*, 1:463, 529–30; ACS, *Eighteenth Annual Report* (1835), 31; "Monrovia Lot Histories" (notebook), box 6, SHP; "Constitution of the Republic of Liberia," reprinted in ACS, *Thirty-First Annual Report* (1848), 52; Minutes of the Liberian Senate, December 18, 1851, box 4, SHP; *Liberian Law Reports*, 320; U.S. Senate, *Roll of Emigrants*, 406–12.

28. Given that the age distribution among North Carolina emigrants reveals unusually high incidences of ages evenly divisible by five and/or ten, it is very likely that many older individuals did not know their exact age and thus offered estimates to ACS officials that were multiples of five or ten. Also, it is entirely possible that colonization agents made their own guesses about the ages of emigrants. NCER.

29. Ibid. Age statistics are based on the known ages of 2,003 North Carolina emigrants.

30. Ibid.

31. Ibid.; Lavinia Nelson to William McLain, September 30, 1861; Martha Nelson to (?), October 2, 1863, reel 160; and William McLain to Martha Nelson, October 24, 1861, reel 240, RACS; Susan Capart to John Kimberly, March 1, 1857, reprinted in Wiley, *Slaves No More*, 270–71; U.S. Senate, *Roll of Emigrants*, 317; King, *Stolen Childhood*, 2.

32. McDaniel, *Swing Low, Sweet Chariot*, 84–87; Johnson, *Ante-bellum North Carolina*, 723–24; Larkin, *The Reshaping of Everyday Life*, 87–88; Kiple and King, *Another Dimension to the Black Diaspora*, 15, 50, 52; K. David Patterson, "Disease Environments of the Antebellum South," in Numbers and Savitt, *Science and Medicine*, 155; Humphreys, *Malaria*, 8–9, 23; Daniel Rhodes to W. H. Starr, September 19, 1853, reprinted in *African Repository*, May 1854, 141.

33. Humphreys, *Malaria*, 9–10, Kiple and King, *Another Dimension to the Black Di-*

aspora, 15–16; Cowan, *Liberia, as I Found It*, 171–73; Delany, *Official Report*, 50, 66; Lugenbeel, *Sketches of Liberia*, 28.

34. Kiple and King, *Another Dimension to the Black Diaspora*, 16, 55–57; Proceedings of the Board of Managers, May 14, 1832, reel 289, RACS; McDaniel, *Swing Low, Sweet Chariot*, 75–77, 86, 89, 91–92; Delany, *Official Report*, 50, 66; "List of Medicines," April 1851; and "Medicines &c.," June 1, 1853, reel 239, RACS; Lugenbeel, *Sketches of Liberia*, 29–32; Humphreys, *Malaria*, 19; Shick, "A Quantitative Analysis," 45–59; Carlson, *African Fever*, 44–48.

35. NCER; U.S. Senate, *Roll of Emigrants*, 152–306; Kiple and King, *Another Dimension to the Black Diaspora*, 114; Patterson, "Disease Environments of the Antebellum South," 155.

36. NCER; Humphreys, *Malaria*, 9–10; Cowan, *Liberia, as I Found It*, 172; Kiple and King, *Another Dimension to the Black Diaspora*, 65; Williams, *The Liberian Exodus*, 41; Close, *Elderly Slaves*, 67, 69.

37. Tobacco was very popular in Liberia during the nineteenth century, as well as in North Carolina. Its usage among immigrants, and Africans, probably caused or complicated a variety of respiratory illnesses. However, tobacco did suppress hunger, which may have contributed to the demand for it among colonists. NCER; McDaniel, *Swing Low, Sweet Chariot*, 83–88; Kiple and King, *Another Dimension to the Black Diaspora*, 135–36, 140–41; Larkin, *The Reshaping of Everyday Life*, 79–80; Patterson, "Disease Environments of the Antebellum South," 155; Johnson, *Ante-bellum North Carolina*, 733; *Mosby's Medical, Nursing, and Allied Health Dictionary*; *Stedman's Medical Dictionary*.

38. *Stedman's Medical Dictionary*; *Mosby's Medical, Nursing, and Allied Health Dictionary*; NCER; Lugenbeel, *Sketches of Liberia*, 32.

39. Lugenbeel, *Sketches of Liberia*, 35; NCER; Larkin, *The Reshaping of Everyday Life*, 80–81.

40. NCER; Johnson, *Ante-bellum North Carolina*, 732, 738; Larkin, *The Reshaping of Everyday Life*, 77–78; Silvy Franklin (McKay) to William McLain, July 11, 1860, reel 159, RACS; McDaniel, *Swing Low, Sweet Chariot*, 15–16.

41. NCER; U.S. Senate, *Roll of Emigrants*, 167, 195, 310, 343; Sion Harris to Samuel Wilkeson, April 16, 1840, reprinted in Wiley, *Slaves No More*, 220–23.

42. Sion Harris to Samuel Wilkeson, April 16, 1840, reprinted in Wiley, *Slaves No More*, 220–23; Thomas Buchanan to Samuel Wilkeson, April 6, 1840, reprinted *African Repository*, June 15, 1840, 179–82.

43. Inaugural Address of Joseph J. Roberts, January 3, 1848, reprinted in Guannu, *The Inaugural Addresses*, 2–8.

44. The ACS had long sought to annex contiguous lands between Cape Palmas and Cape Mount. In their 1842 annual report, colonization officials stated, "Every individual must be convinced that we ought to strain every nerve to gain possession of this continuous coast." ACS, *Twenty-Fifth Annual Report* (1842), 8; J. J. Roberts to George C. Read, December 14, 1846, reel 172, RACS; "Annual Message of President Roberts," *African Repository*, April 1854, 100–104; Williams, *The Liberian Exodus*, 55; Sawyer, *The Emergence of Autocracy*.

45. In an 1854 letter to William McLain, George Seymour lamented that "some of

the most inteligant" immigrants in Bexley had assimilated with indigenous people to the point that they were "living in violation of the laws." George Seymour to William McLain, July 28, 1854, reel 156, RACS; "Dr. Hall's Answers to Mr. Key's Questions," *African Repository*, November 1842, 341–42; Lugenbeel, *Sketches of Liberia*, 29–32; Williams, *The Liberian Exodus*, 41; Alexander, *A History of Colonization*, 320; Huberich, *The Political and Legislative History*, 2:1030; Martin, "How to Build a Nation," 15–38; Cowan, *Liberia, as I Found It*, 143.

46. Stepp, "Interpreting a Forgotten Mission," 104; Williams, *The Liberian Exodus*, 46; NCER; U.S. Senate, *Roll of Emigrants*, 376; John H. Smyth to Mr. Evarts, April 26, 1879, in U.S. House, *Executive Documents*, 46th Cong., 713–17; Williams, *Four Years in Liberia*, 16, 38–39, 59; *Liberian Law Reports*, 320; Sawyer, *The Emergence of Autocracy*, 185–89.

47. A published 1842 letter of Governor Joseph J. Roberts characterizing intermarriage between Africans and colonists as "quite common" has to be viewed as suspect, given the abundance of contradictory evidence and his own political interest in publicly portraying African-immigrant relations as amicable and equitable. "Governor Roberts' Letter to Dr. Hodgkin," October 1842, reprinted in *African Repository*, November 1843, 331–32; Diana Skipwith to Louisa Clark, May 20, 1839, reprinted in Miller, "*Dear Master*," 91–92; Nesbit, *Four Months in Liberia*, 48; Alexander, *A History of Colonization*, 511; Johnston, *Liberia*, 1:275.

48. Joseph J. Roberts served as colonial governor (1842–48) and president of Liberia (1848–54, 1872–76). James S. Payne served as president (1868–70, 1876–78). John Day served as chief justice of the Liberian Supreme Court during the 1850s. Reginald A. Sherman was appointed secretary of navy and war during the late nineteenth century. Louis Sheridan, discussed earlier, was appointed superintendent of commercial operations in Bassa Cove during the colonial period. Richardson, *Liberia's Past and Present*, 86–89; Dunn and Holsoe, *Historical Dictionary of Liberia*, 137, 147, 159; Lowenkopf, *Politics in Liberia*, 22–23; Edward W. Blyden to William Coppinger, October 19, 1874, reprinted in Lynch, *Selected Letters of Edward Wilmot Blyden*, 173–78; "Eulogy of Rev. Edward W. Blyden on the Rev. John Day," *African Repository*, May 1861, 154–58; Barfield, "Thomas and John Day," 1–31; Williams, *The Liberian Exodus*, 57; "Liberian Judge at White Sulphur Springs," *Knoxville Whig*, [late 1859?], reel 87, RACS; NCER; "United States Historical Census Data Browser," ‹http://fisher.lib.Virginia.edu/census/›; U.S. Bureau of the Census, *Negro Population in the United States*, 220.

49. John H. Smyth to Mr. Evarts, April 26, 1879, in U.S. House, *Executive Documents*, 46th Cong., 713–17; Huberich, *The Political and Legislative History*, 1:630–32; Howard, *American Slavers*, 52–53, 71, 138–39, 218–22, 248; "The Voyage of the Frigate Niagara," *New York Times*, December 13, 1858, 2; John Seys to Lewis Cass, November 11, 1860, U.S. State Department, Record Group No. 59, M169, reel 2, NACPM; Boyd, "The American Colonization Society," 166, 120; Brittan, *Scenes and Incidents*, 288–90; ACS, *Forty-Fourth Annual Report* (1861), 16; Cowan, *Liberia, as I Found It*, 166.

50. James Deputie to [William McLain?], February 12, 1861, reel 160; and J. J. Roberts to William McLain, June 25, 1846, reel 172, RACS; John Seys to Lewis Cass, November 11, 1860, U.S. State Department, Record Group No. 59, M169, reel 2,

NACPM; "The Africans by the Pons," *African Repository*, January 1847, 25; "The Six Decades of Liberia," *African Repository*, July 1881, 96–97; Sawyer, *The Emergence of Autocracy*, 187–88; Lavinia Nelson to William McLain, August 23, 1862, reel 160, RACS.

51. Lowenkopf, *Politics in Liberia*, 20–23; *New York Times*, December 29, 1875, 4; "Letter from a Colonist," *African Repository*, November 1845, 337; Richard Judkins to William Blount Rodman, April 13, 1853, box 76.6, William Blount Rodman Papers, NCSA; and Williams, *The Liberian Exodus*, 27.

52. Johnston, *Liberia*, 1:354; G. S. Stockwell, *The Republic of Liberia*, 249; Holsoe, Herman, and Belcher, *A Land and Life Remembered*.

53. "Some Statistics of Liberia," *African Repository*, October 1850, 300; "The Republic of Liberia," *African Repository*, April 1848, 100; Syfert, "The Liberian Coasting Trade," 218–28.

CHAPTER EIGHT

1. NCER; "United States Historical Census Data Browser," ‹http://fisher.lib.Virginia.edu/census/›; Watson, *Bertie County*, 12, 16; Thomas, *Divided Allegiance*, xiv, 13, 17, 48–55, 78, 87–93, 107, 109, 116–19, 131; Escott, *Many Excellent People*, 35–36, 52–54, 143–44; *The Federal and State Constitutions*, 1419, 1421, 1430–32.

2. Browning, "The North Carolina Black Code," 465–67; Wilson, *The Black Codes of the South*, 105–7; "North Carolina," *New York Times*, October 11, 1866, 2; Escott, *Many Excellent People*, 124; Lefler and Newsome, *North Carolina*, 495.

3. NCER; Jonathan S. Taylor to President of the Colonization Society, April 11, 1868, reel 102; John Tayloe to Alonzo Hoggard, October 29, 1869, reel 105; and John S. Shepperd to William Coppinger, May 13, 1869, reel 104, RACS.

4. According to William McLain, the ACS had over four thousand applications for passage to Liberia as of April 1868. William McLain to F. W. Bell, April 30, 1868, reel 206, RACS; ACS, *Forty-Seventh Annual Report* (1864), 35; ACS, *Fifty-First Annual Report* (1868), 45; ACS, *Fiftieth Annual Report* (1867), 8–9, 63–64; ACS, *Fifty-Fifth Annual Report* (1872), 47.

5. Emphasis in original Arthington quotes. Robert Arthington to William Coppinger, August 30, 1868, reel 102; Robert Arthington to William Coppinger, November 11, 1868, reel 103; William Coppinger to Robert Arthington, October 23, 1868; William Coppinger to Robert Arthington, November 26, 1869, reel 212; and William Coppinger to William McLain, August 23 and 26, 1869, reel 104, RACS.

6. William Coppinger to William McLain, August 23 and 26, 1869; John S. Shepperd to William Coppinger, July 7 and September 11, 1869, reel 104; William Coppinger to William McLain, September 6, 1870, reel 106; and Journal of the Executive Committee, November 19, 1869, reel 293, RACS.

7. The Pennsylvania Colonization Society contributed $7,500.00 to the outfitting and settlement of the Brewer party in Liberia. John S. Shepperd to William Coppinger, November 1, 1869; William Coppinger to William McLain, November 3 and 8, 1869, reel 105; William Coppinger to Franklin Lightfoot, November 24, 1869, reel 212; Journal of the Executive Committee, November 19, 1869, reel 293; William Coppinger to William McLain, November 26, 1869, reel 212; and William McLain to Robert Arthington, July 30, 1870, reel 207, RACS.

8. NCER; Lefler and Newsome, *North Carolina*, 500–501; *The Federal and State Constitutions*, 1447–51; "Let Us Have a Fair Count," *New York Times*, December 3, 1876, 1; Taylor, "The Great Migration," 26 (nn. 22, 31); Logan, "The Movement of Negroes," 51; "The Negro's New Bondage," *New York Times*, September 23, 1879, 1; Steelman, *The North Carolina Farmers' Alliance*, 1; "How the Colored Exodus Is Managed," *New York Times*, December 24, 1879, 1; U.S. Senate, *Report to Investigate the Causes of the Removal of the Negroes*, 63, 115; Athearn, *In Search of Canaan*, 217–18.

9. Robert Orr to William Coppinger, September 1, 1877, reel 116A; and Rev. John Wilkins to [William Coppinger?], November 12, 1877, reel 116B, RACS; "Constitution of the Elizabeth City (N.C.) Freedmen's Emigrant Aid Society," *African Repository*, May 1871, 152–55.

10. A. W. Power to [William Coppinger?], December 10, 1869, reel 105; Miles A. Bright to [William Coppinger?], December 10, 1877, reel 116B; Harry Roberts to William Coppinger, October 12, 1879, reel 119; and Peter Mountain to William Coppinger, October 26, 1870, reel 107, RACS.

11. Edward Sawyer to [William Coppinger?], September 4, 1877, reel 116A; William Coppinger to C. W. Jones, July 13, 1877, reel 217; R. S. Lewis to William Coppinger, November 19, 1877, reel 116B; Jerry Jones to [William Coppinger?], April 10, 1878; Cain Gibbs to William McLain, March 7, 1878, reel 117; and Rev. John Wilkins to [William Coppinger?], November 12, 1877, reel 116B, RACS.

12. Livingstone College was originally known as Zion Wesley Institute. The enrollment of Mrs. Cartwright's schools included teachers and superintendent. Logan, *The Negro in North Carolina*, 148–49; Mrs. Caroline R. S. Cartwright letter, March 24, 1888, reprinted in *African Repository*, October 1888, 133; Williams, *Black Americans and the Evangelization*, 58–59, 150–54, 158; NCER.

13. NCER; Whitted, *A History of the Negro Baptists*, 53–60, 150–53; Logan, *The Negro in North Carolina*, 148; "Freedmen's Great Mass Convention" flier, 1877, reel 116B, RACS; "Constitution of the Elizabeth City (N.C.) Freedmen's Emigrant Aid Society," *African Repository*, May 1871, 152–55; Sherwood Capps to [William Coppinger?], December 17, 1877, reel 116B; Sherwood Capps to William Coppinger, May 7, 1879, reel 119; James Hays to William Coppinger, October 3, 1874, reel 113; James O. Hayes to William Coppinger, February 27, 1878, reel 117; and Alexander Hays et al. to Officers and members of the collinazation societey, October 27, 1879, reel 164, RACS.

14. Among the emigrants of the *Azor* were Alfred Hood of Charlotte, his wife, and three children. Williams, *The Liberian Exodus*; Logan, *The Negro in North Carolina*, 121, 131–32; J. C. Price to T. F. Bayard, March 5, 1888, reprinted in *African Repository*, July 1888, 95–96; Tindall, "The Liberian Exodus of 1878," 133–45; Painter, *Exodusters*, 137–45; Crow, Escott, and Hatley, *A History of African Americans*, 104.

15. NCER; Isaac Skinner to William Coppinger, October 10, 1877, reel 116B; Edmund D. Sawyer to William Coppinger, January 10 and February 23, 1878, reel 117; William Coppinger to William McLain, November 1870, reel 107; E. D. Sawyer to [William Coppinger?], December 28, 1877; Charles W. Jones to William Coppinger, December 28, 1877, reel 116B; J. R. Etheridge to William Coppinger, January 18, 1878, reel 117, RACS; Logan, *The Negro in North Carolina*, 133; "Negroes Leaving a State," *New York Times*, August 10, 1889, 5.

16. J. C. Stevens to J. Ormond Wilson, October 11, 1894, reprinted in *Liberia*, No-

vember 1894, 2; Thomas S. Malcom to William Coppinger, October 21, 1870, reel 107; "Arthington, Liberia," *African Repository*, November 1873, 337–38; Alonzo Hoggard et al. to William Coppinger, May 19, 1870, reel 161; Alonzo Hoggard to William Coppinger, July 16, 1870, reel 161; Alonzo Hoggard to William Coppinger, March 19, April 21, May 4, and August 14, 1871, reel 162; Alonzo Hoggard to William Coppinger, March 18, 1873, reel 162; and June Moore to William Coppinger, December 20, 1880, reel 164, RACS.

17. NCER; John B. Roulhac to William Coppinger, October 6, 1871; Peter Mountain to William Coppinger, August 9, 1872, and April 22, 1873, reel 162; Charles R. Branch to William Coppinger, December 20, 1886, reel 167; H. W. Dennis to William Coppinger, May 9 and November 7, 1871, reel 162, RACS; "Liberian Affairs," *African Repository*, December 1872, 367; J. C. Stevens to J. Ormond Wilson, October 1, 1894, reprinted in *Liberia*, November 1894, 2; "Arthington Settlement," *African Repository*, May 1881, 60–61; Stewart, *Liberia*, 38.

18. H. W. Dennis letter, reprinted in *African Repository*, June 1870, 189; ACS, *Fifty-Fourth Annual Report* (1871), 14–15; NCER; J. B. Munden to William Coppinger, April 22, 1874, and August 25, 1876, reel 163; J. B. Munden to William Coppinger, January 26, 1880, reel 164; John B. Munden to C. T. O. King, June 14, 1883, reel 165, RACS; "Returned Emigrants," *African Repository*, July 1883, 91.

19. Holsoe, "A Portrait of a Black Midwestern Family," 41–52; "The Fifth President of the Republic of Liberia," *African Repository*, April 1870, 121–23; John Seys to William Seward, May 11, 1867, in U.S. House, *Executive Documents*, 40th Cong., 330; Montserrado County, Court of Quarter Sessions and Common Pleas, November 1871–February 1872 (typescript copy in notebook), box 22, SHP; Henry W. Dennis to William Coppinger, May 6, June 3, August 24, December 14, 1871, and May 16, 1872, reel 162, RACS; John Lewis to J. Milton Turner, October 23, 1871, in U.S. Department of State, Record Group No. 84, M170, reel 2, NACPM; Kremer, *James Milton Turner*, 63–64; J. Milton Turner to Hamilton Fish, October 30, 1871, in *Papers Relating to the Foreign Relations of the United States* (1873), 324–26; "Condemnation and Subsequent Escape, and Death by Drowning, of the Late President Roye," *African Times* (London), May 23, 1872, 132; "The Late Ex-President Roye of Liberia," *African Times*, March 23, 1872; Dunn and Holsoe, *Historical Dictionary of Liberia*, 149–50, 174–75; Edward W. Blyden to William Coppinger, October 19, 1874, reprinted in Lynch, *Selected Letters of Edward Wilmot Blyden*, 173–78; *New York Times*, December 29, 1875, 4; John B. Munden to William Coppinger, January 31 and September 19, 1881, reel 164, RACS.

20. NCER; S. S. Hardy et al. to H. Dennis, June 28, 1875, reel 163; Alexander Hays et al. to Officers and members of the collinazation societey, October 27, 1879, reel 164; and Norfleet Brown to William Coppinger, February 7, 1883, reel 165, RACS.

21. The 1886 emigrant tally does not include the 5,722 recaptives who were landed in Liberia during the nineteenth century. Alonzo Hoggard letter, July 18, 1870, reprinted in *African Repository*, October 1870, 317–18; John B. Munden letter, April 19, 1871, reprinted in *African Repository*, July 1871, 218–19; ACS, *Sixty-Ninth Annual Report* (1886), 24–25.

22. NCER.

23. West, *Back to Africa*, 253–54; J. Milton Turner to William Evarts, September 3, 1877, in U.S. House, *Executive Documents*, 45th Cong., 370–75; Johnston, *Liberia*, 1:371–72, 444; "Liberia and the Native Tribes," *African Repository*, April 1884, 61–62;

Huberich, *The Political and Legislative History*, 2:1107; John Smyth to William Evart, February 22, 1881, in U.S. House, *Executive Documents*, 47th Cong., 733; Martin, "How to Build a Nation," 15–42; Gershoni, "The Formation of Liberia's Boundaries, Part 1: Agreements," 25–45; Edward W. Blyden et al. to William Coppinger, October 1, 1869, reel 105, RACS; "Assimilation," *African Repository*, April 1882, 63.

24. NCER; ACS, *Seventy-Seventh Annual Report* (1894), 5–6; ACS, *Seventy-Ninth Annual Report* (1896), 4–5; John Smyth to Mr. Frelinghuysen, January 17, 1883, in *Papers Relating to the Foreign Policy of the United States* (1884), 615; Padgett, "Ministers to Liberia," 73–91; *African Repository*, July 1888, 96; Logan, *The Negro in North Carolina*, 43–44; "Emigration," *Liberia*, February 1893, 2.

25. ACS, *Eighty-First Annual Report* (1898), 5; ACS, *Eighty-Sixty Annual Report* (1903), 13; Seifman, "The Passing of the American Colonization Society," 7.

EPILOGUE

1. Kenneth B. Noble, "Liberia President Captured by Foes," *New York Times*, September 10, 1990, A1, A9; Liebenow, *Liberia*, 85; Tim Sullivan, "Liberia's Old Elite Finds New Favor," *Washington Post*, December 16, 2001, A33.

2. Inaugural Address of William R. Tolbert, Jr., January 5, 1976, in Guannu, *The Inaugural Addresses*, 409; Noble, "Liberia President Captured," A1, A9; Kenneth B. Noble, "Liberian President's New Plane 'An Immense Waste of Money,'" *Charlotte Observer*, April 8, 1990, 31A; Howard Witt, "Liberia in Chaos, Decay," *Charlotte Observer*, June 10, 1990, 24A; "Navy Ship on Standby off Liberia in Case Americans Must Evacuate," *Charlotte Observer*, June 1, 1990, 6A; Kenneth B. Noble, "Liberian Insurgents Kill President, Diplomats and Broadcasts Report," *New York Times*, September 11, 1990, A1, A4; Jeffrey Bartholet, "A Big Man in Africa," *Newsweek*, May 14, 2001, 28.

3. "Rebels Advance on Liberian Capital," *Charlotte Observer*, June 3, 1990, 2A; "Leader of Liberian Revolt Bullish on Capitalism—Not Democracy," *Charlotte Observer*, June 3, 1990, 2A; Reno, "Reinvention of an African Patrimonial State," 113–14; "Rebels Seize U.S. Rubber Plantations," *Charlotte Observer*, June 6, 1990, 14A; Human Rights Watch, *Easy Prey*, 2–4; Bartholet, "A Big Man in Africa," 31; Brennan, "Charles Taylor," 210; Norimitsu Onishi, "In Ruined Liberia, Its Despoiler Sits Pretty," *New York Times*, December 7, 2000, A18.

4. Sullivan, "Liberia's Old Elite," A33; NCER; and "One Day to Graduation: UL Students Threaten Suicide," *NEWS*, December 18, 2001; "Taylor Denies Beating Wife before She Left for US," PANA Press, December 26, 2001, ⟨http://www.panapress.com⟩; Brennan, "Charles Taylor," 210.

5. Lia Burns, "Ambassador Diggs Visit to Winston-Salem," *Winston-Salem Journal*, July 13, 1999; Wonkeryor, *Liberia Military Dictatorship*, 18–22; Somini Sengupta, "Peacekeeping Unit Arrives in Liberia," *New York Times*, August 5, 2003, A1, A4; Sengupta, "The Haves and Have-Nots Reside on Both Sides of Liberian Capital," *New York Times*, August 6, 2003, A1, A8; Sengupta, "Vice President Prepares to Take Control," *New York Times*, August 10, 2003, 6; Sengupta, "Leader of Liberia Surrenders Power and Enters Exile," *New York Times*, August 12, 2003, A1, A8; Sengupta, "With Calls for Reconciliation, New Liberian Leader Takes Office," *New York Times*, October 15, 2003, A8.

BIBLIOGRAPHY

MANUSCRIPT COLLECTIONS

Bloomington, Indiana
Archives of Traditional Music, Indiana University
  Svend Holsoe Papers

Chapel Hill, North Carolina
Southern Historical Collection, University of North Carolina
  Manumission Society Papers
  Pettigrew Family Papers
  Weedon and Whitehurst Family Papers

Charlottesville, Virginia
Special Collections Department, University of Virginia Library
  Lucas Brothers of Liberia Letters

Chicago, Illinois
Chicago Historical Society
  American Colonization Society Papers

College Park, Maryland
National Archives II
  General Records of the U.S. Department of State, Record Group No. 59
  Records of the Foreign Service Posts of the U.S. Department of State, Record
    Group No. 84

Durham, North Carolina
Special Collections Library, Duke University
  C. W. Andrews Papers
  Henry Harrison Papers
  Edward L. Hartz Papers
  Henry Huntington Papers
  John Richardson Kilby Papers

Ellis Malone Papers
John Moore McCalla Papers
Montgomery D. Parker Papers
James Redpath Papers
James H. Robeson Papers
William Norwood Tillinghast Papers

Greensboro, North Carolina
Hege Library, Guilford College
  Friends Historical Collection

Nashville, Tennessee
Tennessee State Library and Archives
  Russwurm Papers

Raleigh, North Carolina
North Carolina State Archives
  McKay-Robeson Papers
  Pattie Mordecai Papers
  North Carolina General Assembly, Session Records
  William Blount Rodman Papers

Washington, D.C.
Library of Congress
  Records of the American Colonization Society (microfilm)

NEWSPAPERS

African Intelligencer
African Luminary (Monrovia)
African Repository
African Times (London)
American Museum
Charlotte Observer
Colonizationist and Journal of Freedom
Colored American
Elizabeth-City Star and North Carolina Eastern Intelligencer
Freedom's Journal
Genius of Universal Emancipation (and Baltimore Courier)
Greensboro [Greensborough] Patriot
Liberator
Liberia
Liberia Herald
Maryland Colonization Journal
Missionary Herald
New York Times

NEWS (Liberia)
Norfolk Herald
North Carolina Whig (Charlotte)
PANA Press, ‹http://www.panapress.com›
Raleigh Register
Republican (Monrovia)
Rights of All
Sun (Baltimore)
Times (London)
Western Democrat (Charlotte)
Wilmington Post
Winston-Salem Journal

BOOKS

Alexander, Archibald. *A History of Colonization on the Western Coast of Africa.* 1846. Reprint. New York: Negro Universities Press, 1969.

American Slavery as It Is: Testimony of a Thousand Witnesses. New York: The American Anti-Slavery Society, 1839.

Anderson, Benjamin. *Narrative of a Journey to Musardu . . . Together with Narrative of the Expedition Despatched to Musahdu.* 1870 and 1912. Reprint. London: Frank Cass & Co., 1971.

Andriot, Donna, ed. *Population Abstract of the United States.* McLean, Va.: Documents Index, Inc., 1993.

Aptheker, Herbert, ed. *A Documentary History of the Negro People in the United States.* 3 vols. New York: Carol Publishing Co., 1951.

————. *One Continual Cry: David Walker's Appeal to the Colored Citizens of the World, 1829–1830.* New York: Humanities Press, 1965.

Arnett, Ethel S. *Greensboro, North Carolina: The County Seat of Guilford.* Chapel Hill: University of North Carolina Press, 1955.

Ashmun, Jehudi. *History of the American Colony in Liberia, from December 1821 to 1823.* Washington, D.C.: Way & Gideon, 1826.

————. *Memoir of the Life and Character of the Rev. Samuel Bacon.* Washington, D.C.: Jacob Gideon, 1822.

Athearn, Robert G. *In Search of Canaan: Black Migration to Kansas, 1879–80.* Lawrence: Regents Press of Kansas, 1978.

Barnes, Jay. *North Carolina's Hurricane History.* Rev. ed. Chapel Hill: University of North Carolina Press, 1998.

Bennett, Norman R., and George E. Brooks Jr., eds. *New England Merchants in Africa: A History through Documents, 1802–1865.* Boston: Boston University Press, 1965.

Berlin, Ira. *Slaves without Masters: The Free Negro in the Antebellum South.* New York: The New Press, 1974.

Beyon, Amos J. *The American Colonization Society and the Creation of the Liberian State.* Lanham, Md.: University Press of America, 1991.

Blackburn, Robin. *The Overthrow of Colonial Slavery, 1776–1848.* New York: Verso, 1988.

Blassingame, John W., ed. *The Frederick Douglass Papers*. 5 vols. New Haven, Conn.: Yale University Press, 1982.

Bogger, Tommy L. *Free Blacks in Norfolk, Virginia, 1790–1860*. Charlottesville: University Press of Virginia, 1997.

Boley, G. E. Saigbe. *Liberia: The Rise and Fall of the First Republic*. New York: St. Martin's Press, 1983.

Bowden, James. *The History of the Society of Friends in America*. London: Charles Gilpin, 1850.

Brittan, Harriette G. *Scenes and Incidents of Every-day Life in Africa*. 1860. Reprint. New York: Negro Universities Press, 1969.

Brooks, George E., Jr. *The Kru Mariner in the Nineteenth Century: An Historical Compendium*. Newark, Del.: Liberian Studies Monograph Series, 1972.

———. *Landlords and Strangers: Ecology, Society, and Trade in Western Africa, 1000–1630*. Boulder, Colo.: Westview Press, 1993.

———. *Yankee Traders, Old Coasters and African Middlemen: A History of American Legitimate Trade with West Africa in the Nineteenth Century*. Boston: Boston University Press, 1970.

Brown, Isaac V. *Biography of the Rev. Robert Finley*. 1856. Reprint. New York: Arno Press, 1969.

Bruns, Roger, ed. *Am I Not a Man and a Brother?: The Antislavery Crusade of Revolutionary America, 1688–1788*. New York: Chelsea House, 1983.

Buckingham, J. S. *The Slave States of America*. 2 vols. London: Fisher, Son & Co., 1842.

Butler, Lindley S., and Alan D. Watson, eds. *The North Carolina Experience: An Interpretive and Documentary History*. Chapel Hill: University of North Carolina Press, 1984.

Campbell, Penelope. *Maryland in Africa: The Maryland State Colonization Society, 1831–1857*. Urbana: University of Illinois Press, 1971.

Campbell, Stanley W. *The Slave Catchers: Enforcement of the Fugitive Slave Law, 1850–1860*. Chapel Hill: University of North Carolina Press, 1970.

Carlisle, Rodney. *The Roots of Black Nationalism*. Port Washington, N.Y.: Kennikat Press, 1975.

Carlsen, Dennis G. *African Fever: A Study of British Science, Technology, and Politics in West Africa, 1787–1864*. Canton, Mass.: Science History Publications, 1984.

Catterall, Helen T., ed. *Judicial Cases concerning American Slavery and the Negro*. 5 vols. Washington, D.C.: Carnegie Institution of Washington, 1926–37.

Cecelski, David S. *The Waterman's Song: Slavery and Freedom in Maritime North Carolina*. Chapel Hill: University of North Carolina Press, 2001.

Cecil-Fronsman, Bill. *Common Whites: Class and Culture in Antebellum North Carolina*. Lexington: University Press of Kentucky, 1992.

Censer, Jane T. *North Carolina Planters and Their Children, 1800–1860*. Baton Rouge: Louisiana State University Press, 1984.

Clayton, Thomas H. *Close to the Land: The Way We Lived in North Carolina, 1820–1870*. Chapel Hill: University of North Carolina Press, 1983.

Close, Stacey K. *Elderly Slaves of the Plantation South*. New York: Garland Publishing, 1997.

Coffin, Levi. *Reminiscences of Levi Coffin.* 1876. Reprint. New York: Arno Press, 1968.

Cone, Sydney M., Jr., ed. *The History of Guilford County, North Carolina, U.S.A., to 1980, A.D.* Guilford, N.C.: n.d.

Cooke, Jacob E. *Frederic Bancroft, Historian.* Norman: University of Oklahoma Press, 1957.

Corbitt, David L. *The Formation of the North Carolina Counties, 1663–1943.* Raleigh: North Carolina Department of Archives and History, 1950.

Correspondence Relative to the Emigration to Hayti, of the Free People of Colour, in the United States. New York: Mahlon Day, 1824.

Cowan, Alexander M. *Liberia, as I Found It, in 1858.* Frankfort, Ky.: A. G. Hodges, 1858.

Crow, Jeffrey J. *The Black Experience in Revolutionary North Carolina.* Raleigh: North Carolina Department of Cultural Resources, Division of Archives and History, 1977.

Crow, Jeffrey J., and Flora J. Hatley, eds. *Black Americans in North Carolina and the South.* Chapel Hill: University of North Carolina Press, 1984.

Crow, Jeffrey J., Paul Escott, and Flora J. Hatley. *A History of African Americans in North Carolina.* Raleigh: North Carolina Department of Cultural Resources, Division of Archives and History, 1992.

Crummell, Alexander. *The Future of Africa.* 1862. Reprint. New York: Negro Universities Press, 1969.

Cyclopedia of Eminent and Representative Men of the Carolinas of the Nineteenth Century. 2 vols. Madison, Wis.: Brant & Fuller, 1892.

Davis, David B. *The Problem of Slavery in Western Culture.* New York: Oxford University Press, 1966.

Davis, Ronald W. *Ethnohistorical Studies on the Kru Coast.* Newark, Del.: Liberian Studies Monograph Series, 1976.

De Bow, J. D. B. *Statistical View of the United States . . . Being a Compendium of the Seventh Census.* Washington, D.C.: A. O. P. Nicholson, 1854.

Delany, Martin R. *The Condition, Elevation, Emigration and Destiny of the Colored People of the United States.* 1852. Reprint. New York: Arno Press and New York Times, 1969.

———. *Official Report of the Niger Valley Exploring Party.* In *Search for a Place: Black Separatism and Africa, 1860,* introduction by Howard H. Bell. Ann Arbor: University of Michigan Press, 1969.

Dillon, Merton L. *Benjamin Lundy and the Struggle for Negro Freedom.* Urbana: University of Illinois Press, 1966.

Dixon, Chris. *African America and Haiti: Emigration and Black Nationalism in the Nineteenth Century.* Westport, Conn.: Greenwood Press, 2000.

Dow, George F. *Slave Ships and Slaving.* New York: Dover Publications, 1970.

Drake, Thomas E. *Quakers and Slavery in America.* Gloucester, Mass.: Peter Smith, 1965.

Drew, Benjamin. *The Refugee: Or the Narratives of Fugitive Slaves in Canada.* 1856. Reprint. New York: Negro Universities Press, 1968.

Dunn, D. Elwood. *A History of the Episcopal Church in Liberia, 1821–1980.* Metuchen, N.J.: American Theological Library Association and Scarecrow Press, 1992.

Dunn, D. Elwood, and Svend E. Holsoe. *Historical Dictionary of Liberia*. Metuchen, N.J.: Scarecrow Press, 1985.

Egerton, Douglas R. *Charles Fenton Mercer and the Trial of National Conservatism*. Jackson: University Press of Mississippi, 1989.

Emmons, William R. *Establishing African Homelands for Black Americans*. Los Angeles: Johnson, Pace, Simmons & Fennell Publishers, 1992.

Escott, Paul D. *Many Excellent People: Power and Privilege in North Carolina, 1850–1900*. Chapel Hill: University of North Carolina Press, 1985.

Foner, Eric, ed. *Nat Turner*. Englewood Cliffs, N.J.: Prentice-Hall, 1971.

Ford, Paul L., ed. *The Writings of Thomas Jefferson*. 8 vols. New York: G. P. Putnam's Sons, 1892–99.

Fox, Early L. *The American Colonization Society, 1817–1840*. Baltimore, Md.: Johns Hopkins University Press, 1919.

Fox, George T. *A Memoir of the Rev. C. Colden Hoffman, Missionary to Cape Palmas, West Africa*. New York: A. D. F. Randolph, 1868.

Franklin, John H. *The Free Negro in North Carolina, 1790–1860*. 1943. Reprint. Chapel Hill: University of North Carolina Press, 1995.

Frazier, Thomas R., ed. *Afro-American History: Primary Sources*. New York: Harcourt Brace Jovanovich, 1971.

Fredrickson, George M. *The Black Image in the White Mind: The Debate on Afro-American Character and Destiny, 1817–1914*. Middletown, Conn.: Wesleyan University Press, 1987.

Free African-Americans of North Carolina. Udhailiyah, Saudi Arabia: Paul Heinegg, 1992.

Freehling, William W. *The Reintegration of American History: Slavery and the Civil War*. New York: Oxford University Press, 1994.

Friedman, Lawrence J. *Gregarious Saints: Self and Community in American Abolitionism*. New York: Cambridge University Press, 1982.

Gara, Larry. *The Liberty Line*. Lexington: University Press of Kentucky, 1961.

Garraty, John A., and Jerome L. Sternstein, eds. *Encyclopedia of American Biography*. 2d ed. New York: HarperCollins, 1996.

Garrison, William L. *Thoughts on African Colonization*. 1831. Reprint. New York: Arno Press, 1968.

Goodheart, Lawrence B., and Hugh Hawkins, eds. *The Abolitionists: Means, Ends, and Motivations*. Lexington, Mass.: Heath and Co., 1995.

Griffin, William A. *Ante-bellum Elizabeth City: The History of a Canal Town*. Elizabeth City, N.C.: Roanoke Press, 1970.

Griggs, Earl L. *Thomas Clarkson: The Friend of Slaves*. Ann Arbor: University of Michigan Press, 1938.

Griggs, Earl L., and Clifford H. Prator, eds. *Henry Christophe and Thomas Clarkson: A Correspondence*. Berkeley: University of California Press, 1952.

Grimstead, David. *American Mobbing, 1828–1861: Toward Civil War*. New York: Oxford University Press, 1998.

Guannu, Joseph S., ed. *The Inaugural Addresses of the Presidents of Liberia*. Hicksville, N.Y.: Exposition Press, 1980.

Gurley, Ralph R. *Life of Jehudi Ashmun, Late Colonial Agent in Liberia.* 1835. Reprint. New York: Negro Universities Press, 1969.

Hadden, Sally E. *Slave Patrols: Law and Violence in Virginia and the Carolinas.* Cambridge, Mass.: Harvard University Press, 2001.

Hamilton, J. G. de Roulhac, ed. *The Papers of Thomas Ruffin.* 4 vols. Raleigh, N.C.: Edwards & Broughton Printing Co., 1918.

Harris, Sheldon H. *Paul Cuffe: Black America and the African Return.* New York: Simon and Schuster, 1972.

Henries, A. Doris Banks. *The Life of Joseph Jenkins Roberts (1809–1876) and His Inaugural Addresses.* London: Macmillan, 1964.

Higginbotham, A. Leon, Jr. *In the Matter of Color: Race and the American Legal Process.* Vol. 1, *The Colonial Period.* New York: Oxford University Press, 1978.

Hilty, Hiram H. *By Land and By Sea: Quakers Confront Slavery and Its Aftermath in North Carolina.* Greensboro: North Carolina Friends Historical Society, 1993.

———. *New Garden Friends Meeting: The Christian People Called Quakers.* Greensboro: North Carolina Friends Historical Society, 1983.

———. *Toward Freedom for All: North Carolina Quakers and Slavery.* Richmond, Ind.: Friends United Press, 1984.

Hinks, Peter P. *To Awaken My Afflicted Brethren: David Walker and the Problem of Antebellum Slave Resistance.* University Park: Pennsylvania State University Press, 1997.

———, ed. *David Walker's Appeal to the Coloured Citizens of the World.* University Park: Pennsylvania State University Press, 2000.

Hinshaw, Seth B. *The Carolina Quaker Experience, 1665–1985: An Interpretation.* Davidson, N.C.: Briarpatch Press, 1984.

Hinshaw, William W. *Encyclopedia of American Quaker Genealogy.* 5 vols. Baltimore, Md.: Genealogical Publishing Co., 1969.

Hoff, Advertus A. *A Short History of Liberia College and the University of Liberia.* Monrovia, Liberia: Consolidated Publications, 1962.

Holsoe, Svend E., Bernard L. Herman, and Max Belcher. *A Land and Life Remembered: Americo-Liberian Folk Architecture.* Athens: University of Georgia Press, 1988.

Horton, James O., and Lois E. Horton. *In Hope of Liberty: Culture, Community and Protest among Northern Free Blacks, 1700–1860.* New York: Oxford University Press, 1997.

Howard, Warren S. *American Slavers and the Federal Law, 1837–1862.* Berkeley: University of California Press, 1963.

Huberich, Charles H. *The Political and Legislative History of Liberia.* 2 vols. New York: Central Book Co., 1947.

Human Rights Watch. *Easy Prey: Child Soldiers in Liberia.* New York: Human Rights Watch, 1994.

Humphreys, Margaret. *Malaria: Poverty, Race, and Public Health in the United States.* Baltimore, Md.: Johns Hopkins University Press, 2001.

Hunt, John G., ed. *The Essential Abraham Lincoln.* New York: Gramercy Books, 1993.

Innes, William. *Liberia; or the Early History and Signal Preservation of the American*

Colony of Free Negroes on the Coast of Africa. Edinburgh: Waugh and Innes, 1831.

Jacobs, Sylvia M., ed. *Black Americans and the Missionary Movement in Africa.* Westport, Conn.: Greenwood Press, 1982.

Jefferson, Thomas. *Notes on the State of Virginia.* Edited by William Peden. New York: W. W. Norton, 1972.

Johnson, Guion G. *Ante-bellum North Carolina: A Social History.* Chapel Hill: University of North Carolina Press, 1937.

Johnston, Harry. *Liberia.* 2 vols. London: Hutchinson & Co., 1906.

Kappel, Robert, Werner Korte, and R. Friedegund Mascher. *Liberia: Underdevelopment and Political Rule in a Peripheral Society.* Hamburg, Germany: Institut Für Afrika-Kunde, 1986.

Katz, William L., ed. *Five Slave Narratives.* New York: Arno Press, 1968.

Kay, Marvin L. M., and Lorin L. Cary. *Slavery in North Carolina, 1748–1776.* Chapel Hill: University of North Carolina Press, 1995.

King, Wilma. *Stolen Childhood: Slave Youth in Nineteenth-Century America.* Bloomington: Indiana University Press, 1995.

Kinshasa, Kwando M. *Emigration versus Assimilation: The Debate in the African American Press, 1827–1861.* Jefferson, N.C.: McFarland & Company, 1988.

Kiple, Kenneth F., and Virginia H. King. *Another Dimension to the Black Diaspora: Diet, Disease, and Racism.* New York: Cambridge University Press, 1981.

Kock, Bernard. *Statement of Facts in Relation to the Settlement on the Island of A'Vache, Near Hayti, W.I.* New York: William C. Bryant & Co., 1864.

Konneh, Augustine. *Religion, Commerce, and the Integration of the Mandingo in Liberia.* Lanham, Md.: University Press of America, 1996.

Kremer, Gary R. *James Milton Turner and the Promise of America.* Columbia: University of Missouri Press, 1991.

Larkin, Jack. *The Reshaping of Everyday Life, 1790–1840.* New York: Harper & Row, 1988.

Latrobe, John H. B. *Maryland in Liberia.* Baltimore, Md.: N.p., 1885.

Lefler, Hugh T., and Albert R. Newsome. *North Carolina: The History of a Southern State.* Chapel Hill: University of North Carolina Press, 1963.

Liberian Law Reports, Vol. 1, *1908.* Reprint. Ithaca, N.Y.: Cornell University Press, 1955.

Liebenow, J. Gus. *Liberia: The Quest for Democracy.* Bloomington: Indiana University Press, 1987.

Logan, Frenise A. *The Negro in North Carolina, 1876–1894.* Chapel Hill: University of North Carolina Press, 1964.

Logan, Rayford W. *The Diplomatic Relations of the United States and Haiti, 1776–1891.* Chapel Hill: University of North Carolina Press, 1941.

Lowenkopf, Martin. *Politics in Liberia: The Conservative Road to Development.* Stanford, Calif.: Hoover Institution Press, 1976.

Lugenbeel, J. W. *Sketches of Liberia: Comprising a Brief Account of the Geography, Climate, Productions, and Diseases, of the Republic of Liberia.* Washington, D.C.: C. Alexander, 1853.

Lundy, Benjamin. *The Life, Travels and Opinions of Benjamin Lundy.* 1847. Reprint. New York: Negro Universities Press, 1969.

Lynch, Hollis R., ed. *Black Spokesman: Selected Published Writings of Edward Wilmot Blyden.* New York: Humanities Press, 1971.

————. *Selected Letters of Edward Wilmot Blyden.* Millwood, N.Y.: KTO Press, 1978.

Masur, Louis. *1831: Year of Eclipse.* New York: Hill and Wang, 2001.

Maugham, R. C. F. *The Republic of Liberia.* New York: Charles Scribner's Sons, 1920.

Mayer, Henry. *All on Fire: William Lloyd Garrison and the Abolition of Slavery.* New York: St. Martin's Press, 1998.

McDaniel, Antonio. *Swing Low, Sweet Chariot: The Mortality Cost of Colonizing Liberia in the Nineteenth Century.* Chicago: University of Chicago Press, 1995.

McKee, Charles. *Vital Records of Bladen County, North Carolina, 1753–1915.* Gastonia, N.C.: C. F. McKee, 1995.

McKiever, Charles F. *Slavery and the Emigration of North Carolina Friends.* Murfreesboro, N.C.: Johnson Publishing Co., 1970.

McPherson, James. *Ordeal by Fire.* Vol. 2, *The Civil War.* New York: McGraw-Hill, 1993.

Miller, Floyd J. *The Search for a Black Nationality: Black Emigration and Colonization, 1787–1863.* Urbana: University of Illinois Press, 1975.

Miller, Randall M., ed. *"Dear Master": Letters of a Slave Family.* Ithaca, N.Y.: Cornell University Press, 1978.

Montague, Ludwell L. *Haiti and the United States, 1714–1938.* Durham, N.C.: Duke University Press, 1940.

Moore, John W. *Historical Sketches of Hertford County.* 1877–78. Reprint. Winston, N.C.: Liberty Shield Press, 1998.

Morison, Samuel E. *"Old Bruin": Commodore Matthew C. Perry, 1794–1858.* Boston: Atlantic Monthly Press, 1967.

Mosby's Medical, Nursing, and Allied Health Dictionary. 4th ed. St. Louis, Mo.: Mosby, 1994.

Moses, Wilson J. *Alexander Crummell: A Study of Civilization and Discontent.* New York: Oxford University Press, 1989.

————, ed. *Liberian Dreams: Back-to-Africa Narratives from the 1850s.* University Park: Pennsylvania State University Press, 1998.

Murray, Elizabeth R. *Wake: Capital of North Carolina.* Raleigh, N.C.: Capital County Publishing Co., 1983.

Nesbit, William. *Four Months in Liberia: Or African Colonization Exposed.* Pittsburgh, Pa.: J. T. Shryock, 1855.

Northampton County Bicentennial Committee. *Footprints in Northampton: 1741–1776–1976.* Rich Square, N.C.: The Committee, 1976.

North Carolina Department of Agriculture. *North Carolina and Its Resources.* Winston, N.C.: N. I. and J. C. Stewart, 1896.

Numbers, Ronald L., and Todd L. Savitt, eds. *Science and Medicine in the Old South.* Baton Rouge: Louisiana State University Press, 1989.

Oates, Stephen B. *The Fires of Jubilee: Nat Turner's Fierce Rebellion.* New York: Mentor, 1975.

Officer, Morris. *Western Africa, a Mission Field.* Pittsburgh, Pa.: W. S. Haven, 1856.

Painter, Nell I. *Exodusters: Black Migration to Kansas after Reconstruction.* New York: W. W. Norton, 1976.

Parker, Freddie L. *Running for Freedom: Slave Runaways in North Carolina, 1775–1840.* New York: Garland Publishing, 1993.

———, ed. *Stealing a Little Freedom: Advertisements for Slave Runaways in North Carolina, 1791–1840.* New York: Garland Publishing Co., 1994.

Parker, Roy, Jr. *Cumberland County: A Brief History.* Raleigh: North Carolina Department of Cultural Resources, Division of Archives and History, 1990.

Parramore, Tom C., with Peter C. Stewart and Tommy L. Bogger. *Norfolk: The First Four Centuries.* Charlottesville: University Press of Virginia, 1994.

Peterson, Merrill D. *The Great Triumvirate: Webster, Clay, and Calhoun.* New York: Oxford University Press, 1987.

Powell, William S. *Dictionary of North Carolina Biography.* 6 vols. Chapel Hill: University of North Carolina Press, 1979–96.

Price, Richard, ed. *Maroon Societies.* Baltimore, Md.: Johns Hopkins University Press, 1979.

Quarles, Benjamin. *Black Abolitionists.* New York: Oxford University Press, 1969.

Rawick, George P., ed. *The American Slave: A Composite Autobiography.* Vol. 14, pts. 1–2. Westport, Conn.: Greenwood Publishing Co., 1972.

Reichel, Levin T. *The Moravians in North Carolina: An Authentic History.* Baltimore, Md.: Genealogical Publishing Co., 1968.

Richardson, Nathaniel R. *Liberia's Past and Present.* London: Diplomatic Press and Publishing Co., 1959.

Sanneh, Lamin. *Abolitionists Abroad: American Blacks and the Making of Modern West Africa.* Cambridge, Mass.: Harvard University Press, 1999.

Savitt, Todd L., and James H. Young. *Disease and Distinctiveness in the American South.* Knoxville: University of Tennessee Press, 1988.

Sawyer, Amos. *The Emergence of Autocracy in Liberia.* San Francisco: ICS Press, 1992.

Sensbach, Jon F. *A Separate Canaan: The Making of an Afro-Moravian World in North Carolina, 1763–1840.* Chapel Hill: University of North Carolina Press, 1998.

Shick, Tom W. *Behold the Promised Land: A History of Afro-American Settler Society in Nineteenth-Century Liberia.* Baltimore, Md.: Johns Hopkins University Press, 1980.

Singleton, William H. *Recollections of My Slavery Days.* Edited by Katherine M. Charron and David S. Cecelski. Raleigh: North Carolina Department of Cultural Resources, Division of Archives and History, 1999.

Slaughter, Philip. *The Virginian History of African Colonization.* 1856. Reprint. Freeport, N.Y.: Books for Libraries Press, 1970.

Smith, James W. *Sojourners in Search of Freedom: The Settlement of Liberia by Black Americans.* Lanham, Md.: University Press of America, 1987.

Sprunt, James. *Chronicles of the Cape Fear River, 1660–1916.* Raleigh, N.C.: Edwards & Broughton Printing Co., 1916.

Staudenraus, P. J. *The African Colonization Movement, 1816–1865.* New York: Columbia University Press, 1961.

Stebbins, G. B. *Facts and Opinions Touching the Real Origin, Character, and Influence of the American Colonization Society.* 1853. Reprint. New York: Negro Universities Press, 1969.

Stedman's Medical Dictionary. 22d ed. Baltimore, Md.: Williams & Wilkins Co., 1972.

Steelman, Lala C. *The North Carolina Farmers' Alliance: A Political History, 1887–1893*. Greenville, N.C.: East Carolina University Publications, 1985.

Stephenson, E. Frank. *Murfreesboro, North Carolina: 200 Years on the Meherrin River*. Murfreesboro: Town of Murfreesboro, 1987.

Stetson, George. *The Liberian Republic as It Is*. Boston: A. Williams & Co., 1881.

Stewart, T. McCants. *Liberia: The Americo-African Republic*. New York: Edward O. Jenkins' Son, 1886.

Stockwell, G. S., comp. *The Republic of Liberia: Its Geography, Climate, Soil, and Productions, with a History of Its Early Settlement*. New York: A. S. Barnes & Co., 1868.

Stoesen, Alexander R. *Guilford County: A Brief History*. Raleigh: North Carolina Department of Cultural Resources, Division of Archives and History, 1993.

Tadman, Michael. *Speculators and Slaves: Masters, Traders, and Slaves in the Old South*. Madison: University of Wisconsin Press, 1989.

Thomas, Gerald W. *Divided Allegiances: Bertie County during the Civil War*. Raleigh: North Carolina Department of Cultural Resources, Division of Archives and History, 1996.

Thomas, Lamont D. *Rise to Be a People: A Biography of Paul Cuffe*. Urbana: University of Illinois Press, 1986.

Thornbrough, Emma L. *The Negro in Indiana before 1900: A Study of a Minority*. 1957. Reprint. Bloomington: Indiana University Press, 1993.

Watson, Alan D. *Bertie County: A Brief History*. Raleigh: North Carolina Department of Cultural Resources, Division of Archives and History, 1982.

Watson, Alan D. *A History of New Bern and Craven County*. New Bern, N.C.: Tryon Palace Commission, 1987.

———. *Perquimans County: A Brief History*. Raleigh: North Carolina Department of Cultural Resources, Division of Archives and History, 1987.

Weeks, Stephen B. *Southern Quakers and Slavery: A Study in Institutional History*. Baltimore, Md.: Johns Hopkins University Press, 1896.

West, Richard. *Back to Africa: A History of Sierra Leone and Liberia*. New York: Rinehart and Winston, 1971.

Whitted, J. A. *A History of the Negro Baptists of North Carolina*. Raleigh, N.C.: Edwards & Broughton Printing Co., 1908.

Wiggins, Rosalind C. *Captain Paul Cuffe's Logs and Letters, 1808–1817*. Washington, D.C.: Howard University Press, 1996.

Wiley, Bell I., ed. *Slaves No More: Letters from Liberia, 1833–1869*. Lexington: University Press of Kentucky, 1980.

Wilkeson, Samuel. *A Concise History of the Commencement, Progress and Present Condition of the American Colonies in Liberia*. Washington, D.C.: The Madisonian Office, 1839.

Williams, Alfred B. *The Liberian Exodus*. Charleston, S.C.: News and Courier Book Presses, 1878.

Williams, Samuel. *Four Years in Liberia: A Sketch of the Life of the Rev. Samuel Williams*. Philadelphia, Pa.: King & Baird, 1857.

Williams, Walter L. *Black Americans and the Evangelization of Africa, 1877–1900*. Madison: University of Wisconsin Press, 1982.

Wilson, Charles M. *Liberia: Black Africa in Microcosm.* New York: Harper & Row, 1971.

Wilson, Ellen G. *The Loyal Blacks.* New York: Capricorn Books, 1976.

Wilson, Theodore B. *The Black Codes of the South.* University: University of Alabama Press, 1965.

Windsor Bicentennial Commission. *The Windsor Story, 1768–1968.* Windsor, N.C.: Windsor Bicentennial Commission, 1968.

Winks, Robin W. *The Blacks in Canada: A History.* 2d ed. Montreal: McGill-Queen's University Press, 1997.

Winslow, Raymond A., Jr. *Perquimans County History.* Hertford, N.C., 1984.

Wonkeryor, Edward L. *Liberia Military Dictatorship: A Fiasco "Revolution."* Chicago: Strugglers' Community Press, 1985.

Woodson, Carter G., ed. *Free Negro Owners of Slaves in the United States in 1830.* 1924. Reprint. New York: Negro Universities Press, 1968.

ARTICLES

Africa, Philip. "Slaveholding in the Salem Community, 1771–1851." *North Carolina Historical Review* 54 (July 1977): 271–307.

Akingbade, Harrison O. "The Settler-African Conflicts: The Case of the Maryland Colonists and the Grebo, 1840–1900." *Journal of Negro History* 66 (Summer 1981): 93–106.

Akpan, M. B. "Black Imperialism: Americo-Liberian Rule over the African Peoples of Liberia, 1841–1964." *Canadian Journal of African Studies* 7 (1973): 217–36.

———. "The Liberian Economy in the Nineteenth Century: Government Finances." *Liberian Studies Journal* 6 (1975): 129–61.

———. "The Liberian Economy in the Nineteenth Century: The State of Agriculture and Commerce." *Liberian Studies Journal* 6 (1975): 1–24.

Allen, Jeffrey B. "Did Southern Colonizationists Oppose Slavery?: Kentucky 1816–1850 as a Test Case." *Register of the Kentucky Historical Society* 75 (April 1977): 92–111.

———. "The Racial Thought of White North Carolina Opponents of Slavery, 1789–1876." *North Carolina Historical Review* 59 (January 1982): 49–66.

Aptheker, Herbert. "The Quakers and Negro Slavery." *Journal of Negro History* 25 (July 1940): 331–62.

Barfield, Rodney D. "Thomas and John Day and the Journey to North Carolina." *North Carolina Historical Review* 78 (January 2001): 1–31.

Baur, John E. "Mulatto Machiavelli: Jean Pierre Boyer, and the Haiti of His Day." *Journal of Negro History* 32 (July 1947): 307–53.

Beal, M. Gertrude. "The Underground Railroad in Guilford County." *Southern Friend* 2 (Spring 1980): 18–29.

Beeth, Howard. "Between Friends: Epistolary Correspondence among Quakers in the Emergent South." *Quaker History* 76 (Fall 1987): 108–27.

Bell, Howard H. "Negro Nationalism: A Factor in Emigration Projects, 1858–1861." *Journal of Negro History* 47 (January 1962): 42–53.

Bishir, Catherine W. "Black Builders in Antebellum North Carolina." *North Carolina Historical Review* 61 (October 1984): 423–61.

Boyd, Willis D. "The American Colonization Society and the Slave Recaptives of 1860–61: An Early Example of United States–African Relations." *Journal of Negro History* 47 (April 1962): 108–26.

———. "Negro Colonization in the Reconstruction Era, 1865–1870." *Georgia Historical Quarterly* 40 (December 1956): 360–82.

Brennan, Carol. "Charles Taylor." *Contemporary Black Biography* 20 (1999): 210.

Brooks, George E., Jr. "A. A. Adee's Journal of a Visit to Liberia in 1827." *Liberian Studies Journal* 1 (1968): 56–72.

———. "The Providence African Society's Sierra Leone Emigration Scheme, 1794–1795: Prologue to the African Colonization Movement." *International Journal of African Historical Studies* 7 (1974): 183–202.

———. "A Salem Merchant at Cape Palmas, Liberia, in 1840." *Essex Institute Historical Collection* 98 (July 1962): 161–74.

Browne, George D. "History of the Protestant Episcopal Mission in Liberia up to 1838." *Historical Magazine of the Protestant Episcopal Church* 39 (March 1970): 17–27.

Browning, James B. "The North Carolina Black Code." *Journal of Negro History* 15 (October 1930): 461–73.

Bruce, Dickson D., Jr. "National Identity and African-American Colonization, 1773–1817." *The Historian* 58 (Autumn 1995): 15–28.

Burrowes, Carl P. "Black Christian Republicans: Delegates to the 1847 Liberian Constitutional Convention." *Liberian Studies Journal* 14 (1989): 64–87.

———. "Economic Relations within Pre-Liberian Societies." *Liberian Studies Journal* 13 (1988): 76–103.

Cadbury, Henry J. "Negro Membership in the Society of Friends." *Journal of Negro History* 22 (January 1936): 151–213.

Clark, Ernest J., Jr. "Aspects of the North Carolina Slave Code, 1715–1860." *North Carolina Historical Review* 39 (April 1962): 148–64.

Corby, Richard A. "Manding Traders and Clerics: The Development of Islam in Liberia to the 1870s." *Liberian Studies Journal* 13 (1988): 42–66.

Crow, Jeffrey J. "Slave Rebelliousness and Social Control in North Carolina, 1775 to 1802." *William and Mary Quarterly*, 3d ser., vol. 37 (January 1980): 79–102.

Dorsey, Bruce. "A Gendered History of African Colonization in the Antebellum United States." *Journal of Social History* 34 (Fall 2000): 77–103.

Eaton, Clement. "A Dangerous Pamphlet in the Old South." *Journal of Southern History* 2 (August 1936): 323–34.

Egerton, Douglas R. "Averting a Crisis: The Proslavery Critique of the American Colonization Society." *Civil War History* 43 (1997): 142–56.

———. "'Fly across the River': The Easter Slave Conspiracy of 1802." *North Carolina Historical Review* 68 (April 1991): 87–110.

———. "'Its Origin Is Not a Little Curious': A New Look at the American Colonization Society." *Journal of the Early Republic* 5 (Winter 1985): 463–80.

Elliott, Robert N. "The Nat Turner Insurrection as Reported in the North Carolina Press." *North Carolina Historical Review* 38 (January 1961): 1–18.

Fisher, Miles M. "Lott Cary: The Colonizing Missionary." *Journal of Negro History* 7 (October 1922): 380–418.

Friedman, Lawrence J. "Purifying the White Man's Country: The American Colonization Society Reconsidered, 1816–1840." *Societas* 6 (Winter 1976): 1–24.

Gatewood, Willard B., Jr. "'To Be Truly Free': Louis Sheridan and the Colonization of Liberia." *Civil War History* 29 (1983): 332–48.

Gershoni, Yekutiel. "The Formation of Liberia's Boundaries, Part I: Agreements." *Liberian Studies Journal* 17 (1992): 25–45.

Hamer, Philip M. "Great Britain, the United States, and the Negro Seamen Acts, 1822–1848." *Journal of Southern History* 1 (February 1935): 3–28.

Haskell, Thomas L. "Capitalism and the Origins of the Humanitarian Sensibility, Parts 1–2." *American Historical Review* 90 (April, June 1985): 339–61, 547–66.

Hatcher, Susan T. "North Carolina Quakers: Bona Fide Abolitionists." *Southern Friend* 1 (Autumn 1979): 81–99.

Hendrix, Thomas C. "A Half Century of Americo-Liberian Christianity: With Special Focus on Methodism, 1822–1872." *Liberian Studies Journal* 19 (1994): 243–74.

Hickey, Damon D. "'Let Not Thy Left Hand Know': The Unification of George C. Mendenhall." *Southern Friend* 3 (Spring 1981): 3–24.

Hinshaw, Seth. "Friends Culture in Colonial North Carolina, 1672–1789." *Southern Friend* 22 (Autumn 2000): 3–81.

Holsoe, Svend E. "A Portrait of a Black Midwestern Family during the Early Nineteenth Century: Edward James Roye and His Parents." *Liberian Studies Journal* 3 (1970–71): 41–52.

———. "A Study of Relations between Settlers and Indigenous Peoples in Western Liberia, 1821–1847." *African Historical Studies* 4 (1971): 331–62.

Hutton, Frankie. "Economic Considerations in the American Colonization Society's Early Effort to Emigrate Free Blacks to Liberia, 1816–36." *Journal of Negro History* 68 (Fall 1983): 376–89.

Kerr, Norwood A. "The Mississippi Colonization Society (1831–1860)." *Journal of Mississippi History* 43 (February 1981): 1–30.

Landon, Fred. "The Negro Migration to Canada after the Passing of the Fugitive Slave Act." *Journal of Negro History* 5 (January 1920): 22–36.

Laughon, Samuel W. "Administrative Problems in Maryland in Liberia—1836–1851." *Journal of Negro History* 26 (July 1941): 325–64.

Logan, Frenise A. "The Movement of Negroes from North Carolina, 1876–1894." *North Carolina Historical Review* 33 (January 1956): 45–65.

Love, Edgar F. "Registration of Free Blacks in Ohio: The Slaves of George C. Mendenhall." *Journal of Negro History* 69 (Wointer 1984): 38–47.

Martin, Jane J. "How to Build a Nation: Liberian Ideas about National Integration in the Later Nineteenth Century." *Liberian Studies Journal* 2 (1969): 15–42.

Mehlinger, Louis R. "The Attitude of the Free Negro toward African Colonization." *Journal of Negro History* 1 (July 1916): 276–301.

Mitchell, Memory F., ed. "Freedom Brings Problems: Letters from the McKays and the Nelsons of Liberia." *North Carolina Historical Review* 70 (October 1993): 430–65.

———. "Off to Africa—with Judicial Blessing." *North Carolina Historical Review* 53 (July 1978): 265–87.

Mitchell, Memory F., and Thompson W. Mitchell. "The Philanthropic Bequests of

John Rex of Raleigh." Parts 1–2. *North Carolina Historical Review* 49 (July, October 1972): 254–79, 353–76.

Mooney, Chase C. "Some Institutional and Statistical Aspects of Slavery in Tennessee." *Tennessee Historical Quarterly* 1 (September 1942): 195–228.

Morris, Charles E. "Panic and Reprisal: Reaction in North Carolina to the Nat Turner Insurrection, 1831." *North Carolina Historical Review* 62 (January 1985): 29–52.

Opper, Peter K. "North Carolina Quakers: Reluctant Slaveholders." *North Carolina Historical Review* 52 (January 1975): 37–58.

Padgett, James A. "Ministers to Liberia and Their Diplomacy." *Journal of Negro History* 22 (January 1937): 50–92.

Patton, Adell, Jr. "The 'Back-to-Africa' Movement in Arkansas." *Arkansas Historical Quarterly* 51 (Summer 1992): 164–77.

Poe, William A. "Georgia Influence in the Development of Liberia." *Georgia Historical Quarterly* 57 (Spring 1973): 1–16.

———. "A Look at Louisiana Colonization in Its African Setting." *Louisiana History* 13 (Summer 1972): 111–24.

Rachleff, Marshall. "David Walker's Southern Agent." *Journal of Negro History* 62 (January 1977): 100–103.

Reno, William. "Reinvention of an African Patrimonial State: Charles Taylor's Liberia." *Third World Quarterly* 16 (1995): 109–20.

Rosen, Bruce. "Abolition and Colonization, the Years of Conflict: 1829–1834." *Phylon* 33 (1972): 177–92.

Saillant, John. "The American Enlightenment in Africa: Jefferson's Colonizationism and Black Virginians' Migration to Liberia, 1776–1840." *Eighteenth-Century Studies* 31 (1998): 261–82.

Scheips, Paul J. "Lincoln and the Chiriqui Colonization Project." *Journal of Negro History* 37 (October 1952): 418–53.

Seifman, Eli. "The Passing of the American Colonization Society." *Liberian Studies Journal* 2 (1969): 1–7.

Shepard, E. Lee, Frances S. Pollard, and Janet B. Schwarz. "'The Love of Liberty Brought Us Here': Virginians and the Colonization of Liberia." *Virginia Magazine of History and Biography* 102 (January 1994): 89–100.

Sherrill, P. M. "The Quakers and the North Carolina Manumission Society." *Historical Papers* (Trinity College Historical Society), Series 10 (1914): 32–51.

Sherwood, Henry N. "Early Negro Deportation Projects." *Mississippi Valley Historical Review* 2 (March 1916): 484–508.

———. "Formation of the American Colonization Society." *Journal of Negro History* 2 (July 1917): 209–28.

———. "Paul Cuffe." *Journal of Negro History* 8 (April 1923): 153–229.

Shick, Tom W. "A Quantitative Analysis of Liberian Colonization from 1820 to 1843 with Special Reference to Mortality." *Journal of African History* 12 (1971): 45–59.

Singler, John V. "Language in Liberia in the Nineteenth Century: The Settlers' Perspective." *Liberian Studies Journal* 7 (1976–77): 73–85.

Sowle, Patrick. "The North Carolina Manumission Society, 1816–1834." *North Carolina Historical Review* 42 (January 1965): 47–69.

Stopak, Aaron. "The Maryland State Colonization Society: Independent State Action in the Colonization Movement." *Maryland Historical Magazine* 63 (September 1968): 275–98.

Streifford, David M. "The American Colonization Society: An Application of Republican Ideology to Early Antebellum Reform." *Journal of Southern History* 45 (May 1979): 201–20.

Sullivan, Jo M. "Mississippi in Africa: Settlers among the Kru, 1835–1847." *Liberian Studies Journal* 8 (1978–79): 79–94.

Sundiata, Ibrahim K. "The Rise and Decline of Kru Power: Fernando Po in the Nineteenth Century." *Liberian Studies Journal* 6 (1975): 25–41.

Syfert, Dwight N. "The Liberian Coasting Trade, 1822–1900." *Journal of African History* 18 (1977): 217–35.

——. "The Origins of Privilege: Liberian Merchants, 1822–1847." *Liberian Studies Journal* 6 (1975): 109–29.

Taylor, Joseph H. "The Great Migration from North Carolina in 1879." *North Carolina Historical Review* 31 (January 1954): 18–33.

Taylor, Rosser H. "The Free Negro in North Carolina." *James Sprunt Historical Publications* 17 (1920): 5–26.

——. "Humanizing the Slave Code of North Carolina." *North Carolina Historical Review* 2 (July 1925): 323–31.

——. "Slave Conspiracies in North Carolina." *North Carolina Historical Review* 5 (January 1928): 20–34.

——. "Slaveholding in North Carolina: An Economic View." *James Sprunt Historical Publications* 18 (1926): 1–103.

Temperley, Howard. "African-American Aspirations and the Settlement of Liberia." *Slavery and Abolition* 21 (August 2000): 67–92.

Tindall, George B. "The Liberian Exodus of 1878." *South Carolina Historical Magazine* 53 (1952): 133–45.

Turner, Wallace B. "Kentucky Slavery in the Last Ante Bellum Decade." *Register of the Kentucky Historical Society* 58 (October 1960): 291–307.

Tyler-McGraw, Marie. "Richmond Free Blacks and African Colonization, 1816–1832." *Journal of American Studies* 21 (August 1987): 207–24.

Wagstaff, H. M., ed. "Minutes of the N.C. Manumission Society, 1816–1834." *James Sprunt Historical Publications* 22 (1934): 1–230.

White, Julia S. "The Quakers of Perquimans." *North Carolina Booklet* 7 (April 1908): 278–89.

DISSERTATIONS, THESES, AND UNPUBLISHED PAPERS

Akingbade, Harrison O. "The Role of the Military in the History of Liberia, 1822–1947." Ph.D. diss., Howard University, 1978.

Burin, Eric A. "The Peculiar Solution: The American Colonization Society and Antislavery Sentiment in the South, 1820–1860." Ph.D. diss., University of Illinois, 1999.

Grant, Minnie S. "The American Colonization Society in North Carolina." Master's thesis, Duke University, 1930.

Hoff, Joanna T. D. "The Role of Women in National Development in Liberia, 1800–1900." Ph.D. diss., University of Illinois, 1989.

Holsoe, Svend E. "The Cassava-Leaf People: An Ethnohistorical Study of the Vai People with a Particular Emphasis on the Tewo Chiefdom." Ph.D. diss., Boston University, 1967.

Newman, Debra L. "The Emergence of Liberian Women in the Nineteenth Century." Ph.D. diss., Howard University, 1984.

Oliver, Albert G. "The Protest and Attitudes of Blacks toward the American Colonization Society and the Concepts of Emigration and Colonization in Africa, 1817–1865." Ph.D. diss., St. John's University, 1978.

Park, Eunjin. "Black and White American Methodist Missionaries in Liberia, 1820–1875." Ph.D. diss., Columbia University, 1999.

Parramore, Tom. "A Passage to Liberia." Paper delivered at Chowan College, Murfreesboro, N.C., 1973.

Shay, John M. "The Antislavery Movement in North Carolina." Ph.D. diss., Princeton University, 1971.

Sims-Alvarado, F. Karcheik. "The African Colonization Movement in Georgia: The Expatriation of Freeborn and Emancipated Blacks, 1819–1860." Master's thesis, Clark Atlanta University, 2001.

Stepp, Eddie. "Interpreting a Forgotten Mission: African-American Missionaries of the Southern Baptist Convention in Liberia, West Africa, 1846–1860." Ph.D. diss., Baylor University, 1999.

Tyler-McGraw, Marie. "The American Colonization Society in Virginia, 1816–1832: A Case Study in Southern Liberalism." Ph.D. diss., George Washington University, 1980.

ORGANIZATIONAL REPORTS

American Colonization Society. *The Annual Reports of the American Society for Colonizing the Free People of Colour of the United States.* Vols. 1–91. 1818–1910. Reprint. New York: Negro Universities Press, 1969.

Third Annual Report of the Ladies' Liberia School Association. Philadelphia: Lydia R. Bailey, 1835.

Thirty-Fifth Annual Report of the Missionary Society of the Methodist Episcopal Church. New York: Conference Office, 1854.

Twenty-Sixth Annual Report of the Missionary Society of the Methodist Episcopal Church. New York: J. Collord, 1845.

GOVERNMENT DOCUMENTS

American State Papers: Documents, Legislative and Executive, of the Congress of the United States. 5 vols. Washington, D.C.: Gales and Seaton, 1834.

Clark, Walter, ed. *The State Records of North Carolina.* 26 vols. Raleigh: P. M. Hale, 1886–1907.

Congressional Globe. 46 vols. Washington, D.C., 1834–73.

The Federal and State Constitutions, Colonial Charters, and Other Organic Laws of the United States. Part 1. Washington, D.C.: Government Printing Office, 1878.

Journal of the Senate of the General Assembly of the State of North Carolina. 1830–31 sess. Raleigh, N.C.: Lawrence & Lemay, 1831.

Papers Relating to the Foreign Relations of the United States. Washington, D.C.: Government Printing Office, 1873, 1884.

Resolutions of the Legislature of Georgia, in Relation to the American Colonization Society. 28th Cong., 1st sess. Washington, D.C.: Duff Green, 1828.

U.S. Bureau of the Census. *Negro Population in the United States, 1790–1915.* 1918. Reprint. New York: Arno Press, 1968.

———. *Fourth Decennial Census. Table 5: Population of the 61 Urban Places, 1820.* ‹http://www.census.gov/population/documentation/twps0027/tab05.txt›.

———. *Fifth Decennial Census. Table 6: Population of the 90 Urban Places, 1830.* ‹http://www.census.gov/population/documentation/twps0027/tab06.txt›.

U.S. Congress. House. *African Colonization.* 27th Cong., 3d sess., 1843. H. Rept. 283.

U.S. Congress. House. *Executive Documents.* 40th Cong., 2d sess., 1867–68.

U.S. Congress. House. *Executive Documents.* 45th Cong., 2d sess., 1877–78. Vol. 1.

U.S. Congress. House. *Executive Documents.* 46th Cong., 3d sess., 1880–81. Vol. 1.

U.S. Congress. House. *Executive Documents.* 47th Cong., 1st sess., 1881.

U.S. Congress. House. *House Executive Documents.* 28th Cong., 1st sess., 1844. H. Doc. 162.

U.S. Congress. House. House Report. 16th Cong., 1st sess., ser. 40. 1820. H. Rept. 97.

U.S. Congress. House. House Report. 19th Cong., 2d sess., 1827. H. Doc. 64.

U.S. Congress. House. House Report. 19th Cong., 2d sess., 1827. H. Rept. 160.

U.S. Congress. House. House Report, 20th Cong., 1st sess., 1830. H. Rept. 348.

U.S. Congress. House. *Miscellaneous Documents.* 30th Cong., 2d sess. 1848. H. Rept. 54.

U.S. Congress. House. Reports of Committees. 37th Cong., 2d sess., 1862. H. Rept. 148.

U.S. Congress. Senate. *Executive Documents.* 31st Cong., 1st sess., 1850. S. Doc. 75.

U.S. Congress. Senate. *Report and Testimony of the Select Committee of the United States Senate to Investigate the Causes of the Removal of the Negroes from the Southern States to the Northern States.* Part I. 46th Cong., 2d sess., 1880. S. Rept. 693.

U.S. Congress. Senate. *Roll of Emigrants That Have Been Sent to the Colony of Liberia. . . .* 28th Cong., 2d sess., 1844. S. Rept. 150.

U.S. Congress. Senate. Senate Document. 20th Cong., 1st sess., 1828. S. Doc. 178.

"United States Historical Census Data Browser." ‹http://fisher.lib.Virginia.edu/census/›.

INDEX

Abolitionism, 4, 20, 26, 42–43, 70–72, 74, 130, 136–37, 140, 141–42, 151, 158, 161, 174, 184, 188, 196, 198

Adams, John Quincy, 192

African Americans, 1–7, 18–20, 30, 34–35, 42, 58, 143, 148, 150, 172–74
—in Liberia: unfamiliarity with conditions, 78–79, 200, 203, 259; difficulties experienced by, 80–81, 86–88, 145, 155–56, 182–83, 185, 187, 199–200, 203–4, 211, 221–22, 226–27, 245–46, 260–65; lands allotted to, 86, 89, 145, 157, 203, 252; and development of immigrant identities, 96–98, 99, 110–11, 140, 238–48, 261–62; literacy among, 205–6, 223–24; and color prejudices, 244–45, 246, 263–64
—in North Carolina: as slaves, 9–10, 18–19, 47, 54–55, 66, 152, 164–71, 176–77, 198, 244, 249–50; among Quakers, 10–17, 25, 40–41, 46–51, 55–56, 58, 60–61, 69, 74, 75, 135–37; free blacks, 18–19, 48, 52, 131–33, 152–55, 162, 164, 168, 198, 244; and repression of free blacks, 66, 72–73, 131–33, 153–54, 173, 195–96; as slaveholders, 138, 153; westward migration of, 256, 260, 268
—and views of Africa and Africans: 24, 59, 60, 94–98, 110–11, 143, 183–84, 202, 238–44, 246–48, 257–59, 261–62

African Methodist Episcopal Zion (AMEZ) denomination, 258, 259

African Repository, 61, 64, 92, 102, 134, 139, 151, 157, 158, 160, 167, 169, 180, 200, 202, 209, 265

Africans: resistance to Liberian colonization, 37–38, 74, 84, 103–11, 144–47, 207, 238–39, 267; interactions with immigrants, 77, 79, 94–96, 210, 214–17, 219, 237, 242–44, 261, 266–67, 298–99 (n. 45); trade with immigrants, 87, 207, 242, 247; employed as laborers, 94, 243; as apprentices of immigrants, 94–96, 219, 237, 242–43, 247–48; and pawning, 95, 105, 242; sexual encounters and intermarriage with immigrants, 95–96, 237, 243–44, 266, 299 (n. 47); and ACS renaming practices, 100; medicinal knowledge of, 140, 232, 237, 242. *See also* Dei; Gola; Grebo; Krahn; Kru; Mandingo; Pessay; Vai

African sleeping sickness, 79, 237

Aggrey, James, 258

Allen, Richard, 4, 35

American (ship), 136–37, 138–39, 288 (n. 12)

American Civil War, 5, 142, 147, 196–97, 200; in North Carolina, 249–50

American Colonization Society (ACS), 2, 4–5, 31–34, 59, 64, 74, 89, 99–103, 132, 139–52, 157–59, 186, 190–91, 200, 252–53; appeal of, 4, 33–34, 39, 55, 137; and Quakers, 27, 33, 38–39, 44, 50–51, 55, 58, 60–62, 64–65, 137–38, 158;

founding of, 31–32; opposition of free blacks to, 34–35, 70, 71, 74–75, 142, 161–62, 181–82, 200; land acquisitions in Africa by, 37–38, 84, 101–3; as critical of Haitian emigration, 51; colonial vision of, 62, 82–84, 89, 96, 99–103, 253; decline of, 140–62, 196–97, 200, 255–56, 268–69; influence of northern auxiliaries in, 141, 151, 155, 200, 300 (n. 7); splintering of, 143–51, 155; revival of, 173–200 passim, 252–53; racial prejudice in, 186–87, 253; dissolution of, 268–69

—and North Carolina: auxiliary branches in, 32, 39–40, 42, 55, 60–61, 65, 66, 76, 141, 151–52, 169, 174, 282 (n. 23); support for colonization in, 39, 51, 65, 132, 151, 169, 171, 173; opposition to colonization in, 65, 66, 69, 70, 73, 75, 140–41, 161–62, 187, 193, 254, 259–60; emigrant agents in, 65–67, 161–62, 166, 174–75, 177–78, 191; decline of organizational activity in, 76, 140–43, 151–52, 161–62, 196–97; revival of colonization activity in, 174–79, 182–200 passim

American Revolution, 14, 19, 21, 22, 24, 26, 29

Anasarca, 159, 233, 236

Anasarca exanthem, 233, 236

Anderson, Hull (N.C. emigrant), 219–20

Andres, William S., 188, 189–90

Appeal to the Colored Citizens of the World (1829), 70–73, 76, 130, 153

Arthington (Liberia), 99, 260–62, 273

Arthington, Robert, 253–55

Ashmun, Jehudi, 63, 81, 82, 84, 87, 88, 102–3

Ayres, Eli, 37

Azor (ship), 259, 301 (n. 14)

Bacon, Samuel, 39

Banshee (ship), 208

Baptists, 14, 26, 33, 170, 206, 211, 214–15, 224, 243, 252, 258–59, 265; Southern Baptist Convention, 214

Bassa Cove (Liberia), 145, 146, 147, 154, 155–56, 157, 159, 178, 184, 206–10, 242

Beaufort County, N.C., 173

Benezet, Anthony, 25

Bertie County, N.C., 9, 18, 54, 56, 85, 89, 214, 249–65 passim, 273

Bexley (Liberia), 155, 156, 206, 209–10; naming of, 296 (n. 8)

Bissell, Mary, 189, 190

Black Codes, 250–51

Bladen County, N.C., 152–53, 188, 192–94, 203, 207

Blah, Moses Z., 274

Blyden, Edward W., 98, 183, 263–64

Bopolu (Liberia), 104, 202

Bowe, Matthias (N.C. emigrant), 88

Boyer, Jean Pierre, 44–46, 48, 58

Branch, John, 32, 40

Brewer, Charles, 253

Brewerville (Liberia), 99, 258, 259, 262–65

Bridgestone Firestone, 273

Brown, John, 196

Brumley, Kai Pa (Dei king), 105–12, 162

Brumley, Peter (Dei king), 103–4, 105–6

Brunswick County, N.C., 152

Bryant, Charles G., 274

Buchanan (Liberia), 99, 207–9; immigrant mortality in, 208–9

Burgess, Ebenezer, 37, 89

Caldwell (Liberia), 57, 58, 64, 67, 103, 106, 107, 109, 134, 210–14, 235; immigrant mortality in, 68, 139, 149, 211, 238; founding of, 84–89; naming of, 85, 99; North Carolinians in, 85–89, 107

Caldwell, Elias B., 30–32, 38, 85

Caldwell, Joseph, 40

Camden County, N.C., 56, 58, 85, 88, 213, 236, 257

Canada, 22, 131, 165, 171, 174

Capehart, Susan (N.C. emigrant), 184, 226

Capehart, Tristram, 169

Cape Palmas (Liberia): Maryland colony in, 97, 144–45, 147, 159, 217

Capps, Sherwood (N.C. emigrant), 258–59, 263
Carey, Lott, 39, 87, 88, 89, 285 (n. 17)
Careysburg (Liberia), 100, 209, 226
Cartwright, Andrew (N.C. emigrant), 258
Charleston, S.C., 9, 18, 70
Chowan County, N.C., 53, 85, 88, 188, 222
Christophe, Henri, 44
Civil War, U.S. *See* American Civil War
Clarkson, Thomas, 44
Clay, Henry, 30–35, 64, 143, 149–50, 181
Clay-Ashland (Liberia), 99
Coffin, Aaron, 43, 45–47
Coffin, Levi, 42, 43
Collins, Josiah, 40
Colonization, 2–7, 291 (n. 4); as remedy for racial conflict, 3, 20–21, 24, 33, 200, 252–53; movement in North Carolina, 4–6; early proposals for, 21–22, 25; early black interest in, 22–25; black reaction to, 24–25, 34–36; as encouraging abolition of slavery, 25, 30, 32, 34, 38, 61, 141–42, 144, 149, 188, 198; as civilizing Africa, 30, 33, 39, 96, 102, 111, 217, 239–43, 261–62, 269, 277 (n. 22); as making slavery more secure, 30, 34, 36, 71, 144, 173; as means of removing free blacks, 30–32, 75, 133, 144, 146, 148, 149–50, 173, 175, 180, 188, 191; as reform movement, 32–33, 39, 100, 142, 145
—federal support of, 36, 37, 75, 149, 197
—state support of: Virginia, 21, 32, 147–48; Connecticut, 32; Maryland, 32, 144–45; New Jersey, 32; Ohio, 32; Tennessee, 32, 150; Kentucky, 149–50
The Condition, Elevation, Emigration and Destiny of the Colored People of the United States (1852), 181–82
Consumption. *See* Tuberculosis
Coppinger, William, 252–64 passim
Cornish, Samuel, 70, 159
Council of Liberia, 147
Craven County, N.C., 18, 72, 138, 140, 163–68, 265

Cresson, Elliott, 145, 154
Criterion (ship), 91
Croom, Mingo, 167
Crozer, Samuel, 37
Crummell, Alexander, 98, 217
Cuffe, Paul, 22–25, 35, 37
Cumberland County, N.C., 152, 176–77, 211
Currituck County, N.C., 256, 258, 265, 295 (n. 42)

Dei, 37, 82, 84, 85, 88, 89, 94, 100, 103–12; and conflict with settlers, 103, 105–12, 162; slavery among, 105–6
Delany, Martin R., 4, 181–83
Demery, Bennett (N.C. emigrant), 88, 237–38
Dessalines, Jean-Jacques, 22
Dickinson, Andrew (N.C. emigrant), 165–68, 171, 217, 291 (n. 5)
Dimrey, John, 42
Diseases, 195; in Liberia, 88–90, 159–60, 227–37, 264, 298 (n. 37); in North Carolina, 227, 233. *See also* African sleeping sickness; Anasarca; Anasara exanthem; Malaria; Pleurisy; Tuberculosis
Doe, Samuel, 271–72, 274
Doris (ship), 63–65, 67, 68, 70, 74, 213
Douglass, Frederick, 4, 174, 181
Dred Scott case (1857), 172, 174, 195, 196
Duplin County, N.C., 173

Edgecombe County, N.C., 17
Edina (Liberia), 99, 155–56
Edmundson, William, 12, 13
Ehringhaus, John, 60, 130–31
Elizabeth (ship), 37, 42, 57, 69, 147, 197
Elizabeth City, N.C., 53–54, 65, 74, 164, 175–76, 184, 256, 258
Elizabethtown, N.C., 152, 153, 155
Elvira Owen (ship), 195
Enfield, N.C., 132, 258
Episcopalians, 166, 217, 224

Fayetteville, N.C., 18, 65, 69, 132, 152, 176–79, 209, 215

Fillmore, Millard, 171
Finley, Robert, 39, 146–47
Fletcher, Diver (N.C. emigrant), 213
Forten, James, 35
Four Months in Liberia (1855), 182
Four Years in Liberia (1857), 182–83
Franklin County, N.C., 189
Freedom's Journal, 70, 145, 153
Free Soil movement, 34, 171, 196, 197, 253
Fugitive Slave Law (1850), 171–74, 195
Fundamental Constitutions of the Carolinas, 10

Gales, Joseph, 40, 61, 70, 151, 154, 155, 158, 289 (n. 29)
Garrison, William L., 130, 137, 158, 174, 181
Gola, 106–9, 202, 216, 272
Golconda (ship), 252, 254–55
Gotorah, 238–39
Grand Bassa County (Liberia). *See* Bassa Cove; Bexley; Buchanan
Gray, Joseph, 132–33
Great Dismal Swamp, 53–55, 91
Grebo, 144, 147, 217, 267
Greensboro, N.C., 8, 40, 161
Greenville (Liberia), 146–47
Guilford, first earl of (Lord Francis North), 7
Guilford County, N.C., 7–17, 42–43, 48, 69, 75, 144, 227, 279 (n. 28)
Gurley, Ralph R., 39, 60, 61, 63, 66, 67, 69, 70, 73, 74, 107, 132–34, 161

Haiti, 22, 44–51, 59, 71, 75, 135, 184, 197
Haitian emigration, 22, 44–51, 55, 58, 197
Halifax, N.C., 131–32
Halifax County, N.C., 9, 18, 54, 131–35, 138, 164
Harper (Liberia), 99, 144
Hayes, James O. (N.C. emigrant), 258–59, 264
Heddington (Liberia), 238, 247–48
Hertford County, N.C., 18, 40, 61, 168–70
Hoggard, Alonzo (N.C. emigrant), 249–54, 260–62

Hollister, Sally Ogon (N.C. emigrant), 99, 225
Hood, James W., 259
Hooper, Emily (N.C. emigrant), 177–79, 187–88
Hooper, Marshall (N.C. emigrant), 177–79, 187–88, 248, 293 (n. 21)
Hopkins, Moses A., 268
Hunter (ship), 1–3, 51–52, 57, 67, 192
Hunter, Charity (N.C. emigrant), 1–3, 51, 57

Île a'Vache, 197
Indiana, 42, 44, 47, 58, 137, 151, 174, 256, 281 (n. 10)
Indian Chief (ship), 56–58, 60, 62, 67, 107, 238
Iredell, James, 65, 66, 283 (n. 38)
Iredell County, N.C., 17

Jackson, Andrew, 31, 149
James, Frederick (N.C. emigrant), 214
James, Jonathan (N.C. emigrant), 89
James Perkins (ship), 134–35, 138
Jamestown, N.C., 8
Jamesville, N.C., 254, 257, 262
Jefferson, Thomas, 3, 21–22, 33, 147
Johnson, Prince, 272
Joseph Maxwell (ship), 179, 209
Julius Pringle (ship), 135–36, 288 (n. 12)
Jupiter (ship), 135

Kennedy, John, 63
Kennedy, William P. (N.C. emigrant), 215–16
Kentucky (Liberia), 149–50
Key, Francis S., 31
Keyauwee, 7
Krahn, 271
Kru, 52, 77–79, 83, 104, 112, 146, 165, 246, 247, 267
Ku Klux Klan, 251

Ladies Liberia School Association, 82
Latrobe, John H. B., 144, 200, 253
Liberator, 130, 157, 158, 181